T0305346

MERGERS AND ACQUISITIONS

Strategic Management Society Book Series

The Strategic Management Society Book Series is a cooperative effort between the Strategic Management Society and Blackwell Publishing. The purpose of the series is to present information on cutting-edge concepts and topics in strategic management theory and practice. The books emphasize building and maintaining bridges between strategic management theory and practice. The work published in these books generates and tests new theories of strategic management. Additionally, work published in this series demonstrates how to learn, understand, and apply these theories in practice. The content of the series represents the newest critical thinking in the field of strategic management. As a result, these books provide valuable knowledge for strategic management scholars, consultants, and executives.

Published

Strategic Entrepreneurship: Creating a New Mindset
Edited by Michael A. Hitt, R. Duane Ireland, S. Michael Camp, and Donald L. Sexton

Creating Value: Winners in the New Business Environment
Edited by Michael A. Hitt, Raphael Amit, Charles E. Lucier, and Robert D. Nixon

Strategy Process: Shaping the Contours of the Field
Edited by Bala Chakravarthy, Peter Lorange, Günter Müller-Stewens, and Christoph Lechner

The SMS Blackwell Handbook of Organizational Capabilities: Emergence, Development and Change
Edited by Constance E. Helfat

Mergers and Acquisitions: Creating Integrative Knowledge
Edited by Amy L. Pablo and Mansour Javidan

Forthcoming

Strategy in Transition
Edited by Richard Bettis

Restructuring Strategy: New Networks and Industry Challenges
Edited by Rene Abate, Karel Cool, and James Henderson

Mergers and Acquisitions

Creating Integrative Knowledge

Edited by

Amy L. Pablo
Mansour Javidan

350 Main Street, Malden, MA 02148-5020, USA
108 Cowley Road, Oxford OX4 1JF, UK
550 Swanston Street, Carlton, Victoria 3053, Australia

The right of Amy L. Pablo and Mansour Javidan to be identified as the Authors of the Editorial Material in this Work has been asserted in accordance with the UK Copyright, Designs, and Patents Act 1988.

First published 2004 by Blackwell Publishing Ltd

Library of Congress Cataloging-in-Publication Data

Mergers and acquisitions : creating integrative knowledge/edited by
Amy L. Pablo and Mansour Javidan.
   p. cm. – (Strategic Management Society book series)
Includes bibliographical references and index.
   ISBN 1-4051-1623-4 (cloth : alk. paper)
1. Consolidation and merger of corporations. I. Pablo, Amy L.
II. Javidan, Mansour. III. Strategic Management Society. IV. Series.

   HD2746.5.M456 2004
   658.1′62–dc22   2003020736

A catalogue record for this title is available from the British Library.

For further information on
Blackwell Publishing, visit our website:
http://www.blackwellpublishing.com

Contents

Part I   M&A Performance

Figures

Tables

Contributors

Arikan, Asli Musaoglu
Boston University
e-mail: *aarikan@bu.edu*

Ben-Hur, Shlomo
DaimlerChrysler Services Academy, DaimlerChrysler Services, AG
e-mail: *Shlomo.Ben-hur@daimlerchrysler.com*

Bower, Joseph L.
Harvard Business School
e-mail: *jbower@hbs.edu*

Brousseau, Kenneth R.
Decision Dynamics LLC
e-mail: *ken@decdynamics.com*

Brush, Thomas
Krannert Graduate School of Management, Purdue University
e-mail: *brusht@mgmt.purdue.edu*

Driver, Michael J.
Marshall School of Business, University of Southern California
e-mail: *mdriver@marshall.usc.edu*

Ellis, Kimberly M.
Eli Broad Graduate School of Management, Michigan State University
e-mail: *elliski@msu.edu*

Erez, Miriam
Faculty of Industrial Engineering and Management, Technion, Israel Institute
of Technology
e-mail: *merez@ie.technion.ac.il*

Erez-Rein, Noa
Australian Graduate School of Management
e-mail: *noare@agsu.edu.au*

Greenberg, Danna
Faculty of Management, Babson College
e-mail: *dgreenberg@babson.edu*

Guinan, P.J.
Faculty of Information and Technology, Babson College
e-mail: *guinan@babson.edu*

Hartog, Vera
Vlerick Leuven Gent Management School, Universiteit Gent
e-mail: *vera.hartog@zeelandnet.nl*

Hitt, Michael A.
Mays School of Business, Texas A&M University
e-mail: *mhitt@cgsb.tamu.edu*

Javidan, Mansour
Haskayne School of Business, University of Calgary
e-mail: *mansour.javidan@haskayne.ucalgary.ca*

Jemison, David
McCombs School of Business, University of Texas at Austin
e-mail: *david.jemison@bus.utexas.edu*

Larsson, Rikard
School of Economics and Management, Lund University
e-mail: *rikard.larsson@fek.lu.se*

Maital, Shlomo
Faculty of Industrial Engineering and Management, Technion, Israel Institute
of Technology
e-mail: *maital@ie.technion.ac.il*

Mudde, Paul A.
Siedman School of Business, Grand Valley State University
e-mail: *muddep@gvsu.edu*

Pablo, Amy L.
Haskayne School of Business, University of Calgary
e-mail: *amy.pablo@haskayne.ucalgary.ca*

Pisano, Vincenzo
Arizona State University
e-mail: *pisano@tiu.it*

Reuer, Jeffrey J.
Fisher College of Business, Ohio State University
e-mail: *reuerj@cob.ohio-state.edu*

Shen, Jung-Chin
Strategy and Management Department, INSEAD
e-mail: *jung-chin.shen@insead.fr*

Singh, Harbir
The Wharton School, The University of Pennsylvania
e-mail: *singhh@wharton_upenn.edu*

Sitkin, Sim B.
Center for Organizational Research at the Fuqua School of Business,
Duke University
e-mail: *sim.sitkin@duke.edu*

Sweet, Patrick L.
Decision Dynamics AB
e-mail: *patrick.sweet@decisiondynamics.se*

Thomas, L. Todd
DaimlerChrysler Services Academy, DaimlerChrysler Services, AG
e-mail: *ltt2@daimlerchrysler.com*

Waldman, David A.
School of Management at Arizona State University – West
e-mail: *waldman@asu.edu*

Introduction

Amy L. Pablo and Mansour Javidan

The year 2000 witnessed the eighth successive record year for announced merger and acquisition (M&A) activity: almost 37,000 global M&A transactions with a combined value of close to $3.5 trillion (Thomson Financial 2001). North America is by far the largest M&A market, but other areas of the world are experiencing pronounced increases in the numbers of transactions. During the period 1990–99, North America had a 10 percent compound annual growth rate in the number of M&As, Asia Pacific had a growth rate of 27 percent, and Europe, a rate of 13 percent (Sirower 1997). Still, the highest profile mergers have primarily involved American companies. Exxon-Mobil ($80 billion), BP-AMOCO ($50 billion) and Daimler-Chrysler ($40 billion) are a few notable examples.

Here's an interesting paradox: Corporations and executives are obviously in love with M&As. They have been buying up other companies at dizzying speed. At the same time, the academic and consulting worlds are quite pessimistic about M&As. Booz Allen and Hamilton (1985) recently reported that at least 30 to 50 percent of M&As fail to produce the expected benefits. The latter report indicates that odds are particularly bad for mergers of companies of equal size. The latest report, produced by *Business Week*, concludes that 61 percent of acquiring companies destroyed shareholder value (Henry 2002: 72).

The academic literature is somewhat contradictory about the effect of M&As. Some authors have concluded that M&As destroy value for the shareholders of acquiring companies (Datta and Puia 1995, Loughran and Vijh 1997, Sirower 1997), while others show that M&As have positive consequences for acquiring firms (Lubatkin 1987, Jensen 1988, Shelton 1988, Morosini, Shane, and Singh 1998, Hitt et al. 1991). Still others have shown a zero effect (Copeland, Koller, and Murrin 1988, Loderer and Martin 1992, Healy, Palepu, and Ruback 1997). Despite such a wide range of findings, the general view towards M&As is negative and is best captured in the following comment by Warren Buffet (1981), the guru of investments:

> Many managers were apparently over-exposed in impressionable childhood years to the story in which the imprisoned, handsome prince is released from the toad's body by a

kiss from the beautiful princess. Consequently they are certain that the managerial kiss will do wonders for the profitability of the target company…. Absent the rosy view, why else should the shareholders of company A want to own an interest in company B at a takeover cost that is two times the market price they'd pay if they made direct purchases on their own? In other words investors can always buy toads for the going price for toads. If investors instead bankroll princesses who wish to pay double for the right to kiss the toad, those kisses better pack some real dynamite. We've observed many kisses, but very few miracles.

So how can we explain the apparent divergence between academic conventional wisdom and executive practice? Our response to this question is that existing research on M&As provides a limited and insufficient understanding of this important phenomenon. We believe that a major drawback of existing literature is that, while the construct of M&A is multidimensional and cross-disciplinary, much of the research tends to be single-discipline based and one-dimensional, producing only partial understanding of the phenomenon. This is why we hosted a Strategic Management Society Mini-conference on mergers and acquisitions. The conference, called M&A Summit 2002, was held in Calgary, Canada, during June 6–9, 2002. Academics, senior executives, and consultants from all over the world came together to share their views, experiences, and knowledge about M&As. A primary objective of this conference was to take an integrative and multidisciplinary approach, and to set the stage for a more collaborative research initiative to better understand this important phenomenon. All the submitted papers were blind reviewed with a total of 50 papers accepted for presentation. In addition, 12 keynote speeches were provided by distinguished academics in the field. There were also a variety of speeches by CEOs and other senior executives.

To share the conference learnings with a broader audience, we decided to produce an edited book of readings containing a select set of papers from the conference. This book includes four chapters based on six keynote speeches, as well as 10 papers that we selected from the set of 50 presented papers. We then worked with the authors to finalize each chapter.

The book is in six parts. Part I: M&A Performance consists of two papers examining the notion of success in M&As. In Chapter 1, "The secrets of merger and acquisition success", Larsson et al. review the literature on M&A performance and discuss their findings on a case survey of 61 M&A cases. They conclude that synergy realization in M&As depends to a large extent on high strategic potential, high organizational integration, and low employee resistance. They propose a "co-competence and motivational approach" to help corporations succeed on all three fronts.

Chapter 2 is called "Mind the gap: Key success factors in cross-border acquisitions" by Erez-Rein and her colleagues. The authors use three cases of acquisitions by an American company in Israel to explore the determinants of M&A performance. Through interviews with main executives and review of documents, they identify seven key success factors that seem to distinguish the successful international mergers from the unsuccessful ones. They explain each key success factor and make suggestions on how they can be implemented.

Part II: M&A Strategy contains three chapters focused on strategic issues involved in M&As. In Chapter 3, "Cross-border mergers and acquisitions: Challenges and opportunities", Hitt and Pisano review the logic for the increasing popularity of cross-border mergers and explain the reasons why corporations are buying firms in other countries. They identify the opportunities presented by cross-border mergers and explain the specific challenges that firms face in such initiatives. They also discuss the difficulties researchers interested in cross-border mergers must overcome.

In Chapter 4, "Firm competitiveness and acquisition: The role of competitive strategy and operational effectiveness in M&A," Mudde and Brush explore the relationship between an acquiring firm's business-level strategy and operational effectiveness, and its ability to achieve post-acquisition synergies. Based on a study of over 200 bank acquisitions in the United States, they conclude that companies with strong cost leadership strategies succeed in achieving major cost synergies while those with mixed strategies seem to achieve high levels of growth in sales.

Jung-Chin Shen and Jeffrey Reuer's paper, in Chapter 5 "Acquisition of entrepreneurial firms: How private and public targets differ", compares private and public firms as potential targets of acquisition. Using the Securities Data Corporate database, they show that acquiring firms tend to prefer public targets over private firms both within their own industry and across industries. They also show that buying firms are particularly reluctant to acquire young private firms with intangible assets. The authors discuss the implications of their findings for both acquiring firms and private firms that may be interested in being acquired.

Part III focuses on the implementation and integration issues in M&As and consists of two chapters. In Chapter 6, "The role of the corporate academy in mergers and acquisitions", Thomas and Ben-Hur, based on their experience at Daimler-Chrysler, define the concept of corporate academies and present a set of roles that an effective corporate academy can play in the successful implementation of a merger or acquisition. These are: focus on the big picture, change management coaching and training, assessment experience, career development and discussion, relationship with key leaders, e-learning, and internal–external perspective in organizational development. They make a few suggestions on how corporate academies can successfully play these roles.

In Chapter 7 "Managing the acquisition process: Do differences actually exist across integration approaches?" Kimberly Ellis surveys the executives involved in over 300 merger transactions among large and related firms and shows four different types of integration strategies pursued by different companies: preservation, absorption, symbiotic, and transformational. She explains each approach and describes its distinguishing characteristics and identifies the conditions under which each approach is suitable.

Part IV consists of two chapters and focuses on knowledge transfer. In Chapter 8 "Mergers and acquisitions in technology-intensive industries: The emergent process of knowledge transfer", Greenberg and Guinan use a case study methodology to examine the knowledge transfer process in high technology firms after acquisition. Their findings highlight the important role that individual organization members (integrating entrepreneurs) play in facilitating such transfer, and caution that care be taken in integration so as to create an enabling environment for the activities of these integrating entrepreneurs.

Chapter 9 is entitled "Does it pay to capture intangible assets through mergers and acquisitions?". The author, Arikan, uses a database of mergers to compare the 60-month average buy-and-hold abnormal returns of the firms that acquired highly tangible assets with those that acquired highly intangible assets. Her findings show that on average, buyers of tangible assets break even over the five-year period while the buyers of intangible assets show a large economic loss. She discusses the potential reasons and the implications of her findings.

Part V deals with cultural and leadership issues in M&As. In Chapter 10 Sitkin and Pablo present a theoretically based leadership framework for conceptualizing and studying the effect of leadership on M&A success. In this work, they suggest how M&A leaders can, through focusing their actions on effectively handling the problems and facilitating factors that arise in the M&A process, beneficially influence the M&A outcome.

In Chapter 11, Waldman discusses "The role of CEO charismatic leadership in the effective implementation of mergers and acquisitions". He provides a summary of the literature on charismatic leadership and develops a theoretical model showing how charismatic leadership at the CEO level can play a critical role in the effective implementation of a merger. He suggests that pre-merger cultural and organizational differences impact the company's success in integrating organizational systems and cultures and influence the extent to which employees resist change. He further explains how charismatic leaders can use their skills and attributes to minimize resistance to change and maximize the chances of merger success.

Chapter 12 "The impact of perceived uncertainty on culture differences in the post-acquisition process to strategy realization" by Hartog focuses on why and how, in the post-acquisition integration process, culture differences impact strategy realization. In this work, she suggests how the personal and organizational uncertainty concomitant with integration impacts on individuals' interpretations of culture. These changed personal cultural understandings ultimately affect employee behavior and at the end of the day, strategy realization at the firm level.

Part VI, the last part of the book, consists of two chapters. Chapter 13 "When we study M&A, what are we learning?" by Bower reviews the various research methodologies employed in measuring M&A success. The author examines the work of a variety of researchers and concludes that much work has yet to be done. He explains the shortcomings of several streams of research and concludes that the most fruitful research approach to M&As is a methodology that combines case analysis and large-scale empirical work. He cautions against research that is purely data driven and suggests a multidisciplinary approach that would help us better understand the complex issues involved in M&As.

Chapter 14, the last chapter in the book, represents a rather unique feature of this conference. The last session of the conference consisted of two parts. The first part was a panel presentation. Harbir Singh made a presentation titled "As of June 5, 2002, what did we know and not know about M&As?". He was followed by David Jemison who made a presentation titled "What did we learn in this conference?" and the third speaker was Michael Hitt whose talk was titled "What needs to be done to further our knowledge about M&As?" After a broad-based discussion of these topics, the conference attendants were split into small groups and were asked to discuss and answer three questions: (1) What are the top five burning questions in M&As? (2) How do we go about finding the answers to these questions; and (3) Where do we go from here?

Chapter 14 is a summary of the discussions during the last session of the conference. It summarizes the panel presentations and the outcomes of small group discussions. This chapter is intended to help provide more clear and unified direction to M&A research.

We argued earlier in this section that an important step in closing the apparent gap between academic research and executive practice in M&As is to engage in more cross-disciplinary research. Our intent in organizing the M&A Summit 2002 and in creating this book was to take a step in this direction. We'll have to hear from the readers to know whether we succeeded.

References

Booz Allen and Hamilton Inc. 1985. Diversification: A survey of European chief executives. Executive summary. In S. Cartwright and C. Cooper (eds.). 1993. The role of culture in successful organizational marriage. *Academy of Management Executive*, 7(20): 57–70.

Buffet, W. 1981. *Annual Report to Shareholders*. Berkshire Hathaway Corporation.

Copeland, T., Koller, T., and Murrin, J. 1988. *Valuation: Measuring and Managing the Value of Companies*. New York: Wiley.

Datta, D.K. and Puia, G. 1995. Cross-border acquisitions: An examination of the influence of relatedness and cultural fit on shareholder value creation in U.S. acquiring firms. *Management International Review*, 35: 337–59.

Healy, P.M., Palepu, K.G., and Ruback, R.S. 1997. Which takeovers are profitable? Strategic or financial? *Sloan Management Review*, 38(4): 45–57.

Henry, D. 2002. Mergers: Why most big deals don't pay off. *Business Week*, October 14: 72–8.

Hitt, M.A., Hoskisson, R.E., Ireland, R.D., and Harrison, J.S. 1991. Effects of acquisitions on R&D inputs and outputs. *Academy of Management Journal*, 3(3): 693–706.

Jensen, M.C. 1988. Takeovers: Their causes and consequences. *Journal of Economic Perspectives*, 2(1): 21–48.

Loderer, C. and Martin, K. 1992. Post acquisition performance of acquiring firms. *Financial Management*, autumn, 69–79.

Loughran, T. and Vijh, A.M. 1997. Do long-term shareholders benefit from corporate acquisitions? *Journal of Finance*, 5: 1765–90.

Lubatkin, M. 1987. Merger strategies and stockholder value. *Strategic Management Journal*, 8: 39–53.

Morosini, P., Shane, S., and Singh, H. 1998. National cultural distance and cross-border acquisition performance. *Journal of International Business Studies*, 29(1): 137–58.

Shelton, L.M. 1988. Strategic business fits and corporate acquisition: Empirical evidence. *Strategic Management Journal*, 9: 279–87.

Sirower, M. 1997. *The Synergy Trap*. New York: The Free Press.

Thomson Financial, The world grows while Europe slows, www.tfibcm.com, accessed November 10, 2001.

M&A Performance

PART
M&A Performance

The Secrets of Merger and Acquisition Success: A Co-Competence and Motivational Approach to Synergy Realization

Rikard Larsson, Kenneth R. Brousseau, Michael J. Driver, Patrick L. Sweet

Abstract

Why do some mergers and acquisitions (M&A) succeed while others fail? This chapter offers a practical summary of M&A research, including a case survey of 61 M&As. A pattern has emerged that clearly differentiates highly successful and less successful M&As. As much as 60–70 percent of synergy realization in M&As is explained by high strategic potential, high organizational integration, and low employee resistance. While many corporations appear to have learned the key strategic and organizational factors, the human elements of M&A remain the most difficult to manage. This is due to the challenge of managing employee resistance on collective, interpersonal, and individual levels. A "co-competence and motivational approach" to the human component of M&A is presented as an effective way to achieve all three key factors of synergy realization. Special emphasis is focused on cultural, communication, and career solutions that work to prevent employee resistance.

Introduction

The successful M&A has eluded countless corporations during the last century. Failure rates are reported as high as 50–75 percent (e.g. Marks and Mirvis 1998), although with typically debatable scientific specification and support. Contradictory advice and fragmented theories have also been offered (Schweiger and Walsh 1990, Haspeslagh and Jemison 1991). As the debate continues on whether M&As are

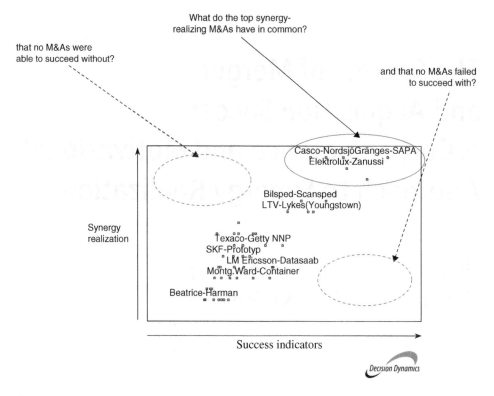

What do the top synergy-
realizing M&As have in common?

that no M&As were
able to succeed without?

and that no M&As failed
to succeed with?

Casco-NordsjöGränges-SAPA
Elektrolux-Zanussi

Bilsped-Scansped
LTV-Lykes(Youngstown)

Synergy
realization

Texaco-Getty NNP
SKF-Prototyp
LM Ericsson-Datasaab
Montg.Ward-Container

Beatrice-Harman

Success indicators

Decision Dynamics

Figure 1.1   A study of synergy realization in 61 M&As

"good or bad", it is acknowledged that M&As will continue to occur. However, we
must recognize that M&As are likely the most volatile of corporate events. They
present an opportunity for value-added organizational synergy to value-destroying
disaster. Therefore, learning systematically how to increase the likelihood of success is
essential.

In a study that Professor Kathleen Eisenhardt of Stanford University expects "to
become a defining paper in M&A research", Larsson and Finkelstein (1999: 1) compared 61 in-depth cases of synergy realization in M&A. They found key contributors
and commonalities among successful M&As. They also found that M&As without
these key factors often failed to realize any synergy at all. Figure 1.1 shows the case
survey sample (including some of the corporate names) in a diagram with synergy
realization on the (vertical) Y-axis and the success indicators on the (horizontal)
X-axis, which will be discussed throughout the chapter.

How is synergy realization measured? Sixty-one substantive M&A case studies
were each examined and scored by two to three raters. Each rater coded cost savings and revenue increases during at least a 12-month period of integration from
11 different potential sources of synergy for each case. Sources of synergy included
consolidating purchasing, production, marketing, administration and/or vertical
supplier/customer relationships, market power, new market access, cross-selling,

transfer of existing expertise, and joint creation of new "know how". The case survey method is a unique combination of quantitative analysis of entire samples of qualitative case studies (Larsson 1993b). Substantial analysis demonstrated quite satisfactory reliability and validity of the raters' case codings (Larsson and Finkelstein 1999).

To understand success one must also look at failure. Searching only for excellence rarely reveals the "mistakes" made by others. Without a comparison between success and failure, we don't know if the supporting evidence drawn from successful models might actually highlight the determinant factors of success and failure. Not surprisingly, advice related to success stories only tends to fail rather quickly (cf. Aupperle, Acar, and Booth 1986). Thus, it is important to ask what the necessary requirements are that separate M&As with high synergy realization from those with low synergy realization.

There are, of course, no simple answers. Complex understanding comprises fragmented strategic, organizational, human resource, financial, and economic M&A factors regarding selection as well as integration issues across different levels. This chapter offers a practical review of this research and addresses these factors with an aim to provide as many useful answers to these questions as possible.

Synergy Factors that Transcend the Performance Controversy

M&A research can be characterized as resulting in a controversy between skeptical economic and enthusiastic financial research. In other words, does M&A create or destroy value in general? Summarizing more than 50 years of primarily economic findings, Goldberg (1983: 207, 209) finds "shareholders of the acquiring firm tend to lose from mergers ... Earnings of firms in mergers decline after consolidation" (cf. Ravenscraft and Scherer 1987). In contrast, financial researchers claim that acquiring firms do not lose and earnings do not decline in the years following integration (e.g. Weston and Chung 1983, Jensen 1984).

This performance disparity reflects the different methods and perspectives of economic and financial M&A research (cf. Datta, Narayanan, and Pinches 1992) that seem to bias the respective findings. However, continuing the controversy of whether M&As are good or bad in general, is of very limited practical use as previously stated.

A more practical approach is to instead look at what the factors are that determine high versus low M&A performance. Rather than "choosing" sides between economic accounting and financial stock-market performance measures and their respective biases, Larsson and Finkelstein (1999) focused on actual *synergy realization* as a useful performance measure of value creation in M&As. The chapter will now review strategic, organizational, and human resource factors that can determine this synergy realization.

Strategic synergy factors: Selecting the right combination upfront

Strategic M&A research has focused primarily on *selection* factors as determinants of M&A performance. The initial choice of organizations to be combined is posited as a key determinant of M&A outcomes. Different types of corporate combinations are suggested to represent different strategic synergy potentials (e.g. Lubatkin 1983,

Singh and Montgomery 1987, Bower 2001). The more related firms are, the greater their synergy potential from a strategic perspective.

Relatedness is typically viewed in terms of similarity of markets, products, and production. The greatest potential for combined organizations is often attributed to so-called horizontal M&As that unite competing entities with overlapping operations. These overlapping operations often lead to redundancies, which are trimmed from the newly combined organization. In essence, value is extracted from the combination through increased marginal outputs per marginal inputs, using scale economics. Synergies are not only limited to "economies of sameness"; Larsson (1990) also points towards the "economies of fitness" between complementary operations. These include vertical combinations between supplier and customer firms and market or product extension combinations, where one firm adds either new markets or new products to the other. In such complementary combinations, value is added which increases the breadth and scope of the total operation. (For a treatment of value-adding vs. value-extracting development strategies, see Sweet 2001a, 2001b.)

Distinguishing between the high strategic combination potential of overlapping operations (that offer value extraction potential) and the low potential of completely unrelated operations (i.e. pure conglomerate M&A) is relatively easy. In contrast, the potential of complementarities (offering potentially value-adding synergies) is likely to vary greatly from high to insignificant and therefore is harder to predetermine. Larsson and Finkelstein (1999) found that both strategic similarities and complementarities were the key selection determinants of synergy realization. In short, significant value must be capable of being extracted and added by a combination for potential synergy to be realized.

Organizational selection factors: A case of "fool's gold"?

Many M&A researchers warn against considering mere strategic factors when selecting corporate combinations. The *potential* for extracting and/or adding value via M&A is not the same as realizing it. These kinds of so-called cultural clashes are seen as substantial barriers to synergy realization in M&As (e.g. Chatterjee et al. 1992, Cartwright and Cooper 1996). Therefore, it is usually recommended that combinations having different corporate cultures be avoided. This is the case even if they have high strategic combination potential in terms of value extraction or value adding.

This recommendation to more or less sacrifice strategic potential in favor of the selection of culturally similar combinations is questioned by other M&A researchers. Larsson (1990) points out that organization cultures include strong defense mechanisms that maintain the shared norms and values of the employees. These cultural defense or maintenance mechanisms are mobilized by external threats like M&A. This can be most clearly seen by the "we versus they" interpretations that are found in almost all M&A *irrespective* of how similar or different the cultures were beforehand.

Consequently, there is little justification in sacrificing strategic potential in favor of selecting culturally similar combinations. Cultural defense mechanisms almost invariably rally in defense of "we and our ways" as being better than "they and their ways". Larsson and Lubatkin (2001) found that cultural clashes and/or acculturation between joining firms were primarily determined by what happened during the ensuing integration process, not by initial similarities at the point of combination selection. In other words, no matter how good the combination "looked on paper and in spirit", the process of integration emerged as a heavier determinant of success/failure.

Another organizational selection issue is whether to specifically choose "good or bad" firms to merge. Yet, there are several reasons for caution in acquiring peak performance firms especially during boom periods. High-performing firms cost more and the risk of employee resistance is greater in the high-priced, high-performing company. High-performing managers and employees are more likely to believe in the superiority of their methods. In turn, they may be less willing to adjust during the integration process. And, during boom periods, increased external employment opportunities may encourage these high-performing employees to seek other opportunities. On this basis, selecting a "good" company can easily become a bad M&A.

On the other hand, "bad" companies can naturally become "good" M&As. For example, some troubled companies offer tremendous opportunity. While shaky economic periods may create, temporarily, poor performers from otherwise stable and profitable entities, the acquiring company may be able to fill in the few missing pieces such as access to other markets to boost performance. In addition to the advantages of lower prices and hidden values, employees may also see opportunity in an M&A and be supportive of the acquisition.

Human resource selection factors: Neglected recruitment issues

One of the least considered sets of M&A selection factors is that corporate combinations actually represent, by far, the greatest source of employee recruitment for most large firms. Anecdotal evidence suggests that companies recruit as much as 10 or more times as many employees through M&A than the usual methods of recruitment such as outsourced headhunting services. This can be a damaging lack of insight from the perspective of corporations and academics since recruitment by M&A is dramatically different from regular recruitment. Regular recruitment, handled internally or outsourced to headhunting firms, typically involves careful assessment and selection among many willing applicants for few specific positions. In contrast, recruitment by M&A involves an acquisition of one large bundle of more or less unknown, unknowing, and even unwilling employees. In turn, another company already employs them and there has usually been little assessment, selection, and participation of human resource professionals in the combination process.

Regular recruitment is recognized as sufficiently difficult to sustain in relation to an entire human resource industry that offers headhunting services. The recruitment nightmare that most M&As seem to experience should be expected in order to explain some of the high M&A failure rates. However, neither practitioners nor academics have given any recognition to these recruitment difficulties as sources of combination failures. And, this dilemma is often made worse because one of the most immediate integration issues facing combining corporations is the selection of who will do what and who will become redundant (cf. Hunsaker and Coombs 1988). If there is any time to buy selection specialist services, it is in relation to solving people selection problems between joining organizations. Yet, there are indications that less than 10 percent of headhunting business refers to such people selection services in M&As.

In other words, companies may be spending more than 90 percent of their purchased selection services on relatively simple regular recruitment that makes up perhaps 10 percent of their total number of recruited employees. At the same time, they may be spending less than 10 percent on the more difficult recruitment by M&A that makes up, perhaps, 90 percent of the total number of recruited employees. But, there may be some light in this human resource selection tunnel. The decision style and career concept models are two important integration tools, presented below, that the world's leading headhunter firm Korn/Ferry International and its subsidiary Korn/Ferry Futurestep have begun using for scalable recruitment and management assessment services. This opens the door for effective selection and integration services to enhance the future human side of M&A.

In any event, neither strategic combination nor organizational and human resource selection factors are sufficient by themselves to realize synergies in M&A. The strategic combination potential is a necessary precondition determined by the chosen selection, but the extent to which this potential is actually realized is determined by the subsequent integration process.

Organizational integration factors: Doing it right afterwards

Synergy realization is highly volatile, risky, and could even be considered rare. However, there are many examples of very high levels of synergy realization being achieved. Different approaches to organizational integration following the legal combination (cf. Pablo 1994) clearly influence if, when, and how much synergy is eventually realized. There are several different integration typologies (e.g. Napier 1989, Haspeslagh and Jemison 1991). Larsson (1990, 1993a) synthesizes some of these typologies into three major organizational integration types: soft/avoiding, hard/controlling, and co-competence.

The *soft* or *avoiding* integration approach aims at mainly preserving existing values of joining firms. Organizational integration, in this case, is largely put on hold. Integration develops slowly as the joining firms learn about each other and establish trust. This approach minimizes employee resistance at the expense of sacrificing integration.

The *hard* or *controlling* integration approach attempts, instead, to crush possible cultural clashes and employee resistance as fast as possible. It employs immediate, forceful, and one-sided implementation of the acquirer's ways of operating. This approach recognizes that synergy realization requires substantial organizational integration, thus reducing uncertainties, takes charge, and builds a forceful momentum for change. It is built on a basic foundational principle (or belief) in building an organization based on the acquirer's superior competence.

These *soft* and *hard* approaches constitute a classic M&A integration dilemma. There are proponents for both sides that prioritize either the soft preservation of existing values, thus minimizing employee resistance (e.g. Chatterjee et al. 1992) or the hard implementation of the acquirer's control to begin quickly realizing intended synergies and assimilate acquired employees (e.g. Searby 1969).

This is a true dilemma. Both sides are right about the other approach being inadequate. Both are also wrong about their own approach being the best. Our research clearly shows that following a soft or a hard approach is systematically undermined by each approach's weaknesses (Larsson 1990, Larsson and Finkelstein 1999). The soft approach sacrifices organizational integration requirements. The hard approach may achieve functional, organizational integration, but at great cost in relation to employee resistance, which can undermine gains hoped for by organizational/functional integration.

The *co-competence* integration approach, on the other hand, has proven to be a superior way of accomplishing the required organizational integration. This approach focuses on exploiting the competences of *both* firms. While the hard approach sacrifices the competence of the acquired firm, an equality approach of so-called "merger of equals" sacrifices some of the competences of the better firm. The assumption is that by dividing positions and authorities on a 50–50 basis, both firms will have equal competence in all areas. The co-competence approach avoids the pitfall of distributing control based on which company employees once belonged to and focuses instead on combining the best, complementary competences from both.

The co-competence approach is not without difficulties. It is common to recognize most of one's own competences while neglecting those of the other firm. A battle for control in the name of competence can ensue. In certain complementary combinations, it may be clear that both companies contribute unique and valuable competences. This can, in turn, guide organizational integration. In less clear cases, such as a company with 20 percent market share that acquires a competitor with 10 percent market share, it is tempting to attribute most if not all "market" competence to the larger acquirer with perceived superior management, production, and marketing. From a co-competence point of view, however, the acquirer should ask if this competitor has inferior management, production, marketing, how did they gain half of our market share? In other words, the competitor must know some things as well as and even better than us.

It is important to identify and respect the competences of both firms in order to pursue the superior co-competence approach to organizational integration. This requires constructive and learning interaction between the joining firms, which leads us to better management of the human side of M&A. A key source of the many advantages of the co-competence approach is that it is far superior in managing the third major synergy determinant of employee resistance.

Human resource integration factors: Avoiding resistance and achieving cooperation

Most employees tend to react negatively to being acquired. However, the strength, duration, and dysfunctional effects of such reactions vary between different M&As. One major reason for this variation is the different organizational integration approaches (i.e. soft/hard/co-competence) discussed above. These approaches offer striking differences between perspectives on the human side of M&A.

Negative employee reactions in M&As can be viewed in terms of *cultural clashes* (e.g. Nahavandi and Malekzadeh 1988, Buono and Bowditch 1989, Chatterjee et al.

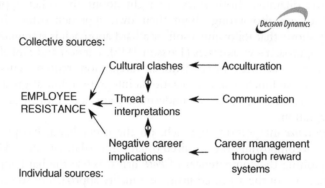

Figure 1.2   Different sources of employee resistance

1992, Cartwright and Cooper 1996). Employee resistance is seen as originating from different corporate cultures at a collective level. Researchers and practitioners who adhere to this perspective claim that (in addition to trying to reduce cultural clashes by selecting combinations with similar cultures) it is essential to develop and foster a new, joint corporate culture. However, other research indicates that this is much easier to state than to accomplish (Larsson 1990, 1993a, Larsson and Lubatkin 2001).

Employee resistance also can be viewed as stemming from *communication* problems (Brousseau 1989, Schweiger and DeNisi 1991, Driver, Brousseau, and Hunsaker 1993). Lack of information, misunderstanding, interpreted threats, and negative rumors interfere with employee perceptions and trust. This leads to resistance and conflict at the interpersonal level. Communication solutions include more precise, extensive, early sharing of real information and team-building initiatives, which are also hard to achieve between parties with initially limited knowledge and trust of one another.

A third and more individual perspective is to view employee reactions in terms of *career* implications (e.g. Hirsch 1987, Walsh 1989). From this point of view, individual employees may resist M&A because of anticipated or actual negative effects on their own careers or working lives. This includes less job security, reduced benefits, blocked advancement opportunities, greater workloads, upset career planning, and so on (Larsson et al. 2001). Career solutions typically involve having reward systems that counteract these negative implications and instead support the integration process. However, this is no simple feat either (Schweiger, Ivancevich, and Power 1987, Larsson, Eneroth, and König 1996).

These cultural, communication, and career perspectives span the collective, interpersonal, and individual levels and sources of employee resistance in M&As as illustrated by Figure 1.2. While all three sources are relevant, researchers as well as practitioners tend to focus on only one of them. This is unfortunate since they represent *simultaneous* sources of employee resistance and focusing on only one is likely to result in two negative surprises. For example, trying to reduce cultural clashes through joint socialization efforts at the collective level can still lead to resistance.

This stems from lack of information and/or negative career implications at the interpersonal and individual levels. Alternatively, if one focuses solely on achieving employee cooperation through improved communication, there is still the risk of cultural clashes and negative career implications at the two other levels.

Employee resistance is also an important determinant of synergy realization. The key to reducing employee resistance is to manage all collective, interpersonal, and individual levels with joint acculturation, communication, and career development efforts (Larsson 1990). This is possible by combining the co-competence approach for accomplishing organizational integration with multiple, mainly "co-motivational" human resource considerations at all three levels to achieve employee cooperation.

A Co-Competence and Motivational Approach to Acculturation in M&A

Larsson and Lubatkin (2001) tested six alternative determinants of achieved acculturation (i.e. the development of a jointly shared, constructive culture and overcoming cultural clashes) in 50 M&As. None of the four selection-based determinants of relatedness, relative size, domestic versus cross-border, and acquirer nationality was found to have statistically significant effects. Nor did the imposition of formal controls through autonomy removal have a negative impact. The only strong determinant for achieving acculturation was "social controls". That is, socialization and coordination efforts like cross-visits, introduction and training programs, joint social events, celebrations, transition teams, job rotation, and other motivational human resource exchanges between the joining firms were shown to enhance acculturation.

Acculturation in joined organizations is difficult. Individual organizations develop and retain their cultures through socialization and maintenance mechanisms (cf. Berger and Luckmann 1966). M&As face dual barriers to acculturation as separate social cohesion mechanisms tend to be maintained. They perpetuate "we-versus-they" interpretations and often lack joint socialization mechanisms to create jointly shared norms and values (Larsson 1990). Development of joint socialization mechanisms in M&As is a long-term endeavor that requires overcoming persistent defenses of the separate cultural maintenance mechanisms. This typically requires more immediate integration efforts on the interpersonal and individual levels. Next, we examine an approach to communication in M&A.

A Co-Competence and Motivational Approach to Communication in M&A

There are several barriers to effective communication to manage uncertainty and threat interpretations at the interpersonal level in M&A. On one hand, the acquiring company initially has only limited knowledge about the acquired company and how integration will occur. Some of this knowledge may also be viewed as "secret" in attempts to establish advantages under conditions of uncertainty for the individuals of the acquired firm. The acquiring company is often located some distance away from the acquired company. Thus, the initial communication from the acquiring firm tends to be minimal and often limited to promises of "no changes" (Austin 1970).

There is rarely any event that creates more uncertainty among employees than becoming acquired. What will happen? Will we stay or be moved? Who will do what? Will there be lay-offs? Who will be my boss? Will we have to change our name? Will the sales forces be kept separate or integrated? Almost everything is up in the air and the need for detailed information is greater than ever. At the same time, the acquirer often provides very little information. Distrust grows and undermines whatever information is shared. Promises of "no changes" don't tend to ring true in the face of the very real change that has occurred with many more likely to come. This misinformation and dearth of information are usually filled, and countered, with negative rumors (e.g. Pritchett 1985) as people try to make sense of uncertainty.

Resulting suspicion and resistance from acquired employees can disappoint even the most well-intended acquirer. This disappointment can, in turn, further limit the acquirer's communication, creating a vicious communication circle, representing a strong interpersonal source of employee resistance. Given that most of the acquired corporate value and synergy potentials are sustained and realized by the acquired employees, a more effective communication approach is needed, e.g. information sharing that considers and values the acquired employees through:

- Voice – timely, honest communication that reduces employee uncertainty, active listening to their thoughts and feelings to learn how to best integrate the combining companies;
- Involvement in the integration process by retaining as much of the acquired corporate values as possible and by seeking ideas and suggestions from employees about their integration and improvement solutions; and
- Precision in two-way communication and integration because people process information in different ways, have different career motives, experience threats in different ways and therefore need different information and solutions.

Driver and Brousseau developed the decision style model as a conceptual, assessment, communication, and team-building tool that is helpful in avoiding common misunderstandings. Precision of the two-way VIP communication approach in M&A (Brousseau 1989, Driver, Brousseau, and Hunsaker 1993) can also be increased. It is based on how people differ when processing information.

The first dimension where people differ significantly is in the amount of *information use*. That is, does the individual settle for using only small or moderate amounts of information – satisfice – or does he/she use as much information as possible – maximize? Which is the best way to process information and make decisions? The correct answer is that it depends on the situation that sometimes favors the fast action of satisficing and, at other times, rewards the complex analysis of maximizing.

| | Information use | |
	Satisficer	Maximizer
Unifocus	**Decisive** fast, action-oriented loyal efficient	**Hierarchic** analytic logical quality-oriented
Multifocus	**Flexible** fast, action-oriented social adaptable	**Integrative** analytic team-oriented creative

(Solution focus labels the rows: Unifocus and Multifocus.)

Figure 1.3   Decision style matrix

However, a satisficer tends to view a maximizer as slow and prone towards analysis paralysis, while a maximizer often sees a satisficer as hasty and irresponsible. Even though their strengths could offset each other's weaknesses, satisficers and maximizers typically consider the other way of processing information as stupid.

The second decision style dimension is *solution focus*. Does the person generate one single solution to a problem and stick to it over time – unifocus – or does he/she generate several different solutions that are all entertained and/or changed over time – multifocus? Again, neither unifocus nor multifocus is generally better than the other. This also depends on the situation. Stability may make unifocus more efficient and multifocus may be more able to deal with changing conditions. However, a unifocus person tends to view a multifocus as "wishy-washy" and unreliable, while a multifocus individual often sees a unifocus as rigid and narrow-minded. They are more likely to view each other as stupid than as having complementary information-processing skills.

The combination of these two dimensions creates a matrix with four major types of decision styles – decisive, flexible, hierarchic, and integrative (Driver, Brousseau, and Hunsaker 1993) as shown in Figure 1.3. The diagonal relationships between the decision styles represent the worst, most "toxic" style clashes, where two persons can view each other as "doubly stupid". For example, a flexible person can see a hierarchic as both slow and rigid, while the hierarchic person considers the flexible as both hasty and unreliable.

The decision style model helps interacting persons to understand themselves and others in more constructive ways by pointing out that differences in processing information are complementary rather than stupid. This also helps people to understand the benefits of mutual accommodation to each other's decision styles. This becomes highlighted in M&A where there are strong tendencies to view "the others" and their ways as stupid (Brousseau 1989). Learning the decision style model and the style profiles of oneself and interacting others can greatly improve communication and teamwork in corporate combinations and during other periods of strategic change (Driver, Brousseau, and Hunsaker 1993, Driver et al. 1996).

A Co-Competence and Motivational Approach to Career Development in M&A

Negative career implications can result in employee resistance at the individual level (e.g. Hirsch 1987). Benefits can be cut, job security reduced by threatening lay-offs, advancement opportunities thwarted by losing one's boss, and career planning upset by the surprise of the M&A (Larsson et al. 2001). At the same time, most employees are asked to contribute more during integration, on top of existing work. Synergies are also realized by reducing the number of employees in the joint organization, who, in turn, end up doing the work of the two separate companies together. This is "value extraction" gained from hopefully increased efficiencies of the two firms combined. What this basically boils down to is that most employees have to do more for less. The M&A tends to make them "double losers" from a career perspective, generating a sufficiently strong motive for resistance (cf. increasing contributions and decreasing inducements in the Barnard–Simon model of organizational participation; March & Simon 1956).

Motivating employees to contribute additional integration effort requires inducement. This can be done in two major ways. First, the expensive way, offering employees extrinsic rewards. In other words, "bribing" employees with more money so they won't resist the M&A integration. Unfortunately, this approach rewards or pays employees not to resist. In contrast, the use of intrinsically rewarding integration efforts actually increases employee motivation. This approach enables employees to do more tasks they believe are exciting.

However, the difficulty of intrinsically motivating integration efforts is that employees perceive motivators differently. In other words, what one employee feels is a motivating task, another will feel is a demotivating punishment. For example, some appreciate stability and are demotivated by changes. Others appreciate change and novelty to the extent that they will leave an organization which merely offers secure stability. We therefore need to better understand different individual motives if we are to increase the motivational precision of integration efforts in M&A. The career concept model is a suitable framework for doing so (Driver 1980, Brousseau et al. 1996). It distinguishes between four major career and motivational patterns:

- **Expert** that strives to remain within one occupation and become as good as possible at this during the whole work life. Expert motives include security, being allowed to refine one's expertise and being recognized for this expertise.
- **Linear** that strives to climb upward on the corporate ladder towards positions of higher authority. Linear motives include power and achievement.
- **Spiral** that periodically (every 5–10 years) moves laterally to related occupations where previous experience can be applied in new ways. Spiral motives include creativity and personal growth.
- **Transitory** that frequently (every 2–4 years) changes to new and unrelated occupations. Transitory motives include variety and independence.

A major contribution of the career concept model is that it provides four different perspectives on one's own and others' working lives. This is generally speaking and in

	Expert	Linear	Spiral	Transitory
Focus	+ islands of stability + true security + maintaining existing value creation + corporate memory	opportunities for: + corporate growth + leadership + efficiency improvements + promotion + achievement/ winning	+ applying existing competences in new areas + integrating new and existing operations + strategic renewal + long-term creative teamwork + personal growth	+ network with many new people + fast and novel action + short-term transition teams/projects + travel + quick learning
Avoid	- uncertainty - insecurity - turbulence	- relative demotion - delayering - downsizing	- non-involvement	- non-involvement - long-term commitment

Figure 1.4   Co-competence and motivational division of integration work

relation to M&A in particular. Even at the individual career level, there are different reasons or motives to resist M&A. An expert person can resist them due to all the destabilizing changes they tend to bring. A linear person can resist them if they demote him/her to lower hierarchic levels while spiral and transitory persons can resist because they are not being sufficiently involved.

If we only try to manage one type of negative career implication at the individual level, we are likely to get three other negative surprises. However, if we try to protect everybody from everything, there will be no integration at all. The more motivationally precise career management of M&A includes protecting an individual from what is most demotivating to him/her individually. At the same time, more integration work that is intrinsically motivating to that particular person can be offered. The career concept model may offer an effective basis for precise division of the broad array of needed integration activities according to the individuals' different motivational profiles, as illustrated in Figure 1.4 (Larsson et al. 2001).

Requiring the same integration efforts from everybody and offering them all the same rewards produces, at best, one winner and two/three losers from a career perspective. Forcing expert employees to change, demoting or downsizing linear employees, or neglecting to involve spiral and transitory employees become even more imprecise and demotivating integration approaches where almost everybody loses. However, this seems to be common practice. The two most involved categories appear to be expert employees identified with the functions to be integrated and linear managers who make the hard decisions to demote, delayer, and downsize redundant employees.

The high-precision career motivational solution to integration is intended to let individuals with primarily expert motives take care of "islands of stability" and existing value creation. Those with linear motives focus on growth and achievement opportunities; spiral-motivated employees create bridges between the old and the new; and those with transitory motives enact short-term and novel activities involved in the integration process. This career concept-based co-competence and motivational integration approach builds upon a complementary diversity of career motives to accomplish a wide range of needed integration activities for both maintaining and creating joint value.

It is of course quite unrealistic to conduct personal career coaching with all employees as an integration tool for large M&As. Time is scarce for most involved in corporate combinations and the cost of bringing in sufficient career coaching would be prohibitive. However, the current era of e-learning enables organizations to implement both time and cost-efficient solutions. Now any number of employees can get personalized career e-coaching at any time. The Internet has already enabled more than 500,000 people to be assessed using the career concept model, mostly through Korn/Ferry International's e-cruitment website Futurestep.com and Sweden's largest white collar union SIF (see www.DecisionDynamic.se for a corporate version of this career e-coaching called the Career Adventure®).

Conclusion

Co-competence and motivational realization of synergies in M&A

The complete co-competence and motivational approach for realizing M&A synergies then is to combine the three major synergy determinants of selecting high strategic combination potential, while managing high organizational integration and high employee cooperation/low resistance during the subsequent post-combination process. Achieving high employee cooperation/low resistance is, in turn, dependent on managing acculturation at the collective level. This includes cultural clashes, communication at the interpersonal level of uncertainties, misunderstandings and rumors, and career development at the individual level in relation to different negative working-life implications such as job insecurity, demotions, and non-involvement. Figure 1.5 summarizes this integrative framework for synergy realization in M&A that as a whole can account for at least 60–70 percent of the variance in performance.

Timing is essential. Prior to the combination, it is primarily the choice of companies with high strategic combination potential that creates the future opportunities to realize synergies. Mainly anecdotal evidence suggests that corporate combinations made in late recessions have the advantages of lower prices, less organizational integration overload, and less employee resistance compared to those made during boom periods.

Once the combination is made, *both speed and long-term orientation* become paramount. Integration efforts are necessary for synergy realization and should not be delayed for pacifying purposes. However, it is better to start with positive integration efforts of the co-competence and motivational approach that give resources, influence, and opportunities to the acquired firm rather than taking them away. One of the few easy things in M&A is to actualize positive surprise in acquired employees with two-way communication, career development, opportunities to influence, and organizational investments, given their prevalent negative expectations, fears, and rumors. Especially high-precision communication and team-building at the interpersonal level and also high-precision career development and division of integration

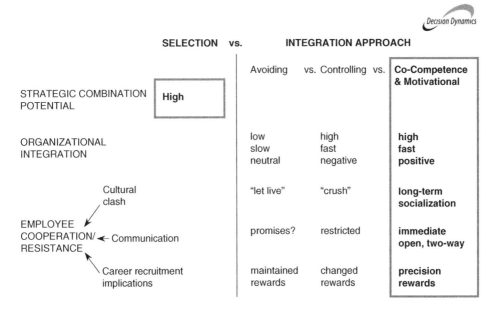

Figure 1.5   A framework for synergy realization through a co-competence and motivational approach

work according to different motivational profiles at the individual level are important co-competence and motivational approaches to turn employee resistance into cooperation as soon as possible.

At the same time, it is not only what is done immediately that matters to synergy realization in M&A. Operational synergies are typically realized on a continual, long-term basis rather than as quick fixes. Initial speed is essential so that strategic momentum is not lost to competitors. This includes the commencement of organizational coordination and avoidance of the vicious circle of employee resistance. However, M&A integration should never be viewed as something that can be completed in "X" months. Good M&As are both "now" and "forever". It is impossible to know all synergy potentials and the best ways to realize them immediately. Thus, high synergy-realizing M&As often discover new potentials and better ways to achieve them over time through additional long-term orientation of the co-competence and motivational approach (Larsson 1990). The achievement of acculturation is also clearly a long-term task to replace persistent "we and our better ways versus they and their worse ways" with a common "we with the best of both ways".

For example, Tetra Laval Prepared Food was still suffering from culturally clashing "we versus they" views two years after Tetra Pak's acquisition of Alfa Laval (Larsson et al. 2001). This unit was formed by an approximately equal number of employees from each of the combined corporations. Their respective views of themselves and each other were firmly anchored in their diverse corporate histories. However, through the use of the career concept model, they began adopting a career perspective that was more future-oriented and individualized. The collective defense of their past identities gave way to a more shared view of a joint organization with common goals as well as motivational diversity. By measuring their individual career profiles and organizational career culture, they were able to manage the subsequent integration process with greater precision and mutual understanding.

References

Aupperle, K.E., Acar, W., and Booth, D.E. 1986. An empirical critique of in search of excellence: How excellent are the excellent companies? *Journal of Management*, **12**: 499–512.

Austin, D.V. 1970. Merger myths: We contemplate no changes in personnel. *Mergers and Acquisitions*, **5**(5): 20–1.

Berger, P.L. and Luckmann, T. 1966. *The Social Construction of Reality*. New York: Anchor Books.

Bower, J.L. 2001. Not all M&As are alike – and that matters. *Harvard Business Review*, March: 93–101.

Brousseau, K.R. 1989. Navigating the merger transition. *Journal of Organizational Change Management*, **2**(1): 72–8.

Brousseau, K.R., Driver, M.J., Eneroth, K., and Larsson, R. 1996. Career pandemonium: Realigning organizations and individuals. *Academy of Management Executive*, **10**(4): 52–66.

Buono, A.F. and Bowditch, J.L. 1989. *The Human Side of Mergers and Acquisitions*. San Francisco: Jossey-Bass.

Cartwright, S. and Cooper, C.L. 1996. *Managing Mergers, Acquisitions, and Alliances: Integrating People and Cultures*. Oxford: Butterworth Heinemann.

Chatterjee, S., Lubatkin, M., Schweiger, D.M., and Weber, Y. 1992. Cultural differences and shareholder value. *Strategic Management Journal*, **13**: 319–34.

Datta, D.K., Narayanan, V.K., and Pinches, G.E. 1992. Factors influencing wealth creation from mergers and acquisitions: A meta-analysis. *Strategic Management Journal*, **13**: 67–84.

Driver, M.J. 1980. Career concepts and organizational change. In C.B. Derr (ed.), *Work, family, and the Career*. New York: Praeger.

Driver, M.J., Brousseau, K.R., and Hunsaker, P.L. 1993. *The Dynamic Decision Maker: Five Decision Styles for Executive and Business Success*. San Francisco: Jossey-Bass.

Driver, M.J., Svensson, K., Amato, R.P., and Pate, L.E. 1996. A human information processing approach to strategic change: Altering managerial decision styles. *International Studies of Management and Organization*, **26**(1): 41–58.

Goldberg, W.H. 1983. *Mergers: Motives, Modes, Methods*. Aldershot: Gower.

Haspeslagh, P.C. and Jemison, D.B. 1991. *Managing Acquisitions: Creating Value through Acquisition Activity*. New York: Free Press.

Hirsch, P.M. 1987. *Pack Your Own Parachute: How to Survive Mergers, Takeovers, and Other Corporate Disasters*. Reading, MA: Addison-Wesley.

Hunsaker, P.L. and Coombs, M.W. 1988. Mergers and acquisitions: Managing the emotional issues. *Personnel*, March: 56–63.

Jensen, M.C. 1984. Takeovers: Folklore and science. *Harvard Business Review*, **60**(6): 109–21.

Larsson, R. 1990. *Coordination of Action in Mergers and Acquisitions: Interpretive and Systems Approaches towards Synergy*. Lund, Sweden: Lund University Press.

Larsson, R. 1993a. Barriers to acculturation in mergers and acquisitions: Strategic human resource implications. *Journal of European Business Education*, **2**(2): 1–18.

Larsson, R. 1993b. Case survey methodology: Quantitative analysis of patterns across case studies. *Academy of Management Journal*, **36**: 1515–46.

Larsson, R., Driver, M.J., Holmqvist, M., and Sweet, P.L. 2001. Career disintegration and reintegration in mergers and acquisitions: Managing the competence and motivational intangibles. *European Management Journal*, **19**: 609–18.

Larsson, R., Eneroth, K., and König, I. 1996. On the folly of rewarding domestic stability while hoping for international expansion. *International Studies of Management and Organization*, **26**(1): 105–33.

Larsson, R. and Finkelstein, S. 1999. Integrating strategic, organizational, and human resource perspectives on mergers and acquisitions: A case survey of synergy realization. *Organization Science*, **10**: 1–26.

Larsson, R. and Lubatkin, M. 2001. Achieving acculturation in mergers and acquisitions: An international case survey study. *Human Relations*, **54**: 1573–607.

Lubatkin, M. 1983. Mergers and the performance of the acquiring firm. *Academy of Management Review*, **8**: 218–25.

March, J.G. and Simon, H.A. 1956. *Organizations*. New York: Wiley.

Marks, M.L. and Mirvis, P.M. 1998. *Joining Forces: Making One Plus One Equal Three in Mergers, Acquisitions, and Alliances*. San Francisco: Jossey-Bass.

Nahavandi, A. and Malekzadeh, A.R. 1988. Acculturation in mergers and acquisitions. *Academy of Management Review*, **13**: 79–90.

Napier, N.K. 1989. Mergers and acquisitions, human resource issues and outcomes: A review and suggested typology. *Journal of Management Studies*, **26**: 271–89.

Pablo, A.L. 1994. Determinants of acquisition integration level: A decision-making perspective. *Academy of Management Journal*, **37**: 803–36.

Pritchett, P. 1985. *After the Merger: Managing the Shockwaves*. Dallas, TX: Dow Jones-Irwin.

Ravenscraft, D.J. and Scherer, F.M. 1987. *Mergers, Sell-offs, and Economic Efficiency*. Washington, DC: Brookings Institution.

Schweiger, D.M. and DeNisi, A.S. 1991. Communication with employees following a merger: A longitudinal field experiment. *Academy of Management Journal*, **34**: 110–35.

Schweiger, D.M., Ivancevich, J.M., and Power, F.R. 1987. Executive actions for managing human resources before and after acquisition. *Academy of Management Executive*, **12**: 127–38.

Schweiger, D.M. and Walsh, J.P. 1990. Mergers and acquisitions: An interdisciplinary view. *Research in Personnel and Human Resource Management*, **8**: 41–107.

Searby, F.W. 1969. Control of postmerger change. *Harvard Business Review*, **47**(5): 4–12, 154–5.

Singh, H. and Montgomery, C.A. 1987. Corporate acquisition strategies and economic performance. *Strategic Management Journal*, **8**: 37–86.

Sweet, P. 2001a. Strategic value configuration logics and the "new economy": A service economy revolution? *International Journal of Service Industry Management, Special Issue on Service Quality in the New Economy: Interdisciplinary and International Dimensions*, **12**(1): 70–83.

Sweet, P. 2001b. *Designing Interactive Value Development: Perspectives and Strategies for High-precision Marketing*. Ph.D. Dissertation. Lund University.

Walsh, J.P. 1989. Doing a deal: Merger and acquisition negotiations and their impact upon target company top management turnover. *Strategic Management Journal*, **10**: 307–22.

Weston, J.F. and Chung, K.S. 1983. Do mergers make money: A research summary. *Mergers & Acquisitions*, **18**(3): 40–8.

CHAPTER TWO

Mind the Gap: Key Success Factors in Cross-Border Acquisitions

Noa Erez-Rein, Miriam Erez, Shlomo Maital

Abstract

The purpose of the research was to identify gaps in non-financial factors between two partners in international mergers and acquisitions (IM&As) using case study methodology. Three Israeli companies that had been acquired, or invested in, by a large American-based global company participated in the study. Specifically, we interviewed 31 managers at different managerial levels from the acquired and acquiring organizations. The content analysis of the interviews, together with company documents, served as a basis for three written case studies, generation of the results, and the model for this study. Seven key success factors (KSFs) were identified in the gap analysis, portraying the differences between the acquired and acquiring companies, and hence, causing potential conflicts in business environment, deal motives, deal strategy, processing of the deal, leadership, organizational culture, and national culture. Actions taken by the companies, as part of the integration process, to close the gap with respect to these seven factors were found to be crucial for the success of the deal.

Introduction

There is a fundamental paradox in the growth strategies of many technology-intensive global companies. In addition to internal organic growth – building labor, capital, and productive capacity – growth by acquisition (merger and acquisition: "M&A") is often a key part of competitive strategy. Yet, it is now widely understood by senior managers that the post-merger performance of companies has generally (though not always) been poor. Most mergers do not achieve their objectives and the stock-market performance of merged companies has been much poorer than the market average. A study by Deloitte, Touche Worldwide of 540 companies, mainly American, with sales revenues totaling $500 billion, revealed that only about a third of the CEOs of acquiring companies were satisfied with the results. Cited in *Haaretz* (2002), the subjective probability that a merger will be successful was only 9 percent.

A study by Bridgewater Associates reveals "... the 20 companies with the greatest merger-and-acquisition activity over the past four years, a group that includes Cisco Systems, AT&T, and General Electric, are now being punished by Wall Street. Through February 4, 2002, their stocks were down, on average 15 percent, since the beginning of 2002 compared with a decline of 5 percent for the companies in the Standard & Poor's 500-stock index. Of the most acquisitive companies, those who took on the heaviest debt loads to support their acquisitions were down more than 20 percent through February 4" (*Business Week* 2002). For example, America On Line (AOL) rose to #271 (by sales revenue) on the *Fortune* 500 list for 2000, with sales of $6.886 billion (up 44 percent from 1999) and net profits of $1.232 billion. With the largest number of subscribers, AOL positioned itself strongly to dominate the ISP market, not only in the United States but also internationally, where its growth has been even stronger. After AOL's merger with Time-Warner in 2001, AOL-Time Warner posted the largest corporate loss ($54 billion) in history due to write-downs of merger-related assets. The merged firm continues to struggle.

On the opposite pole is Cisco Systems based in San Jose, California, specializing in networking hardware and software. Cisco and its CEO John Chambers are studied intensively by scholars and managers alike, because of their remarkable M&A growth strategy. Cisco has of late fallen on hard times, largely because the telecom and net-working market has collapsed during the current U.S. and world recession. However, its growth and profitability record during the 1990s were universally admired. In 2000, Cisco had sales of $19 billion, up 55.7 percent from 1999, and earned $2.688 billion in profits, up 28 percent from 1999. Between 1990 and 2000, earnings per share rose at a remarkable annual rate of 59 percent, while total return to investors (capital gains and dividends) averaged 73.4 percent yearly. Cisco achieved this rapid growth using consummate skill in acquiring companies with the knowledge and human resources it needed. During some years, 30 such acquisitions were made. Cisco had a systematic, well-defined approach for integrating a newly acquired firm into Cisco's business strategy and culture. One key aspect of this approach was in "pairing" a Cisco manager with a counterpart in the acquired company, ensuring that the Cisco manager integrated the new employee in every possible way. Many compa-nies sought to imitate Cisco's strategy of "growth by acquisition", but lacked the model, skills, and focus such strategy required.

Why have mergers proven difficult and strategically disappointing? One reason is that a substantial proportion of M&As involve cross-border deals. This adds issues of communication, culture, and management style that differ across countries, to the already formidable task of merging two companies. According to the *Economic Report of the President* (2002: 103), "During the second half of the 1990s the United States witnessed a remarkable surge in merger activity ... In 2001, 29 percent of all announced mergers and acquisitions in which a U.S.-headquartered firm was a party also involved either a foreign buyer or a foreign seller. This was a markedly higher percentage than was common during much of the 1970s and 1980s."

Often M&A deals are led principally by the financial side of management and enormous effort is invested in the financial structuring – valuation, deal structure, compensation for employees who leave or who remain, etc. But, in many ways, finance is the easy part. Ultimately it is people, not money, who merge, bond, ally, and work together; and it is from a people perspective that successful cross-border M&A integration should focus.

The current study focuses on the non-financial factors involved in international mergers and acquisitions (IM&As). The approach we take is on gap analysis consisting of *identifying* the non-financial factors – both at the organizational and the national level; *analyzing* the gaps between the combined organizations on each one of these factors; and *evaluating* the extent to which these gaps are managed and resolved in the integration process.

Review of the Literature

Unsuccessful M&As are not a new phenomenon. Since the 1970s, extensive evidence has shown that between 50–80 percent of M&As are financially unsuccessful (Ellis and Pekar 1978, British Institute of Management 1986, Marks 1988). Ravenscroft and Scherer (1989) found that the profitability of target companies, on average, declines after an acquisition. McManus and Hergert (1988) reported that in the first 12 months following a merger or acquisition, companies typically experienced a loss in market value of 1–10 percent. A McKinsey and Co. study (Hunt 1988, McManus and Hergert 1988) found evidence to suggest that most organizations would have received a better rate of return on their investment if they had merely banked their money rather than acquired another company (adapted from Cartwright and Cooper 1996). Furthermore, there is evidence of adverse effects of M&As on an array of behaviors and applications: lowered productivity, worsened strike records, higher absenteeism, and poorer accident rates (Meeks 1977, Sinetar 1981).

Perception of M&As as a financial transaction

A review of M&A literature shows a clear bias in viewing M&As as mainly, if not exclusively, financial transactions. The issues that attract most of the attention in identifying suitable acquisition targets or during due diligence are taxes, financial statements, marketing, R&D, shareholding details, management and industrial relations etc. (e.g. Hill Samuel Bank 1989). There are few or no recommendations in relation to human aspects of the acquired company. Jemison and Sitkin (1986) differentiated between making an M&A decision and making an M&A work. Making an M&A decision has to do with the selection process (i.e. recognizing the synergistic potential). Making an M&A work, on the other hand, has to do with management of the integration process (i.e. releasing that potential). The traditional perception of M&As as mostly financial transactions affects the decision-making process from the formation of the acquisition team. The team, usually composed of five or more lawyers and accountants primarily with technical or functional experience (Free 1983, Hunt 1988, McManus and Hergert 1988), evaluates the financial and legal feasibility of the deal, including issues of availability, price, potential economies of scale, and projected earning ratios (Jemison and Sitkin 1986). However, assessing people and their intangible assets is often overlooked in the process of deciding whether to acquire an organization (Cartwright and Cooper 1996).

The non-financial factors – the human side of M&As

Levinson (1970) used the metaphor of marriage to describe M&As, meaning that M&As, like marriage, have all the problems of integrating two separate entities into one working combination. Davy et al. (1988) attributed "employee problems" as being responsible for 33–50 percent of all merger failures. A discussion paper prepared by the British Institute of Management (1986) identified 16 factors associated with unsuccessful mergers and acquisitions, nearly half of which directly related to people and people management issues: (1) Underestimating the difficulties of merging two cultures; (2) Underestimating the problems of skill transfer; (3) Demotivation of employees of acquired company; (4) Departure of key people in acquired company; (5) Too much energy devoted to "doing the deal", not enough to post-acquisition planning and integration; (6) Decision-making delayed by unclear responsibilities and post-acquisition conflicts; and (7) Neglecting existing business due to the amount of attention going into the acquired company (adapted from Cartwright and Cooper 1996: 28).

There is no single factor that determines whether an acquisition will fail or succeed. Interestingly, Hunt (1988) found that company experience in former acquisitions is not a significant factor in predicting current acquisition success. Datta (1991) found a correlation between poor merger performance and differences in management style.

Integration

In most M&A transactions the focus is usually on the deal opportunity, overlooking "the morning after". "Most deals are driven by conceptual strategies and not by operational realities. When the deal is done there is no blueprint for implementation" (Feldman and Spratt 1987: 411). The implementation stage of the deal entails integrating the two companies into one new synergetic company including organizational structures, management styles, employee expectations, policies, and culture. "This is the human side of the post-merger equation. It drives performance, consumes most of the operating costs and suffers the most severe and debilitating impact from a merger" (Feldman and Spratt 1987: 410).

Because of neglect in the initial planning stage, many integration processes suffer from delay and confusion. Key decisions take much time and effort resulting in an erosion of the strategic and economic value of the acquisition, delays, and reduction of shareholder returns (Feldman and Spratt 1987).

The few studies that focused on the human side of M&As led to the conclusion that the key to M&A success was essentially the way in which the "transitional process" was managed and the quality of the working relationship between the partnering organizations. Studies that investigated failed mergers showed that in 81 percent of these cases reporting relationships were said to be unclear or frequently changed (Kitching 1967), and that the cost of culture collisions resulting from poor integration may be as high as 25–30 percent of the performance of the acquired organization (Walter 1985). The acquisitions of Chrysler by Daimler-Benz, and of Nixdorf by Siemens are good illustrations. Even though entrepreneurial Nixdorf and bureaucratic Siemens are both German companies, the cultural clash was enormous making the integration process far longer and costlier than Siemens originally imagined. Differences in national cultures, as in the case of Daimler-Benz and Chrysler, make the integration even harder.

Culture

The definition of culture ranges from the specific view of Schweder and LeVine (1984) that culture is a set of shared meaning systems to Hershkovits' (1955: 305) broad view that "culture is the man-made part of the environment" (in Erez and Earley 1993). Culture can be defined at different levels: national, organizational, and group (Erez and Earley 1993). Any definable group with a shared history can have a culture. Thus, in one nation or one organization there can be a number of sub-cultures (Triandis 1972, Schnieder 1975, Schein 1990, Cartwright and Cooper 1996). "Once a group has learned to hold common assumptions about adaptation to the environment, its members respond in similar patterns of perception, thought, emotion, and behavior to external stimuli" (Erez and Earley 1993: 23). Cross-cultural business interactions such as cross-border M&As comprise both national culture and organizational culture, interwoven, a concept Barkema, Bell, and Pennings (1996) termed a "doubled-layered acculturation process".

Cultural differences have been associated with lower commitment and cooperation of acquired employees (Sales and Mirvis 1984, Buono, Bowditch, and Lewis 1985), diminished relative standing and increased turnover among acquired executives (Hambrick and Cannella 1993, Lubatkin, Schweiger, and Weber 1998), and lower financial success (Nahavandi and Malekzadeh 1988, Datta 1991, Haspeslagh and Jemison 1991, Chatterjee et al. 1992). Culture clashes are likely to be more prominent in cross-national acquisitions than in domestic ones (Schneider 1988, Very, Calori, and Lubatkin 1993), since such mergers bring together not only two firms that may have different organizational cultures but also organizational cultures rooted in different national cultures (Veiga et al. 2000).

Mergers and acquisitions generate change and thus uncertainty and instability that often result in culture clash (Cartwright and Cooper 1996). As in any human interaction, M&As impact both the macro level (organizational) and micro levels (individual). Incongruity of person–organization fit (P–O fit) has been shown to negatively impact job satisfaction and stress which, in turn, affects physical and mental well-being, in turn affecting organizational performance and quality of work life (Cartwright and Cooper 1996). Therefore, if organizational cultures of merging or acquiring companies differ greatly, there is a high probability that employees may no longer "fit" into the new cultural environment, and negative consequences will be felt (Cartwright and Cooper 1996).

Furthermore, there is an atmosphere of "winning" or "losing" surrounding M&As (mainly acquisitions) as one side is "conquered" by the other. Hambrick and Cannella (1993) showed that there was a great pressure on managers to "break the bond with the way things were and conform to the culture of the buying firm" (1993: 735), causing the "acquired manager" to experience a "culture clash".

Since companies are competing in a global market, the probability of merging two different types of organization is quite high. Cross-border M&As bring with them change and unrest that hoist cultural issues to the surface in everyday interactions. Therefore, leadership that actively manages the cultural dimensions in the integration stage of an M&A may determine the success of the transaction.

Some researchers clearly distinguished between cultural distance and the way it was being treated. They viewed cross-cultural distance in routines and in the repertoires of activities between two merging companies as a competitive advantage of the new venture (Morosini 1998, Morosini, Shane, and Singh 1998). International M&As enabled accessibility to new knowledge, and ways of operations that did not exist in the home company. In their study, Morosini, Shane, and Singh (1998) demonstrated that cultural distance between the two partners positively affected performance of the new venture, depending on the steps taken after the M&As. Flexible integration strategies that did not undermine the routines and repertoires of behaviors in the acquired company, and strong communication links were crucial for the success of the integration.

Leadership

Leaders of both organizations are the key players in the acquisition transaction. Managing the transitional process and the quality of the working relationship between the two organizations were found to be crucial for the success of the deal (Kitching 1967). The perceptions of the leader, and the actions taken by him/her, affect the organizational strategies and culture (Malekzadeh and Nahavandi 1998). Leaders of both organizations are representatives of their national and organizational culture. Therefore, respect and acknowledgment of cultural differences – national and organizational – are important factors in the successful integration throughout the post-acquisition process.

In summary, our review of the literature has pointed to key non-financial factors, all of them related to the beliefs and values of people involved, and to the leadership that drives M&A success or failure. Also addressed are the potential conflicts embedded in the differences in motives, perceptions, and values between the two merging organizations. The literature also emphasizes the importance of the integration phase for overcoming these conflicts. Building upon the literature review we further developed the conceptual framework of the current study.

The conceptual framework

The development of the conceptual framework was an inductive-interpretive process (Van Maanen 1998). While we initially identified the overall problem (i.e. the failure of a majority of M&As) and had a tentative research focus (i.e. the influence of non-financial human factors for determining success), construction of the subsequent framework was based on the variables that surfaced from the data. While extant literature was used to obtain an initial understanding of the field, we attempted to go into the companies with a clear slate (Eisenhardt 1989).

The current research focuses on the non-financial human factors that influence the success of the M&A transaction. The underlying conceptual framework that directs this study consists of two major components: gap analysis and the integration process.

First, we argue that through the analysis of gaps between involved parties in key factors to the success of the deal, conflicts, clashes, and crises can be anticipated and addressed by the two parties, thus enhancing chances for success. For example, gaps in leaders' perceptions, and expectations, and lack of respect for differences in organizational and cultural values have the potential to cause the transaction to fail. Second, we argue that recognizing those gaps and then acting to close them, can significantly improve chances of success. Therefore, the integration process, and the extent to which it manages to bridge the gaps and minimize potential clashes, is crucial for the success of the M&As.

Method

The multiple case study approach

In line with our conceptual framework, we adopted the multiple case study approach, which allows us to conduct an in-depth inquiry of the gaps in the most salient factors in each case. This, in turn, enables us to identify the common factors across all cases that are crucial for the success of the deal.

The case-based research is one type of qualitative research focusing on "understanding the dynamics present within single settings" (Eisenhardt 1989: 534). It focuses more on specific cases and exceptions rather than on abstractions and generalizations, and uses an inductive-interpretive approach rather than the hypothetical-deductive research model (Van Maanen 1998).

In the multiple case study approach, each case serves as an independent experiment that provides support for the conceptual insights (Shona and Eisenhardt 1997). The case-based qualitative methodology is guided by a research problem and potentially important variables, with some reference to the extant literature (Eisenhardt 1989: 536). In the current study we focused on two research problems: (a) Identifying the gaps between cross-border merging companies in non-financial variables such as motives, culture, and leadership, that appeared in the research literature; and (b) analyzing the extent to which gaps in these factors were taken into consideration in the integration process. Comparisons among the three cases in the current study will enable the identification of common factors in the gap and integration analysis.

The participating organizations (represented by fictitious names)

Three Israeli companies and an American-based international conglomerate AMERIGROUP participated in the study. The three companies were each acquired (partially or fully) by AMERIGROUP through its various divisions. Two of the companies are in the medical imaging industry (ISRASOUND and MEDITECH), and one is in financial services for car sales and leasing (EZYCAR).

ISRASOUND was the first company to be contacted, followed by EZYCAR and finally MEDITECH. The companies participating were initially chosen because the same American company was involved in all three cases. This allowed for comparisons between the three cases while holding the foreign partner as a constant. It was assumed that the three companies varied in success factors. In other words, to the untrained eye, EZYCAR was an unsuccessful acquisition because the deal dissolved after one year. At the same time, ISRASOUND and MEDITECH were successful acquisitions, based on the evaluation of the managers on both sides.

Studies of cross-border mergers have typically used one of two types of metrics to measure success: market-based measures (e.g. percentage rise in stock price: Singh and Montgomery 1987, Chatterjee et al. 1992) or growth in sales (Morrison and Roth 1992, Morosini, Shane, and Singh 1998, Woo, Willard, and Daellenbach 1992). These measures were not feasible for our three cases, either because such data were unavailable or inappropriate. In the current study, evaluation of the deal by top managers of both sides served as the measure of success. In listening closely to the managers involved, we realized that ISRASOUND and MEDITECH were successful. EZYCAR was a success from the perspective of AMERIGROUP because the deal achieved its target amount of profit for AMERIGROUP. Yet, it was less successful from the perspective of the Israeli managers who aimed for a long-term acquisition and financial support from AMERIGROUP.

We propose that even when quantitative performance measures for merger success are available, it is important to "read" the perceptions of those involved and determine whether they believe the merger succeeded or not. This is because their behavior is largely driven by these perceptions.

A short description of the companies (represented by fictitious names)

MEDISOUND was an international company that developed and manufactured ultrasound (ULS) diagnostic systems (uses sound waves to create an image of internal organs thus assisting with medical diagnosis). MEDISOUND had divisions in Israel (headquarters for ISRASOUND), Norway, and the USA with distribution systems in Europe and Latin America. MEDISOUND was acquired fully from INVESTECH, an Israel defense-focused company, on April 1, 1998 by AMERIMED, the medical division of AMERIGROUP. ISRASOUND was acquired as a part of the MEDISOUND "package". AMERIMED initially needed only the Norwegian division, which specialized in cardiac ULS systems – a niche into which AMERIMED wanted to expand.

EZYCAR was an auto finance and operational leasing company, owned by an Israeli investment company (IIG). AMERICAP, the investment capital division in AMERIGROUP, represented by three of its businesses, acquired a minority stake in EZYCAR in March 1999. In April 2000, IIG acquired the stock held by AMERI-CAP. The deal was thus terminated.

MEDITECH was a joint venture for the development and manufacturing of Gamma cameras, between the nuclear medicine (NM) division of ISRATECH and the NM modality in AMERIMED. (ISRATECH is a pioneering Israeli firm specializing in medical imaging.) The new company (created on July 1, 1997) through the joint venture – MEDITECH – was equally owned by the partners. The two companies were partners in the development and manufacturing of the Gamma cameras but remained competitors in the sale and marketing of the products. In November 1998 the competitive phase came to an end when AMERIMED acquired the

MRI unit, and NM sales and services unit from ISRATECH. On December 31, 2000 AMERIMED bought all MEDITECH stocks held by ISRATECH.

Participants

In each of the cases, participants from all levels of management from both partners were interviewed: 22 from the Israeli companies and nine from AMERIGROUP. Participants were chosen by their role in the transaction. At the time of the interview some participants had moved to other jobs in the company. They were interviewed about the events pertaining to their previous job. Contact with relevant participants was achieved by asking each participant interviewed to recommend others who fit the research needs ("snowball"). All persons we approached agreed to be interviewed.

The research instruments

1. *The semi-structured interview*: This served as the main instrument for identifying key factors that account for success or failure of the acquisition. The semi-structured interview is guided by pre-established questions, not standardized with wording that may change depending on the direction the interview takes. This interview strategy is more flexible than the structured interview. It enables an in-depth interview where the framing and direction are set by preplanned questions, however, questions and directions that are not pre-established are welcome (Fontana and Frey 1994). Each interview contained four major issues: personal data; the story of the transaction and integration from the participants' perspective; salient differences between the companies as perceived by the participants; and personal comments.
2. *Documentation*: Additional sources of information consisted of: (1) publication sources such as books, journals, and daily newspaper articles; (2) financial documents, documentation of strategic decisions, and of procedures that were implemented during the integration process; and (3) company archives and intranet served to document the corporate culture, leadership characteristics, and communication structure and content. Use of internal data was based on company consent.

Case writing. Based on the interviews and company documents, three cases were written by the first author. The two other authors commented on the case writing and shaped it in its final form. There was complete agreement by the three researchers on the final cases. The cases were reviewed and verified by the respective companies.

Procedure.   The research was conducted in four stages: data collection; case writing; analysis of data; interpretation and generation of the integrated model. The data were collected by a group of three researchers, mainly through semi-structured in-depth interviews of the key people involved in the acquisition on both sides of the transaction. Each interview session took between 60 to 90 minutes. Present at the interview were one to three interviewers from the research team. During the interview the interviewers took notes, highlighting both verbal and non-verbal occurrences. The interviews were recorded and transcribed with the permission of the person interviewed (four of the 31 interviews were not recorded: two at the request of the participant and two due to technical failure). Interviews were collected within one month in each company. Altogether, the interviews continued for a period of six months. The transcripts of the interviews and the additional documentation served for writing three cases, one for each company.

Data analysis. The methodology we used led to the development of a tool that served two purposes: (a) assessing the factors that were brought up by each of the two partners as crucial for the success or failure of the deal; and (b) analyzing the gaps in these factors between the two sides. The process of analysis consisted of the following steps:

1. *Within-case analysis* – Each case underwent separate content analysis where key issues within the case were identified and key factors to which the transactions' outcome was attributed. Three independent researchers reviewed the issues and factors for inter-judge reliability.
2. *Between-case analysis* – The three cases were analyzed horizontally, comparing them on the key factors that were identified in the single-case analyses.

Factors from all three cases were collapsed into major categories, leading to the identification of seven key factors that accounted for the transaction outcome with some additional subcategories that emerged from the data, and were consistent with the literature. Three independent researchers reviewed the seven key factors and their subcategories, for inter-judge reliability.

For each separate case, the perspective of each participating company was analyzed for each one of the key success factors (KSFs). Potential gaps stemming from different perspectives on each one of the seven factors were identified and classified. An attempt was made to limit occurrences of unknown issues to some of the participants by re-interviewing them. Three independent researchers reviewed the analysis for inter-judge reliability. The potential gaps were analyzed horizontally, across the three cases, attempting to identify differences and similarities over and above all three cases. For each gap variable, companies were classified as: D (different); C (complementary); and UK/NR (unknown, not relevant). Again, three independent reviewers reviewed the analysis for inter-judge reliability.

Findings

Step 1: Identifying the key success factors

The within and between case analysis resulted in the identification of seven key success factors (KSFs) in and across all three cases that served as explanation of the outcome of the transaction. These factors are: business environment, deal motives, deal strategy, processing of the deal, leadership, organizational culture, and national culture.

1. *Business environment (BE)*: In an international transaction this factor represents the local geopolitical, economic, social, and cultural environment in which the deal takes place. The environment defines the potential and limitations of businesses, for example, legislative restrictions. In the case of EZYCAR, local legislative restrictions limited the Israeli investment companies' opportunities for capital recruitment. In the case of MEDITECH, investments made by the Israeli Chief Scientist Office became a crucial issue in acquisition negotiations. There was a chance, in this case, that the invested capital would need to be returned to the Chief Scientist Office or the deal would not be authorized. This was an issue AMERIMED would not necessarily have agreed to. The business environment is especially crucial in Israel, where the local market is both relatively small (compared with the United States) and given to geopolitical instability.

2. *Deal motive (DM)*: The motive of the deal is defined as *the participants' perspective on the desired outcome of the deal*. If, in the case of ISRASOUND, the motive of the Israeli parent organization (INVESTECH) was to achieve a high exit, then its objective was met, and the deal was deemed a success. Similarly within EZYCAR, the motive of AMERICAP was to find a financial investment that would yield high returns, and create a potential stepping-stone towards emerging markets. Thus, when the deal terminated a year after commencement it was not viewed by either side as a failure. AMERICAP achieved a high exit, recognizing that the chances for emerging markets in the geopolitical environment are quite low, while EZYCAR obtained much knowledge and confidence.

   In all cases, the need for a multi-level analysis was accentuated as motives of the owners were different from the management's motives. Thus, in the case of ISRASOUND, the selling of the company to AMERIMED yielded high returns for the owning parent company. However, this could have potentially resulted in the shut down of ISRASOUND which, at the time of the acquisition, were competitors of AMERIMED ULS.

3. *Deal strategy (DS)*: DS determines the *architecture of the deal* and is, seemingly, the most straightforward of the factors. It relates to the strategy used in the transaction: minority investment joint venture, merger, acquisition, etc. Yet, even an objective factor describing the actual architecture of the deal may be perceived in different ways by the two partners. An analogy that may clarify the relationship between DS and perception is the age-old example of the cup that is half-empty or half-full. There is no argument about the existence of the cup and the liquid. It is the choice of perceiving it as half-full or half-empty that we assume will affect behavior. Thus, in the case of EZYCAR, the deal was seen by EZYCAR as potential acquisition and by AMERICAP as an investment. Both parties fully understood the DS, but viewing it as an investment or potential acquisition meant, for example a different time perspective (short vs. long). This, in turn, created different expectations for commitments and eventually raised issues of mistrust between board members. The perception of the deal molded expectations and behavior of both sides, creating major clashes whose

origin remained elusive throughout the deal and long after its termination. The elusive character of this gap seemed to derive from the fact that participants assumed that since the deal strategy was straightforward and understood by both parties, it was not revisited as a potential factor for misunderstanding. Yet, through the investigative process, it became clear that the way the deal strategy was perceived had a substantive effect on the behavior of the participants.

4. *Processing of the deal (PoD)*: It is the process that unfolds as the deal is implemented. For instance, the EZYCAR deal was rife with misunderstandings, management inconsistencies, and overall negative atmosphere of interactions. Short-term objectives of AMERICAP coupled with local financial business seg-mentation, a problematic contract, and poor interpersonal relationships, created an atmosphere where differences had a high profile. In MEDITECH, on the other hand, the effort for achieving a relationship based on trust was accentuated. Much effort was put into it, including the involvement of management who were to implement the deal, heightened continuous communications, and personal effort on both sides. Long-term objectives of developing and manufacturing technology that has a global market facilitated common goals and objectives in the PoD.

5. *Leadership (L)*: This factor relates to the role played by various levels of management in the deal. A multi-level analysis of leadership was obtained by ana-lyzing the perspectives of the different levels of management involved. Different leadership levels have different roles in the various stages of transactions. At the root of any organizational transaction are individual people filling organizational roles. When organizations merge or ally it is individuals in managerial roles that design the deal, implement it, and are among those affected by it. It is the char-acteristics of these individuals and the teams they comprise that greatly affect the proceedings and outcome of the deal. In the case of ISRASOUND, proactive leadership on the part of the CEO and his team and the willingness to take a cal-culated risk on the part of the AMERIMED ULS CEO resulted, not only in the sustaining of ISRASOUND, but also the realization of the hidden value of the deal. ISRASOUND's PC-based systems (a paradigm shift in the ULS systems field) were subsequently implemented in all AMERIMED ULS systems and potentially gave AMERICAP a competitive advantage in a very mature market.

6&7. *Organizational and national culture (CU)*: We combined organizational and national culture into one factor because, in international transactions, both fac-tors shape the cultural differences between the partners. Culture represents the shared values and behavioral norms of its members. In all three cases, national identity was very strong and a source of pride. Organizations are embedded within nations. Therefore, in the present study, cultural differences between the two partners represent both national and organizational factors.

Step 2: Gap analysis

Gaps between partners, in their perceptions of the key success factors, were inter-preted and classified into one of three major categories: *Differences (D)* – differences in perceptions and expectations that created potential for clashes; *Complementary*

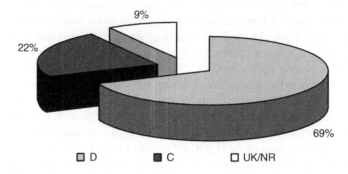

Figure 2.1 Frequencies of gap category: differences across the three cases

(C) – factors deemed as similar or synergetic; *Unknown (UK)* or *Not Relevant (NR)* – issues on which there was either insufficient data (UK) or were irrelevant to the specific case or partner (NR). Gaps were further aggregated within each category, and presented in the form of percentages. Our objective of quantifying the qualitative data is to permit an overall impression of the dominance of the gap category in terms of D, C, or UK/NR, for each of the seven factors. The findings show that overall there were more differences identified (69 percent) than complementary issues (22 percent) (Figure 2.1).

An overall comparison of the three companies in terms of the gap categories D, C, or UK/NR (Figure 2.2) showed that EZYCAR accounted for most of the differences (41 percent) with ISRASOUND accounting for 28 percent and MEDITECH accounting for 31 percent. ISRASOUND accounted for most of the similarities (48 percent) with MEDITECH accounting for 39 percent of the similarities and EZYCAR accounting for 13 percent of similarities.

In all three cases, differences exceeded complementary issues (Figure 2.3) with EZYCAR holding the highest rate of differences (84 percent D vs. 9 percent C). MEDITECH held a rate of 63 percent D vs. 26 percent C and ISRASOUND held 59 percent D vs. 30 percent C.

The highest percentage of differences (100 percent) compared to complementary issues was found for deal strategy (DS) (Figure 2.4). An example is in the case of ISRASOUND. The strategy was a full acquisition. Seemingly, this strategy limits differences in the perception of the deal. Yet, for ISRASOUND, which was not the focus of the deal, it was unclear whether AMERIMED had long-term goals for it or whether it was the beginning of its demise. All that was known was it had been acquired – not if it would survive. Next to DS the highest percentage of differences, compared to complementary, was found in the culture factor (CU) (87 percent D vs. 5 percent C) followed by the business environment (BE) factor (70 percent D vs. 30 percent C), leadership (L) (63 percent D vs. 26 percent C), processing of the deal (PoD) (56 percent D vs. 33 percent C), and deal motives (DM) (54 percent D vs. 38 percent C).

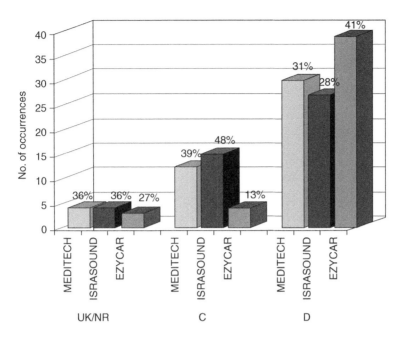

Figure 2.2 Comparison of companies by gap categories (in % & occurrences)

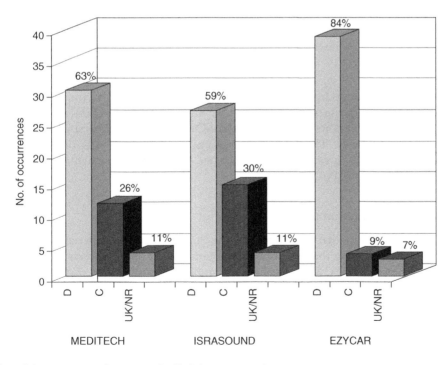

Figure 2.3 Frequency of gap categories (in % & occurrences)

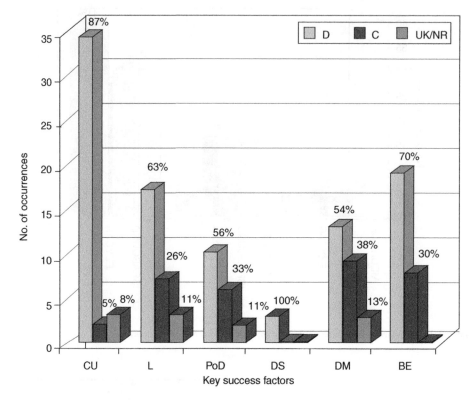

Figure 2.4   Key success factors by gap category

The primary findings from these results are that, overall, there are more differences than complementary issues. EZYCAR had the higher percentage of differences, compared with the other companies, while ISRASOUND had the highest percentage of complementary issues. The highest percentage of differences was observed with respect to DS and CU, whereas the highest percentage of complementary issues was found in DM and the PoD.

Step 3: The integration process

The three companies that participated in this study underwent different integration processes, accentuating the influence that integration has on the success of the acquisition. The case of EZYCAR exemplified the implications of the lack of an integration process. The deal strategy, which was a minority investment, and the short-term intentions of AMERICAP did not require integration. EZYCAR management expected AMERICAP to invest in training and knowledge transfer, and to acquire the company in the long run. However, there was no structured process for identifying gaps in expectations between the players. Failure to identify and deal with the differences resulted in the escalation of mistrust, accompanied by tension and dissatisfaction, that finally terminated the deal. The EZYCAR case demonstrated that even a change in the balance of owners, which does not include majority holdings or full acquisition, brings change and uncertainty into the company and therefore requires a structured transition management process.

MEDISOUND was a complete acquisition and underwent a full integration process which was delayed by six months. The case demonstrated that timing is a very important factor in the integration process. Delay of integration, interacting with strategic uncertainties, created unrest and apprehension for the acquired company. The effectiveness of the transition management was identified as another important factor in the integration process, in particular, during the first period of high ambiguity. The effective management team at ISRASOUND counterbalanced the negative impact of the delayed process of integration. The transformational leadership of the CEO and his management team managed not only to hold the company together through the long period of uncertainty but also to actively participate in the molding of the new organizational identity and integration of organizational procedures. The CEO of ISRASOUND did not use a structured process to identify gaps, doing so intuitively, attempting to find strategies to bridge them. One of the major gaps concerned the mission of ISRASOUND. The decision in AMERIMED was that ISRASOUND would concentrate on a small market niche that had very low growth potential. It meant a gradual demise of the company. There was another issue. The team at ISRASOUND believed the PC-based technology could be achieved and did not wish to shelve it. This new technology had huge market potential and would literally change the way things were done in ULS technology. The CEO of ISRASOUND turned the threat into an opportunity by negotiating a cardiac niche and the opportunity to develop a new technology in ISRASOUND.

Following this successful negotiation process, a full integration took place. This process consisted of merging the organizational structure of the acquired company with the acquiring company, forming one integrative organizational system: integrating the line structure and integrating the communication channels. The use of a matrix organizational structure facilitated the integration of the local entity with the global conglomerate. Functional managers in the Israeli site reported not only to their local CEO but also to their functional manager located in the regional headquarters. Yet, integration into the organizational hierarchy was not equally implemented in all units. The units that, from the beginning, reported to the global modality in the matrix structure were finance and HR. These units experienced more conflicts and tension than others because they were more closely controlled and centralized. Thus, these units may need relatively more coaching and support throughout the integration. Information technology played an important role in the integration process. The Israeli companies were logged onto the AMERIGROUP intranet enabling them to share knowledge, information, and cultural values with the rest of the global company. The intranet facilitated communication with professional counterparts in other countries. This included sending out inquiries concerning day-to-day problems like shortage of parts necessary for manufacturing, or as benchmarks for quality standards in other locations. The opportunity to communicate with others who were holding similar jobs or professions facilitated the integration process. Cultural differences were also encountered during the integration phase. For example, the emphasis on innovation in the Israeli companies versus the emphasis on quality, rules, and procedures in the U.S.-based multinational company. To overcome this gap, Israeli managers participated in training courses, studying methods for quality improvement, and implementing them upon return to their jobs. The Israeli company was acquired because of its technological innovation. Training programs in quality improvement served to bridge the gap in the quality-oriented culture and know-how. Yet, AMERIMED showed flexibility with respect to the local leadership and repertoires of behavior, allowing ISRASOUND to maintain its local cultural values.

MEDITECH went through a gradual process of structured integration. Initially, organizational processes (e.g. processes in manufacturing) were integrated. The third stage of the deal, which included full integration, exemplified several points. MEDITECH integration was the product of an organizational learning process that AMERIMED had undergone, implementing the experience that had been acquired from ISRASOUND integration, and other acquisitions undergone at the time. A strong capable integration manager was appointed. He had worked for AMERIMED for many years in various locations around the globe, but he was originally from Israel and understood the local culture very well. Early on in the process integration teams for each division began working together on a regular basis. The teams worked with web-based tools enabling efficient communication. The procedure deployed in MEDITECH is congruent with literature recommendations such as appointing strong transition management, appointing small efficient work teams, and having a detailed "blueprint" of the integration process (Feldman and Spratt 1987, Harbison, Viscio, and Asin 1999, Adolph, Buchanan, and Hornery 2001). Comparison between MEDITECH and ISRASOUND exemplifies the impact that an experienced integrator, leading the integration process, has on the process of the deal and its potential for success.

The integration process is also a stage where the acquiring company can reassess the initial perceived value of the acquired company, eliminate overlapping assets and capabilities, and identify hidden values (Feldman and Spratt 1987, Harbison, Viscio, and Asin 1999). ISRASOUND was a "speck of dust" to the AMERIGROUP elephant. Its hidden value to AMERIGROUP may have easily remained unidentified had the combination of active leadership on both sides and integration process not occurred.

The interviews with the AMERIGROUP participants created one salient impression on the research team – an awareness of the sensitivity needed in the transition period. This was especially emphasized in the MEDITECH case, but also found in ISRASOUND. For EZYCAR, it was acknowledged that there had been problematic interpersonal relationships on both sides, lessening the sensitivity expressed. Another action that seemed to limit the "shaking" due to uncertainty was that the acquiring company kept the core professional team. By doing so, they communicated the message that the knowledge base is important to AMERIGROUP.

In summary, the integration process was facilitated by an effective transition management, and by an integrator who was specifically responsible for the integration phase. The integration involved merging two organizational structures, merging the hierarchy of commands, connecting the acquired company with the communication system of the acquiring company, and resolving existing gaps in expectations and cultural differences.

Discussion

The current study was aimed at identifying the crucial non-financial factors that affect the success (or failure) of structural cooperations. The striking statistics, showing the failure of a majority of cross-border M&As to realize expectations of companies and investors, suggested that financial factors, per se, were not enough for predicting IM&As success (British Institute of Management 1986, Cartwright and Cooper 1996, Weber, Shenkar, and Raveh 1996).

Based on the literature review, we adopted a gap analysis approach for study-ing the differences in motives, expectations, leadership styles, and cultural values between the two partners; and the extent to which these gaps were bridged during the integration phase.

This research was based on multiple case studies using "replication logic" while treating each case as an independent experiment (Yin 1984, Eisenhardt 1989). Each case is an example of a transaction of an Israeli company with an American-based international conglomerate. Comparisons between the cases aided in the generation of the theory, by creating a scope that enabled extraction of factors relevant in all three cases, and ultimately drawing a model of the relationships between the KSFs and the outcomes. Ultimately, the case study methodology enabled us to obtain knowledge not only on the predetermined research question but also on constructs and dimensions not considered initially by the research team.

The multiple case study qualitative methodology consisted of three phases. The first phase focused on identifying the factors that were brought up by the two part-ners as crucial to the outcome of the deal in each of the three cases. The second phase focused on comparative analyses within and between the three cases. The within-case analysis revealed the existing gaps between the two sides with respect to each of the KSFs. These gaps were classified into three categories: differences that may lead to clashes; complementary that pointed at the added value of joing forces; and unknown or not relevant. The between-case analysis identified the common fac-tors that appeared in all three cases, and the differences between the three cases with respect to the gaps. This analysis revealed seven key factors that served to explain the deal success or nearly failure by both partners, in all three cases: business environ-ment, deal strategy, deal motive, processing of the deal, leadership, organizational and national culture.

The analysis of the KSFs revealed that they were interrelated and interacted with each other. For example, the deal motive affected the deal strategy, and then, later affected the processing of the deal. For example, in the case of EZYCAR, the AMERICAP motive to maximize gain in a short period of time resulted in a deal strategy of minor-ity holding. This affected the lack of integration phase in the processing of the deal. Furthermore, a change in one factor has a dynamic effect on the other factors. Thus, as an executive in AMERICAP on the EZYCAR case stated, if motivations for doing

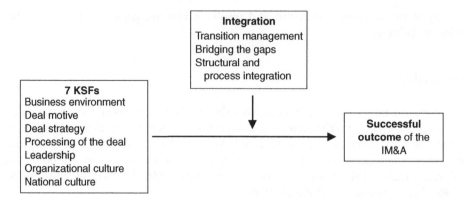

Figure 2.5   The generated model: relationship between KSFs, integration, and IM&A success

the deal had changed (e.g. changes in the market or changes in company strategy), they possibly would have exercised their option to acquire a majority holding in the company and abandoned the option to realize the 13 percent average return on their initial investment. This change would have triggered changes in both DS and PoD. We therefore propose to take a system approach for analyzing the gaps in M&As, recognizing the interdependence among the crucial factors for the success of the deal (Ackoff 1974, 1999).

Gap identification and analysis were found to be necessary, but not sufficient, for enhancing a successful outcome. Thus, the third phase focused on the assessment of the integration of gaps through planned transition management and a clear process of integration. As such, the complete process of inquiry has evolved from the identification phase to the analytical phase, and finally, to the synthesis stage of integrating and bridging the gaps. The research model that has emerged from the inquiry process consists of the following factors and their interrelationships (see Figure 2.5): the gaps between partners with respect to the KSFs influence the success of the deal. The amount of gaps signal as to the complexity of the deal, but do not by themselves determine success. It is enough to leave one gap unattended (e.g. the issue of the Chief Scientist Office's loan to the acquired companies was a potential deal breaker) for an unsuccessful outcome. It is the integration process that moderates the effect of the gaps on the deal success. An effective integration process that acknowledges and attempts to resolve the gaps (problems) between the two partners, attenuates the negative impact of potential conflicts resulting from the gaps. Lack of integration, or failure to bridge the gaps, accelerates the negative impact of the gaps and results in the failure of the IM&A.

A successful integration process may treat cultural differences as an asset rather than a threat to the success of the deal. This is because acquisitions provide access to innovative routines and repertoires of behaviors that did not exist in the home culture (Morosini, Shane, and Singh 1998). Recognizing the differences, demonstrating respect for the partners' culture, and being flexible in the integration process may turn the differences into a competitive advantage that is hard to imitate.

All three cases showed that the companies involved had more differences than similarities in key variables. The case of EZYCAR had the highest frequency of gaps. It was also the one that did not implement an integration process, resulting in a deal that did not last long. ISRASOUND was the case with the lowest frequency of gaps. Yet, it failed to uncover the hidden value of the deal as a result of a delay in the implementation of the integration phase. The strong and transformational transition management counterbalanced the negative impact of the delay, resolved some of the crucial gaps with respect to the deal motive, and successfully implemented the delayed integration process. The case of MEDITECH demonstrated that an effective implementation of the integration process, on time, and with an integration leader, helped overcome the potential gaps and resulted in successful integration. We conclude that a high rate of differences between merging or acquired companies decreases the potential for a successful outcome because it increases the potential for conflict. But, intervening between the M&A outcome and the gaps in KSFs is the crucial integration factor/skill in bridging the gaps. Thus, having many gaps and differences in the KSFs does not, in itself, determine the outcome of the transaction.

To increase chances for success, the partners need to design and implement a clear, explicit integration process that, in essence, is a strategic plan to overcome the identified gaps.

Using the term coined by Lester Thurow (1992), "a successful outcome is enhanced by the participating companies' ability to 'adapt and adopt'". If two words could summarize a long period of research on successful acquisitions it would be these two. "Adopting" is the process of identifying the required changes (gaps), essentially an analytical process. "Adapting" is strategizing action plans to reduce identified gaps, accomplishing a proper integration between the companies.

Understanding the analytic and synthetic nature of these processes is the key to achieving a successful outcome. A successful merger is far more than the sum of its parts; it is the creation of a new entity. Challenges and obstacles accompany all acts of creation. By systematically analyzing gaps and acting to reduce them, merger partners improve the likelihood that they will indeed realize the potential financial gains that underlie nearly all such deals.

Notes

Partial funding was provided by The Davidson Fund, Technion, and by TIM-Technion Institute of Management. The authors wish to express their gratitude for the help and cooperation of the managers of the American company in Israel, the CEOs of the Israeli companies, and their senior management, who participated in the study. Special thanks to Dr. Josef Rein, whose input and support were invaluable.

Dedication

To my one and only Ima – I just wish you were here, Noa.

References

Ackoff, R.L. 1974. *Redesigning the Future: A Systems Approach to Societal Problems*. New York: Wiley.

Ackoff, R.L. 1999. *Re-creating the Corporation: A Design of Organizations for the 21st Century*. New York: Oxford University Press.

Adolph, G., Buchanan, I., and Hornery, J. 2001. *Merger Integration: Delivering on the Promise*. Booz, Allen & Hamilton Inc.

Barkema, H.G., Bell, J.H., and Pennings, J.M. 1996. Foreign entry, cultural barriers, and learning. *Strategic Management Journal*, 17: 151–66.

Booz, Allen & Hamilton Inc. 1985. *Diversification: A Survey of European Chief Executives – Executive Summary*. Booz, Allen & Hamilton Inc.

British Institute of Management. 1986. *The Management of Acquisitions and Mergers* (Discussion paper No.8). Economics Department, September.

Buono, A.F., Bowditch, J.L., and Lewis, J.W. III. 1985. When cultures collide: The anatomy of a merger. *Human Relations*, 38(5): 477–500.

Cartwright, S. and Cooper, C.L. 1996. *Managing Mergers, Acquisitions and Strategic Alliances: Integrating People and Cultures*. Oxford: Butterworth-Heineman.

Chatterjee, S., Lubatkin, M., Schweiger, O., and Weber, Y. 1992. Cultural differences and shareholder value in related mergers: Linking equity and human capital. *Strategic Management Journal*, 1(5): 319–34.

Cisco Systems Inc. Economic report of the president: *Annual Report* 2002, p. 103.

Datta, D.K. 1991. Organizational fit and acquisition performance: Effects of post-acquisition integration. *Strategic Management Journal*, 12(4): 281–97.

Davy, J.A., Kinicki, A., Kilroy, J., and Scheck, C. 1988. After the merger: Dealing with people's uncertainty. *Training and Development Journal*, 42(8): 57–61.

Economic Report of the President. 2002. Washington, DC: U.S. Government Printing Office.

Eisenhardt, K.M. 1989. Building theories from case study research. *Academy of Management Review*, 14(4): 532–50.

Ellis, D.J. and Pekar, P. 1978. Acquisitions: Is 50/50 good enough? *Planning Review*, 6(4): 15–19.

Erez, M. and Earley, P.C. 1993. *Culture, Self-identity, and Work*. New York: Oxford University Press.

Feldman, M.L. and Spratt, M.F. 1987. Postmerger integration. In M.L. Rock, R.H. Rock, and M. Sikora (eds.), *The Mergers and Acquisitions Handbook*, 2nd edn. New York: McGraw-Hill, pp. 409–17.

Fontana, A. and Frey, J.H. 1994. Interviewing: The art of science. In N.K. Dezin and Y.S. Linciln (eds.), *Handbook of Qualitative Research*. Thousand Oaks, CA: Sage Publications, pp. 361–76.

Free, V. 1983. CEOs and their corporate cultures: New game plans. *Marketing Communications*, 311(3): 21–7.

Hambrick, D. and Cannella, B. 1993. Relative standing: A framework for understanding departures of acquired executives. *Academy of Management Journal*, 36(4): 733–62.

Harbison, J.R., Viscio, A.J., and Asin, A.T. 1999. *Making Acquisitions Work: Capturing Value after the Deal*. Booz, Allen & Hamilton Inc.

Haaretz. 2002. Tel Aviv, April 21: 13c.

Haspeslagh, P.C. and Jemison, D.B. 1991. *Managing Acquisitions: Creating Value Through Corporate Renewal*. New York: Free Press.

Hershkovits, M.J. 1955. *Cultural Anthropology*. New York: Knopf.

Hill Samuel Bank Limited. 1989. *Mergers, Acquisitions and Alternative Corporate Strategies.* London: W.H. Allen & Co.

Hunt, J. 1988. Managing the successful acquisition: A people question. *London Business School Journal,* summer: 2–15.

Jemison, D. and Sitkin, S.B. 1986. Corporate acquisitions: A process perspective. *Academy of Management Review,* **11**(1): 145–63.

Kitching, J. 1967. Why do mergers miscarry? *Harvard Business Review,* **45**(6): 84–101.

KPMG. 2001. Review of M&A activity worldwide. *KPMG Corporate Finance Dealwatch,* December.

Levinson, H. 1970. A psychologist diagnoses merger failures. *Harvard Business Review,* **48**(2): 139–47.

Lubatkin, M., Schweiger, D., and Weber, Y. 1998. Top management turnover in related M&As: An additional test of the theory of relative standing. *Journal of Management,* **25**(1): 39–52.

Malekzadeh, A.R. and Nahavandi, A. 1998. Leadership and culture in transitional strategic alliances. In M.C. Gertsen, A.M. Soderberg, and J.E. Torp (eds.), *Cultural Dimensions of International Mergers and Acquisitions.* Berlin: Walter de Gruyter, pp. 111–27.

Marks, M.L. 1988. How to treat the merger syndrome. *Journal of Management Consulting (Netherlands),* **4**(3): 42–51.

McManus, M.L. and Hergert, M.L. 1988. *Surviving Merger and Acquisition.* Glenview, IL: Scott, Foresman & Co.

Meeks, G. 1977. *Disappointing Marriages: A Study of the Gains from Merger.* Cambridge: Cambridge University Press.

Morosini, P. 1998. *Managing Cultural Differences: Effective Strategy and Execution Across Cultures in Global Corporate Alliances.* Oxford: Pergamon Press.

Morosini, P., Shane, S., and Singh, H. 1998. National cultural distance and cross-border acquisition performance. *Journal of International Business Studies,* **29**(1): 137–58.

Morrison, A. and Roth, K. 1992. A taxonomy of business-level strategies in global industries. *Strategic Management Journal,* **13**: 399–418.

Nahavandi, A. and Malekzadeh, A.R. 1988. Acculturation in mergers and acquisitions. *Academy of Management Review,* **13**(1): 79–90.

Ravenscroft, D.J. and Scherer, F.M. 1989. The profitability of merger. *International Journal of Industrial Organization,* **7**(1): 101–16.

Sales, A.L. and Mirvis, P.H. 1984. Acquisition and the collision of cultures. In R. Quinn and J. Kimberly (eds.), *Managing Organizational Transitions.* New York: Dow-Jones, pp. 107–33.

Schein, E.H. 1990. Organizational culture. *American Psychologist,* **45**: 109–19.

Schnieder, B. 1975. Organizational psychology: An essay. *Personal Psychology,* **28**: 447–79.

Schneider, S.C. 1988. National versus corporate culture: Implications for human resources management. *Human Resource Management,* **27**(1): 231–46.

Schweder, R.A. and LeVine, R.A. 1984. *Culture Theory: Essays on Mind, Self and Emotion.* New York: Cambridge University Press.

Sinetar, M. 1981. Mergers, morale and productivity. *Personnel Journal,* **60**: 863–7.

Singh, H. and Montgomery, C.A. 1987. Corporate acquisition strategies and economic performance. *Strategic Management Journal,* **8**: 377–86.

Shona, L.B. and Eisenhardt, K.M. 1997. The art of continuous change: Linking complexity theory and time paced evolution in relentlessly shifting organizations. *Administrative Science Quarterly,* **42**(1): 1–34.

Thurow, L. 1992. *Head to Head.* New York: William Morrow.

Triandis, H.C. 1972. *The Analysis of Subjective Culture.* New York: Wiley.

Van Maanen, J. 1998. Different strokes: Qualitative research in the *Administrative Science Quarterly* from 1956 to 1996. In J. Van Maanen (ed.), *Qualitative Studies of Organizations*. Thousand Oaks, CA: Sage and Administrative Science Quarterly, pp. xi–xxxii.

Veiga, J., Lubatkin, M., Calori, R., and Very, P. 2000. Measuring organizational culture clashes: A two-nation posthoc analysis of a cultural compatibility index. *Human Relations*, 53(4): 539–57.

Very, P., Calori, R., and Lubatkin, M. 1993. An investigation of national and organizational cultural influences in recent European mergers. In P. Shrivastava, A. Huff, and J. Dutton (eds.), *Advances in Strategic Management* 9th edn. Greenwich: JAI Press, pp. 323–46.

Walter, G.A. 1985. Culture collisions in mergers and acquisitions. In P.J. Frost, L.F. Moore, M.R. Louis, C.C. Lundberg, and J. Martin (eds.), *Organizational Culture*. Beverly Hills, CA: Sage Publications, pp. 301–14.

Weber, Y., Shenkar, O., and Raveh, A. 1996. National and corporate cultural fit in mergers and acquisitions: An exploratory study. *Management Science*, 42(8): 1215–27.

Woo, C.Y., Willard, G.E., and Daellenbach, U.S. 1992. Spin-off performance: A case of overstated expectations? *Strategic Management Journal*, 13: 433–47.

Yin, R.K. 1984. *Case Study Research: Design and Methods*. Beverly Hills, CA: Sage.

M&A Strategy

CHAPTER THREE

Cross-Border Mergers and Acquisitions: Challenges and Opportunities

Michael Hitt, Vincenzo Pisano

Abstract

Merger and acquisition (M&A) has come to be a truly ubiquitous occurrence in the corporate world. Although this popular strategy has been particularly prevalent within North America, other areas of the world have experienced dramatically increasing growth rates, in terms of both the number and value of these transactions. While most M&A occur between firms within the same country, the numbers involving firms head-quartered in different countries have increased to a substantial percentage of the total. The difficulties of M&A management within a single country are such that at least 50 percent are considered to be failures, and the added complexity of a cross-border situation has the potential to either increase or decrease that number. This chapter explores both the challenges and opportunities presented by cross-border M&A, and thus not only highlights for managers levers that may benefit their odds in this high stakes game, it also calls attention to areas where future research on cross-border mergers will be high value-added work in this field.

Introduction

Mergers and acquisitions have long been a popular strategy for many firms, particularly in North America. However, in the fifth merger wave of the twentieth century in the decade of the 1990s, the popularity of this strategy spread to other parts of the world, including Europe, Asia, and Latin America. Additionally, while a majority of the mergers and acquisitions involved two firms within the same country, over 40 percent of the mergers and acquisitions that were completed in 1999 and 2000 involved firms headquartered in two different countries (Hitt, Harrison, and Ireland 2001). Certainly, the growth in cross-border mergers and acquisitions was fed by activity in Europe with firms preparing for the full implementation of the European Union. However, the cross-border M&A trend has been observed in many regions throughout the world, including North America, Asia, and Latin America, in addition to Europe. While the occurrence of cross-border M&A has grown dramatically in the last few years, academic research on this type of strategic action has not kept pace with the changes. Because of their importance and complexity, we need to more carefully examine and understand the opportunities and challenges provided by cross-border M&A.

While the research is not extensive, data suggest that cross-border M&A can produce positive returns, especially because of the benefits of international diversification (Fatemi and Furtado 1987). For example, cross-border M&A provide the opportunity for a firm to enter and to have immediate impact in a new market. By acquiring an existing business in the market the firm desires to enter, it obtains existing products, customers, and critical relationships with suppliers, distributors, and government officials (Hitt, Ireland, and Hoskisson 2003). Having existing customers and relationships can be especially critical for a foreign firm because it would be more difficult for this firm to enter the market without these relationships and the requisite knowledge of that market.

Increasing globalization of business has heightened the opportunities for, and the pressures to engage in, cross-border M&A (Hitt, Keats, and DeMarie 1998, Hitt 2000). Acquiring businesses headquartered in other countries helps firms take advantage of growth opportunities in international markets. These opportunities become especially important as firms encounter limits to growth in the current markets in which they compete. Horizontal acquisitions across country borders may be completed to enhance the firm's market power in global markets. Such acquisitions may be undertaken partly in response to continued consolidation within industries – a recent global trend (Hitt, Harrison, and Ireland 2001). Additionally, cross-border acquisitions may also help the firm more effectively compete with other businesses operating in multiple geographic markets. In fact, multi-market competition has become increasingly common in recent years (Smith, Ferrier, and Ndofor 2001).

Regardless of the opportunities presented by, and the pressures for, cross-border acquisitions, recent evidence suggests they are not highly successful. For example, in 1999, a study by KPMG found that only approximately 17 percent of cross-border acquisitions created shareholder value while 53 percent destroyed shareholder value (*Economist* 1999). Cross-border acquisitions are highly complex strategic transactions with many challenges that the acquiring firm managers must overcome. Given the increasing number of cross-border acquisitions and their growing importance in global markets, a better understanding of their opportunities and challenges is required.

We begin with a discussion of the opportunities presented by cross-border M&A.

Opportunities

Cross-border M&A present a number of potential opportunities for the acquiring firm. Among these opportunities are access to new and lucrative markets, as well as the expansion of the market for a firm's current goods. Additionally, acquisition of firms headquartered in other countries presents an especially good opportunity for the acquiring firm to learn new knowledge and capabilities. Acquiring firms may also gain access to valuable and complementary resources that they may not currently possess but need in order to gain or maintain a competitive advantage. Certainly, cross-border M&A often enhance the acquiring firm's market power. Finally, acquiring a firm headquartered in another country can provide several forms of support for the acquiring firm's innovation. We explore each of these opportunities in the following paragraphs.

It is often difficult to enter new markets in foreign countries because of the multiple entry barriers. In addition to the entry barriers common to the particular industry and competitive profile in the market, countries often have regulations that discourage market entry by foreign firms. Additionally, foreign firms are unlikely to have relationships with suppliers and distributors thereby making it difficult to enter a new market and operate successfully. However, acquiring a firm that already exists in that market overcomes these entry barriers. Therefore, the acquisition provides access to these markets (Hitt, Ireland, and Hoskisson 2003) that may not be accessible in other ways.

Moving into new markets provides a form of geographic diversification. Geographic diversification expands the market for a firm's current goods. As such, it provides economies of scale and lower cost per item sold. As a result, cross-border acquisitions provide a form of potential rapid growth to the firm and can enhance its profits, assuming that the costs of the acquisition do not offset its benefits (Hitt et al. 2003). Growth by geographic expansion into new international markets also spreads the risk for a firm such that there is less reliance on any one market. Furthermore, it often balances revenue flows because of the different economic conditions in regional economies across the globe.

Because of the growth and access to new markets, cross-border acquisitions can provide the acquiring firm with market power. The economies of scale and scope can make firms more efficient and allow them to become increasingly effective in the use of their resources. Market power may be especially important in consolidation of global industries. Such consolidation and the importance of market power can be seen in the global automobile industry with Daimler's acquisition of Chrysler and Renault's controlling ownership position in Nissan (Hitt, Harrison, and Ireland 2001).

Vermeulen and Barkema (2001) argue that acquisitions can help revitalize acquiring firms and thereby foster their long-term survival. The revitalization potential is because of the opportunity to learn new knowledge and capabilities (Barkema, Bell, and Pennings 1996, Barkema and Vermeulen 1998). The opportunity to learn is especially strong in cross-border acquisitions. This is because the societal and corporate cultures along managerial practices often differ across country borders. Thus, the acquiring firm may learn new capabilities and managerial practices from the acquired firm. This new knowledge may come from new product or process technologies, marketing, logistics, or other important areas within the firm. Very and Schweiger (2001) describe acquisitions as a learning process. They especially emphasize the potential learning opportunities of cross-border acquisitions. Therefore, it seems that all mergers and acquisitions present opportunities to learn but that cross-border acquisitions provide heightened opportunities.

Entry into new international markets exposes firms to a number of different activities, practices, knowledge bases, and capabilities. However, the mode of entry can affect the probability of learning from these new stimuli. For example, greenfield ventures may present problems for learning because of the lack of needed absorptive capacity (Cohen and Levinthal 1990). In other words, the firm may have inadequate knowledge bases to understand and absorb the new knowledge. Alternatively, strategic alliances as a mode of entry into those markets provide access to the knowledge bases that may help the entering firm to understand and absorb the new knowledge. Still, alliances do not provide adequate control and there are a number of barriers to the transfer of knowledge between alliance partners. However, in acquisitions, the knowledge bases and capabilities are internalized and thus under the control of the acquiring firm. As such, the knowledge transfer and diffusion becomes an internal process. While not simple, the probability of knowledge transfer and diffusion should be greater in these circumstances (Vermeulen and Barkema 2001).

Linked closely with acquiring new knowledge is the opportunity to access valuable and complementary resources in the acquired firm (Harrison et al. 1991, 2001). Few if any firms have all of the resources they need to implement major strategies. This is especially true with regard to entering new international markets. Additionally, as markets have become more global, the competition has become stronger (Hitt et al. 1998). In order to compete in global markets, firms often need substantial resources. Additionally, Barney (1991) argues that firms must have valuable and unique resources if they are to gain a competitive advantage. Also, these resources must be difficult to imitate and nonsubstitutable if the competitive advantage is to be sustainable. Thus, firms must search for valuable and unique resources and/or valuable resources that, when integrated with their own resource base, provide unique resource bundles that are difficult to imitate. Uniquely valuable resources may be better obtained outside of a firm's domestic markets. Therefore, cross-border acquisitions provide an opportunity to obtain and internalize valuable and unique resources that complement a firm's own resource base (Hitt, Harrison, and Ireland 2001).

Harrison et al. (1991) found empirical support for the notion that acquiring different but complementary resources had positive effects on the acquiring firm's performance. In fact, acquiring similar resources may contribute to economies of scale. However, economies of scale are rarely enough to offset the other costs of acquisition or alone to produce a competitive advantage. Rather, the different but complementary resources provide a unique, and difficult to imitate, resource bundle. Thus, cross-border acquisitions can provide access to new knowledge, new technology, and/or new markets, all of which can be valuable to the acquiring firm (Hitt et al. 2001).

Finally, cross-border acquisitions can enhance a firm's innovation capabilities and productivity. First, a firm may acquire a business with greater innovation capability than it has. Furthermore, it can acquire firms with new products that are developed and ready to enter the market (Hitt et al. 1996). However, firms that acquire businesses in different international markets also may gain access to new knowledge and other types of resources in the acquired firm that support its innovation capabilities (Kotabe 1990). For example, Hitt, Hoskisson, and Kim (1997) found that internationally diversified firms had higher levels of innovation. While firms entering international markets are exposed to new ideas and new product development processes, international diversification provides larger markets in which to earn returns from innovative products. Because of the fast pace of innovation in many industries and the short life cycle of products, firms must recoup their investment in new products rapidly. A larger market for the new product increases the probability that they can recoup their investment in developing that product and earn a return on it. Additionally, the cost of developing new products in many industries has increased rather dramatically in the last several years. As a result, larger and diverse markets may provide greater revenues to invest in the development of innovation (Kobrin 1991). Of course, acquisition of other firms provides an instant access and new market opportunities for the acquiring firm. Furthermore, because of the internalization, the acquiring firm also has access to the acquired firm's innovation capabilities and new products in the pipeline. As a result, cross-border acquisitions provide especially positive opportunities for enhancement of the acquiring firm's innovation.

Thus, we conclude that cross-border acquisitions provide a number of positive opportunities for acquiring firms. However, these acquisitions also present a number of substantial challenges to managers in the acquiring firms. We examine these challenges next.

Challenges in Cross-Border Acquisitions

There are a number of challenges to completing successful cross-border acquisitions. These include the challenges of evaluating acquisition targets, managing cultural differences, overcoming the liabilities of foreignness, dealing with institutional distances, understanding differing strategic orientations, ensuring adequate absorptive capacity to learn, and avoiding paying excessive premiums.

To identify appropriate acquisition targets and to negotiate and effectively complete acquisitions require a thorough due diligence process. Due diligence is a complex process in all mergers and acquisitions (Hitt, Harrison, and Ireland 2001). However, it is greatly complicated by cross-border acquisitions (Angwin 2001). For example, evaluating the financial assets of target firms can be difficult. This is because of differing accounting standards in separate countries and issues of fluctuating exchange rates. The due diligence process, however, must go beyond examination of the financial assets and health of the firm to be acquired. Importantly, the firm's intangible assets must be evaluated. Again, this is complicated even in domestic acquisitions, but even more difficult in acquisitions of firms headquartered in different countries. Accurate evaluation of intangible resources may require understanding the educational system and skills and capabilities of the work force, for example. Additionally, the acquired firm's reputation is often an important factor in the acquisition. In fact, the firm's reputation may be even more critical in cross-border than in domestic acquisitions. Finally, assessment of critical environmental conditions in which the firm operates is often important. As an example, an understanding of the government regulations with which this firm must deal and how effectively it responds to those regulations can be important in particular industries (where there may be especially heavy or sensitive regulations such as in high technology products). As a result, managers must pay special attention to the due diligence process in evaluating acquisition targets in cross-border acquisitions (Kissin and Herrera 1990, Harris and Ravenscraft 1991).

A second potential challenge in cross-border acquisitions is that of post-merger integration. Post-merger integration is a major potential problem in most acquisitions, regardless of whether they are domestic or involve firms from different countries. However, post-merger integration is likely to be more difficult to achieve between firms with home bases in different countries. The challenges of integration are affected by cultural differences, the institutional distance between the two home countries and the differing strategic orientation/intent of the executives in the two firms. The potential cultural problem is referred to by Barkema, Bell, and Pennings (1996) as double-layered acculturation. Double-layered acculturation is necessary because of the separate corporate cultures and national cultures represented in the two firms. Because there are two layers of culture with which the acquiring firm must contend in the integration process, there is greater potential for conflict based on these cultures. Of course, the potential for conflict on cultural bases depends upon the degree of integration required between the two firms (Nahavandi and Malekzadeh 1988). The more integration required and thus the closer the coordination, the more important cultural differences become. Chatterjee et al. (1992) found that the degree of cultural differences negatively affected shareholder value when strong integration was required. Weber, Shenkar, and Raveh (1996) found that differentials in corporate culture affected the cooperation between the top managers in the two firms. As such, they found negative attitudes toward the merger when there were greater differences in corporate culture. Similarly, Very, Lubatkin, and Calori (1996) found that acculturative stress was more likely to occur in cross-border acquisitions than in domestic acquisitions. Furthermore, they found this form of stress to be disruptive and a key obstacle to integration. Specifically, Very, Lubatkin, and Calori (1996) found acculturative stress to be associated with lower commitment and cooperation by the acquired firm employees and increased turnover of acquired firm executives. As a result, there was lower financial success in mergers between firms where acculturative stress was high.

Calori et al. (1997) suggested that a nation's social and political institutions form the context in which managerial practices develop and are applied. Thus, differences in these institutions across countries can result in different managerial practices. National culture is part of the institutional context, but this context contains other elements as well. The government regulations and support for individual industries, access to financial resources through financial institutions, and the general resources available in the environment all contribute to the institutional infrastructure (Newman 2000, Zahra et al. 2000). Where the institutional distance (differences) between two countries is high, there is a greater likelihood of conflict between the managers and employees in the acquiring and acquired firms. While both cultural differences and institutional distance create sometimes substantial challenges for the acquiring firm managers in integrating the acquired firm, they also present important opportunities. As noted earlier, Harrison et al. (1991, 2001) found that different but complementary resources produced the highest performance in acquisitions. Therefore, the greater these differences, the higher the probability that a firm may learn and/or gain value from the acquired assets. As a result, there are more opportunities but also increased challenges in realizing these opportunities where cultural and institutional differences are greater in cross-border acquisitions.

The cultural and institutional contexts in which firms operate have a significant effect on the strategic orientations developed and applied by the top managers in firms (Hitt et al. 1997, Child et al. 2001). For example, Hitt et al. (1997) found important differences in the strategic orientations between Korean and U.S. top executives. While U.S. top executives placed strong importance on financial returns, Korean executives emphasized growth more than returns. While these two foci may not necessarily be in conflict, they presented a definitive problem in the GM and Daewoo joint venture that failed during the late 1980s. Daewoo executives wanted to expand the joint venture to achieve greater growth even though the venture was experiencing net losses. However, GM executives wanted to reduce operations in hopes of earning a net profit. Eventually, these differences led to the dissolution of the unsuccessful joint venture and major losses in the investments made by both firms (Hitt et al. 1997).

A manager's strategic orientation also includes the propensity to take risks. Pablo and Javidan (2002) argue that differences in managers' risk-taking propensity can have a major effect on the outcome of acquisitions. If the acquired firm managers have a high propensity for risk taking but the acquiring firm managers are more conservative, there is likely to be conflict in the types of strategies and actions desired by these sets of managers. For example, if a firm acquires another firm because of its innovative capabilities but then integrates it into a conservative environment and incentive system, investments in R&D are likely to decrease and there may be a lower commitment to innovation in the merged firm (Hitt, Hoskisson, and Ireland 1990, Hitt et al. 1996). Thus, in summary, the cultural and institutional context shapes managerial strategic orientations and practices. These managerial strategic orientations and practices, in turn, affect the ability of acquiring firm managers to effectively integrate the acquired firm and to create value from the new merged firm (Lubatkin et al. 1998, Kostova 1999, Uhlenbruck and DeCastro 2000).

Earlier, we noted that cross-border acquisitions present a major opportunity to learn new knowledge from the acquired firm. In fact, if the knowledge bases of both the acquired and acquiring firms are different, each can learn from the other. This integrated knowledge base could help provide the firm with a unique and difficult-to-imitate set of resources that contribute to a competitive advantage. However, the differences in the knowledge bases also present difficulties for the managers. Specifically, firms must have the capacity to absorb the new knowledge available. Cohen and Levinthal (1990) refer to this capability as the absorptive capacity. Thus, if the knowledge bases are substantially different, neither firm may have the appropriate absorptive capacity to learn the knowledge stocks of the other. In these circumstances, learning may only occur where managers in each firm coordinate fully in the transfer of the knowledge (Tsai 2001). Transfer of knowledge requires substantial cooperation between the parties involved (Hitt et al. 2000). Thus, managers must be willing to transfer the knowledge to the other parties. Such transfer is more likely in friendly as opposed to hostile acquisitions (Hitt, Harrison, and Ireland 2001).

These arguments suggest that the integration process is critical to organizational learning in acquisitions but that there are significant challenges and barriers to overcome in cross-border acquisitions to achieve the learning. Another important challenge in cross-border acquisitions is the liability of foreignness (Zaheer and Mosakowski 1997). Essentially, the liability of foreignness is a challenge faced by all firms operating in international markets. Research on this concept suggests that such firms face certain unavoidable costs that firms operating in their home countries do not. The sources of these costs include higher coordination, lack of knowledge about local markets, lack of relationships in critical networks (i.e. political), along with cultural differences and institutional distance. Because of the liabilities of foreignness, firms operating in international markets have certain disadvantages and extra costs as compared to firms with which they compete operating only in the local domestic markets. As such, foreign firms competing against local domestic firms have certain competitive disadvantages (Miller and Parkhe 2002).

All of the challenges noted above contribute to the difficulty of determining an appropriate price for acquiring a firm. Many firms pay a premium over the current market value to acquire a firm. To determine an appropriate price (and thus premium), requires an estimation of the future market value of the assets to be acquired. Of course, the future market value is partially based on the extent to which potential synergies between the acquired firm and acquiring firm assets exist and can be achieved. The challenges described above make it difficult to accurately estimate the future market value because they complicate the ability of the firm to achieve the potential synergies. Some of them make it difficult to even estimate the synergies, much less the ability of the firm to achieve those synergies. In these cases, firms are more likely to pay excessive premiums. Sirower (1997) suggests that any premium greater than 25 percent of the firm's market value is excessive. Of course, the extent to which a premium is excessive depends on the potential synergies and the ability of the firm to realize those synergies. If a firm cannot realize synergies, even a 10 percent premium may be excessive. As such, we conclude that there is a higher probability of paying an excessive premium in cross-border acquisitions.

In summary, while cross-border acquisitions present a number of opportunities, there are also significant challenges. To deal with and overcome these challenges requires experienced, knowledgeable, and highly effective managers.

Making Cross-Border Mergers and Acquisitions Work

There are several actions that managers can take to increase the probability of a successful outcome in cross-border mergers and acquisitions. These actions focus on the negotiation process, the integration process, the structure and routines as well as the managerial mindset. Below, we examine each of these areas.

The preparations for negotiations of a cross-border acquisition must be substantial. Much care must be taken to ensure a fair and equitable price is paid for the acquired firm and in the development of the contractual arrangements to complete the acquisition. As noted earlier, there are multiple challenges that create ambiguities in cross-border acquisitions. Most significant among those are the problems in valuing the financial worth of a firm's assets and in identifying its intangible resources. Often because of the differences in language and culture, special care must be taken in the valuation process. In fact, firms often seek help from financial and legal advisors in the country where the target firm is headquartered. Undoubtedly, the negotiators must have clarity of purpose before they enter the negotiation process.

Additionally, firms that make multiple cross-border acquisitions can learn from their prior experiences. In fact, research has shown that firms learning from their prior acquisition experience are more likely to make successful acquisitions (Hitt et al. 1998). Hayward (2002) found that firms learn best from prior acquisitions that are not highly similar or dissimilar to the focal acquisition, experience only small losses, and are not too temporally close to or distant from the focal acquisition. Some have argued that firms should institute formal processes designed to facilitate learning from major strategic decisions and their outcomes. For example, the U.S. military conducts after-action reviews. Firms making acquisitions could conduct after-acquisition reviews (AARs). As such, all key managers involved in the acquisition process from the beginning through integration should hold a retreat and discuss the key challenges they encountered and the actions they took to meet those challenges. Furthermore, they should explore actions they might change to increase the effectiveness of a future acquisition.

As implied from prior discussions herein, the integration process is critical to the success of a cross-border acquisition. Clearly, firms must achieve an effective integration in order to capture synergy and create value (Haspeslagh and Jemison 1991). To do so requires that managers in the acquiring firm take positive actions to avoid conflict and to encourage cooperation and coordination during the integration process. For example, they must overcome both national and corporate cultural differences and hopefully achieve a form of cultural fit (different but complementary). Haspeslagh and Jemison (1991) suggest that the integration process is likely to be incremental and interactive in which key personnel from both organizations learn to cooperate and to transfer their strategic capabilities to others in their organization. Managers must avoid an atmosphere of "we versus them". Rather, there should be a collective "we" where all see themselves as members of the same team (Olie 1994). Some competencies may be culture-specific and therefore not easily transferred. This will increase the coordination costs in cross-border acquisitions (Datta and Puia 1995). Haspeslagh and Jemison (1991) argue that these acquisitions need to be symbiotic.

Interestingly, a recent study by Morosini, Shane, and Singh (1998) found that firms may acquire businesses in which there is significant cultural distance and yet enhance the performance of the acquisition. Their logic suggests that firms are likely to learn more new knowledge from businesses operating in distinct and different cultures. This logic fits with the arguments presented earlier about seeking partners with different but complementary resources. However, it also requires identifying businesses in which the knowledge bases are similar enough for the acquiring firm to have adequate absorptive capacity. Such cross-border acquisitions also place significant pressure on the integration process. Without effective integration in these cases, the synergy and learning are unlikely to be realized.

Of critical concern to the success of cross-border acquisitions is retaining intangible resources such as knowledge, capabilities, and reputation. Turnover can be relatively high following an acquisition, especially in the acquired firm. Some of the turnover occurs through natural layoffs designed to achieve expected economies of scale. However, research shows that top executives of the acquired firm often leave quickly after the merger is completed. Furthermore, even more junior managers from the acquired firm leave within a few years. If these managers are able to transfer their tacit knowledge prior to leaving, the acquiring firm may be able to retain the intangible resources it acquired. However, firms must emphasize the importance of retaining the key talent from the acquired firm to avoid losing these intangible resources included in the valuation and price of the acquisition (Krug and Nigh 2001). Some firms have been taking special actions to retain key managers and professionals from the acquired firm. For example, Cisco makes the top executive of the acquired firm a vice president reporting directly to the CEO. Furthermore, no employees from the acquired firm can be laid off without the agreement of both the Cisco CEO and the former CEO of the acquired firm (Killick, Rawoot, and Stockport 2003).

Research has shown that managers from separate countries are likely to implement different control systems and use different managerial practices in acquired firms. For example, Child, Falkner, and Pitkethly (2001) found that managers from Asian, North American, and European firms acquiring firms in the United Kingdom all practiced different forms of control. While Child, Falkner, and Pitkethly also found that any set of these controls could be successful, we argue that strategic control is likely the most effective means for integrating an acquired firm (for further discussion see Hoskisson and Hitt 1994). The exercise of strategic control requires managers to understand the business and to exercise control by monitoring the strategies employed as opposed to overemphasizing financial control targets.

It has become increasingly common for firms actively engaged in mergers and acquisitions to form integration teams. The purpose of these integration teams is to plan, coordinate, and implement the integration process (Inkpen, Sundaram, and Rockwood 2000). Although the composition and responsibility of integration teams may vary, effective cross-border acquisitions normally have representatives from both firms on the integration team. The integration teams chart out the specific actions required for effective integration and likely even evaluate many of the personnel in both organizations to decide who should stay and who should be laid off after the acquisition is completed. This team also recommends any structural and process changes along with new routines necessary to effectively integrate the acquired firm's assets and resources.

As noted above, the organizational structure and routines should be carefully evaluated and changed if necessary in order to effectively implement the merger and integrate the acquired firm's resources. In some cases, effective integration may require changes in reporting relationships and in authority assigned to different managerial positions (e.g. increasing the decentralization of authority). Routines, on the other hand, relate to the organizing of activities and include policies and procedures, such as those for scanning the environment, obtaining approval for new products developed by R&D, and supervising and evaluating subordinates. The integration process requires that the appropriate routines be used in integrating the resources and in the continuing operations of the merged firm. Some of these routines are likely to be formal, while others are informal. The integration team should ensure that all routines, formal and informal, are known and understood by all parties, especially the employees from the acquired firm. In particular, integration teams should identify and evaluate the routines used by both firms and attempt to select the best routines from both firms to use in the merged firm. In other words, they should not use only the routines of the acquiring firm unless it is certain that they are the most effective for the merged firm. The acquired firm may have some valuable routines that should be continued and used in the merged firm. Oftentimes, these valuable routines are embedded in national cultures and thus, cross-border acquisitions are more likely to produce valuable routines in the merged firm.

Finally, Hitt, Harrison, and Ireland (2001) argue that successful cross-border acquisitions require managers and other key personnel in the acquiring firm to develop a global mindset. In this way, they do not view the acquired firm from an idiosyncratic cultural perspective. Managers with a global mindset understand and appreciate the value of diversity of culture and thought. As such, they search for value in the differences between the acquired firm and their firm. In so doing, managers using a global mindset are more likely to identify and create the synergy between different but complementary resources.

Conclusions and Future Research

Cross-border acquisitions have become an increasingly important strategy used by a large number of firms in multiple regions across the globe. However, there has been little research on this type of strategic action. Our intent has been to examine cross-border mergers and acquisitions to identify the opportunities they present as well as the challenges that must be confronted for effective strategic action. While cross-border mergers and acquisitions have a number of characteristics in common with domestic mergers and acquisitions, they also have unique and important differences.

Cross-border mergers and acquisitions present several unique and valuable opportunities. For example, they provide the opportunity to enter new and different geographic global markets. Additionally, cross-border mergers and acquisitions present special opportunities for learning and accessing different but complementary resources. These opportunities are potentially more valuable than in domestic mergers and acquisitions because of the unique cultural and institutional differences that often exist between the firms involved in these transactions. As such, they can contribute more strongly to a firm's competitive advantages.

However, cross-border mergers and acquisitions also present greater challenges for managers than do the same strategic actions in a domestic context. Given the low success rate of domestic mergers and acquisitions, the challenges of cross-border mergers and acquisitions are highly salient to managers. One of those challenges, the ability to achieve double acculturation (integrating both different national and corporate cultures) is a special challenge. Differences in institutional infrastructures in the countries where the two firms are headquartered also can present special challenges for managers of the acquiring firm. The difficulties in valuing assets of potential target firms headquartered in other countries increase the probability of paying excessive premiums for the acquisitions as well. If the acquiring firm pays an excessive premium, the likelihood of success (e.g. earning positive returns from the acquisition) may be dramatically lower.

Because of the special opportunities and the substantial challenges involved in cross-border acquisitions and their increasing importance in the global competitive landscape, more research is required to understand this phenomenon. For example, we need to better understand the effects of cultural and institutional differences on the post-merger integration process and on the success of cross-border mergers and acquisitions. Furthermore, we need to better understand the effects of differences in the strategic orientations of managers in the acquiring and target firms. How do these differences affect negotiating the deal and achieving the synergies after the acquisition is completed? We also should better understand the pressures for cross-border mergers and acquisitions (e.g. globalization of markets and industry consolidations).

Future research on cross-border mergers and acquisitions should examine in more detail how to effectively identify potential targets for acquisition, the due diligence process, negotiating the deal, the post-merger integration process, and how to best create organizational learning and new knowledge. For example, research should be conducted to help us better understand how to evaluate non-financial and intangible resources, especially in foreign firms targeted for acquisition. Research should increase our understanding of valuing target assets and avoiding excess premiums in the prices paid for acquisitions. Additionally, research should be conducted on how to identify and evaluate potential complementary resources in target firms. Future research could help answer the question, "What actions can be taken to enhance a firm's learning from acquisitions that would contribute to more effective negotiations on future acquisitions?"

With regard to the post-merger integration process, research is needed on the double acculturation process, identifying effective structures and routines, retaining critical human capital, the use of integration teams and actions to increase the realization of potential synergies. We also need to better understand the importance of trust in the post-merged integration process. Research is needed to understand the internalization and diffusion of knowledge in merged firms.

Future research might also address the role of corporate governance in cross-border mergers and acquisitions. Furthermore, we should better understand the role of investment bankers and consultants in cross-border acquisitions. Also, the make versus buy decision (i.e. innovation as opposed to acquiring new products and processes) requires further research, especially in a cross-border context. Finally, research could be useful to understand if mergers and acquisitions could be used to be more entrepreneurial in international markets.

Overall, our work concludes that cross-border mergers and acquisitions have become an important strategy employed by firms in the global competitive landscape. As such, managers must be better informed as to the potential opportunities and challenges presented by this significant strategic action. Furthermore, they must understand how to increase the probability of successful cross-border merger and acquisition actions. In this light, we have identified a number of important areas needing future research. We hope that this work serves as a catalyst for future research on cross-border mergers and acquisitions.

Notes

This chapter is based on an article previously published in *Management Research*, **2**(1) (spring 2003): 133–44. Reprinted by kind permission of M.E. Sharpe Inc.

References

Angwin, D. 2001. Mergers and acquisitions across European borders: National perspectives on preacquisition due diligence and the use of professional advisors. *Journal of World Business*, **36**(1): 32–57.

Barkema, H.G., Bell, J.H.J., and Pennings, J.M. 1996. Foreign entry, cultural barriers and learning. *Strategic Management Journal*, **17**: 151–66.

Barkema, H.G. and Vermeulen, F. 1998. International expansion through start-up or acquisition: A learning perspective. *Academy of Management Journal*, **41**: 7–26.

Barney, J.B. 1991. Firm resources and sustained competitive advantage. *Journal of Management*, **17**: 99–120.

Calori, R., Lubatkin, M., Very, P., and Veiga, J.F. 1997. Modeling the origins of nationally bound administrative heritages: A historical institutional analysis of French and British firms. *Organization Science*, **8**(6): 681–96.

Chatterjee, S., Lubatkin, M.H., Schweiger, D.M., and Weber, Y. 1992. Cultural differences and shareholder value in related mergers linking equity and human capital. *Strategic Management Journal*, **13**: 319–34.

Child, J., Falkner, D., and Pitkethly, R. 2001. *The Management of International Acquisitions*. Oxford: Oxford University Press.

Cohen, W.M. and Levinthal, D.A. 1990. Absorptive capacity: A new perspective on learning and innovation. *Administrative Science Quarterly*, **35**: 128–52.

Datta, D. and Puia, G. 1995. Cross-border acquisitions: An examination of the influence of relatedness and cultural fit on shareholder value creation in U.S. acquiring firms. *Management International Review*, **35**(4): 337–59.

Economist, 1999. Business: faites vos jeux. *Economist*, 4 December: 63.

Fatemi, A.M. and Furtado, E.P.H. 1987. An empirical investigation of the wealth effects of foreign acquisitions. In S.J. Khoury and A. Ghosh (eds.), *Recent Developments in International Banking and Finance*. Lexington, MA: Lexington Books, pp. 363–79.

Harris, R.S. and Ravenscraft, D. 1991. The role of acquisitions in foreign direct investment: Evidence from the U.S. stock market. *Journal of Finance*, **46**(3): 825–44.

Harrison, J.S., Hitt, M.A., Hoskisson, R.E., and Ireland, R.D. 1991. Synergies and post-acquisition performance: Similarities versus differences in resource allocations. *Journal of Management*, **17**: 173–90.

Harrison, J.S., Hitt, M.A., Hoskisson, R.E., and Ireland, R.D. 2001. Resource complementarity in business combinations: Extending the logic to organizational alliances. *Journal of Management*, **27**: 679–90.

Haspeslagh, P.C. and Jemison, D.B. 1991. *Managing Acquisitions: Creating Value through Corporate Renewal*. New York: Free Press.

Hayward, M.L.A. 2002. When do firms learn from their acquisition experience? Evidence from 1990–1995. *Strategic Management Journal*, **23**: 21–39.

Hitt, M.A. 2000. The new frontier: Transformation of management for the new millennium. *Organizational Dynamics*, **28**: 6–17.

Hitt, M.A., Dacin, M.T., Levitass, E., Arregle, J.L., and Borza, A. 2000. Partner selection in emerging and developed market contexts: Resource-based and organizational learning perspectives. *Academy of Management Journal*, **43**: 449–67.

Hitt, M.A., Dacin, M.T., Tyler, B.D., and Park, D. 1997. Understanding the differences in Korean and U.S. executives' strategic orientations. *Strategic Management Journal*, **18**: 159–67.

Hitt, M.A., Harrison, J.S., and Ireland, R.D. 2001. *Mergers and Acquisitions: A Guide to Creating Value for Stakeholders*. New York: Oxford University Press.

Hitt, M.A., Harrison, J.S., Ireland, R.D., and Best, A. 1998. Attributes of successful and unsuccessful acquisitions of US firms. *British Journal of Management*, **9**: 91–114.

Hitt, M.A., Hoskisson, R.E., and Ireland, R.D. 1990. Mergers and acquisitions and managerial commitment to innovation. *Strategic Management Journal*, **11**(Special Issue): 29–47.

Hitt, M.A., Hoskisson, R.E., Johnson, R.A., and Moesel, D.D. 1996. The market for corporate control and firm innovation. *Academy of Management Journal*, **39**: 1084–119.

Hitt, M.A., Hoskisson, R.E., and Kim, H. 1997. International diversification: Effects on innovation and firm performance in product-diversified firms. *Academy of Management Journal*, **40**: 767–98.

Hitt, M.A., Ireland, R.D., Camp, S.M., and Sexton, D.L. 2001. Strategic entrepreneurship: Entrepreneurial strategies for creating wealth. *Strategic Management Journal*, **22**(Special Issue): 479–91.

Hitt, M.A., Ireland, R.D., and Hoskisson, R.E. 2003. *Strategic Management: Competitiveness and Globalization*. Cincinnati, OH: SouthWestern, in press.

Hitt, M.A., Keats, B.W., and DeMarie, S.M. 1998. Navigating in the new competitive landscape: Building strategic flexibility and competitive advantage in the 21st century. *Academy of Management Executive*, **12**(4): 22–42.

Hoskisson, R.E. and Hitt, M.A. 1994. *Downscoping: How to Tame the Diversified Firm*. New York: Oxford University Press.

Inkpen, A.C., Sundaram, A.K., and Rockwood, K. 2000. Cross-border acquisitions of U.S. technology assets. *California Management Review*, **42**(spring): 50–70.

Killick, M., Rawoot, I., and Stockport, G.J. 2003. Cisco Systems Inc.: Growth through acquisitions. In M.A. Hitt, R.D. Ireland, and R.E. Hoskisson (eds.), *Strategic Management: Competitiveness and Globalization*. Cincinnati, OH: SouthWestern, in press.

Kissin, W.D. and Herrera, J. 1990. International mergers and acquisitions. *Journal of Business Strategy*, **11**(July/August): 51–5.

Kobrin, J. 1991. An empirical analysis of the determinants of global integration. *Strategic Management Journal*, **12**(Special Issue): 17–37.

Kostova, T. 1999. Transnational transfer of strategic organizational practices: A contextual perspective. *Academy of Management Review*, **24**: 308–24.

Kotabe, M. 1990. The relationship between offshore sourcing and innovativeness of U.S. multinational firms: An empirical investigation. *Journal of International Business Studies*, **21**: 623–38.

Krug, J.A. and Nigh, D. 2001. Executive perceptions in foreign and domestic acquisitions: An analysis of foreign ownership and its effect on executive fate. *Journal of World Business*, **36**(1): 85–105.

Lubatkin, M., Calori, R., Very, P., and Veiga, J.F. 1998. Management mergers across borders: A two-nation exploration of a nationally bound administrative heritage. *Organization Science*, **9**(6): 670–84.

Miller, S.R. and Parkhe, A. 2002. Is there a liability of foreignness in global banking? An empirical test of banks' x-efficiency. *Strategic Management Journal*, **23**: 55–75.

Morosini, P., Shane, S., and Singh, H. 1998. National cultural distance and cross-border acquisition performance. *Journal of International Business Studies*, **29**: 137–58.

Nahavandi, A. and Malekzadeh, A.R. 1988. Acculturation in mergers and acquisitions. *Academy of Management Review*, **13**: 79–90.

Newman, K.L. 2000. Organizational transformation during institutional upheaval. *Academy of Management Review*, **25**: 602–19.

Olie, R. 1994. Shades of culture and institutions in international mergers. *Organization Studies*, **15**: 381–405.

Pablo, A.L. and Javidan, M. 2002. Thinking of a merger … Do you know their risk propensity profile? *Organizational Dynamics*, **30**(3): 206–22.

Sirower, M.L. 1997. *The Synergy Trap*. New York: Free Press.

Smith, K.G., Ferrier, W.J., and Ndofor, H. 2001. Competitive dynamics research: Critique and future directions. In M.A. Hitt, R.E. Freeman, and J.S. Harrison (eds.), *Handbook of Strategic Management*. Oxford: Blackwell, pp. 315–61.

Tsai, W. 2001. Knowledge transfer in intraorganizational networks: Effects of network position and absorptive capacity on business unit innovation and performance. *Academy of Management Journal*, **44**: 996–1004.

Uhlenbruck, K. and DeCastro, J.O. 2000. Foreign acquisitions in Central and Eastern Europe: Outcomes of privatization in transitional economies. *Academy of Management Journal*, **43**: 381–402.

Vermeulen, F. and Barkema, H.G. 2001. Learning through acquisitions. *Academy of Management Journal*, **44**: 457–76.

Very, P., Lubatkin, M., and Calori, R. 1996. A cross-national assessment of acculturative stress in recent European mergers. *International Studies of Management and Organizations*, **26**: 59–88.

Very, P. and Schweiger, D.M. 2001. The acquisition process as a learning process: Evidence from a study of critical problems and solutions in domestic and cross-border deals. *Journal of World Business*, **36**(1): 11–31.

Weber, Y., Shenkar, O., and Raveh, A. 1996. National and corporate fit in M&A: An exploratory study. *Management Science*, **4**: 1215–27.

Zaheer, S. and Mosakowski, E. 1997. The dynamics of the liability of foreignness: A global study of survival in financial services. *Strategic Management Journal*, **18**: 439–64.

Zahra, S.A., Ireland, R.D., Gutierrez, I., and Hitt, M.A. 2000. Privatization and entrepreneurial transformation: Emerging issues and a future research agenda. *Academy of Management Review*, **25**: 509–24.

CHAPTER FOUR

Firm Competitiveness and Acquisition: The Role of Competitive Strategy and Operational Effectiveness in M&A

Paul A. Mudde, Thomas Brush

Abstract

This chapter explores the relationship between an acquirer's business-level strategy and operational effectiveness and its realization of performance improvements in acquisitions. It develops theory arguing that the capabilities associated with an acquirer's competitive strategy condition its acquisition activity. Specifically, we argue that the competitive strategy and operational effectiveness of an acquirer affect the selection, evaluation, and integration of its targets, which ultimately affect the type of performance improvement realized in acquisitions. Based on an empirical analysis of 207 bank acquisitions occurring within an industry sample of 8,881 U.S. banks, we find evidence that high levels of cost leadership in acquirers are associated with reductions in post-acquisition costs. High levels of mixed strategies (combinations of both cost leadership and differentiation) and/or operational effectiveness are found to be associated with significant growth in post-acquisition revenues. Thus, this study develops important theory linking business-level competitiveness with success in corporate-level strategies and provides empirical evidence that competitive strategies and operational effectiveness contribute to better performance in acquisitions.

Introduction

The purpose of this research is to expand the realm of strategic management theory in explaining M&A activity. It focuses on issues of business-level strategy – competitive strategy and operational effectiveness – and their role in acquisitions. This research is motivated by linking competitive strategy theory and corporate strategy theory. Building on Porter's (1996) arguments that business strategy and operational effectiveness are important for superior firm performance, we examine whether an acquirer's business-level competitiveness, defined by its competitive strategy and operational effectiveness, affects its acquisition outcomes. We argue that M&A may serve as an important mechanism for acquirers to exploit the existing strengths of their competitive strategies and/or operational effectiveness. Likewise, acquirers can benefit by correcting deficiencies in the competitive strategies and/or operational effectiveness of targets.

This study is motivated by Bower's (2001) arguments that all M&As are not alike and that the strategic intent of the acquirer is important in determining the distinct activities used in the integration of acquirers and targets. Consequently, this research focuses on differences between acquirers and how these differences affect acquisition outcomes. We hypothesize that an acquirer's competitive strategy influences its selection decisions and shapes the synergies achieved in its acquisitions. Acquirers with high levels of cost leadership are expected to select targets that can benefit from their cost leadership capabilities and to emphasize cost reductions in their acquisitions. Acquirers with high levels of differentiation are expected to select targets that can benefit from their differentiation capabilities and to emphasize revenue growth in their acquisitions. Thus, an acquirer's business-level strategy influences the strategic intent of its corporate strategy action and corporate strategy can serve to reinforce a firm's business-level competitiveness.

This research complements and extends previous strategy research on M&A, which focuses on heterogeneity in acquisition activity, progressing from topics such as diversification and M&A (Lubatkin 1983, 1987, Singh and Montgomery 1987, Shelton 1988, Seth 1990a, 1990b), the role of resource positions in M&A (Harrison et al. 1991), resource redeployment in M&A (Capron, Dussauge, and Mitchell 1998, Capron 1999), and most recently, on differences in the strategic intent of acquirers (Bower 2001). It also extends the economic research that examines how firm efficiency affects whether a company experiences a change in ownership and whether inefficiencies in targets are associated with post-acquisition performance improvements (Lichtenberg and Siegel 1987, Ravenscraft and Scherer 1987, Brush 1996). These previous studies do not directly examine, or control for, the effects of variations in the competitive strategy and operational effectiveness of the firms involved in M&A, although it is clear that these effects are part of all types of acquisitions.

Acquirer competitiveness has had an important position in many of the existing theoretical perspectives on M&A, but has not previously been the focus of a research study. For example, economic studies of M&A explore the ability of M&A to improve the productivity or profitability of the acquired firm, or business unit (Lichtenberg and Siegel 1987, Ravenscraft and Scherer 1987, Brush 1996). Finance theory argues that equity markets facilitate acquisitions where strong competitors acquire weak, poorly managed competitors using the "market for corporate control" (Manne 1965, Jensen and Ruback 1983). Within strategy theory, researchers argue that the competitive nature of the acquisition market results in a selection process where firms with uniquely advantaged resource positions are expected to be the highest bidders (Barney 1988, Seth 1990a).

The empirical analysis within this study examines M&A activity within the U.S. banking industry to explore how business-level competitiveness affects acquisition outcomes. It focuses on an acquirer's ability to gain synergies from acquisitions.

The competitive strategy and operational effectiveness of 8,881 U.S. banks and bank-holding companies (BHCs) are measured along continuous scales of differentiation, cost leadership, and focus/breadth. Two hundred and thirty bank acquisitions from within the larger bank population are analyzed in order to understand how an acquirer's competitive strategy contributes to its ability to realize synergies in horizontal acquisitions.

This study makes a number of important contributions to our understanding of M&A. First, it shows that an acquirer's competitive strategy and operational effectiveness are important in shaping the strategic intent of an acquirer's horizontal acquisitions and in determining the extent of value creation in acquisitions. Second, it shows that an acquirer's competitive strategy influences the types of synergies realized in acquisitions, suggesting a link between an acquirer's strategy, its selection process, its post-acquisition integration activities, and its redeployment of resources. Third, it presents evidence that acquirers can be economically motivated and successful in generating significant post-acquisition revenue growth or cost reductions, yet their acquisitions can still fail to improve post-acquisition return on assets (ROA).

This chapter is organized into the following sections: (1) a discussion of previous empirical research; (2) developing the theory of how business-level strategy and operational effectiveness affect M&A; (3) the model and data sources; (4) a presentation of the empirical findings; and (5) a discussion of the findings.

Previous Empirical Research

This research addresses limitations in previous research on M&A. It follows a progression of research on M&A that examines the heterogeneity of acquisition activity. Much of this research has focused on performance differences associated with different types of acquisitions. Other research has emphasized resource differences between acquirers and targets and resource transfers between acquirers and targets. As noted, no previous research has focused on examining how differences in the competitive strategies of acquirers affect acquisition outcomes. This section summarizes the previous research and reviews the findings of empirical research on competitive strategies and studies that examine M&A performance. It also provides a brief review of related strategy research on M&A. Since the theory motivating this research weaves together differing research streams, this section provides an overview of existing studies that border on the topic of how acquirer competitiveness affects M&A outcomes. We start by discussing the research on the relationship between competitive strategy and firm performance.

Empirical research on competitive strategies has focused on two main issues. First, competitive strategies research identifies business-level strategies based on the operational characteristics of firms (Hambrick 1983, Dess and Davis 1984, Miller and Freisen 1986). Second, competitive strategies research examines the relationship between competitive strategy and firm performance (Hambrick 1983, Dess and Davis 1984, Miller and Freisen 1986, Miller and Dess 1993).

Early research on competitive strategies explores the association between a firm's characteristics and capabilities and its business-level strategy. These studies show an association between capabilities such as operating efficiency, high capacity utilization, and low input costs, and cost leadership strategies (Hambrick 1983, Dess and Davis 1984, Miller and Friesen 1986). Differentiation strategies are shown to be associated with R&D capabilities, marketing capabilities, and above-average levels of advertising expense.

This body of research also examines the relationship between competitive strategy and firm profitability. There is general support for Porter's assertions that competitive strategy contributes to higher performance. The empirical evidence on the performance effects of mixing cost leadership and differentiation strategies has not been conclusive (Miller and Dess 1993, Mudde, unpublished dissertation), suggesting that the relationship between strategy and performance is complex and may depend on industry context. Finally, in the only empirical study of competitive strategy that accounts for variation in firm efficiency, operational effectiveness was found to have a strong positive effect on firm performance in the U.S. banking industry (Mudde, unpublished dissertation).

In the following theory section, we argue that competitive strategy research can be applied to M&A research to better understand how business-level strategy contributes to success in M&A. Mudde's (unpublished dissertation) study of competitive strategy and operational effectiveness in the banking industry suggests that banks can improve financial performance by using mixed strategies (combinations of cost leadership and differentiation), improving their operational effectiveness, and increasing the breadth of their competitive strategy. This implies that acquisitions that focus on improving these aspects of competitiveness are likely to produce post-acquisition performance improvements. Another extension of competitive strategy research relevant to M&A relates to the ability of acquirers to utilize the capabilities associated with their competitive strategies and apply these capabilities to their M&A activity. This will be discussed in more detail in the section discussing theory.

Next, we review the empirical research on M&A. First, we discuss studies that focus on the target as the unit of analysis and examine heterogeneity in the target's level of competitiveness. Lichtenberg and Siegel (1987) examine the effect of a target's pre-acquisition productivity level on M&A performance. Within their sample of manufacturing plants, they find that plants experiencing an ownership change had productivity levels that were below the industry average before being acquired. Their study shows that ownership changes of manufacturing plants are associated with improvements in the target's productivity in the period after the ownership change occurs. Consistent with these findings, Brush (1996) finds that acquired firm performance improves in the post-acquisition period. He finds that the market share of the acquired firm increases after acquisition. Brush's study did not control for the pre-acquisition competitiveness (relative efficiency, market share, or profitability) of the acquired firms.

Ravenscraft and Scherer (1987) measure pre-acquisition profitability to assess the acquired firm's competitiveness. Their sample included firms that, on average, had above-average performance prior to being acquired. They present evidence that a firm's accounting performance declines after being acquired. Post-acquisition performance (one-year and three-year measures of ROA adjusted by industry average) was compared to pre-acquisition performance and showed that financial performance declined in the post-acquisition period.

These studies focus solely on the performance changes occurring in an acquired firm and do not control for the competitive strength of the acquirer. This makes it difficult to draw clear conclusions about how competitiveness affects the realization of synergies. Lichtenberg and Siegel's sample (1987) shows that acquisitions involving targets with low levels of competitiveness result in performance improvements. Ravenscraft and Scherer's sample (1987) shows that acquisitions involving targets with high levels of competitiveness fail to achieve performance improvements and actually result in declining performance. These studies suggest questions regarding the role that acquirer competitiveness plays in acquisition success. Do their results differ based on the strength or weakness of the acquired firm or due to the variation in the competitiveness and capabilities of acquirers? This study attempts to address this issue by focusing attention on how acquirer competitiveness affects acquisition outcomes.

Next, this section provides an overview of strategy research on M&A and presents a context for understanding how the topic of acquirer competitiveness and M&A fits within the larger body of empirical research on M&A. A main area of strategy research in M&A examines how diversification strategy affects acquisition outcomes. Recently, attention has also been given to a second area of interest: the role of learning or experience in M&A. A third recent stream of strategy research on M&A has focused on horizontal acquisitions.

As noted in the introduction, much of the empirical research conducted by strategy researchers in the area of M&A has focused on whether diversification strategy has an effect on acquisition performance (Lubatkin 1983, 1987, Singh and Montgomery 1987, Shelton 1988, Seth 1990a, 1990b). Reviews by Datta, Pinches, and Narayanan (1992) and Sirower (1997) support the general consensus that related acquisitions perform better than conglomerate acquisitions, but the evidence is mixed.

It is interesting to consider the role of firm competitiveness and business strategy in diversifying M&A. Although previous studies do not control for variations in the competitive strategies and operational effectiveness of the firms involved in diversifying M&A, it is clear that issues related to firm competitiveness are part of all types of acquisitions. This study, by focusing on horizontal acquisitions, takes a first step in identifying how firm competitiveness affects acquisition outcomes and may explain some of the factors that confound our understanding of the performance effects of diversification strategies.

Acquisition experience has also been an area of interest in the strategy field (Singh and Zollo 1998, Hayward 2002). Similar to the studies on diversification strategies, the evidence on the effect of acquisition experience and learning is mixed (Hitt, Harrison, and Ireland 2001, Hayward 2002). These studies also do not account for differences in the competitive strategies and operational effectiveness of the combining firms, which may contribute to their mixed results. There is evidence that different types of acquisitions affect the acquirer's ability to learn from its acquisition experience (Hayward 2002), suggesting that a better understanding of firm competitiveness and its effect on M&A may shed light on how acquirers benefit from their experience.

Finally, a third body of strategy research on M&A has focused its attention on horizontal acquisitions. Similar to this study, this research focuses on M&A within a single industry to understand how horizontal acquisitions create value. These studies cover a range of issues exploring M&A effects on performance in declining industries (Anand and Singh 1997), the use of resource transfers and asset restructuring in horizontal M&A (Capron, Dussauge, and Mitchell 1998, Capron 1999, Capron, Mitchell, and Swaminathan 2001), and how M&A affects technology and innovation (Ahuja and Katila 2001). These previous studies of horizontal acquisitions have not specifically looked at competitive strategies and effectiveness. As noted previously, case studies of horizontal acquisitions have given evidence to the important role competitive strategies can play in the M&A (Kaplan, Mitchell, and Wruck 2000, Vlasic and Stertz 2000).

This study complements previous work on horizontal acquisitions, acquisition experience, and diversification strategies. It fills an important void in the existing strategy research on M&A and expands the realm of theory explaining how strategy affects acquisitions. In the next section, we develop the theory and hypotheses regarding how acquirer competitiveness affects acquisition outcomes.

Theory and Hypotheses Development

In this section, we use competitive strategy theory and M&A process theory to make the following arguments regarding the role of competitive strategy in M&A: (1) an acquirer's competitive strategy contributes to its ability to create synergies in acquisitions; and (2) the particular competitive strategy of the acquirers (whether it is predominately differentiation or cost leadership) shapes the acquirer's selection decision and type of post-acquisition performance improvements that occur in acquisitions. Operational effectiveness is also expected to contribute to the realization of synergies in acquisitions. We argue that acquirers with greater operational effectiveness will achieve greater levels of synergy in acquisitions.

For the purpose of this chapter, competitive strategy is defined along the three dimensions of Porter's (1980) competitive strategy typology. Similar to Miller and Dess (1993), we define a firm's competitive strategy along three continuous dimensions: cost leadership, differentiation, and focus/breadth. A firm's level of *cost leadership* is determined by its use of low cost inputs and low pricing relative to its competitors. A firm's level of *differentiation* is defined by its use of high quality inputs, ability to offer premium products, and its ability to charge higher prices relative to competitors. The level of *focus/breadth* in a firm's competitive strategy is defined by the degree it is limited in its geographic, product, or customer markets.

Porter (1996) argues that firm competitiveness can be strengthened by improving a firm's business strategy, operational effectiveness, or by improving both strategy and effectiveness simultaneously. It follows that horizontal acquisitions may serve as an important mechanism for improving the strategy and operational effectiveness of the firms involved in the acquisition. An acquirer can create value by improving the competitive strategy of the combining firms. In doing so, the acquirer's pre-acquisition competitive strategy is important in determining the type of synergy resulting from acquisition. Operational effectiveness is expected to have an independent, positive effect on post-acquisition synergies. Improvements in operational effectiveness reflect the acquirer's ability to raise the combined firm's efficiency in transforming its inputs into outputs and are independent of the specific competitive strategy of the firms involved in an acquisition (Mudde, unpublished dissertation). We begin by discussing how different competitive strategies (cost leadership, differentiation, and focus/breadth) contribute to acquisition success. Following this discussion, we develop hypotheses on how operational effectiveness supports value creation in acquisitions.

Competitive strategy theorists argue that firms with cost leadership strategies are characterized by low cost inputs, process technology that improves efficiency, large scale, administrative and incentive systems that reward cost reduction and efficiency, and a culture that emphasizes reducing overhead, eliminating waste, and using experience to drive down unit costs (Porter 1980). These traits are likely to also affect a firm's acquisitions strategy.

Acquirers with high levels of cost leadership are expected to select targets that complement a low-cost strategy. The target can contribute to the acquirer's ability to create value through cost leadership in one of two ways. First, it can allow the acquirer to employ its existing resource advantage toward new markets (Harrison et al. 1991) and/or inefficiencies inherent in the target. Second, it may obtain under-utilized resources in the target that can enhance its existing cost leadership position. This can occur through resource redeployment or asset divestiture (Capron, Dussauge, and Mitchell 1998, Capron 1999, Capron, Mitchell, and Swaminathan 2001). The market for corporate control also makes this argument, suggesting that acquirers with strong competitive positions acquire targets that have underutilized or mismanaged their assets (Jensen and Ruback 1983).

In general, strategy theory argues that acquisitions result from market failures regarding the exchange of specific resources (Harrison et al. 1991, Capron, Dussauge, and Mitchell 1998). Individual firms face constraints in their abilities to adapt and improve their competitive positions due to the rigidity of existing routines and bounded rationality (Nelson and Winter 1982). Lacking the ability to develop new resources internally or deploy existing resources toward existing growth opportunities, businesses turn to M&A to obtain new resources or employ existing resources toward new products or markets (Capron, Dussauge, and Mitchell 1998, Harrison et al. 1991). Acquirers are expected to make acquisitions where their existing resources complement those of the target, allowing the acquirer to make use of acquired resources or employ its competitive strengths toward new opportunities (Penrose 1959, Harrison et al. 1991). Consistent with this reasoning, research on M&A process typically emphasizes the role of the acquirer and the acquirer's selection process as an important component in successful acquisition outcomes (Haspeslagh and Jemison 1991, Hitt, Harrison, and Ireland 2001).

From the perspective of competitive strategy theory, acquirers using cost leadership strategies are likely to identify opportunities for cost reductions in their acquisitions. They are expected to focus on eliminating redundancies and waste, centralizing operations, downsizing staff functions and cutting overhead, and standardizing products.

Cost leader acquirers are likely to eliminate poor performing products, operations, and sales or service locations. Examples of this type of acquirer and acquisition process include Cooper Industries (Collis and Stuart 1995) and Wells Fargo (Schmitt 1986).

Strategy theory argues that a firm's management capabilities create and shape its opportunities for expansion (Penrose 1959). Thus, the acquirer's managerial resources, administrative systems, low cost operating, sales, marketing, and distribution processes reflected in its cost leadership competitive strategy are expected to contribute to acquisition success. Similarly, an acquirer's selection decisions may be influenced by its cost leadership strategies. Cost leader acquirers are expected to target firms with deficiencies in cost leadership or resources that will contribute to reducing the combined firm's costs. Research on M&A process typically emphasizes the acquirer's ability to select complementary targets (Salter and Weinhold 1981), gain consensus regarding goals (Shanley and Correa 1992), and implement the appropriate integration processes (Pablo 1994). Thus, the characteristics of the acquirer are expected to determine the amount and type of post-acquisition synergies. These arguments result in the following hypothesis:

Hypothesis 1:   An acquirer's level of cost leadership is expected to be positively associated with reductions in post-acquisition expense and overall improvements in post-acquisition ROA.

According to competitive strategy theory, differentiators are characterized by high quality inputs, specialized labor, above-average investments in R&D and marketing, and high quality and brand reputation (Porter 1980). In contrast to cost leaders' emphasis on cost management, differentiators are expected to develop a culture that emphasizes and rewards revenue growth through sales and marketing, premium customer service, and brand image.

Acquirers with high levels of differentiation are expected to select targets that complement a differentiation strategy. Similar to the case of cost leader acquisitions, the target can contribute to the acquirer's ability to create value through differentiation by: (1) allowing the acquirer to employ its existing resource advantage toward new markets and/or products (Harrison et al. 1991); and (2) it may obtain underutilized resources in the target that can enhance its existing differentiation position. This may occur through resource redeployment (Capron, Dussauge, and Mitchell 1998, Capron 1999, Capron, Mitchell, and Swaminathan 2001).

From the perspective of competitive strategy theory, acquirers utilizing differentiation strategies are likely to identify opportunities for synergistic revenue growth in their acquisitions. They are expected to focus on making use of superior sales, marketing, and distribution capabilities. Differentiators may also improve product quality and features and increase product innovation (Harrison et al. 1991). Lastly, brand reputation may be transferred between firms, increasing the sales of the combined firms. Examples of this type of acquirer and acquisition process include Banc One (Uyterhoeven and Hart 1993) and Cisco Systems Inc. (Wheelwright et al. 1999).

As in the case of acquisitions made by cost leader acquirers, the acquirer's managerial resources, administrative systems, operating, sales, marketing, and distribution processes reflected in its differentiation strategy are expected to contribute to acquisition success. Similarly, an acquirer's selection decisions are influenced by its differentiation strategies. Differentiation acquirers are expected to target firms with deficiencies in differentiation or resources that will contribute to improving the combined firm's revenues. Thus, the characteristics of the acquirer are expected to determine the amount and type of post-acquisition synergies.

Hypothesis 2:   An acquirer's level of differentiation is expected to be positively associated with increases in post-acquisition revenue and overall improvements in post-acquisition ROA.

These arguments mainly follow Porter's assertions suggesting that improvements to competitive strategy translate to value creation (Porter 1980). We deviate from Porter's theory when considering the role of focused and broad strategies in acquisitions. Porter argues that focused strategies are associated with high performance. Firms using focused strategies achieve high performance by targeting their most profitable product, geographic, or customer segments. In general, acquisitions are not expected to be compatible with most focused strategies and may signal a retreat from pursuing a focused strategy. Thus, focused strategies in acquirers are expected to negatively affect acquisition performance.

Acquisitions are likely to contribute to the growth and expansion required to achieve broad strategies. Thus, we argue that acquirers with broad strategies are likely to be active in making acquisitions and to view acquisitions as a critical part of their competitive success. Acquirers with broad competitive strategies are expected to have developed the infrastructure and experience needed to achieve positive outcomes in their acquisitions. As a result, we hypothesize that acquirers with broad competitive strategies will achieve greater synergies in acquisitions.

Hypothesis 3:   An acquirer's level of breadth is expected to be positively associated with post-acquisition improvements in ROA.

Lastly, we focus on the role of an acquirer's operational effectiveness in contributing to acquisition success. Operational effectiveness is defined by a firm's technical efficiency in transforming its critical inputs into revenue creating outputs. This is independent of an acquirer's competitive strategy. Operational effectiveness differs from strategy in that it reflects a firm's ability to align its competitive strategy with its external competitive environment (Mudde, unpublished dissertation). High levels of operational effectiveness in acquirers reflect the capability of fine-tuning their competitive strategies to most closely fit the preferences of a given customer segment.

Porter (1996) argues that high levels of operational effectiveness contribute to better firm performance. As argued with competitive strategies, high levels of operational effectiveness in acquirers are expected to contribute to the realization of synergies in acquisitions. High levels of operational effectiveness in an acquirer indicate capabilities that allow it to adjust its competitive strategy to suit the needs of its specific markets. Similar to the capabilities supporting competitive strategies of cost leadership and differentiation, we hypothesize that the capabilities that support operational effectiveness can be utilized and transferred to create value in acquisitions. Acquirers with high levels of effectiveness are expected to utilize these capabilities in integrating their acquisitions and as a result achieve high levels of synergies from their acquisitions. These synergies are expected to be independent of the acquirer's competitive strategy and therefore are not predicted to be specifically based on post-acquisition cost reductions or revenue growth. This results in the following hypothesis:

> Hypothesis 4:   An acquirer's level of operational effectiveness is expected to be positively associated with improvements in post-acquisition ROA.

In summary, acquirers' competitive strategy and operational effectiveness provide the means for realizing the potential synergies. Mergers driven by competitive strategies of cost leadership are likely to realize synergies through cost reductions. For example, in these acquisitions we expect that the combined firm's cost level would be reduced post acquisition. In a similar fashion, mergers driven by differentiation strategies are expected to realize revenue growth.

Model and Sample Description

The model used to explore the relationships between acquirer characteristics and acquisition outcomes is described below:

$$\text{Post-acquisition performance} = f(\text{acquirer's cost leadership,}$$
$$\text{differentiation, focus/breadth,}$$
$$\text{and operational effectiveness}).$$

The competitive strategies of acquirers and targets are measured relative to industry competitors along dimensions of cost leadership, differentiation, and focus/breadth. Operational effectiveness is a fourth measure of acquirer competitiveness. Post-acquisition performance improvements are measured as changes in accounting performance between the pre-acquisition period and post-acquisition period. These measures are described in greater detail later in this section.

The sample is drawn from the population of U.S. commercial and savings banks operating between 1993 and 1998. Accounting data were acquired from the Federal Reserve and include data provided by all U.S. banks via FDIC call reports. Call reports are required by regulation and used by federal and state bank examiners to assess the safety and soundness of U.S. financial institutions (Siems and Barr 1998). This database has the benefit of including information on the entire population of U.S. banks and containing high quality accounting information due to its scrutiny by bank examiners.

The sample contains observations on 8,881 banks and bank holding companies (BHC). Accounting information is aggregated to the parent entity (when a BHC existed) under the assumption that acquisition activity is associated with the highest level of a banking organization. The sample of acquirers and targets includes 230 matched pairs from bank acquisitions that occurred in 1994 and 1995.

Information on mergers and acquisitions in the banking industry is drawn from the *M&A Journal* and includes all acquisitions with information on both acquirers and targets in the sample of 8,881 banks. The sample of acquisitions was reduced by 23 observations, which were identified as outliers and eliminated from the sample, resulting in a final sample of 207 bank acquisitions (Neter et al. 1996).

Dependent variables

Three measures of post-acquisition performance improvements are used in this study: change in ROA (ΔROA), change in cost (ΔCOSTS), and change in revenue (ΔREV). These measures are consistent with measures of economic value used in M&A studies into strategy (Seth 1990b, Harrison et al. 1991) and economic research (Ravenscraft and Scherer 1987). Each is calculated by netting the aggregate accounting performance of the individual firms during the year prior to acquisition from the accounting performance during the three years after the acquisition. The change in ROA is calculated as follows: $\Delta\text{ROA} = (\Sigma\text{Net Income}_C/\Sigma\text{Assets}_C)_{t,t+1,t+2} - (\text{Net Income}_A + \text{Net Income}_T)_{t-1}/(\text{Assets}_A + \text{Assets}_T)_{t-1}$, where: Net Income$_A$, Net Income$_T$, Net Income$_C$ are the values of net income associated with acquirers, targets, and combined banks (post-acquisition), respectively.

The change in costs (ΔCOSTS) and revenues (ΔREV) are calculated likewise using the pre-acquisition $(t-1)$ and post-acquisition (year of acquisition plus two years following acquisition) cost levels and revenues levels. The equation would be identical to the calculation for ΔROA with either total costs or total revenue substituted for net income. Using a three-year period to evaluate post-acquisition synergies is similar to Ravenscraft and Scherer's study (1987).

Independent variables

The independent variables used in the models include four instruments: three measuring dimensions of competitive strategy and one measuring operational effectiveness. These measures capture the acquirer's differentiation, cost leadership, focus/breadth, and operational effectiveness prior to making the acquisition. These measures and their proposed effects on acquisition synergies are summarized in Table 4.1.

The measures of competitive strategy are based on Porter's typology (1980) and include continuous measures of cost leadership, differentiation, and focus/breadth. The level of a bank's cost leadership is operationalized as a cumulative measure of the degree its property and equipment expense, personnel expense, other operating expense, cost of funds, and product pricing are below industry average. The level of a bank's differentiation is operationalized as a cumulative measure of the degree its property and equipment expense, personnel expense, other operating expense, product pricing, and level of fee income are above industry average. The level of a bank's focus/breadth is measured as the natural log of its asset size and generally reflects the extent of the breadth of its geographic markets.

The independent variable used to measure the operational effectiveness of the banks within the sample is based on a DEA analysis (Charnes, Cooper, and Rhodes

Table 4.1   Hypothesized relationships between competitiveness and acquisition synergies

Acquirer characteristics	Hypothesized effect on acquisition performance	Hypothesized source of synergy
Cost leadership (COSTLEAD)	+ (H1)	Cost reductions (H1)
Differentiation (DIFF)	+ (H2)	Revenue growth (H2)
Breadth (BREADTH)	+ (H3)	
Operational effectiveness (OPSEFF)	+ (H4)	

1978) for all of the 8,881 banks in the full sample (Mudde, unpublished dissertation). As previously noted, it reflects a bank's technical efficiency in converting five critical inputs into three income-generating outputs. This model is based on Siems and Barr (1998). Sample statistics and correlations are shown in Table 4.2.

The methodology used to test the proposed hypotheses uses OLS regression models. Model 1 uses ΔROA as its dependent variable. It includes independent variables of acquirers' competitive strategy and operational effectiveness. Model 2 is similar to Model 1 but uses ΔCOSTS as the dependent variable. Model 3 uses ΔREV as its dependent variable.

Results

Before proceeding to examine the specific hypotheses, we first test whether acquiring banks have accounting performance that differs from that of non-acquiring banks. Comparing the changes between pre-acquisition ROA and post-acquisition ROA for each acquisition with the change in ROAs from the same time periods for banks not involved in acquisitions shows no significant difference in accounting performance between acquisition banks and non-acquisition banks ($F = 1.09$, $p < 0.298$). Both populations experience slight declines in ROA during these periods. This evidence shows that, in general, bank acquisitions offered no measurable performance improvements when comparing performance in the year prior to the acquisition with the three-year period following acquisition.

This does not mean that all bank acquisitions fail to produce synergies. The results of our analysis show that significant variations in acquisition performance exist (see Table 4.3). Model 1 shows the relationship between acquirer competitive strategy and operational effectiveness and post-acquisition ROA. Two of the four hypothesized independent variables have significant effects on post-acquisition ROA. Hypothesis 1 predicts a positive association between an acquirer's level of cost leadership and post-acquisition ROA. Hypothesis 1 is not supported with respect to post-acquisition profitability – higher levels of cost leadership have no significant effect on post-acquisition ROA. Differentiation also did not have a significant effect

Table 4.2 Descriptive statistics and Pearson correlation coefficients

	N	Mean	StDev	Min	Max	1	2	3	4	5	6	7
1. ΔROA	207	-0.00022	0.00163	-0.00501	0.00354							
2. ΔCOSTS	207	-0.00349	0.00717	-0.02599	0.0207	-0.164 (0.018)						
3. ΔREV	207	-0.00551	0.00542	-0.02416	0.00981	0.098 (0.161)	0.874 (0.000)					
4. DIFF	207	1.761	1.61	0	7.988	-0.121 (0.082)	0.043 (0.541)	-0.063 (0.364)				
5. COSTLEAD	207	1.0318	0.6473	0	4.2999	-0.02 (0.775)	-0.169 (0.015)	-0.149 (0.032)	-0.2 (0.004)			
6. BREADTH	207	15.181	1.726	10.722	19.023	0.097 (0.163)	-0.259 (0.000)	-0.275 (0.000)	0.503 (0.000)	-0.127 (0.068)		
7. DIFF*COSTLEAD	207	1.61	1.877	0	12.28	-0.161 (0.02)	0.069 (0.323)	0.001 (0.992)	0.556 (0.000)	0.454 (0.000)	0.29 (0.000)	
8. OPSEFF	207	0.6459	0.10107	0.48495	0.87859	0.117 (0.092)	0.035 (0.621)	0.147 (0.034)	-0.049 (0.487)	0.456 (0.000)	0.009 (0.898)	0.314 (0.000)

Cell contents: Correlation coefficients; p values.

Table 4.3   Results for OLS regression models 1, 2, and 3

Independent variables	Model 1 (Dependent variable = ΔROA) Coefficients	Model 2 (Dependent variable = ΔCOSTS) Coefficients	Model 3 (Dependent variable = ΔREV) Coefficients
Constant	−0.004648*** (0.000)	0.01957*** (0.000)	0.006134 (0.123)
DIFF	−0.0000796 (0.470)	−0.0002643 (0.558)	−0.0005215 (0.124)
COSTLEAD	−0.000049 (0.845)	−0.005167*** (0.000)	−0.0041716*** (0.000)
BREADTH	0.0001969** (0.008)	−0.001673*** (0.000)	−0.00113*** (0.000)
DIFF*COSTLEAD	−0.0002114* (0.034)	0.001494*** (0.000)	0.0009643** (0.002)
OPSEFF	0.002891* (0.020)	0.008875 (0.081)	0.01422*** (0.000)
R–sq	9.0	21.2	22.2
F	3.96	10.8	11.48
P	(0.002)**	(0.000)***	(0.000)***
N	207	207	207

†$p < 0.10$; * $p < 0.05$; ** $p < 0.01$; *** $p < 0.001$.
Cell contents: Coefficients; p values.

on post-acquisition ROA. Thus, hypothesis 2 is also not supported with respect to post-acquisition profitability. Hypothesis 3 is supported. Acquirers with broader competitive strategies have significantly higher post-acquisition ROA ($p < 0.008$). Higher levels of operational effectiveness also are associated with post-acquisition performance improvements in bank acquisitions, supporting hypothesis 4 ($p < 0.020$). Although not hypothesized, an interaction term capturing the effect of mixing strategies of cost leadership and differentiation was found to be significant and added to the model. High levels of mixed strategies (combinations of high levels of cost leadership and differentiation) are found to be negatively related to post-acquisition synergy ($p < 0.034$).

These effects are both statistically and economically significant. For the "average" acquiring bank within the sample, holding all other measures constant, the estimated economic value of the improvement in ROA associated with broadening its strategy by one standard deviation is $10.2 million of economic value. A two standard deviation increase in breadth results in improvements in post-acquisition profitability of $98.5 million dollars of economic value. The escalating value of the economic gain results from two conditions. Acquirers with broader strategies benefit from (1) better accounting performance (improved ROA) and (2) the larger size of their asset base, which makes an equivalent change in ROA even more valuable. A one standard deviation improvement in an acquirer's operational effectiveness is predicted to increase post-acquisition synergies by $1.0 million, assuming all other factors remain constant. Acquirers with higher levels of mixed strategies are predicted to reduce post-acquisition profits by $1.4 million (based on a one standard deviation increase in DIFF*COSTLEAD and an average-sized acquirer, holding all other measures constant).

Thus, the evidence supports the following hypotheses regarding the realization of improvements in ROA in acquisitions. First, in general, the acquisition activity occurring within this sample does not appear to result in improvements (or declines) in performance. There was no significant difference in the changes in accounting performance between acquisition banks and non-acquisition banks. But, there was significant variation in the ability of acquirers to improve ROA in their acquisitions. Acquirers with broader strategies realize significantly more returns from their acquisitions. Higher levels of operational effectiveness are also associated with greater post-acquisition synergy. But, acquirers with high levels of mixed strategies realize lower ROA in their acquisitions.

The next line of inquiry relates to the link between the acquirer's strategy and the type of performance improvements generated by acquisitions. Model 2 uses ΔCOSTS as the dependent variable to test the relationship between acquirer characteristics and the realization of post-acquisition cost reduction synergies. Model 3 uses ΔREV as the dependent variable to test the relationship between acquirer characteristics and the realization of post-acquisition revenue growth.

Model 2 shows the relationship between acquirer strategy and operational effectiveness and post-acquisition cost reductions. This model provides additional insight regarding the expected relationships between cost leadership and differentiation strategies and post-acquisition ROA. Model 2 shows that the expected relationship (H1) between an acquirer's cost leadership strategy and post-acquisition cost reductions is supported at a level of high statistical significance ($p < 0.000$). Acquirers with high levels of cost leadership achieve significant cost reduction in acquisitions. Recall that Model 1 showed no significant relationship between cost leadership and post-acquisition ROA.

How can acquirers with high levels of cost leadership be successful at reducing post-acquisition expense, but fail to achieve improvements in overall profitability? Model 3 provides evidence that explains this finding. The results from the analysis in Model 3 show that high levels of cost leadership are associated with declines in post-acquisition revenues, which offset the benefits gained from the realization of post-acquisition cost reductions. Thus, acquirers with high levels of cost leadership achieve significant gains from reducing costs in their acquisitions, but fail to realize improvements in overall profitability due to declines in post-acquisition revenues.

Other significant findings from the analysis in Model 2 show broad strategies also negatively affect (reducing costs) post-acquisition expense ($p < 0.000$). High levels of mixed strategies in acquisitions are positively associated with increased post-acquisition costs ($p < 0.000$) as is operational effectiveness ($p < 0.081$). Although this relationship is not hypothesized, it is consistent with the previous theory suggesting that acquirers with mixed strategies are likely to make investments to increase the level of differentiation in their targets, resulting in higher post-acquisition costs.

Finally, Model 3 shows that the acquirer's level of differentiation does not significantly affect the realization of revenue growth in the post-acquisition period

($p < 0.124$), as predicted by hypothesis 2. Operational effectiveness and mixed strategies have significant positive relationships with post-acquisition revenue ($p < 0.002$, $p < 0.000$, respectively). Thus, differentiation contributes to increased post-acquisition revenue when it is combined with high levels of cost leadership.

Broad strategies and cost leadership strategies negatively affect an acquirer's post-acquisition revenue growth ($p < 0.000$, $p < 0.000$, respectively). The negative relationship between cost leadership and post-acquisition revenue was not hypothesized. However, it is consistent with the types of integration activities that support post-acquisition cost reductions, such as eliminating low margin products and sales and/or distribution outlets. It may also reflect the short-term effects of reducing prices as a result of competing on low prices.

Discussion and Conclusions

These findings tell an interesting story about how acquirer competitiveness affects M&A. First, this study provides additional evidence about the challenges of achieving economic gains through acquisitions. In general, bank acquisitions had no significant effect on financial performance, since there was no measurable difference between the ROA of banks involved in M&A activity and those that were not. There is significant variation in acquirers in terms of their competitive strategies and operational effectiveness and the performance of their acquisitions.

We examined performance variation in acquisitions at two levels. First, we focused on how competitive strategy and operational effectiveness affect acquisition profitability (ΔROA). This analysis showed acquirers with high levels of operational effectiveness achieved greater performance improvements in their acquisitions. Acquisition performance also improved for acquirers with broad competitive strategies. Combinations of cost leadership and differentiation (mixed strategies) are found to have a negative effect on net synergies. Competitive strategies of cost leadership and differentiation did not have a significant effect on acquisition profitability.

The link between acquirer operational effectiveness and acquisition profitability supports our theoretical arguments that capabilities developed by firms to improve their effectiveness in business-level competition can also be used to positive effect in M&A activity. The association between the breadth of an acquirer's strategy and acquisition performance is consistent with our arguments that acquisitions complement and support broad competitive strategies, and may be inconsistent with focused business strategies. The negative association between acquirers with high levels of mixed strategies and acquisition performance was not specifically hypothesized. This finding appears to indicate that the lack of a clear strategic orientation in an acquirer (either dominantly cost leadership or differentiation) creates problems for acquisitions. This discussion continues in the next section.

The second type of performance variation examined in this study dealt with how operational effectiveness and competitive strategy affected post-acquisition costs and revenues. The findings regarding the effect of competitive strategy on the types of synergies realized in acquisitions provide some important insights about value creation in acquisitions. In general, acquirers using differentiation, in combination with cost leadership, were able to gain synergistic revenue growth in their acquisitions. Unfortunately, acquirers with mixed strategies also had significant increases in post-acquisition costs, negating the value of their synergistic revenues.

Acquirer operational effectiveness also contributed to the realization of growth in revenues during the post-acquisition period. This was also associated with increases in post-acquisition costs. However, in the case of operational effectiveness, its positive effects on revenue exceeded its effect on costs, resulting in net synergies. Cost leadership was associated with post-acquisition cost reductions and revenue decreases. As a result, cost leadership had a non-significant effect on net synergies. Breadth and operational effectiveness were the only measures of acquirer competitiveness that resulted in improvements in post-acquisition ROA.

This study adds to our understanding of cost-reduction and revenue-enhancing synergies (Capron 1999). Unlike Capron's study that found these two types of synergy were complementary, the findings of this research show that acquirers tend to specialize in either post-acquisition revenue growth or cost reduction. This supports the view that cost and revenue synergies are fundamentally different and, in some cases, appear to be mutually exclusive.

There are a number of possible explanations for the evidence that post-acquisition revenue improvements are associated with increasing costs and post-acquisition cost reductions are associated with declines in revenue. The first is Porter's arguments that pursuing cost leadership and differentiation require tradeoffs (Porter 1980). This explanation suggests that altering the competitive strategy of the acquired firm (or combined firms) has a cost associated with the change. In the case of a shift toward more differentiation, additional expense is required to support the development of revenue-enhancing capabilities. In banking, differentiation acquirers may be especially concerned about customer defection during the turbulence of post-acquisition integration. Additional marketing and sales expense may be required to reassure acquired customers and generate brand awareness in a new geographic market. Investment may also be necessary to upgrade the acquired bank's existing facilities and train its personnel to support a differentiation strategy.

In the case of a shift toward cost leadership, some revenue loss may be associated with cost-reducing activities. For example, closing redundant or unprofitable locations and eliminating non-standard products are likely to result in the loss of some customers, resulting in a decline in revenue. A cost leader may reduce the fees and rates charged for the acquired bank's products and services to align with a low price strategy, causing a near-term decline in revenues.

Another explanation is that poor management or implementation, not strategic tradeoffs, is to blame. Cost-leader acquirers may be myopic in their attention to achieving cost-reduction synergies during post-acquisition and not recognize the corresponding reduction in revenues. Target management, lacking experience with the acquirer's cost leadership strategy, may be inclined to unnecessarily waive fees to retain customers. Unanticipated employee and management turnover at the acquired firm may contribute to customer defection and reduced revenues. The acquirer's management and control systems may be overly geared toward tracking variances in expenses. Likewise, the goals and incentives associated with acquisition integration may be exclusively oriented toward expense reduction.

Similarly, differentiation acquirers may be myopic in their pursuit of revenue growth. Lack of controls during post-acquisition integration may allow high levels of expense growth while the combined bank attempts to meet its aggressive goals for synergistic revenue growth. Goals, incentives, and reporting systems supporting the acquisition integration process may be exclusively oriented toward revenue growth and fail to control for increases in post-acquisition expense.

This study with its measures based on Porter's typology of competitive strategy and firm-level operational effectiveness is limited in its ability to diagnose specific failures in the M&A process. Future research is needed to better understand under what conditions post-acquisition revenue growth and cost reduction are mutually exclusive and under what conditions are they complementary (Capron 1999). Additional research is also needed to understand the reasons that revenue growth or cost reduction do not translate into overall improvements in ROA. If strategic tradeoffs are to blame, it suggests greater caution on the part of banks considering acquisition as a strategy for growth. If poor implementation is to blame, it suggests an integration process that focuses on managing both costs and revenues.

This study also identifies some of the information that bidders should take into account if they are attempting to achieve abnormal returns from their acquisitions. Barney (1988) argues that bidders need to understand the value of targets to both themselves and all other bidding firms in order to avoid overpaying for acquisitions. Given the lack of evidence regarding how acquirer characteristics and acquisition characteristics affect synergies, this advice has been difficult to put into practice.

The inability of cost leadership and differentiation to support net synergies suggests that the resources supporting these strategies may not be unique enough to allow for abnormal returns from M&A. Broad strategies and operational effectiveness on the other hand do contribute to the creation of synergies. This research suggests that bidders should focus on the competitive strategies and operational effectiveness of rival bidders to gain abnormal returns from acquisition activity. It also suggests that banks with broad strategies and high operational effectiveness have an advantage in making acquisitions.

The conclusions of this study are subject to several possible limitations. First, this study examines M&A in a single industry, U.S. banking. The use of a single industry sample allows for a more precise focus on measuring firm competitiveness and how competitiveness affects M&A performance. A single industry study is limited in its ability to be generalized to M&A in other industries or across industries. The findings of this study suggesting that broad strategies and operational effectiveness provide advantages to acquirers is consistent with the battle for scale that is evident in the general M&A market. A second limitation is due to the cross-sectional nature of the study, which limits its ability to determine the dynamic, or causal, relationships between the constructs used in the study.

The contribution of business-level competitiveness in realizing synergies in M&A is an important finding for many areas of research in M&A. While firm competitiveness is a central concern in horizontal acquisitions, it is also likely to be important in diversifying acquisitions. It suggests another finer grained dimension of relatedness that explains performance variation within groups such as related, unrelated, horizontal, or vertical M&A. Understanding the competitive strategy and operational effectiveness of acquirers and targets in diversifying acquisitions may explain variation that currently confounds the conclusions of research on how relatedness affects M&A performance (Lubatkin 1987, Shelton 1988, Seth 1990b).

Business-level competitiveness may also be useful in understanding the M&A process. This study has used M&A process theory to develop its propositions but has not directly examined M&A process or integration directly. The evidence that different competitive strategies result in different selection decisions and different types of post-acquisition synergies raises interesting questions for research in the M&A process. Do the competitive strategies of acquirers affect their selection, negotiation, planning, and integration processes?

It also may be useful in other areas of M&A research. Topics such as top management teams (Shanley and Correa 1992), the effect of learning and experience in M&A (Hayward and Hambrick 1997, Singh and Zollo 1998), cultural conflicts and acculturation in M&A (Pablo 1994, Jemison and Sitkin 1986), post-acquisition resource sharing and restructuring activities (Capron, Dussauge, and Mitchell 1998), and many others could benefit from an understanding of how acquirer competitiveness influences M&A.

This study also makes a contribution to strategy research at a more general level. It is one of the first studies to show how business-level strategy and corporate-level strategy interact. Specifically, it shows that business-level competitiveness influences corporate strategy decisions (M&A selection) and that the decision to acquire (an action of corporate strategy) can potentially improve the competitiveness and profitability of a firm at the business level. This important interaction between business and corporate strategy is not likely to be limited to M&A. Corporate strategy decisions related to alliances, vertical integration, and diversification may also be influenced by business-level competitiveness, and vice versa.

This research offers several important implications for managers. First, it adds to the mounting evidence on how difficult it is for acquirers to achieve positive synergies in acquisitions. It suggests would-be acquirers focus on improving their operational effectiveness prior to making acquisitions. This has two potential benefits: (1) it can contribute to immediate improvements in financial performance (Mudde, unpublished dissertation) and (2) it can contribute to improved acquisition outcomes. The benefit of a broad strategic position presents a "catch 22" for acquirers. To achieve large size, acquisitions may be necessary, but acquisitions' results are expected to be poor until significant breadth is achieved. This finding is consistent with the patterns of M&A activity in the banking industry, where the larger banks continue to increase their size in waves of acquisitions.

Another important implication for managers resulting from this study is the findings regarding the realization of synergistic revenues and cost reductions. Are managers misunderstanding their acquisition outcomes? Are managers of differentiation acquirers focusing solely on the creating of synergistic revenue growth, without recognizing that post-acquisition costs are increasing hand in hand with new revenues? Are managers of cost leader acquirers making similar errors in exclusively focusing on post-acquisition cost reductions? These are interesting questions for future research. This may be part of the explanation for the pervasiveness of hubris in M&A decisions (Roll 1986).

There may be potential for improving M&A performance by focusing on both revenue and expense management during post-acquisition integration. If different-iation acquirers can limit the growth of expense without hindering post-acquisition revenue growth, net synergies will result. Similarly, if cost leaders can limit revenue loss, while still achieving post-acquisition cost reductions, net synergies will result. This offers some hope for improving the success of future M&A.

References

Ahuja, G. and Katila, R. 2001. Technological acquisitions and the innovation performance of acquiring firms: A longitudinal study. *Strategic Management Journal*, **22**(3): 197–220.

Anand, J. and Singh, H. 1997. Asset redeployment, acquisitions, and corporate strategy in declining industries. *Strategic Management Journal*, **18**: 99–118.

Barney, J.B. 1988. Returns to bidding firms in mergers and acquisitions: Reconsidering the relatedness hypothesis. *Strategic Management Journal*, **9**: 71–8.

Bower, J. 2001. Not all M&As are alike – and that matters. *Harvard Business Review*, March: 93–101.

Brush, T.H. 1996. Predicted changes in operational synergy and post-acquisition performance of acquired businesses. *Strategic Management Journal*, **17**: 1–24.

Capron, L. 1999. The long-term performance of horizontal acquisitions. *Strategic Management Journal*, **20**: 987–1018.

Capron, L., Dussauge, P., and Mitchell, W. 1998. Resource redeployment following horizon-tal acquisitions in Europe and North America, 1988–1992. *Strategic Management Journal*, **19**: 631–61.

Capron, L., Mitchell, W., and Swaminathan, A. 2001. Asset divestiture following horizontal acquisitions: A dynamic view. *Strategic Management Journal*, **22**: 817–44.

Charnes, A., Cooper, W.W., and Rhodes, E. 1978. Measuring the efficiency of decision-making units. *European Journal of Operational Research*, **2**(November): 429–44.

Collis, D. and Stuart, T. 1995. *Cooper Industries' Corporate Strategy (A)*. Boston, MA: Harvard Business School Publishing, pp. 61–86.

Datta, D.K., Pinches, G.E., and Narayanan, V.K. 1992. Factors influencing wealth creation from mergers and acquisitions: A meta-analysis. *Strategic Management Journal*, **13**: 67–84.

Dess, G.G. and Davis, P.S. 1984. Porter's (1980) generic strategies as determinants of strategic group membership and organizational performance. *Academy of Management Journal*, **27**(3): 467–88.

Hambrick, D.C. 1983. High profit strategies in mature capital goods industries: A contingency approach. *Academy of Management Journal*, **26**(4): 687–707.

Harrison, J.S., Hitt, M.A., Hoskisson, R.E., and Ireland, R.D. 1991. Synergies and post-acquisition performance: Differences versus similarities in resource allocations. *Journal of Management*, **17**(1): 173–90.

Haspeslagh, P.C. and Jemison, D.B. 1991. *Managing Acquisitions*. New York: Free Press.

Hayward, M.L A. 2002. When do firms learn from their acquisition experience? Evidence from 1990–1995. *Strategic Management Journal*, **23**(1): 21–39.

Hayward, M.L.A. and Hambrick, D.C. 1997. Explaining the premiums paid for large acquisi-tions: Evidence of CEO hubris. *Administrative Science Quarterly*, **42**: 103–27.

Hitt, M.A., Harrison, J.S., and Ireland, R.D. 2001. *Mergers and Acquisitions: A Guide to Creating Value for Stakeholders*. New York: Oxford University Press.

Jemison, D.B. and Sitkin, S.B. 1986. Corporate acquisitions: A process perspective. *Academy of Management Journal*, **11**: 145–63.

Jensen, M.C. and Ruback, R.S. 1983. The market for corporate control. *Journal of Financial Economics*, **11**: 5–50.

Kaplan, S., Mitchell, M., and Wruck, K. 2000. A clinical exploration of value creation and destruction in acquisitions. In S. Kaplan (ed.), *Mergers and Productivity*. Chicago: University of Chicago Press, pp. 179–227.

Lichtenberg, F.R. and Siegel, D. 1987. Productivity and changes in ownership of manufacturing plants. *Brookings Papers on Economic Activity: Microeconomics*, 643–73.

Lubatkin, M. 1983. Mergers and the performance of the acquiring firm. *Academy of Management Review*, **8**: 218–25.

Lubatkin, M. 1987. Merger strategies and shareholder value. *Strategic Management Journal*, **8**: 39–53.

Manne, H.G. 1965. Mergers and the market for corporate control. *Journal of Political Economy*, **73**: 110–20.

Miller, A. and Dess, G.G. 1993. Assessing Porter's (1980) model in terms of its generalizability, accuracy, and simplicity. *Journal of Management Studies*, **30**(4): 553–85.

Miller, D. and Friesen, P.H. 1986. Porter's (1980) generic strategies and performance: An empirical examination with American data. Part 1: Testing Porter. *Organizational Studies*, **7**(1): 37–55.

Nelson, R.R. and Winter, S. 1982. *An Evolutionary Theory of Economic Chance*. Cambridge, MA: Belknap Press.

Neter, J., Kutner, M.H., Nachtsheim, C.J., and Wasserman, W. 1996. *Applied Linear Statistical Models*. Chicago: Irwin.

Pablo, A.L. 1994. Determinants of acquisition integration level: A decision-making perspective. *Academy of Management Journal*, **37**(4): 803–36.

Penrose, E.T. 1959. *The Theory of the Growth of the Firm*. New York: Wiley.

Porter, M. 1980. *Competitive Strategy*. New York: Free Press.

Porter, M. 1996. What is strategy? *Harvard Business Review*, November–December: 3–20.

Ravenscraft, D.J. and Scherer, F.M. 1987. *Mergers, Sell-offs, and Economic Efficiency*. Washington, DC: Brookings Institution.

Roll, R. 1986. The hubris hypothesis of corporate takeovers. *Journal of Business*, **59**: 197–216.

Salter, M.S. and Weinhold, W.A. 1981. Choosing compatible acquisitions. *Harvard Business Review*, **59**(1): 117–27.

Schmitt, R. 1986. Bold banker: Wells Fargo takeover of Crocker is yielding profit but some pain. *Wall Street Journal*, 5 August: A1.

Seth, A. 1990a. Sources of value creation in acquisitions: An empirical investigation. *Strategic Management Journal*, **11**: 431–46.

Seth, A. 1990b. Value creation in acquisitions: A reexamination of performance issues. *Strategic Management Journal*, **11**: 99–115.

Shanley, M. and Correa, M. 1992. Agreement between top management teams and expectations for post-acquisition performance. *Strategic Management Journal*, **13**: 245–66.

Shelton, L.M. 1988. Strategic business fits and corporate acquisition: Empirical evidence. *Strategic Management Journal*, **9**: 279–87.

Siems, T.F. and Barr, R.S. 1998. Benchmarking the productive efficiency of U.S. banks. *Financial Industry Studies*, December: 11–24.

Singh, H. and Montgomery, C.A. 1987. Corporate acquisition strategies and economic performance. *Strategic Management Journal*, **8**: 377–86.

Singh, H. and Zollo, M. 1998. The impact of knowledge codification, experience trajectories, and integration strategies on the performance of corporate acquisitions: Working paper, INSEAD.

Sirower, M.L. 1997. *The Synergy Trap*. New York: Free Press.

Uyterhoeven, H. and Hart, M.M. 1993. *Banc One – 1993*. Boston, MA: Harvard Business School Publishing, pp. 87–108.

Vlasic, B. and Stertz, B. 2000. *Taken for a Ride*. New York: HarperCollins.

Wheelwright, S.C., Holloway, C.A., Tempest, N., and Kasper, C.G. 1999. *Cisco Systems Inc: Acquisition Integration for Manufacturing (A)*. Boston, MA: Harvard Business School Publishing, pp. 1–27.

CHAPTER FIVE

Acquisition of Entrepreneurial Firms: How Private and Public Targets Differ

Jung-Chin Shen, Jeffrey J. Reuer

Abstract
This study compares private and public entrepreneurial firms that are acquisition targets. We develop the argument that private targets tend to involve higher transaction costs in the presence of search and valuation problems than their public counterparts. Consistent with predictions, the empirical evidence indicates that bidders choose to acquire public, rather than private, targets when purchasing firms in industries involving spatially dispersed firms, and when engaging in inter-industry transactions. Acquirers also tend to avoid private targets that are young, have significant intangible assets, and have not signaled the value of these resources through other means, such as collaborative agreements. For entrepreneurial firms, the results shed light on the benefits of being public and the decision-making criteria employed by acquiring organizations.

Introduction

The mergers and acquisition (M&A) phenomenon is a leading cause of industrial change and the rationalization of business organizations in the modern industrial era (e.g. Jensen 1993). Equally significant, entrepreneurial firms have long been recognized as a major source of change within industries (e.g. Schumpeter 2000) because they tend to have higher founding rates, faster and more variable growth, and a greater propensity to fail than established firms (Evans and Leighton 1986). Moreover, entrepreneurial firms also play an important role in M&As. Research has concluded that entrepreneurial firms have a higher likelihood of becoming takeover targets than other firms (e.g. Levine and Aaronovitch 1981, Palepu 1986, Mulherin and Boone 2000). Yet, relatively little systematic research has been devoted to the study of the acquisition of entrepreneurial firms.

The neglect of entrepreneurial firms in the M&A literature is due, in part, to the methods that scholars have used to study core research questions in the field. Throughout the past two decades, one of the chief purposes of M&A studies has been to understand how different acquisition motives influence firm performance (e.g. Andrade, Mitchell, and Stafford 2001). The standard approach used to untangle this question is event study methodology. Event study methodology is based on the assumption of market efficiency that implies the effects of an event such as an acquisition announcement will be reflected immediately in security prices. As a result, the M&A literature tends to use datasets that sample public companies. This work implicitly assumes that conclusions drawn from large, public companies apply equally well to small, private ones. However, given the substantial qualitative differences between public and private companies, the validity of this assumption may be problematic. Drawing conclusions from samples of public targets potentially undermines the generalizability of the interpretations and weakens the external validity of the evidence (Berk 1983).

In fact, recent research provides initial evidence suggesting that the implications of M&A deal structures do vary across private and public targets. Chang (1998), for instance, found that for privately held target firms, the method of payment has a completely different effect on the bidding firm's stock returns. The positive mean abnormal return that bidders obtain when using stock to acquire privately held targets contrasts with the negative average abnormal return documented for bidders using stock to acquire public targets. Recent work has also reported that contingent earnouts, which specify future variable payments to the target firm based on the achievement of performance objectives, are more likely to be used in an acquisition if the target is a private company (Datar, Frankel, and Wolfson 2001). While these studies provide insights into specific financial instruments in M&A, they do not specifically focus on acquisitions of public and private companies per se, nor do they examine the more fundamental differences underlying acquisitions of public and private entrepreneurial firms.

This study therefore seeks to extend prior research on acquisitions in two ways. First, we focus on acquisitions of entrepreneurial firms in particular. Second, we explore essential differences between private versus public targets in order to understand their underlying differences, and the appropriateness of pooling them together or focusing on only public targets in M&A studies. The theory that we propose suggests that searching for a profitable target and assessing its value can pose significant difficulties for buyers (e.g. Stigler 1961, Akerlof 1970). And, this is particularly the case when the target is small and private. The core proposition is that when such search and valuation difficulties are manifest, bidders are more likely to pursue public targets, for which these problems are comparatively less severe. Searching for and valuing entrepreneurial targets is often problematic in general because entrepreneurial firms are difficult to locate as exchange partners (Deeds, DeCarolis, and Coombs 1999). At the same time, entrepreneurial firms tend to find it more difficult to signal their business prospects to investors (e.g. McConnell and Pettit 1984). We develop the argument that these problems are less significant for public, rather than private, entrepreneurial firms due to the enhanced visibility of public firms, the greater information disclosed on them, and the signals attached to being publicly traded.

The chapter is organized as follows: After an overview of background literature, we present the theoretical arguments and research hypotheses, which apply concepts from information economics (e.g. Stigler 1961, Akerlof 1970, Spence 1974) to the M&A setting. A discussion of the empirical findings follows details on the research design, which appear in a subsequent section. The study is based on a sample of over 900 private and public entrepreneurial firms in the manufacturing sector that were acquired between 1996 and 1999. We find that entrepreneurial targets are more likely to be publicly held in industries subject to high search costs. Our findings are also consistent with the view that public targets become more attractive relative to private firms when would-be buyers confront valuation challenges due to information asymmetries in the acquisition process. In particular, buyers tend to prefer public targets over private targets when acquiring younger firms. Moreover, firms are willing to acquire private targets in their core business, but in noncore domains the stock market appears to be useful as a means of screening potential targets that the acquirer would otherwise find more difficult to assess. Furthermore, firms are more willing to acquire public targets that have significant intangible resources than equivalent private firms. We suggest, and find, that strategic alliances may be alternative vehicles to mitigate the effects of information asymmetry accompanying the target's intangible resources. A discussion of the implications of our findings and new avenues for research concludes.

Background Literature

A large body of literature across various disciplines and applied areas has focused on corporate acquisitions (e.g. for a recent review, see Andrade, Mitchell, and Stafford 2001). Researchers interested in the impact of target characteristics on acquisition patterns have used a variety of approaches. We highlight three streams of research that are particularly relevant to this study. The first models the likelihood of acquisition based on firm characteristics. The second examines the implications of information asymmetry for M&A markets. The third investigates the potential implications of going public on the transfer of control rights in M&A markets.

Firm characteristics and the likelihood of acquisition

Numerous theoretical and empirical studies have been conducted in order to understand why acquisitions occur and how they affect bidders and targets (e.g. Bradley, Desai, and Kim 1983, Andrade, Mitchell, and Stafford 2001). To disentangle various motives for corporate acquisitions, one research stream empirically examines the likelihood of acquisition by identifying salient characteristics of target and acquiring firms. Since most studies have found that the gains from acquisitions tend to accrue to targets, identifying target firm characteristics and modeling the takeover likelihood could potentially be a profitable arbitrage strategy. Early research was aimed at developing models for the likelihood of M&A, and this work concluded that there were distinctive characteristics of target and acquiring firms in terms of their financial ratios. Therefore, it was possible to construct a predictive model (e.g. Simkowiz and Monroe 1971, cf. Palepu 1986). However, this stream of research sought to distinguish targets from nontargets rather than to differentiate private and public targets.

Information asymmetry and corporate acquisitions

Other M&A studies have noted that information asymmetry may have a significant impact on the likelihood and performance implications of acquisitions. Akerlof's (1970) classic study of the market for "lemons" in product markets is instructive and, under certain circumstances, it may also be in operation for corporate acquisitions. For instance, an entrepreneur with superior information about the value of the firm will be reluctant to sell above-average assets if he or she cannot credibly convey this information, thereby obtaining a reasonable price. Consequently, bidders discount their offer prices, and the average quality level of acquisitions will be lower in equilibrium. Given the incentives for misrepresentations on the part of target firms, the possibility of adverse selection arises. In turn, this leads to inefficiencies due to additional information gathering and extensive negotiations, and to the failure of firms to consummate attractive deals. Consistent with the application of Akerlof's model to the M&A setting, research has found that under conditions of asymmetric information, firms can benefit from contingent forms of consideration such as stock payments (Eckbo, Giammarino, and Heinkel 1990). That is, firms lengthen their negotiations in acquisitions subject to valuation problems (Coff 1999). They may gain from using joint ventures instead, in order to stimulate credible information revelation through the joint ownership of assets (e.g. Reuer and Koza 2000). We develop the argument that different forms of acquisitions, in particular those involving private versus public targets, are more or less subject to these problems. This is due, in part, to the interdependence between equity markets and the market for corporate control, as suggested below.

IPOs and control rights transfers

Scholars have noted that information asymmetry is not only evident in corporate acquisitions, but it also has implications for transfers of control rights through the use of initial public offering[1] (IPO) markets. While financial economics research on IPOs has largely focused on potential challenges to the efficiency of capital markets due to so-called anomalies such as underpricing, hot issue markets, and the long-run underperformance of newly public companies (e.g. Ibbotson, Sindelar, and Ritter 1988, Allen and Faulhaber 1989), emerging findings also suggest that IPOs have implications for M&A markets since newly public firms exhibit a higher propensity of being acquired (e.g. Pagano, Panetta, and Zingales 1998, Field and Mulherin 1999). In the words of one investment banker, entrepreneurs can use the IPO process as a way of "teeing up" a company for sale (Rock, Rock, and Sikora 1994).

Several theoretical works have similarly noted that the prevailing public decision may have implications for future transfers of control rights in firms. For instance, Ellingsen and Rydqvist (1997) developed a model suggesting that acquiring firms can use the stock market to screen target firms under conditions of information asymmetry. On the sell side, Zingales' (1995) model suggests that the firm can use a two-stage sale in order to maximize its total proceeds by relying on the capital market to auction off cash flow rights, and the market for corporate control to negotiate the sale of private benefits of control. Mello and Parsons' (1998) model reaches a similar conclusion, emphasizing the information the owner obtains regarding the value of the firm by going public. These models identify potential benefits of going public as well as costs of remaining private. Yet, empirical research is needed to determine if being public, in fact, has implications for the efficiency of acquisitions. Because entrepreneurial firms are often difficult to locate as exchange partners (Deeds, DeCarolis, and Coombs 1999) and find it challenging to signal their business prospects (e.g. McConnell and Pettit 1984), it is of particular interest to situate an analysis of acquisitions within the context of entrepreneurial targets.

Theory and Hypotheses

Search for exchange partners

A search occurs when decision makers perceive that profit opportunities lie beyond known exchange partners. Search can be triggered by unsatisfactory performance of existing exchange partners (March and Simon 1958), or by motivation to find more favorable prices or better transaction conditions (Stigler 1961). A variety of changes in industries can therefore stimulate the search for M&A targets. New firms enter the industry, other firms exit or are acquired, firms' strategies are altered, new innovations are introduced, and firm values change over time for other reasons.

Searching for potential exchange partners is costly given the various expenses associated with the scanning of sellers and buyers, the encoding and decoding of signals, and the employment of agents in the process (e.g. Arrow 1974). Prior research notes that these costs tend to increase as spatial dispersion of potential exchange partners grows, creating "a powerful inducement to localize transactions as a device for identifying potential buyers and sellers" (Stigler 1961: 216). Early organized markets, for instance, physically brought together buyers and sellers to economize on search costs (Polanyi 1957). By being in proximity to one another, exchange partners reduce the costs of canvassing buyers and sellers and the costs of sending supply or demand signals. In contrast, research notes that as distance increases, trade tends to fall off dramatically, more so than can be explained by transportation costs and other factors (e.g. McCallum 1995).

When search costs increase with the spatial dispersion of potential exchange partners, acquiring public targets, rather than private firms, becomes more attractive. This is because the process of going public can make the firm more visible to would-be buyers in several ways. For instance, the selling firm engages in an intensive marketing effort lasting several months. During so-called road shows and subsequent registrations and offerings, selling firms not only present themselves to the investment community and attract media attention, they also tap into underwriters' business relationships. Acquiring firms can therefore become aware of the existence of potential targets vis-à-vis a series of informational channels, ranging from the business press and investment banks to social networks in the investment community. Moreover, information such as stock prices and accounting data is widely disclosed for public firms. This can help would-be buyers economize on their attention (March and Simon 1958) and avoid redundant search efforts. Based on these arguments, we suspect that private targets will be more subject to search costs stemming from spatial dispersion than their public counterparts.

> Hypothesis 1:   The likelihood that target firms are public rather than private is positively related to the spatial dispersion of firms in the target's industry.

Valuation of exchange partners

Even if potential buyers have solved the problem of identifying acquisition candidates, they still need to evaluate the opportunities for creating value by acquiring these firms. Valuation difficulties increase with the level of uncertainty about a target's prospects and with information asymmetry between sellers and buyers. As discussed below, the level of asymmetric information hinges upon the would-be buyer's ability to discern the value of the combined business. More specifically, we suggest that the target firm's age, industry of operation, intangible assets, and investments in signaling through collaborative agreements, affect the bidder's valuation challenges and the associated ex ante transaction costs of an acquisition. As in the case of search costs discussed above, we propose that valuation difficulties will be less severe for public targets than privately held concerns.

Firm age

Newly founded organizations will tend to exhibit higher uncertainty and higher degrees of information asymmetry than established firms due, in part, to resource and institutional constraints. Resource shortages often impede young companies from committing to their employees and building trustworthy relationships with customers and suppliers (Stinchcombe 1965). Young companies are also thought to lack reliability and accountability in their organizational routines and performance (Hannan and Freeman 1989). Institutional constraints for young companies include a lack of legitimacy, which arises due to the lack of support from relevant organizations (e.g. Baum 1989), or due to segmentation in the market for interorganizational relationships (Carter and Manaster 1990, Podolny 1993). These factors suggest that it will be difficult to assess the value of young firms due to greater uncertainties associated with such transactions as well as the problems such firms face in credibly conveying their value to potential investors.

The valuation difficulties associated with the acquisition of young companies will tend to be lower for public targets, however. This is because information disclosure regulations and observable stock prices help buyers calibrate their bids, which reduces the riskiness of the acquisition. The presence of a liquid resale market for shares of public firms further reduces the downside risk of an acquisition. Consistent with these arguments, evidence exists that information disclosure reduces the dispersion of investors' forecast errors (Simon 1989) and that restricted stock is discounted 25–45 percent relative to unrestricted stock (Pratt 1989).

Acquiring public targets can also mitigate the effects of information asymmetry associated with young firms. Going public can be viewed as a signaling mechanism that can help buyers discriminate high quality firms from low quality firms (Spence 1974). High quality entrepreneurial firms, for example, can underprice their newly public issues as a way of signaling their healthy quality and differentiating themselves from low quality counterparts (e.g. Allen and Faulhaber 1989). Private entrepreneurial firms, by contrast, will find it more difficult to convey their value credibly since they lack the benefits of the equity market as a screening device and tend to be more subject to resource and institutional constraints.

Hypothesis 2:   The likelihood that target firms are public rather than private is negatively related to the target's age.

Inter-industry transactions

Research has found that acquisitions in new lines of business are especially problematic for several reasons (e.g. Hopkins 1987, Singh and Montgomery 1987). Relative to intra-industry transactions, in which the firm can use its existing routines and rely on the knowledge base it has developed in its core business (Levitt and March 1988), the firm is less knowledgeable about the business in an inter-industry acquisition. Thus, in inter-industry transactions, opportunities for misrepresentation of target firm resources will be greater since the target firm has significantly better information about its resources and prospects than the buyer operating in another industry. Bidders will therefore face a higher likelihood of adverse selection in inter-industry transactions than in intra-industry deals (Reuer and Koza 2000). However, as earlier suggested, the challenges associated with asymmetric information will not be equivalent for public and private targets.

Specifically, public targets will be less sensitive to information asymmetry problems for reasons paralleling those offered above. For example, regulations requiring financial reporting according to generally accepted accounting principles directly reduce information asymmetry for public firms, and share prices in stock markets can incorporate heterogeneous information about assets. It has been suggested that share prices offer performance information that cannot be extracted from the firm's current or future accounting data (Holmstrom and Tirole 1993). As noted above, targets can also use the process of going public to signal their value (e.g. Allen and Faulhaber 1989), and bidders can rely on the stock market to screen attractive targets from less attractive ones (Ellingsen and Rydqvist 1997). Thus, we hypothesize:

Hypothesis 3:   The likelihood that target firms are public rather than private is higher for inter-industry transactions than intra-industry transactions.

Intangible assets

The level of asymmetric information hinges, perhaps most directly, upon the nature of the resources to be acquired. For example, information about the value of undifferentiated physical assets can be conveyed relatively easily, so valuation problems will be relatively low for the acquisition of such resources. By contrast, adverse selection will tend to be more serious for acquisitions of firms with substantial intangible assets because financial data may provide little information regarding the true value of these resources, and the quality of such resources is difficult to codify and verify. This increases the likelihood of ex ante misrepresentations. Uncertainties about what resources can and cannot be transferred ex post are greater, so the synergies obtainable through the combination are more difficult to appraise when intangible resources are involved.

We suspect that the problems associated with asymmetric information due to the target's intangibles are likely to be lower for public targets than privately held firms for several reasons. First, to some extent, public markets can directly reduce asymmetric information. Firms going public face information disclosure requirements for registration and subsequent listing, and the equity market serves to place a price on the firm. The aggregated information and collective judgment of investors may help buyers calibrate their bids (Hellwig 1980). Second, the screening function of equity markets helps discriminate high from low quality firms (e.g. Ellingsen and Rydqvist 1997). Third, investment bankers and other institutions involved in equity markets can certify the quality of participating firms because the repeated nature of investment bankers' business encourages them to refrain from opportunism and build up their reputation capital (e.g. Beatty and Ritter 1986). To the extent that being public can reduce asymmetric information directly, or mitigate its effects by offering signaling opportunities, this can reduce buyers' downside risks and can enhance the efficiency of the market for corporate control.

Hypothesis 4:   The likelihood that target firms are public rather than private is positively related to the target's intangible assets.

Collaborative agreements

Given that going public is expensive and that acquirers may pay higher control premiums for purchasing public targets, the question arises whether alternative vehicles exist for entrepreneurial firms to resolve valuation problems associated with intangible resources. For instance, warranties, hostages, and insurance provide remedies to failures in many product markets otherwise subject to adverse selection, though such institutions are not developed for many one-time decisions made by organizations such as divestiture. Considering asocial remedies such as these and their limitations, Rangan (2000) discusses situations in which firms come to rely heavily on networks for search and deliberation in economic exchange.

Strategic alliances are an alternative form of organizational investment discussed in the literature on external corporate development that are thought to redress adverse selection in the market for firm resources. Alliances permit firms to pool together resources that are difficult to value on a piecemeal basis, avoid the transfer of ownership rights and a terminal sale, and are able to be terminated at lower exit cost (e.g. Balakrishnan and Koza 1993, Reuer and Koza 2000). Repeated contracting and the threat of termination can promote information revelation. Such relationships afford opportunities for first-hand experience with the resources. However, not only can alliances reduce information asymmetries directly for actual collaborators, they can also attenuate the effects of asymmetric information for other would-be acquirers. More specifically, assuming that taking on alliance partners will be more difficult for lower quality firms, alliance investments may provide signals that help potential buyers differentiate attractive and unattractive targets (Stuart, Hoang, and Hybels 1999). Therefore we posit that alliances will reduce valuation problems for private targets with significant intangible assets:

> Hypothesis 5:   For target firms with significant intangible assets, the likelihood that target firms are public rather than private is negatively related to the target's investment in strategic alliances.

Methods

Sample

In order to test the hypotheses developed above, a sample of corporate acquisitions of public and private targets was developed. We used the M&A module of the Securities Data Corporate (SDC) database to obtain a sample of targets in the manufacturing sector (i.e. SICs 2000–3999[2]) that were acquired during the 1996–99 time period. The sample was composed of firms acquired by U.S. bidders (Leveraged buyout[3] (LBO) firms were excluded).

The sectoral distribution of the public and private acquisitions appears in Table 5.1. The percentage of public target firms averages 46.5 percent and ranges from 31.9 to 100 percent for the industries considered. Several studies have reported significant industry clustering in acquisition activities in the 1960s, 1980s, and 1990s (e.g. Mitchell and Mulherin 1996, Mulherin and Boone 2000) and have, therefore, concluded that economic change such as deregulation is a major source of the observed restructuring activity (e.g. Andrade, Mitchell, and Stafford 2001). Our data show that not only does industry clustering exist in public acquisitions and acquisitions overall, as previous research has noted, but significant patterns exist across industries for acquisitions of public versus private targets. For industries with more than 100 transactions in total, those with a majority of acquisitions involving public targets are as follows: textile mill products (58.1 percent); chemicals and allied products (56.3 percent); measuring, analyzing, and controlling instruments (50.4 percent). In contrast, the incidence of acquisitions involving private targets appears to be higher in industries such as rubber and plastics (68.1 percent); fabricated metals (67.3 percent); and stone, clay, glass, and concrete (65.2 percent).

To focus on the impact of problems arising from search and valuation on the means by which entrepreneurial firms are acquired, the dataset was further screened by the size of the target firm. The number of employees was used as an indicator for the size of the firm, where those firms with fewer than 500 employees were selected. This cut-off value for small firms corresponds to the one used by the U.S. Commerce

Table 5.1 Sectoral distribution of public and private targets

I Industry (SIC)	II Public (%)	III Private (%)	IV % Public	V Total (%)
Food and kindred products (20)	153 (4.9)	269 (7.5)	36.3	422 (6.3)
Tobacco products (21)	14 (0.5)	6 (0.2)	70.0	20 (0.3)
Textile mill products (22)	61 (2.0)	44 (1.2)	58.1	105 (1.6)
Apparel (23)	83 (2.7)	75 (2.1)	46.9	177 (2.3)
Lumber and wood products (24)	43 (1.4)	77 (2.1)	35.8	120 (1.8)
Furniture and fixtures (25)	68 (2.2)	70 (1.9)	49.3	138 (2.1)
Paper and allied products (26)	70 (2.2)	77 (2.1)	47.6	147 (2.2)
Printing and publishing (27)	35 (1.1)	0 (0)	100.0	35 (0.5)
Chemicals and allied products (28)	423 (13.5)	329 (9.1)	56.3	752 (11.2)
Petroleum refining (29)	18 (0.6)	0 (0)	100.0	18 (0.3)
Rubber and plastics (30)	81 (2.6)	173 (4.8)	31.9	254 (3.8)
Leather (31)	31 (1.0)	12 (0.3)	72.1	43 (0.6)
Stone, clay, glass, and concrete (32)	46 (1.5)	86 (2.4)	34.8	132 (2.0)
Primary metals (33)	113 (3.6)	153 (4.2)	42.5	266 (4.0)
Fabricated metal products (34)	128 (4.1)	263 (7.3)	32.7	391 (5.8)
Industrial and commercial machinery and computer equipment (35)	497 (15.9)	559 (15.5)	47.1	1,056 (15.7)
Electronic and electrical equipment (36)	540 (17.3)	577 (16.0)	48.3	1,117 (16.6)
Transportation equipment (37)	168 (5.4)	202 (5.6)	45.4	370 (5.5)
Measuring, analyzing, and controlling instruments (38)	467 (14.9)	460 (12.7)	50.4	927 (13.8)
Miscellaneous manufacturing (39)	89 (2.9)	171 (4.7)	34.2	260 (3.9)
Total	3,128 (100)	3,603 (100)	46.5	6,731 (100)

Note: Percentages may not sum to 100 due to rounding.

Department (e.g. Roy and Simpson 1981). Data were obtained from SDC, Compustat, and Standard and Poors. After accounting for missing data, 923 acquisitions were available for analysis, 457 of which involved public targets. Additional details on the sample are contained in the results section.

Model specification

The basic structure of the multivariate model used to differentiate public and private targets is as follows:

$$
\begin{aligned}
\text{Public target} = {} & \beta_0 + \beta_1 \text{Spatial dispersion} + \beta_2 \text{Firm age} \\
& + \beta_3 \text{Inter-industry transaction} + \beta_4 \text{R\&D intensity} \\
& + \beta_5 \text{Strategic alliances} + \beta_6 \text{R\&D intensity strategic} \\
& \text{alliances} + \beta_7 \text{Equity stake} + \beta_8 \text{Industry} \\
& \text{incumbents} + \beta_9 \text{Industry uncertainty} + \varepsilon.
\end{aligned}
\tag{5.1}
$$

The first explanatory variable captures search costs in the industry's M&A market, as reflected in the geographic dispersion of firms in the industry (i.e. spatial dispersion). The next five explanatory variables – firm age, inter-industry transaction, R&D intensity, strategic alliances, and the interaction between R&D intensity and strategic alliances – address adverse selection problems arising from information asymmetries as well as the role of alliances in signaling the value of intangible assets.

While our objective was to develop a parsimonious model to compare acquisitions of public and private targets, we introduced controls that might be related to the type of acquisition as well as to the key, theoretical variables. Specifically, we included controls for the percentage of a target firm's shares being acquired (i.e. equity stake), the number of firms in the target's industry (i.e. industry incumbents), and the uncertainty of the industry in which the target firm operates (i.e. industry uncertainty). The measurement of the variables and the motives for the firm- and industry-level controls are taken up below.

Measures

Public target.   As described earlier, we determined whether the target firm was publicly or privately held. Therefore, public target equals one if the target was a public firm, and zero if the target was a private firm when the acquisition occurred. Given the binary nature of the dependent variable, equation (5.1) was estimated using logistic regression. Data for this variable were obtained from the M&A module of the SDC database.

Explanatory variables.   The first explanatory variable captures the geographic dispersion of firms within an industry across state boundaries. Let P_{ij} be the proportion of firms in target i's industry in state j (i.e. $j \in J$) in 1996. Since the sum of the squared proportions yields a measure of the geographic concentration of firms, and this measure has a lower bound of zero and an upper bound of one, the spatial dispersion of firm i's industry was defined as follows:

$$\text{Spatial dispersion} = 1 - \sum_{j \in J} P_{ij}^2 \qquad (5.2)$$

Data for this variable were obtained from the U.S. Census Bureau and the Office of Advocacy of the Small Business Administration.

Firm age was used as the second explanatory variable to provide an inverse indicator of valuation problems. The age of the targets was measured as the difference between the time of the acquisition and the time of the target's founding, stated in years. Data were obtained from SDC, Compustat, and Standard and Poors.

Another proxy used for information asymmetries between target firms and acquirers is based on their industries of operation. In its primary business, the acquirer is better able to value potential targets because it tends to be more familiar with such firms as well as their technologies, employees, and other resources. By contrast, valuation problems will tend to be more severe when the firm acquires targets operating in other industries. Inter-industry transaction was measured as an indicator that is assigned a value of one if the primary businesses of the acquirer and target differ at the three-digit SIC level; otherwise, it is given a value of zero. Data for this variable were obtained from SDC.

Finally, we used the intangible assets of the target firm's industry as another proxy for the asymmetric information confronting potential acquirers. Specifically, the R&D intensity of the target firm's industry provides a measure of selling parties' intangible assets and the ex ante valuation challenges that would-be acquirers confront. We measured R&D intensity as the ratio of R&D expenditures to sales for the year prior to the divestiture. Data for this variable were obtained from the National Science Foundation's *Research and Development in Industry*.

To measure the firm's investment in strategic alliances, we used the SDC database to count the number of alliances formed by the target firm. The SDC database includes collaborative agreements such as equity joint ventures; minority purchases; R&D contracts; joint manufacturing, marketing, or supply agreements; and licensing and value-added resale agreements as strategic alliances. Data on these alliances were assembled from 1986, the year the database began tracking alliances.

Control variables.   In addition to the theoretical variables discussed above, several additional regressors were incorporated into the specification to control for other firm- and industry-level effects. First, we introduced a control for the percentage of the target firm's equity being acquired in the acquisition process (i.e. equity stake). On the one hand, low equity stakes might be expected to be more likely to accompany acquisitions of private targets than public targets due to the fact that the former suffer from the lack of transparent market prices and greater risk. On the other hand, the greater ownership concentration in private firms may require larger stakes to obtain control (Demsetz and Lehn 1985). Data for this variable were obtained from SDC.

At the firm level, we also incorporated a control for the direct effects of alliances since we are interested in testing the interaction between alliance investments and intangible resources. Inclusion of the control for alliances is also motivated based on the observation that firms enter into alliances to achieve high growth (Dutta and Weiss 1997) and on findings showing that firms tend to go public following a period of expansion (Pagano, Panetta, and Zingales 1998). Prior research has also found that firms with alliances tend to go public sooner and obtain higher IPO valuations (Stuart, Hoang, and Hybels 1999).

At the industry level, we first introduced a control for the number of firms in the focal firm's industry (i.e. industry incumbents). Potential buyers, experienced in the same line of business as the seller, tend to be in a better position than others to make such judgments concerning the value of the acquisition. Thus, when the number of firms in an industry increases, the set of potential acquirers for which information asymmetries are low also tends to increase as will the spatial dispersion of firms in the industry. However, profit opportunities due to concentration and the resulting entry barriers can stimulate acquisitive entries despite possible information asymmetries (e.g. Yip 1982). Data for this variable were obtained from the U.S. Census Bureau and the Office of Advocacy of the Small Business Administration. Finally, we included a control for industry uncertainty to address the predictability of demand as well as product–market conditions potentially shaping firms' investments in

Table 5.2 Descriptive statistics and correlation matrix[a]

Variable	Mean	S.D.	(1)	(2)	(3)	(4)	(5)	(6)	(7)	(8)
(1) Public target	0.42	0.49	–							
(2) Spatial dispersion	0.95	0.01	−0.08*	–						
(3) Firm age	39.06	28.65	−0.09†	0.15**	–					
(4) Inter-industry transaction	0.44	0.50	0.25***	−0.02	−0.07	–				
(5) R&D intensity	4.45	2.41	0.27***	−0.31***	−0.18***	0.13***	–			
(6) Strategic alliances	0.19	0.72	0.28***	−0.03	−0.09*	0.06†	0.11***	–		
(7) Equity stake	89.08	28.85	−0.58***	−0.02	−0.06	0.06	−0.09*	−0.17***	–	
(8) Industry incumbents	22.95	16.98	−0.02	0.19***	−0.04	−0.09**	−0.02	0.01	0.03	–
(9) Industry uncertainty	0.03	0.02	0.08*	−0.14***	−0.05	0.03	0.03	0.00	0.08*	0.06†

[a] $N = 923$.
† $p < 0.10$, * $p < 0.05$, ** $p < 0.01$, *** $p < 0.001$.

internal development projects and external alliances (Eisenhardt and Schoonhoven 1996). Industry uncertainty was calculated as a measure of the volatility of net sales in each industry using regression analysis over the five-year time period 1992–96 (e.g. Dess and Beard 1984). The specification used to develop the proxy for industry uncertainty was as follows:

$$\text{Industry sales} = \gamma_0 + \gamma_1 \text{Year} + \varepsilon \tag{5.3}$$

Industry uncertainty was then measured as the standard error of the slope parameter divided by the mean of industry sales. Data required for estimating the industry-specific regressions and calculating the proxy for industry uncertainty were obtained from Compustat.

Results

Table 5.2 presents descriptive statistics and a correlation matrix for the sample. The average age of the sampled firms is approximately 39 years. Forty-four percent of the deals are inter-industry transactions. The average number of alliances formed by the sampled firms is 0.19. The average percentage of shares being acquired is 89 percent.

The correlation matrix indicates modest correlations among most of the variables. As might be expected, the spatial dispersion of firms in an industry tends to increase as the number of firms in the industry rises ($p < 0.001$). The R&D intensity of spatially dispersed industries tends to be low, while industries with firms that are geographically concentrated are more R&D intensive ($p < 0.001$). The correlation between R&D intensity and the geographic distribution of firms in an industry is consistent with prior research on localization and knowledge spillovers (e.g. Jaffe, Trajtenberg, and Henderson 1993).

Reflecting the use of alliances to exploit existing capabilities or to tap into others' skills in the presence of contractual hazards (e.g. Mowery, Oxley, and Silverman 1998), entrepreneurial firms situated in R&D intensive industries tend to be more actively engaged in collaborative agreements with others ($p < 0.001$). Similar to Dutta and Weiss (1997), no relationship is evident between industry uncertainty and firms' investments in alliances, despite arguments that alliances provide firms with needed flexibility in such settings (e.g. Kogut 1991). Contrary to what has been observed in some single-industry research (e.g. Stuart, Hoang, and Hybels 1999), older firms tend to have fewer alliances ($p < 0.05$) and are situated in industries where R&D intensity is low ($p < 0.001$). This relationship seems to contradict the liability-of-newness argument that young firms lack necessary resources and social relations to build up alliances with other firms (Stinchcombe 1965) and have lower innovation capability (Sorensen and Stuart 2000), but it is consistent with the liability-of-obsolescence argument (Baum 1989).

Although the correlations among the regressors are generally low, inclusion of the interaction between R&D intensity and strategic alliances in the multivariate model resulted in a maximum variance inflation factor (VIF) of 39.1, which is above the rule-of-thumb threshold value of 10 used to indicate multicollinearity problems in regression models (Neter, Wasserman, and Kutner 1985). To alleviate concerns

Table 5.3   Logistic regression estimates[a]

Variable	Model I	Model II	Model III
Equity stake	−2.66***	−2.44***	−2.41***
	(0.17)	(0.21)	(0.21)
Industry incumbents	0.13**	0.00	0.00
	(0.41)	(0.01)	(0.01)
Industry uncertainty	24.47***	7.85[†]	7.62
	(3.72)	(4.77)	(4.81)
Spatial dispersion	–	1.43***	1.74***
		(0.27)	(0.30)
Firm age	–	−0.05***	−0.05***
		(0.01)	(0.01)
Inter-industry transaction	–	0.58**	0.60**
		(0.20)	(0.20)
R&D intensity	–	0.36***	0.03
		(0.10)	(0.15)
Strategic alliances	–	0.74***	1.89***
		(0.21)	(0.54)
R&D intensity · Strategic alliances	–	–	−1.33**
			(0.43)
χ^2	344.99***	576.99***	588.97***
Log likelihood, $L(\beta_k)$	−455.52	−339.53	−333.54
$-2[L(\beta_I) - L(\beta_k)]$	–	232.00***	243.97***
$-2[L(\beta_{II}) - L(\beta_{III})]$	–	–	11.97**

[a] $N = 923$. Positive coefficients indicate that increases in the variable tend to increase the likelihood that the target is public rather than private.
[†] $p < 0.10$, * $p < 0.05$, ** $p < 0.01$, *** $p < 0.001$.

of multicollinearity, the variables R&D intensity and strategic alliances were standard-ized prior to forming the interaction term, which reduced the maximum VIF to 4.9.

Estimation results from models using these transformed variables appear in Table 5.3. Model I presents a baseline specification consisting of three controls. Model II aug-ments this model with the direct effects of the theoretical variables, and Model III represents the full model incorporating the interaction effect between R&D intensity and alliances. All three models are significant at the 0.001 level. Log-likelihood ratio tests demonstrate that Models II and III have significantly more explanatory power than Model I (both $p < 0.001$), and Model III has significantly more explanatory power than Model II ($p < 0.01$). Model III correctly predicts whether the target is public or private for 780 of the 923 transactions (or 84.5 percent). This hit rate improves upon alternatives such as random assignment (i.e. 50 percent) or the value that would obtain if all transactions were assigned to the dominant category of private targets (i.e. 58 percent).

The first hypothesis suggested that public rather than private targets are more likely to be acquired in industries with geographically dispersed firms since public firms enjoy greater visibility and are subject to lower search costs. Consistent with predictions, in industries characterized by greater spatial dispersion, targets tend to be publicly traded ($p < 0.001$ in both Models II and III). Acquisitions of private targets are more likely to take place in industries with firms that are geographically more concentrated.

The second hypothesis predicted that among younger targets, firms will be more willing to acquire public entrepreneurial firms rather than their private counterparts to avoid downside risks associated with adverse selection. Consistent with this hypothesis, acquisitions of private targets are more likely to involve older organizations, whereas younger firms that are acquired tend to have already gone public ($p < 0.001$ in both Models II and III).

The third hypothesis suggested that bidders will be more willing to acquire private targets in the bidder's core business, but in noncore domains involving higher levels of information asymmetry, there is value in using the stock market to help screen targets prior to the acquisition. Consistent with this hypothesis, inter-industry M&A transactions are more likely to involve public targets than intra-industry deals ($p < 0.01$ in Models II and III).

The fourth hypothesis predicted that private targets with substantial intangible resources are apt to experience greater valuation challenges than equivalent public targets. The model with all of the direct effects (i.e. Model II) suggests that there is a tendency for firms to purchase publicly held targets in industries that are R&D intensive ($p < 0.001$). However, the results appearing in Model III indicate that this is true only for the subsample of firms that have modest or no investment in strategic alliances. The negative interaction effect between R&D intensity and strategic alliances provides support for the fifth hypothesis that alliances provide a means of signaling the value of intangible resources ($p < 0.01$).

The results for the control variables also deserve some comment. The negative coefficient estimate on the equity stake variable indicates that full acquisitions are more likely for private firms, and partial acquisitions tend to occur with greater incidence for publicly held targets ($p < 0.001$ in all models). Although the number of firms in an industry and the level of industry uncertainty may initially appear to bear upon the means by which entrepreneurial firms are acquired, it is also evident that these effects disappear when acquisition problems arising from search costs and asymmetric information are accounted for.

Discussion

This study has examined acquisitions of entrepreneurial firms and has explored the differences between private and public targets. Although prior research has indicated that entrepreneurial firms exhibit a high propensity of being acquired, such firms have not received adequate attention in the M&A literature to date. By studying such firms further, future studies may be able to enhance our understanding of sell-side processes in mergers and acquisitions. In fact, M&A researchers have long lamented the fact that target firm considerations have not received their due in the acquisition literature. Our analysis has focused on entrepreneurial targets. Future work might also compare entrepreneurial targets to other firms.

Although different types of entrepreneurial targets tend to experience a similar set of problems such as search costs and signaling difficulties (e.g. McConnell and Pettit 1984, Deeds, DeCarolis, and Coombs 1999), we have developed the argument that such difficulties are not equivalent across public and private targets. The evidence that bidders tend to be sensitive to search and valuation problems in selecting publicly held or private targets, suggests that future M&A studies should carefully consider the implications of pooling public and private targets in analyses or by generalizing findings from samples of public targets to the universe of M&A transactions. Where possible, future studies should examine whether the effects differ across public and private targets. Replications of prior M&A studies could also explicitly examine the extent to which received findings in the literature in fact generalize to acquisitions of entrepreneurial firms and private targets in particular.

For entrepreneurial firms, the results shed light on the benefits of being publicly traded, and on some of the criteria used by bidders in pursuing acquisition candidates. Even though search and valuation difficulties may still loom larger for entrepreneurial firms relative to other organizations, the results suggest that such problems may be less severe for firms that have gone public. Initial public offerings may widen the set of potential bidders by raising the target firm's visibility due to relationships with underwriters, marketing efforts during the IPO, and subsequent press coverage. The results suggest that the increased visibility of being public may be particularly important in industries in which firms are spatially dispersed and search costs in the M&A market are higher as a consequence. Being public may also either reduce information asymmetries in M&A transactions directly, or attenuate the effects of such difficulties for targets. By going public, the firm reveals information in a more credible fashion just as the equity market serves as a screening device, aggregates heterogeneous information to assist bidders in calibrating their bids, and offers a liquid resale market for shares. Going public also allows the firm to signal value through a variety of means such as the relationship it enjoys with an investment banker who, owing to its repeat business, has an incentive to develop reputation capital by avoiding misrepresentations. Our findings are therefore at odds with traditional views of IPOs that portray them either as a natural end-state for entrepreneurial firms or as a choice that addresses purely financial objectives. In fact, going public has potential implications for the transfer of control rights rather than just ownership rights and is therefore a decision that affects the future evolution of firms. The results and interpretations are broadly consistent with recent evidence that capital markets and the market for corporate control are not independent as often assumed (e.g. Pagano, Panetta, and Zingales 1998, Field and Mulherin 1999).

The findings presented here indicate that collaborative agreements are another means of addressing valuation difficulties in M&A markets for entrepreneurial firms. Such relationships among firms can reduce information asymmetries directly and can also mitigate the effects of information asymmetry for other potential acquirers. Future studies might examine other potential means of enhancing the efficiency of M&A transactions, including asocial and social remedies such as alternative deal structures (Datar, Frankel, and Wolfson 2001), other intermediaries such as venture capitalists (Amit, Brander, and Zott 1998), and other members of bidders' and targets' networks (e.g. Haunschild 1993, Rangan 2000). Such research could examine the relative efficiency of alternative solutions such as these to search and valuation problems. It is plausible that some alternatives like alliances may be comparably inexpensive. However, their relatively low cost may also mean that the signaling value attached to them is weaker than other remedies like going public.

Finally, it is worth noting that the current analysis relies on a discrete choice model and the conventional reduced form set-up that it implies. Thus, the chapter is ultimately silent on the actual performance of acquisitions of public and private entrepreneurial targets. Yet, our theoretical arguments do carry empirical implications for the performance of acquisitions of public versus private entrepreneurial firms. Future research could examine the implications of acquisitions of private and public entrepreneurial targets for both bidders and targets when search and valuation problems are present or absent. For example, previous research concludes that corporate takeovers on average generate positive abnormal returns for target firms but zero or negative abnormal returns for bidding firms (e.g. Jensen and Ruback 1983, Andrade, Mitchell, and Stafford 2001). In order to assess the roles played by search costs and information asymmetry, as well as the remedies discussed here, this research could explore whether the dispersion of abnormal returns for firms acquiring public targets is lower than for equivalent private targets. And, whether the "going public" decision, in fact, reduces the risks to bidders under conditions of information asymmetry. Our arguments also imply that for targets with higher intangible assets or those operating in an industry different from acquirers, acquisition of public targets should generate lower dispersion of abnormal returns for the reduced valuation errors for acquisitions of public targets. Research along these lines might enhance our understanding of acquisitions of entrepreneurial firms, sell-side considerations in M&A deals, and the important differences underlying publicly and privately held targets.

Notes

In developing this research, we have benefited from comments and suggestions from Jean Helwege, Mitchell Koza, and Subi Rangan. We also gratefully acknowledge financial support from INSEAD's R&D Department.

1. Initial public offering (IPO) – The first sale of stock by a company to the public.
2. Standard Industrial Classification (SIC) are digit codes used to categorize and uniquely identify business activities. Manufacturing sectors belong to SICs 2000–3999.
3. Leveraged Buyout (LBO) – Takeover of a company or controlling interest in a company, using a significant amount of borrowed money, usually 70 percent or more of the total purchase price.

References

Akerlof, G.A. 1970. The market for "lemons": Qualitative uncertainty and the market mechanism. *Quarterly Journal of Economics*, **84**: 488–500.

Allen, F. and Faulhaber, G.R. 1989. Signaling by underpricing in the IPO market. *Journal of Financial Economics*, **23**: 303–23.

Amit, R., Brander, J., and Zott, C. 1998. Why do venture capital firms exist? Theory and Canadian evidence. *Journal of Business Venturing*, **13**: 441–66.

Andrade, G., Mitchell, M., and Stafford, E. 2001. New evidence and perspectives on mergers. *Journal of Economic Perspectives*, **15**: 103–20.

Arrow, K.J. 1974. *The Limits of Organization*. New York: W.W. Norton.

Balakrishnan, S. and Koza, M.P. 1993. Information asymmetry, adverse selection, and joint ventures. *Journal of Economic Behavior and Organization*, **20**: 99–117.

Baum, J.A.C. 1989. Liabilities of newness, adolescence, and obsolescence in the dissolution of organizational relationships and organizations. *Proceedings of the Administrative Science Association of Canada*, **10**(5): 1–10.

Beatty, R. and Ritter, J.R. 1986. Investment banking, reputation, and the underpricing of initial public offerings. *Journal of Financial Economics*, **15**: 213–32.

Berk, R.A. 1983. An introduction to sample selection bias in sociological data. *American Sociological Review*, **48**: 386–98.

Bradley, M., Desai, A., and Kim, E.H. 1983. The rationale behind interfirm tender offers: Information or synergy? *Journal of Financial Economics*, **11**: 183–206.

Carter, R. and Manaster, S. 1990. Initial public offerings and underwriter reputation. *Journal of Finance*, **45**: 1045–67.

Chang, S. 1998. Takeovers of privately held targets, methods of payment, and bidder returns. *Journal of Finance*, **53**: 773–84.

Coff, R.W. 1999. How buyers cope with uncertainty when acquiring firms in knowledge-intensive industries: Caveat emptor. *Organization Science*, **10**: 144–61.

Datar, S., Frankel, R., and Wolfson, M. 2001. Earnouts: The effects of adverse selection and agency costs on acquisition techniques. *Journal of Law, Economics, and Organization*, **17**: 201–38.

Deeds, D., DeCarolis, D., and Coombs, J.E. 1999. Dynamic capabilities and new product development in high technology ventures: An empirical analysis of new biotechnology firms. *Journal of Business Venturing*, **15**: 211–29.

Demsetz, H. and Lehn, K. 1985. The structure of corporate ownership: Causes and consequences. *Journal of Political Economy*, **93**: 1155–77.

Dess, G.G. and Beard, D.W. 1984. Dimensions of organizational task environments. *Administrative Science Quarterly*, **29**: 52–73.

Dutta, S. and Weiss, A.M. 1997. The relationship between a firm's level of technological innovativeness and its pattern of partnership agreements. *Management Science*, **43**: 343–56.

Eckbo, B.E., Giammarino, R.M., and Heinkel, R.L. 1990. Asymmetric information and the medium of exchange in takeovers: Theory and tests. *Review of Financial Studies*, **3**: 651–75.

Eisenhardt, K.M. and Schoonhoven, C.B. 1996. Resource-based view of strategic alliance formation: Strategic and social effects in entrepreneurial firms. *Organization Science*, **7**: 136–50.

Ellingsen, T. and Rydqvist, K. 1997. *The Stock Market as a Screening Device and the Decision to Go Public*. Unpublished manuscript, Stockholm School of Economics.

Evans, D. and Leighton, L. 1986. Some empirical aspects of entrepreneurship. *American Economic Review*, **79**: 519–35.

Field, L.C. and Mulherin, J.H. 1999. *Newly Public Firms as Acquisition Targets: A Comparison with Established Firms*. Unpublished manuscript, Penn State University.

Hannan, M. and Freeman, J. 1989. *Organizational Ecology*. Cambridge, MA: Harvard University Press.

Haunschild, P.R. 1993. Interorganizational imitation: The impact of interlocks on corporate acquisition activity. *Administrative Science Quarterly*, **38**: 564–92.

Hellwig, M.F. 1980. On the aggregation of information in competitive markets. *Journal of Economic Theory*, **22**: 477–98.

Holmstrom, B. and Tirole, J. 1993. Market liquidity and performance monitoring. *Journal of Political Economy*, **101**: 678–709.

Hopkins, H.D. 1987. Acquisition strategy and the market position of acquiring firms. *Strategic Management Journal*, **8**: 535–47.

Ibbotson, R.G., Sindelar, J.L., and Ritter, J.R. 1988. Initial public offerings. *Journal of Applied Corporate Finance*, **1**: 37–45.

Jaffe, A.B., Trajtenberg, M., and Henderson, R. 1993. Geographic localization of knowledge spillovers as evidenced by patent citations. *Quarterly Journal of Economics*, **108**: 577–98.

Jensen, M.C. 1993. The modern industrial revolution, exit and the failure of internal control systems. *Journal of Finance*, **48**: 831–80.

Jensen, M.C. and Ruback, R.S. 1983. The market for corporate control: The scientific evidence. *Journal of Financial Economics*, **11**: 5–50.

Kogut, B. 1991. Joint ventures and the option to expand and acquire. *Management Science*, **37**: 19–33.

Levine, P. and Aaronovitch, S. 1981. The financial characteristics of firms and theories of merge activity. *Journal of Industrial Economics*, **30**: 149–72.

Levitt, B. and March, J.G. 1988. Organizational learning. *Annual Review of Sociology*, **14**: 319–40.

March, J.G. and Simon, H.A. 1958. *Organizations*. Oxford: Blackwell.

McCallum, J. 1995. National borders matter: Canada–U.S. regional trade patterns. *American Economic Review*, **85**: 615–23.

McConnell, J.J. and Pettit, R.R. 1984. Application of the modern theory of finance to small business firms. In P. Horvitz and R.R. Pettit (eds.), *Problems in Financing of Small Businesses*. Greenwich, CN: JAI Press, p. 42.

Mello, A.S. and Parsons, J.E. 1998. Going public and the ownership structure of the firm. *Journal of Financial Economics*, **49**: 79–109.

Mitchell, M.L. and Mulherin, J.H. 1996. The impact of industry shocks on takeover and restructuring activity. *Journal of Financial Economics*, **41**: 193–229.

Mowery, D.C., Oxley, D.E., and Silverman, B.S. 1998. Technological overlap and interfirm cooperation: Implications for the resource-based view of the firm. *Research Policy*, **27**: 507–23.

Mulherin, J.H. and Boone, A.L. 2000. Comparing acquisitions and divestitures. *Journal of Corporate Finance*, **6**: 117–39.

Neter, J., Wasserman, W., and Kutner, M. H. 1985. *Applied Linear Statistical Models* (2nd edition). Homewood, IL: Irwin.

Pagano, M., Panetta, F., and Zingales, L. 1998. Why do companies go public? An empirical analysis. *Journal of Finance*, **53**: 27–64.

Palepu, K.G. 1986. Predicting takeover targets: A methodological and empirical analysis. *Journal of Accounting and Economics*, **8**: 3–35.

Podolny, J.M. 1993. A status-based model of market competition. *American Journal of Sociology*, **98**: 829–72.

Polanyi, K. 1957. *The Great Transformation*. Boston: Beacon Press.

Pratt, S. 1989. *Valuing a Business*, 2nd Edition. Homewood, IL: Irwin Business One.

Rangan, S. 2000. The problem of search and deliberation in economic action: When social networks really matter. *Academy of Management Review*, **25**: 813–28.

Reuer, J.J. and Koza, M.P. 2000. Asymmetric information and joint venture performance: Theory and evidence for domestic and international joint ventures. *Strategic Management Journal*, **21**: 81–8.

Rock, M.L., Rock, R.H., and Sikora, M. 1994. *The Mergers and Acquisitions Handbook*, 2nd Edition. New York: McGraw-Hill.

Roy, D.A. and Simpson, C.L. 1981. Export attitudes of business executives in the smaller manufacturing firm. *Journal of Small Business Management*, **19**: 16–22.

Schumpeter, J.A. 2000. Entrepreneurship as innovation. In R. Swedberg (ed.), *Entrepreneurship: The Social Science View*. Oxford: Oxford University Press, pp. 51–75.

Simkowiz, M. and Monroe, R.J. 1971. A discriminant analysis function for conglomerate targets. *Southern Journal of Business*, November: 1–16.

Simon, C. 1989. The effect of the 1933 Securities Act on investor information and the performance of new issues. *American Economic Review*, **79**: 295–318.

Singh, H. and Montgomery, C.A. 1987. Corporate acquisition strategies and economic performance. *Strategic Management Journal*, **8**: 377–86.

Sorensen, J.B. and Stuart, T. E. 2000. Aging, obsolescence, and organizational innovation. *Administrative Science Quarterly*, **45**: 81–112.

Spence, A.M. 1974. *Market Signaling: Informational Transfer in Hiring and Related Screening Processes*. Cambridge, MA: Harvard University Press.

Stigler, G.J. 1961. The economics of information. *Journal of Political Economy*, **69**: 213–25.

Stinchcombe, A.L. 1965. Social structure and organizations. In J. March (ed.), *Handbook of Organizations*. Chicago: Rand McNally, pp. 142–93.

Stuart, T.E., Hoang, H., and Hybels, R.C. 1999. Interorganizational endorsements and the performance of entrepreneurial ventures. *Administrative Science Quarterly*, **44**: 315–49.

Yip, G.S. 1982. Diversification entry: Internal development versus acquisition. *Strategic Management Journal*, **3**: 331–45.

Zingales, L. 1995. Insider ownership and the decision to go public. *Review of Economic Studies*, **62**: 425–48.

Merger Implementation and Integration

CHAPTER SIX

The Role of the Corporate Academy in Mergers and Acquisitions

L. Todd Thomas, Shlomo Ben-Hur

Abstract
Corporate academies, while becoming more sophisticated and integrated into their respective businesses, have not frequently been used to facilitate the process of mergers and acquisitions. However, there are specific skill sets and experiences resident in successful corporate academies that could provide more effectiveness and greater returns on the human capital side of integrating companies. Several characteristics of the corporate academy are discussed with an explanation of their application to the merger and acquisition activity of business organizations.

Introduction

The Corporate Leadership Council (1999) reports that the volume of merger and acquisition activity, across almost all industries, has more than tripled since 1990. It is further reported in the same report, that over half of these mergers fail to create substantial returns for shareholders. As many companies have discovered, while precise reasons for underperformance vary across specific mergers, "people issues" (including but not limited to cultural integration) rather than financial or operational issues, are often the root cause of lower than expected results (Corporate Leadership Council 1999).

While recognition of these people issues has not yet resulted in widespread appropriate human resource (HR) department involvement throughout the M&A process, progressive HR departments are beginning to play an extensive role in M&A through active work in both the due diligence and integration phase (Corporate Leadership Council 1999). HR departments are traditionally involved in the integration of compensation plans, benefits, and other personnel issues during the post-merger phase. However, it is our experience that the learning and development areas of HR can add unique and specific value to the pre-merger, planning, and integration processes.

This chapter will examine a variety of characteristics specific to the corporate learning and development functions. Each of these characteristics will be applied in the context of mergers and acquisitions.

Corporate Academies in M&A

For the purpose of discussion, the HR area involved in "learning and development" activities within an organization will be referred to as the corporate academy (CA). We assume that the CA is responsible, within the organization, for traditional training and organizational development activities, and executive coaching and consulting. Research in 2000 (Meister 2000) identified over 1000 companies with corporate universities or academies focused on the customized and specific development of individual employees and executives. Sometimes within the HR departments, CAs are often standalone departments with the unique proposition of providing a direct link between continuous learning and the specific business challenges of the organization. While this model varies by organization, the thesis should be generalizable to most large and mid-sized companies involved in merger or acquisition activity who provide not only training but organizational development activity as well.

The organizational development activity is important because of the unique characteristic of offering a "third-party perspective" on difficult business issues such as mergers and acquisitions. Organizational development (OD) traditionally takes an objective role in addressing concerns while benefiting from the inside knowledge of the organization. The approach is usually process- or behavioral-oriented in order to increase the effectiveness of the company's operation. The most successful CAs have OD departments coupled with the training function, but with responsibilities different than those of departments responsible solely for learning and development (Corporate Leadership Council 1997). Within the effective CA, the focus is on strategic impact, leadership development, employee empowerment, and alignment with the strategies of the business.

In examining the activities of each phase of a merger and acquisition, it would appear that the CA may have a number of unique characteristics that make it an appropriate tool in facilitating successful M&A projects:

- Focus on the "big picture".
- Change management coaching and training.
- Assessment experience.
- Career development and succession.
- Relationships with key leaders.
- E-learning and e-communication technologies.
- Neutral facilitation skills.

The foundation for each of these characteristics will be discussed below with the application of each characteristic to a merger or acquisition.

Focus on the "big picture"

When M&A activity begins, many specialists are normally involved in the process. For example, accountants examine the books, legal representatives focus on trade practices and policies, operations representatives examine the product and market and financial forecasts to determine if the business fit is a good one. If HR is represented at the due diligence phase, it is most often in examining benefits programs, compensation programs, and other employee relations issues. Each of these representatives has a responsibility to the investigating organization to ensure that the specific area of concern is audited in a way that presents a fair picture of the potential post-merger organization.

A representative from the CA of the investigating organization can, with his or her knowledge of the strategy and the "soft" factors within the acquiring company, examine the likelihood of a successful integration in terms of *overall* factors such as attitudes of executives and employees, cultural attributes, and the path the new company will have to follow from a human capital perspective in order to achieve the merger objectives.

One of the primary "core competencies" of the CA today is in a solid understanding of the goals, processes, and operations of the organization (Filipczak 1998). In working with the executives of the organization to identify development needs and create learning solutions, consultants within the CA have the possibility of understanding the overall operational direction, without being focused on any specific operational area within the organization. This approach to business is clearly a unique and beneficial attribute to the M&A team.

Change management coaching and training

Organizational training and coaching in change management is a primary responsibility of CAs. In a cross-industry study of organizations with "value-added" organizational development functions, all profiled companies characterized change management as an important issue that the CA addresses (Corporate Leadership Council 1997).

While continuous change is an element of almost all organizational settings in today's economy, there is no context that is more directly defined as a change process than a merger or acquisition. Because of this, leadership training in change management processes should be an integral part of any leadership development process. Additional training in negotiation skills, audit, and assessment would be appropriate in an organization that grows through acquisition and merger. As part of a development plan, these courses could be included in management and leadership tracks, which are likely to involve participation on an M&A team.

Customized to the M&A process would be just-in-time (JIT) modules focused more on application than theory and designed as a "refresher" for leaders who are actively involved in mergers. Another application of this JIT training is for integration teams during the post-merger phases as members of both organizations come together to plan the strategy and actions of the newly formed company.

As a final area of expertise in change management, CA consultants can work with executives from both sides to effectively and efficiently manage the change process in action. Due to the sheer speed of most planning around M&A activity, executives are challenged to engage in strategic thinking about how to achieve the change necessary to make the new organization work. With this in mind, the internal consultancy or organizational development area within the CA can focus on working with the senior executives from both sides to:

- Correctly position the effort within the communicated objectives of the company.
- Identify the most high-impact levers for mobilizing positive action in the organization.
- Set up transition and integration teams that represent the most involved stakeholders in the future organization.
- Clarify the new leadership roles and organizational infrastructure.
- Create strategies and conditions to accelerate the integration process.
- Maintain a realistic expectation as to the pace of change.

As stated earlier, most members of an M&A team have very specific responsibilities to ensure the soundness and feasibility of the deal. With the CA participant monitoring the change process, the predictable barriers associated with change can be better minimized.

Assessment experience

The ability to construct and administer surveys, interviews, and other data-collecting methods is an inherent characteristic of the CA and another way to inhibit the surprise and sometimes crisis that develops from uncovering problems in skill levels, leadership capabilities, or cultural fit after the deal is done. The needs analysis process related to training and the employee opinion/corporate culture assessments created by organizational development departments are easily applied to an M&A situation. Especially as it relates to the avoidance or mitigation of "culture clash", the survey and assessment techniques used as tools in the CA are invaluable, especially in the pre- and post-merger phases.

Of course, during the pre-merger phase, the data must be gathered from a small population. Surveys are difficult to administer before the approval of the acquisition because of lack of access to the acquired company's employees due to legal reasons and also because there is insufficient time for a comprehensive cultural survey (Marks and Mirvis 1998). However, targeted interviews and observations by CA personnel throughout the process can lead to discovery of potential cultural obstacles. In debriefing sessions or strategy discussions as early as the due diligence phase, the CA representative can listen, observe, and share observations about where he or she thinks there may be issues. Once these issues are stated, other members can validate or invalidate the concern based on additional experiences within the soon to be acquired organization or, if there is a cross-organization M&A team, from experiences with each other.

Once the merger is announced, the CA can administer a fully organizational cultural and/or employee opinion survey. It is widely researched and reported that failure to assess a targeted organizational culture is a major contributor to M&A underperformance (Marks and Mirvis 1998). While traditionally the involvement of HR, and especially the CA function, has been at times an afterthought, this one aspect of cultural assessment can well pay off in either a better prepared integration scheme or, in some cases, the recognition that the M&A deal may not be as good as it seems.

Of course it is difficult to identify what aspects of "culture" are best assessed at the beginning of an M&A process. While there are some M&A failures due to poor strategic fit, most costly post-merger issues seem to result from organizational and human factors (Haspeslagh and Jemison 1991, Marks and Mirvis 1998). Unless a company is purchasing another company solely for acquisition of "hard" assets, the resistance of employees inhibits the success of the overall approach (Cartwright and Cooper 1996). Such cultural issues as communication styles, leadership approaches, and overall satisfaction with each of the separate companies can be solid indicators of the ease (or difficulty) in which a merger will produce fairly rapid benefits (Shweiger and DeNisi 1991).

Career development and succession

Similar to the assessments valuable in the pre- and post-merger phases of M&A, is the need to recognize that the human capital will be concerned, individually and collectively, about career opportunities, changes, and impacts. Larsson et al. (2001) states that, when two organizations integrate, the careers of individual employees tend to disintegrate. For example, key executives in each organization are also the most likely to have clear succession plans in place. The results of a merger can drastically alter those plans (Hirsch 1987). Even in situations where critical leaders and employees are handled in special ways in order to retain their services, the employee body "mass" may become more focused on individual survival than on the objectives of the newly formed organization (Bogdandy 2001).

Bogdandy further states that, while it is important to assess organizational culture with a focus on the future, it is critical to have an evaluation of organizational *climate* as a focus on the present (Bogdandy 2001). While an M&A team may consider the employee body of an organization as one of the elements of the acquisition, the CA team member should be more accustomed to recognizing each individual as a holistic representation *of* the organization. The involvement of CAs in the ongoing succession, development, and identification of high-potential employees within the acquiring organization can be utilized as an assessment of the newly merged members as well. In this case, the concern for individual career can greatly affect the overall impact of the M&A on future success of the organization. Larsson et al. (2001), suggest that it is important to temper the traditional view of M&A from an organizational perspective with the point of view of an M&A impact on individual careers. The researchers further suggest that the individual can be identified on a "career concept" model of two conceptual factors in light of their preferences and perceptions of an ideal environment. These factors (frequency of career change and direction of career movement) might also be predictors of longevity and stability with the employee body of a new organization. Especially when looking at the retention of key people, an approach which prioritizes the identification of work preferences would give the newly merged organization not only an indication of potential areas of resistance, but also the data necessary to formulate a retention plan that takes the career concept dimensions into the practice of M&A.

Relationships with key leaders

Critical to the success of the CA involvement during the M&A process is substantive involvement with the senior management team. The CA must not only leverage the relationships already established within the "home" company, but must also establish the trust and relationships of the senior leadership in the acquired organization. These relationships are much harder to establish if the M&A process has proceeded into the pre-merger or merger implementation stages. If this relationship building is facilitated early in the process, the insights gained by the CA consultant will provide the basis for training, coaching, and consulting throughout the integration.

Scott and Hascall (2001) compare the internal consultant, such as that within an effective CA, with external consultants and point out that one of the primary strengths that make the internal facilitator valuable, is that he or she develops their leadership out of position and character, as opposed to the external provider who is often seen as able to move on to other clients if the specific project does not work out. Adams (2001) points out that the skill in developing relationships with senior executives is a cornerstone to a successful CA and is transferable between various projects and situations.

Although some researchers have surmised that HR and training departments attempting to be involved in the planning stage of an M&A provide relatively feeble influence (Corporate Leadership Council 1999), the establishment of the relationships alone are well worth the investment in early involvement. Fully leveraging relationships with senior leaders, building partnerships for influence, and coaching leaders to model what they espouse are all relationship skills that position the CA as a leading management resource for business issues such as M&A (Adams 2001).

E-learning and e-communication technologies

When an M&A takes place, it is often difficult to organize a simple meeting within the new organization, not to mention some critical training or communication event. The CA within an organization often has technologies available that can quickly be focused on the support and development of the new organization. While the technology to conduct video conferences, tele-conferences, and email are common among organizations today, the more sophisticated aspects of Internet conferencing, web-based technologies and electronic forum and meeting infrastructure are often the purview of the CA.

While these technologies may not be the most effective for the establishment of new personal relationships, they can augment the initial face-to-face time spent between the leadership and employee body of a newly merged organization. Such common CA practices as the establishment of online forums, libraries, and chat rooms can be successfully utilized in the high-paced activity of an M&A. Even e-technologies that have less of an infrastructure demand (servers, intranets, etc.) such as compact disc production, can be utilized to share information, provide orientation, or simply communicate with a large number of employees and/or leaders at one time.

Neutral facilitation skills

While the technology availability in the CA is helpful to address the training and orientation of newly merged organizations, the more personal approach of organizational development consulting is readily available to focus on the relational aspects of a merger. Most successful OD functions within CAs operate as internal consultants – "pseudo" third parties within the organization. This dual internal–external role can add a unique value to the organization considering an M&A. For example, while the OD consultant is expected to be neutral and objective in most facilitations – and certainly those involving parties creating a merger or acquisition – the consultant is also aware of cultural norms that should not be violated, history of the acquiring companies and the pitfalls normally experienced and the traditions that will be questioned in the cultural integration of the two companies (Scott and Hascall 2001).

The Corporate Leadership Council (1999) reports that the internal consultant role often afforded CAs allows for a more integrated and less complicated issue-resolution process, which leaves the executives feeling they can hold the CA more accountable for results than an external consultant and the CA becoming more business focused. Further, the internal consultant from a CA who has established these high-level consulting relationships can be an objective sounding board for M&A members who may have few other resources for openly discussing concerns and issues raised by a potential merger. If the CA consultant is successful in building the additional relationships with the acquired company in the beginning stages of a merger, the ongoing interpersonal aspects can be leveraged in the post-merger and implementation phases.

Conclusion

When placed into the context of a merger and acquisition, the characteristics listed above of innovative CAs can become vital to the effectiveness of business integration. For example, during (and prior to) the due diligence phase, the CA can provide general M&A training, change management, negotiation, and process skill training, while actively being involved in the facilitation of the transition team and in creating an initial cultural assessment used to predict "culture clash" issues that may have a detrimental effect on a successful merger. During the implementation planning phase, the CA can focus on the facilitation of transition teams and the creation of a cultural integration plan. During implementation, the CA can play a key role in leadership team development, vision-mission creation, change management, cultural integration, and a number of other high-impact "people" issues such as the assessment of leadership talent in the merging organizations vs. needs and individuals' career aspirations. All of these activities are done utilizing the CA's unique expertise in the design of assessment centers and management audits, provision of career development consulting, and executive coaching. This opportunity also creates an enormous challenge for the CA of any organization that pursues M&A activity. It is impossible to put in place the support mechanisms that are necessary and to do so on an *ad hoc* basis. If the CA is truly to support M&A activity, there must be a commitment made to provide the necessary resources and focus. Further, and at times more challenging, is the need for the CA's organization to recognize this innovative involvement and allow the CA consultants access to the activities of M&A as they are being conceived and implemented. Many companies have long traditions of a fairly closed team when M&A is being conducted. The change in philosophy necessary to facilitate the success of CA involvement in M&A is perhaps the largest obstacle to overcome.

Of course, the complete and total involvement of the CA in merger and acquisition activity is neither common nor practical in many cases. At least through the late 1990s, the sheer volume of activity for some companies would have made it impossible for a CA to be as involved in M&A activity as depicted above. However, the CA has an opportunity to have very real business impact in whichever area of the M&A process it is able to become involved in. Like most strategies, the creation of the strategy is much easier than the implementation. But for forward-looking CAs, each involvement in an M&A activity provides the learning needed to become more valuable to corporate strategy for the next one.

References

Adams, B. 2001. *OD: The Next 10 Years – It's Still About Relationships.* Conference Proceedings of the 2001 OD Network Annual Conference.

Bogdandy, C. 2001. *Optimizing Merger Value.* Paper presented at the annual Organizational Network Conference. Vancouver, British Columbia, Canada.

Cartwright, S. and Cooper, C.L. 1996. *Managing Mergers, Acquisitions and Alliances: Integrating People and Cultures.* Oxford, UK: Butterworth Heinemann.

Corporate Leadership Council. 1997. *Fact Brief: Creating a Value-Added Organizational Development Function.* (Fact Brief). http://www.clcinteractive.com (Accessed August, 2001).

Corporate Leadership Council. 1999. *Executive Inquiry: The Role of HR in Mergers and Acquisitions.* (Executive Inquiry). http://www.clcinteractive.com (accessed August, 2001).

Filipczak, R. 1998. *The Training Manager in the 90s. Managing Training in the Organization.* Minneapolis, MN: Lakewood Publications.

Haspeslagh, P.C. and Jemison, D.B. 1991. *Managing Acquisitions: Creating Value through Corporate Renewal.* New York: Free Press.

Hirsch, P. 1987. *Pack Your Own Parachute: How to Survive Mergers, Takeovers and Other Corporate Disasters.* Reading, MA: Addison-Wesley.

Larsson, R., Driver, M., Holmqvist, M., and Sweet, P. 2001. *Career Dis-integration and Re-integration in Mergers and Acquisitions: Managing Competence and Motivational Intangibles.* Paper submitted to the *European Management Journal.*

Marks, M.L. and Mirvis, P.H. 1998. *Joining Forces: Making One Plus One Equal Three in Mergers, Acquisitions and Alliances.* San Francisco: Jossey-Bass.

Meister, J.C. 2000. *Corporate Universities: Lessons in Building a World-Class Work Force.* New York: McGraw-Hill.

Scott, B. and Hascall, J. 2001. Transitions and partnerships: The Tao of internal and external consulting. *OD Practitioner,* 33(3): 24.

Schweiger, D.M. and DeNisi, A.S. 1991. Communication with employees following a merger: A longitudinal field experiment. *Academy of Management Journal,* 34: 110–35.

CHAPTER SEVEN

Managing the Acquisition Process: Do Differences Actually Exist Across Integration Approaches?

Kimberly M. Ellis

Abstract

The purpose of this study was to determine if the importance of key process dimensions differed across the four primary integration approaches identified in prior studies of acquisition process management. Attention was focused on three critical areas of the acquisition process: general operating environment; preliminary planning; and transition management structure. Results based on examining integration activities associated with a specific M&A type – those large deals involving related and similar-sized firms – suggest that differences do exist across integration approaches, though sometimes not in ways described in prescriptive literature on the acquisition process.

Introduction

Despite their popularity and occurrence at record levels throughout the 1990s, mergers and acquisitions are a more complex phenomenon than ever. Conditions under which they enhance or destroy firm value still remain unclear in spite of the wealth of research in both management and finance literature. In fact, recent studies by several major consulting and advisory services firms provide evidence that at least one-third to one-half of these deals fail to achieve anticipated benefits, cost savings, and other synergistic outcomes (KPMG 1999, Mergerstat 2000, Pricewaterhouse Coopers 2000). Even more alarming, a recent report released by Booz Allen and Hamilton (2001), indicates that this "failure" to deliver announced benefits increases to 67 percent when examining mergers or acquisitions between comparable sized firms, a special deal type – commonly referred to as mergers of equals – that accounts for over 75 percent of the total dollars spent on merger and acquisition transactions since 1998. Thus, it is more important than ever to seek an answer to the lingering question: What distinguishes mergers or acquisitions that are successful in meeting intended goals and performance improvements from those that are not successful?

To better understand this complex phenomenon, Hitt, Harrison, and Ireland (2001) recently identified key attributes that influence post-acquisition value creation, as well as several impediments to achieving post-acquisition success. After researching hundreds of examples over a 15-year period, these authors infer that acquisition success hinges on the ability to effectively manage and implement activities throughout the entire acquisition decision-making process. Moreover, recent studies by KPMG (1999) and Booz Allen and Hamilton (2001) also point to the importance of effectively managing and executing multiple aspects of the acquisition integration process as the key to creating value following acquisitions. While each of these studies develops a list of attributes observed in those acquisitions deemed to be successful (as measured by various indicators such as stock price and profitability), they do not take into consideration that differences may be required in the integration process because of factors such as acquisition type and relative size of the two firms involved (Lubatkin 1983, Shrivastava 1986, Jemison and Sitkin 1986, Buono and Bowditch 1989, Haspeslagh and Jemison 1991, Schweiger, Csiszar, and Napier 1993). Even though the collective results of these studies provide critical insight into post-acquisition success factors, they tend to offer a "one-size-fits-all" solution. However, the reality is that for any given type of merger or acquisition, the combined firm will choose multiple levels or types of integration based on factors such as task, cultural, and political characteristics (Pablo 1994). Furthermore, the choice of integration has varying implications on the nature and extent of organizational changes required in the acquired and/or the acquiring firm in an effort to combine operations of both firms into a functioning whole (Haspeslagh and Jemison 1991, Marks and Mirvis 1998). Therefore, the importance of specific dimensions of the acquisition integration process is likely to vary depending upon the actual integration approach being utilized. Thus, "one size may not fit all" when making critical decisions about how to effectively integrate operations following an acquisition.

In an effort to increase our understanding of the linkage between integration process management and post-acquisition success, three critical works, based primarily on case studies of selected firms, have focused on discussing the various modes by which the two previous firms' operations can be combined into a cohesive, single entity after the acquisition (Nahavandi and Malekzadeh 1988, Haspeslagh and Jemison 1991, Marks and Mirvis 1998). Though Nahavandi and Malekzadeh (1988) employed a culturally based perspective while Marks and Mirvis (1998) examined the degree of post-combination change in both firms, their resulting integration approaches are quite similar to those described by Haspeslagh and Jemison (1991) who used a capabilities-based perspective.

These three critical works collectively generate useful prescriptions about the effective management of various integration approaches. However, given the dearth of empirical work examining acquisition integration approaches, the veracity and generalizability of these guidelines remain unknown. To address this gap in the acquisition process literature, the current study first draws on these three critical prescriptive works to identify the combined firm's choice of integration approach. It then examines the use of various activities to manage the related post-deal combination process. More specifically, the study utilizes a large sample of deals involving related and similar-sized firms to explore the following research question: Does the emphasis placed on key dimensions of the integration process vary across the primary integration approaches in ways described in prescriptive literature on the acquisition process? Seeking an answer to this question is important because the recognition of the diversity of integration challenges associated with the various integration approaches can have a significant influence on post-M&A outcomes.

Integration Approaches

Prescriptive works[1] on the acquisition integration process are reasonably consistent in terms of their conceptualizations of the various approaches used by firms engaging in this type of transaction. Employing a cultural-based perspective, the seminal work of Nahavandi and Malekzadeh (1988) identified various modes of acculturation based on two primary dimensions from the acquiring firm's perspective: degree of relatedness between the two firms and the degree of tolerance for multiculturalism by the acquiring firm. Moreover, these authors provided a brief description of each mode of acculturation: separation, assimilation, integration, and deculturation. Taking into consideration varying levels of the need for strategic interdependence and the need for organizational autonomy following an acquisition, Haspeslagh and Jemison (1991) developed a capabilities-based contingency framework that identified three primary integration approaches: preservation, absorption, and symbiotic. Recognizing that the set of attributes required to create value and yield the desired benefits varies by approach, these authors provided detailed insight as to what combination of factors is critical to the effective management of each approach. More recently, Marks and Mirvis (1998) also discussed several major methods firms exercise to combine their operations following an acquisition. Using the degree of post-combination change as the basis of their classification scheme, these authors identified and described the organizational attributes necessary to successfully manage five basic integration approaches: absorption as well as reverse merger/assimilation, preservation, best of both, and transformation.

Figure 7.1 provides a graphical depiction of the overlap in integration approaches identified in these three key studies. The authors' initials are indicated beside the terms they used to describe the basic mode of integration represented by each cell. The dimensions along the X-axis, need for strategic interdependence (Haspeslagh and Jemison 1991) and degree of relatedness (Nahavandi and Malekzadeh 1988), reflect the extent to which the two firms involved in the acquisition provide similar product–service offerings and/or target similar customer groups. Higher levels of relatedness between the two firms imply greater strategic interdependence thereby creating the need for more integration of the firms' operations in order to achieve the intended goals of the deal. This in turn leads to significant changes in one of the firms, usually the acquired firm. The two dimensions on the Y-axis, need for organizational autonomy (Haspeslagh and Jemison 1991) and tolerance for multiculturalism (Nahavandi and Malekzadeh 1988), indicate the acquired firm's ability to retain elements of its organizational culture and have continued involvement by its executives in key decision-making activities. Greater autonomy and acceptance of

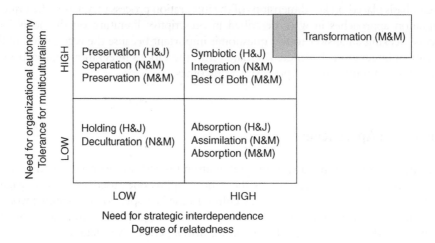

Figure 7.1   Integration approaches
Notes
1. The authors' initials are indicated beside the terms they used to describe the basic type of integration approach identified in the various cells such that: H&J = Haspeslagh and Jemison (1991); N&M = Nahavandi and Malekzadeh (1988); M&M = Marks and Mirvis (1998).
2. Need for organizational autonomy and need for strategic interdependence are the two dimensions used by Haspeslagh and Jemison (1991) in deriving their classification of integration approaches.

   Tolerance for multiculturalism and degree of relatedness are the two dimensions from the acquiring firm's perspective used by Nahavandi and Malekzadeh (1988) to identify modes of integration.

different organizational cultures result in limited plans to combine operations of the two firms.

Executives engaging in acquisitions are likely to apply one of four primary integration approaches described by these three sets of authors when combining operations of the two previously separate firms. One integration approach, typically known as preservation (upper-left quadrant of Figure 7.1), involves both firms continuing to operate autonomously so that their operations, culture, and other organizational characteristics remain intact and independent. Another common integration approach, often referred to as absorption (lower-right quadrant of Figure 7.1), describes a unilateral process where one firm is assimilated into the practices, culture, etc. of the other firm with the eventual goal of full consolidation. In the upper-right quadrant of Figure 7.1 is a third basic integration approach, symbiotic, which requires some degree of change to various aspects of the acquiring and target firms' organizational design and processes, as both firms' leading practices are gradually blended together. The last primary approach (far right, upper quadrant in Figure 7.1) to integrating the firms, a transformation approach, necessitates significant changes in both original firms as the new entity seeks to totally reinvent itself thereby developing new routines, practices, culture, and other organizational attributes.

The integration approach which appears in the lower-left quadrant of Figure 7.1 (holding or deculturation) involves a situation where the acquiring firm acts, basically, as a holding company with no intention of integrating the two firms. According to the respective authors, the acquired firm is likely to be kept completely at arm's length and/or eventually disintegrate as a cultural entity. Moreover, this approach differs from the preservation approach in that the integration choice is not necessarily driven by a strategic need for organizational separation/operational autonomy but results from a lack of concern for the integration decision-making process. Given the absence of integration intention, this general approach will not be considered in this study.

Preservation approach

The preservation approach allows the target firm to continue operating independently following the acquisition. In essence, this approach maintains boundaries between the two firms and, as such, involves very little change in both the acquiring and target firms. Thus, one of the primary drivers of achieving post-acquisition success is the ability to keep intact those strategic resources and capabilities of the target firm, as well as limiting intrusions by the acquiring firm. In order to be effectively implemented, this approach necessitates integration activities such as (1) allowing for continuing differences within the target firm; (2) giving autonomy and decision-making authority to the target firm management; (3) permitting the target firm managers to challenge or refute decisions suggested or made by the acquiring firm; and (4) providing resources to improve the operations of the target firm as needed.

Absorption approach

The absorption[2] approach fully consolidates the activities of both firms, primarily by assimilating the target firm into the acquiring firm's operations. Since this approach involves a significant degree of change in the target firm, it is essential to move in a fairly predetermined and speedy manner to minimize the level of disruption and uncertainty surrounding post-acquisition integration efforts. In order to effectively address the challenges imposed by absorbing the target firm, this approach requires (1) extensive preliminary planning for key integration issues or areas developed before the deal is consummated; (2) communications with employees and other stakeholders throughout the process to minimize uncertainty; (3) a calendar with milestones as well as time pressures for change to lessen the level of disruption in the combined firm; and (4) a limited transition structure to oversee integration efforts, identify best practices after eliminating redundancies/achieving cost savings, and harness complementary capabilities while seeking uniformity.

Symbiotic approach

The symbiotic approach requires both firms to undergo some changes as efforts are made to create a combined firm that reflects the core competencies and leading practices of both previous firms. To accomplish this goal, there needs to be a period of initial preservation where members of both firms first coexist and learn from each other before making the strategic changes necessary to gradually amalgamate the two firms. Because it seeks to blend together the operations of both firms, thereby necessitating autonomy in the target firm as well as strategic interdependence between the firms, the symbiotic integration approach presents additional difficulties during the acquisition decision-making process. As a result, this approach requires (1) creating an atmosphere that fosters cooperation between members of both firms; (2) allowing target firm managers to have some operational responsibility; (3) developing an extensive transition management structure to coordinate integration activities as well as help identify best practices; and (4) maintaining a slower pace to deal with the complex challenges created by balancing the simultaneous need for boundary protection and boundary permeability.

Transformation approach

Finally, while the symbiotic approach necessitates some degree of change in both firms as best practices are adopted and operations gradually blended together, occasionally the integration process associated with an acquisition involves very significant, fundamental changes in the organizational culture and operating practices of both previous firms. In these cases, where both firms are essentially dismantled as a part of integration efforts, the mode of combining operations is referred to as a transformation approach. This approach requires the newly combined firm to abandon old practices and routines while totally reinventing itself through the creation of a new organization, set of values, and way of operating. To facilitate the development of new practices, routines, organizational values, and the like, firms employing this integration approach need to manage the process in an inclusive and inventive manner. This necessitates (1) preparing a blueprint of the new organization's structure, culture, and similar features before completing the deal; (2) clearly articulating the strategic vision and/or purpose of the new company to all stakeholders of both firms; (3) involving managers of both the acquiring and target firms in decision-making activities; and (4) establishing a temporary transition management structure to oversee as well as coordinate integration efforts.

Primary differences in integration approaches

Table 7.1 recaps the critical process dimensions for each integration approach and highlights differences between the four primary integration approaches. The critical activities associated with the various integration approaches appear to emphasize three main dimensions of the post-deal combination process. One group of process dimensions consists of those activities that set the general tone for acquisition decision making. This group, referred to as general operating environment, includes the need for communications, articulation of a shared purpose, the ability of the target firm's managers to refute decisions, and the level of autonomy given to target firm managers. The next set of process dimensions relates to preliminary planning efforts. These activities include the existence, detail, and flexibility of preliminary plans as well as issues considered by the firms when developing such blueprints for combining their operations. The remaining process dimensions discussed in the prescriptive works on acquisition integration approaches relate to transition management efforts. This group of activities includes the composition and structure of the transition management team as well as its primary goals.

Table 7.1   Critical process dimensions of each integration approach

Process dimensions	Integration approaches			
	Preservation	Absorption	Symbiotic	Transformation
General operating environment				
• Shared purpose			*	*
• Bilateral communications		*		*
• Ability to refute	*		*	*
• Autonomy	*		*	
Preliminary planning				
• Existence		*		*
• Level of detail		*		*
• Extent of flexibility				*
• Issues considered				
– Transition process			*	*
– Success factors		*		*
– Management of combined operations				*
– Integration timetable		*		
– Employee communications		*		*
– Restructuring issues		*		*
– Board structure				*
– Name, HQs, etc.				*
Transition management				
• Existence		*	*	*
• Members from both organizations			*	*
• Employees from various levels			*	*
• Specific task forces in key functions			*	*
• Primary goals				
– Design for combined firm				*
– Coordinate integration		*	*	*
– Identify best practices		*	*	
– Foster cooperation			*	*
– Prioritize decisions		*	*	*
– Resolve HR policy differences		*		

* Indicates those dimensions considered to be most critical in effectively implementing a given integration approach (based on prescriptions provided in Haspeslagh and Jemison 1991, Marks and Mirvis 1998, and Nahavandi and Malekzadeh 1988).

Purpose of Study

Consistency across the prescriptive works suggests characteristics of these four approaches represent a central phenomenon such that there appears to be an ideal way to manage each approach. However, to date there are no known empirical studies in the acquisition process literature that investigate differences in how firms manage the post-deal combination process across integration approaches. The primary purpose of this study, then, is to empirically examine whether the use of various process dimensions highlighted in Table 7.1 varies across the primary integration approaches in ways described in prescriptive literature on the acquisition process. In doing so, this study not only adds to the growing literature on the acquisition integration process, but also represents one of the first known empirical investigations of acquisition integration approaches. Better understanding of the link between a combined firm's integration activities and its choice of integration approach may provide critical insight necessary to overcome integration challenges that often represent a major impediment to the combined firm's ability to achieve anticipated deal benefits.

Methodology

Because integration challenges are posited to vary by acquisition type and size of the firms involved (Lubatkin 1983, Jemison and Sitkin 1986, Shrivastava 1986, Buono and Bowditch 1989, Haspeslagh and Jemison 1991, Schweiger, Csiszar, and Napier 1993), this study examines differences in process dimensions across integration approaches within a specific context: large, related mergers or acquisitions involving similar sized firms.[3] This special type of acquisition is selected for several reasons. First, from a practical standpoint there has been a steady increase over the last five years of mega-mergers that bring together firms competing in the same industry and of similar size such that now they account for nearly 75 percent of all deals involving publicly traded firms (Mergerstat 2000, PricewaterhouseCoopers 2000). Moreover, mergers and acquisitions of relatively equal firms are not only popular, they are also phenomenologically unique (Carey 2000). While these deals generate great expectations about synergistic benefits and ultimate performance gains from multiple stakeholders, they also involve high levels of uncertainty as one, and in some cases, both original firms undergo significant changes or dismantlement to create the new combined organization (Carey 2000, Olie 1994). Because of the enormous strategic stakes, complex management challenges, and critical need for success in this special type of acquisition, the effects of the integration process are drawn into high relief. So, it is likely that various integration approaches will be used to combine the firms' operations into a functioning whole in such a way that anticipated synergies are delivered and a multitude of stakeholder expectations are met following these deals.

Sample criteria and final sample size

Focusing on this specific type of acquisition required certain criteria to be established. First, large acquisitions are defined as those with a transaction value of at least $100 million (Hayward and Hambrick 1997, Sirower 1997). Relatedness is based on transactions meeting one of two requirements: the first involves the traditional method of matching both firm's primary SIC code at the two-digit level (Lubatkin 1987) and the second requires that the two firms have at least one four-digit SIC code match among the top six lines of businesses they are operating in at the time of the acquisition (Haleblian and Finkelstein 1999). Consistent with a similar category of mergers identified by Ravenscraft and Scherer (1987), similar size is measured as firms having a relative sales or relative assets ratio between 0.5 and 2.0 where one firm is no more than twice the size of the other firm. Sales and assets of both firms the year prior to the acquisition are used in calculating this ratio. Finally, the time period is limited to transactions completed between 1995 and 1998. This four-year period is appropriate because details of the acquisition are likely to still be fresh in the memory of respondents.

The initial population of interest consisted of 360 acquisitions meeting the estab-lished criteria. After adjustments were made for multiple acquisitions by an acquiring firm during the sample period, subsequent acquisitions of previously acquiring firms, divestitures of a portion of the acquired firm's assets, and spin-offs of combined assets into a separate entity, the working population consisted of 305 transactions. Completed surveys, administered via fax, were received from 101 key informants knowledgeable about the focal acquisition (the vast majority of which were chief exec-utive officers/presidents, chief financial officers, vice presidents of acquisitions, or vice presidents of corporate or business development). This response rate of 33 percent is considered quite high given the time demands placed on top managers and the sensitive nature of this research topic (Singh and Zollo, 1998).[4]

Process dimensions

General operating environment.   The general operating environment consists of four elements: articulation of a shared purpose or vision for the combined firm; bilateral communications between the combined firm and its employees; maintenance of autonomy by the target firm in making strategic and operational decisions; and the ability of the target firm to refute or challenge decisions made by the acquiring firm. These four items were derived from reviewing the prescriptive works on integration approaches. Respondents were asked to assess the extent to which each of these four activities existed. Each item was evaluated along a five-item scale ranging from 1 (not at all) to 5 (very large extent).

Preliminary planning.   Another important aspect of the overall integration process prescribed to vary by approach is preliminary planning. Preliminary planning involves the preparation of a "blueprint" for combining and reconfiguring the firms prior to the actual start of integration efforts. As such, this process includes not only devel-oping combination plans, but also addressing critical issues like the combined firm's name, potential downsizing, and integration timetable before beginning to combine the operations of the two firms.

Existing prescriptive studies based primarily on case and anecdotal research served as the basis for creating survey items to tap preliminary planning activities. First, respondents were asked to indicate whether or not preliminary plans for combining the firms were developed prior to finalizing the merger agreement. If preliminary plans were developed, then respondents assessed two important aspects of pre-liminary planning – the level of detail as well as flexibility – along a five-point scale ranging from 1 (not at all) to 5 (very large extent). Moreover, in those instances where preliminary plans were developed, respondents were provided with a list of eight major issues identified in previous acquisition process studies and asked to select those issues considered in this stage of the acquisition decision-making process.[5]

Transition management. The last set of dimensions that differ across integration approaches pertain to the transition management process. Generally speaking, transition management refers to the oversight of integration efforts necessary to combine the two previously separate firms into a functioning whole. This process encompasses the structure/composition of the transition structure as well as its related goals.

Survey items were constructed based on discussions of transition management activities in existing prescriptive studies about the acquisition integration process and integration approaches. Initially respondents were asked to indicate whether or not a formal transition management structure existed. When replying affirmatively to this item, the respondent was then asked to assess the level of three aspects of the transition structure: (1) involvement by members from both organizations; (2) inclusion of employees from various levels within the firm; and (3) use of specific task forces in key functions. These three items were rated along a five-point scale ranging from 1 (not at all) to 5 (very large extent). Finally, respondents were provided with a list of six primary goals of the transition management structure mentioned in prior studies on the acquisition integration process and asked to check all the goals that applied in the focal acquisition.

Integration approaches

The characteristics of integration approaches consistently described by Haspeslagh and Jemison (1991), Marks and Mirvis (1998), and Nahavandi and Malekzadeh (1988) served as the basis for developing the coding scheme used to classify the manner in which firms combined the operations of the two previously separate companies. To identify the actual integration approach being employed by firms in this study, press releases and annual reports discussing each acquisition were content analyzed. Information used in the content analysis included: (1) the primary motives for the current acquisition; (2) if the combined firm would operate under a new name; (3) whether references were made to a "new" company or just to the name of the acquiring firm; (4) the extent to which the combined firm would follow the operating procedures of the acquiring firm or seek to identify best practices of both firms; (5) the composition of the top management team and board of directors following the acquisition; (6) if any plans existed for restructuring and downsizing initiatives; and (7) whether words such as assimilate, absorb, blend, or retain were used in describing the process of integrating the operations of the two firms.

Based on their assessment of this information as summarized in Table 7.2, two raters well versed in the acquisition process literature then classified the integration approach being used in each acquisition as one of four main approaches: preservation, absorption, symbiotic, or transformation with 92.5 percent agreement. Of the 101 acquisitions in the final sample, 40 firms used the absorption approach, 33 the transformation approach, 24 the symbiotic approach, and only four followed the preservation approach. The fact that only four firms chose the preservation approach is not surprising given the sample criteria established. The primary sources of value creation for firms

Table 7.2   Profile of integration approaches used for content analysis

Approach	Critical components
Preservation (n = 4)	• Revenue growth and market position key motives • Plans to retain majority of target's TMT and/or target brand name • Neither firm changed significantly • No plans to integrate key business areas
Absorption (n = 40)	• Cost savings, increase size, and market position primary motives • Acquiring firm's procedures being used in target firm • Use of the words "assimilate" or "absorb" • Very limited retention of/involvement by managers of the target firm
Symbiotic (n = 24)	• Expand products/geographic areas and increase size primary motives • Use of the words "best of both" or "best practices" • Some retention of/involvement by top managers of the target firm • No plans to integrate or delay in integration efforts in many or most business areas
Transformation (n = 33)	• Complementary nature of businesses, revenue growth, increase size, and cost savings primary motives • Combined firm operates under new name; references to "new" entity • A significant number of individuals from target firm included on the top management team and board of directors of the combined firm • Both firms changed significantly

involved in this special M&A type are likely to be derived from economies of scale, economies of scope, and market power (Carey 2000, Seth 1990). In order to capture such synergistic benefits, it is critical that firms utilize an integration approach that facilitates their ability to combine, share, and/or transfer key resources, know-how, or business activities across the two previously separate organizations. Clearly, this is not consistent with goals of the preservation approach. Given its limited use, the preservation approach was not examined in subsequent analyses.

Results

Multivariate (MANOVA) and one-way analysis of variance (ANOVA) procedures were applied to test whether significant differences existed in critical elements of process management across the three common integration approaches (absorption, symbiotic, and transformation) used by firms included in the current study. First, a MANOVA was performed to test for significant differences among the three common integration approaches when considering all the process dimensions simultaneously. The F value derived from Wilks' lambda was 1.53 with an associated p value of 0.06. Moreover, the computed value of Wilks' lambda statistic is 0.19 – the lower the value of this statistic, the stronger the relationship – which indicates a moderate to strong relationship between integration approaches and the process dimensions of interest (Hatcher and Stepanski 1994).

Given these results from the MANOVA, univariate ANOVAs were performed to identify the specific process dimensions along which there were significant differences between the three integration approaches. Means of the individual process dimensions for each integration approach, shown in columns two through four of Table 7.3, were calculated and compared using Tukey's HSD test. A critical p value of 0.10 was used because of the relatively small sample size (especially the number of firms employing the symbiotic approach) as well as the exploratory nature of the current study (Sauley and Bedian 1989).[6] As reported in the last column of Table 7.3, the F value associated with the ANOVAs was statistically significant for 16 of the 25 process dimensions identified in the current study with associated R-squares ranging from 0.08 to 0.28. Thus, differences do exist between the three integration approaches along several specific process dimensions.

Tukey's HSD test showed that in general, use of the transformation approach led to significantly higher levels along many process dimensions as compared to using either the absorption or symbiotic approaches. First, firms utilizing the transformation approach exhibited significantly higher levels than firms employing both the symbiotic and absorption approach on each of the following process dimensions:

1. Articulation of a shared purpose.
2. Consideration of the combined firm's name and headquarters during the preliminary planning process.
3. Existence of a transition management structure.
4. Involvement by members from both organizations in the transition management structure.
5. Inclusion of employees from various levels within the firm in the transition management structure.
6. Use of specific task forces in key functions as a part of the transition management structure.
7. Design for combined firm as a primary goal of the transition management structure.
8. Identification of best practices as a primary goal of the transition management structure.

Moreover, as compared to firms implementing an absorption approach, firms using the transformation approach engaged to a greater extent in:

1. Establishing bilateral communications.
2. Providing the target firm with the ability to refute decisions.
3. Considering the management of combined operations during the preliminary planning process.
4. Fostering cooperation between members of both firms as a primary goal of the transition management structure.

Table 7.3 ANOVA results of differences in process dimensions across integration approaches

Process dimensions	Absorption	Symbiotic	Transformation	Significant differences at 0.10[†]	F value
General operating environment					
• Shared purpose	3.00	3.42	4.11	T > A, S	11.53***
• Bilateral communications	3.28	3.54	4.06	T > A	5.60**
• Ability to refute	2.26	3.31	3.00	S > A, T > A	8.25***
• Autonomy	1.80	3.48	2.14	S > A, T	19.60***
Preliminary planning					
• Existence	0.63	0.63	0.71		0.38
• Level of detail	2.33	2.17	2.46		0.18
• Extent of flexibility	2.12	2.21	2.43		0.31
• Issues considered					
– Transition process	0.79	0.56	0.96	T > S	5.53**
– Success factors	0.46	0.31	0.73	T > S	4.16*
– Management of combined operations	0.71	0.81	0.96	T > A	3.05*
– Integration timetable	0.79	0.63	0.88		2.01
– Employee communications	0.61	0.75	0.81		1.39
– Restructuring issues	0.82	0.44	0.77	A > S, T > S	4.30*
– Board structure	0.46	0.63	0.58		0.61
– Name, HQs, etc.	0.46	0.44	0.77	T > A, S	3.51*
Transition management					
• Existence	0.70	0.54	0.91	T > A, S	5.80*
• Members from both organizations	2.53	2.38	4.17	T > A, S	9.30***
• Employees from various levels	2.51	2.08	3.63	T > A, S	6.32***
• Specific task forces in key functions	2.91	1.96	4.11	T > A, S	10.03***
Primary goals					
– Design for combined firm	0.25	0.21	0.56	T > A, S	4.59*
– Coordinate integration	1.00	0.93	0.94		1.08
– Identify best practices	0.41	0.43	0.88	T > A, S	10.32***
– Foster cooperation	0.59	0.64	0.88	T > A	3.54*
– Prioritize decisions	0.72	0.71	0.78		0.20
– Resolve HR policy differences	0.38	0.36	0.59		1.94

[†] A = Absorption; S = Symbiotic; T = Transformation.
* $p < .05$, ** $p < .01$, *** $p < .001$.

Finally, as compared to firms using the symbiotic approach, the use of the transformation approach resulted in firms being more likely to consider three key issues when developing preliminary plans:

1. Transition process.
2. Critical success factors.
3. Restructuring issues.

There were a few instances where the use of the absorption or symbiotic approach led to greater emphasis on select process dimensions. Firms utilizing the symbiotic approach did allow the target firm's management to retain significantly more autonomy in strategic and operational decision making than either of the other two integration approaches. Also, as with the transformation approach, firms using the symbiotic approach provided managers of the target firm with more ability to refute decisions as compared to firms employing an absorption approach. Finally, like the transformation approach, the use of the absorption approach led to a greater likelihood of considering restructuring issues during the preliminary planning process as compared to employing a symbiotic approach.

Discussion

In an effort to better understand how firms actually combine their operations following a merger or acquisition, the current study focused attention on the acquisition integration process. In doing so, the primary purpose was to examine whether differences existed in terms of how the integration process is managed across several commonly accepted integration approaches. Moreover, the study was restricted to a special deal type – large, related acquisitions involving similar sized firms – where the need for effective process management is essential given complex challenges and high strategic stakes as well as emerging reports that up to two-thirds of these deals fail to deliver anticipated benefits (Booz Allen and Hamilton 2001).

Generally speaking, results indicate that differences do indeed exist in terms of the importance placed on various process dimensions across three commonly utilized integration approaches: absorption, symbiotic, and transformation. Especially noteworthy was that those firms utilizing a transformation approach where original operations of both firms were dismantled and a completely new, reinvented organization and culture were developed in the combined firm, placed much greater emphasis on communicating the vision and other critical issues to their employees, addressing many critical integration issues during the preliminary planning process, and establishing extensive transition management structures. Firms pursuing this approach appear to take into consideration that it is fraught with more integration difficulties than the other approaches because of the additional complexities created by the significant changes in both previous firms (Marks and Mirvis 1998, Olie 1994). Thus, these firms paid significantly more attention to multiple aspects of the overall acquisition decision-making process as compared to firms using the absorption and symbiotic approaches.

With regard to the general operating environment, specific differences do exist across integration approaches. Those firms using the absorption approach focused less on articulating a shared purpose and involving the target firm in decision-making activities, both of which were expected as the combined firm seeks to eliminate redundancies and achieve cost savings via consolidating operations (Haspeslagh and Jemison 1991). However, contrary to prescriptive works, firms exercising this approach did not spend a significant amount of time communicating with employees of both firms. Moreover, given the importance of preserving initial boundaries between the two firms before blending them together, firms using the symbiotic approach did provide the target firms with decision-making responsibilities via the ability to refute and maintenance of operational autonomy. This is consistent with prescriptive literature that emphasizes the importance of preserving some boundaries between the two firms (Haspeslagh and Jemison 1991). Finally, firms deciding to transform themselves following this special type of acquisition emphasized shared purpose, communications, and the target firm's ability to refute decisions but did not allow managers of the target firm to maintain autonomy in making decisions. Perhaps, firms pursuing this approach valued some involvement by the target firm in making the decisions critical to developing a new organization but thought that providing the target firm with strategic and operational autonomy would hinder their efforts to reinvent the combined firm.

There was no difference in the decision of firms involved in this special type of acquisition to engage in preliminary planning activities. When considering acquisitions in general, this result may be surprising. However, within the context of this special deal type, it is possible that regardless of the integration approach being used, firms spend the necessary time upfront developing a roadmap of how operations will be combined prior to closing the deal given the sheer size of both firms involved as well as power considerations among top managers, heightened levels of uncertainty among employees, and a myriad of other stakeholder concerns (Booz Allen and Hamilton 2001).

Significant differences do emerge across integration approaches in terms of major issues considered when developing preliminary plans for combining the two firms' operations. Consistent with the notion of creating a virtually new company, firms using the transformation approach tend to deal more with critical issues such as success factors, the transition process, restructuring, and the management, name, and headquarters of the combined firm. Moreover, when firms used the absorption approach, it is not surprising that restructuring issues also received significant consideration while other issues garnered less attention during the preliminary planning process. Dealing with restructuring issues is essential given that the target firm is assimilated into the acquiring firm and the critical need to identify opportunities for cost savings. Finally, with regard to the symbiotic approach, not placing much concern on issues such as restructuring, success factors, and the transition process prior to closing the deal seems consistent with the combined firms' goal of initially preserving the organizational boundaries of the two firms involved in the acquisition. After all, allowing both firms at the onset to operate as they did prior to the acquisition should not require the development of a detailed blueprint for combining operations.

Finally, differences also exist when examining transition management efforts. It appears that firms pursuing a transformation approach are more likely to have an extensive, formal transition management structure in place than firms using the other two approaches. The primary goals emphasized as a part of this structure include recommending a design for the combined firm, identifying best practices of the two firms, and fostering mutual cooperation and communications – all likely to be critical in the development of a new organization. It is also important to note that low emphasis being placed on these same goals is consistent with prescriptions for the absorption approach that suggest having a limited transition management structure as the combined firm seeks to fully consolidate the target firm into the acquiring firm (Haspeslagh and Jemison 1991). It was somewhat surprising that firms using the symbiotic approach did not have an extensive transition management structure in place given the need to eventually identify best practices and blend the operations of the two firms together. However, at the time of data collection, firms using this approach may have still been in the initial preservation mode where both firms were co-existing and learning from each other before proceeding with amalgamation. Given the enormous strategic stakes and additional integration challenges created by this special M&A type, it is likely that the time elapsed before encouraging the interactions required to start amalgamating the two firms may be longer than in other types of acquisition.

Contributions

The current study represents one of the first known empirical investigations of acquisition integration approaches. In doing so, its findings offer initial support that, at least within the context of related acquisitions involving similar sized firms, the emphasis placed on various process dimensions does, in fact, vary depending upon the chosen integration approach, although not entirely in ways consistent with guidelines generated in existing prescriptive works on acquisition integration approaches. This study also adds to the emerging management literature examining elements of the actual acquisition integration process. As such, some empirical evidence is found that confirms the need for several key dimensions when implementing specific integration approaches that had been identified in prescriptive and anecdotal work on the acquisition process. Also, while some previous acquisition process literature has implied that acquisitions involving firms operating in the same or similar product markets usually imply the use of an absorption approach (Haspeslagh and Jemison 1991), evidence is provided in support of other researchers' contentions that even for related deals, firms actually utilize multiple integration approaches as they seek to combine operations into a functioning whole (Buono and Bowditch 1989, Marks and Mirvis 1998).

From a practical perspective, findings from this study imply that "one size does not fit all" as it pertains to managing the acquisition integration process. On the contrary, when making critical process-oriented decisions necessary for the effective integration of businesses following an acquisition, managers should first determine which type of integration approach they will use. Then, managers should take into consideration the implications that the chosen approach has on the magnitude and nature of changes taking place in one or both of the original firms in deciding which dimensions of the integration process need to be emphasized (Buono and Bowditch 1989, Haspeslagh and Jemison 1991, Marks and Mirvis 1998). Moreover, as mentioned by

Hitt, Harrison, and Ireland (2001), effective post-acquisition integration does not hinge on incorporating just one particular process dimension, but rather on the ability to simultaneously engage in as well as manage multiple, inter-related activities during the M&A integration process.

Limitations and future research

The current study is not without limitations. One limitation is the potential for retrospective bias that exists when managers are asked to recall past events. To address and minimize this concern, the study focused on recent acquisitions and made efforts to identify the member of the combined firm's top management team that was most involved with the integration process for the focal acquisition. Also, this study focused exclusively on large, related acquisitions involving firms of similar size. While a better understanding of how critical process dimensions differed across integration approaches for this specific type of acquisition was gained, the results of the current study may not be generalizable to acquisitions as a whole.

Future research should examine whether findings observed in this special acquisition type can be generalized to a broader population of acquisitions or if the high strategic stakes and complex management challenges required focus on radically different process dimensions for the respective integration approaches. Other interesting questions that need to be addressed include: Is one integration approach more likely than others to facilitate the combined firm's ability to achieve post-acquisition success? Or can all of the integration approaches generate similar post-acquisition outcomes as long as firms combine multiple process dimensions in ways that address the integration challenges created by the level of changes required in both firms? Also, there are opportunities to expand our understanding of acquisition experience and the programmability of acquisition integration efforts (Eisenhardt and Brown 1998, Haleblian and Finkelstein 1999) by exploring issues such as: What role does the prior acquisition experience of not only the acquiring firm, but also that of the target firm play in managing the integration process? Are managers inclined to pursue the same integration approach used in prior deals even if another approach would be more appropriate given the context of the focal acquisition? Does the significance, as well as directional influence of prior acquisition experience, vary based on the type of integration approach being employed? For example, when using an absorption approach, could high levels of prior experience actually lead to inappropriate application of programmed integration guidelines thereby resulting in ineffective process management, especially within the context of mega-deals involving comparable sized firms that once competed against one another? Answers to these and other questions are critical to advancing our understanding of this complex business phenomenon and developing a more comprehensive theory of acquisitions.

Conclusion

Though the number and dollar value of deals have tapered off since the first half of 2001, continued M&A activity is expected as firms respond to marketplace realities such as increasing industry consolidation, rapidly changing technologies, and intensifying global competition. In addition, many firms that completed acquisitions in 1999 and 2000 are still dealing with integration challenges that have thus far hindered their ability to deliver benefits promised to various stakeholders at the time of deal completion. However, additional studies exploring how firms can effectively manage multiple integration approaches in particular, and the overall acquisition decision-making process in general, thereby increasing the probability of achieving post-acquisition success are definitely warranted.

Notes

1. Because of the more detailed discussion of the effective management of the absorption, preservation, and symbiotic integration approaches, Haspeslagh and Jemison's (1991) classification scheme is used as the main source for describing these three approaches. Marks and Mirvis' (1998) categorization serves as the primary basis for discussing the transformation approach due to their direct identification of this integration approach. It is worth noting that Haspeslagh and Jemison (1991) alluded to this approach on several occasions but did not discuss it in detail.
2. Occasionally the target firm of record assumes the leadership position in terms of managing the integration process. In these instances, the integration approach may be described as reverse merger, reverse absorption, or reverse assimilation. While the roles of the acquiring and target firm are switched, critical components of managing the integration process remain the same.
3. In addition to providing suggestions as to how each approach can be effectively managed, Haspeslagh and Jemison (1991) also imply that each approach is most appropriate for a specific type of acquisition (preservation for unrelated or domain exploration acquisitions; absorption for horizontal or domain strengthening acquisitions; and symbiotic for related, vertical, or domain extension acquisitions). However, as articulated by Buono and Bowditch (1989) and Marks and Mirvis (1998), firms engaged in horizontal and/or related acquisitions may actually use each of the four primary integration approaches.
4. There were no statistically significant differences between respondents and non-respondents in terms of sample criteria used (transaction value, relative sales, and relative assets). In addition, mean comparisons of early and late respondents revealed no significant differences between the two groups along the sample criteria. Thus, the current sample is representative of large, related acquisitions completed between 1995 and 1998 that involved similar sized firms.
5. Responses were coded 0 and 1 for the existence of preliminary planning and a formal transition management structure (YES/NO). In addition, the major issues considered during preliminary planning and the primary goals of the transition structure were also coded 0 and 1 depending upon whether or not the item was checked by the respondent. For preliminary planning, the eight issues listed on the survey included: (1) transition process; (2) critical success factors; (3) management of combined operations; (4) integration timetable; (5) communications with employees; (6) restructuring or downsizing issues; (7) board of directors structure; and (8) the combined firm's name or headquarters. For transition structure, the six goals listed on the survey included: (1) recommend a design for the combined firm; (2) coordinate the integration of functions/areas; (3) identify best practices of both firms; (4) foster mutual cooperation; (5) prioritize combination decisions/initiatives; and (6) resolve firm differences in HR policies. The items for both

lists were generated primarily from a review of prior acquisition process literature, but supplemented by popular press articles and special proxy statements discussing process-related efforts.

6. Differences between all of the pairs shown in column five of Table 7.3 were actually significant at the .05 value except the following four pairs: name, headquarters of the combined firm – T > A and T > S; existence of transition management structure – T > A; and design of combined firms – T > S.

References

Booz Allen and Hamilton. 2001. *Merger Integration – Delivering on the Promise*. July.

Buono, A.F. and Bowditch, J.L. 1989. *The Human Side of Mergers and Acquisitions: Managing Collisions Between People, Cultures, And Organizations*. San Francisco: Jossey-Bass.

Carey, D. 2000. A CEO roundtable on making mergers succeed. *Harvard Business Review*, 78(3): 145–54.

Eisenhardt, K.M. and Brown, S.L. 1998. Time pacing: Competing in markets that won't stand still. *Harvard Business Review*, 76(1): 59–69.

Haleblian, J. and Finkelstein, S. 1999. The influence of organizational acquisition experience on acquisition performance: A behavioral learning perspective. *Administrative Science Quarterly*, 44: 29–56.

Haspeslagh, P.C. and Jemison, D.B. 1991. *Managing Acquisitions: Creating Value Through Corporate Renewal*. New York: Free Press.

Hatcher, L. and Stepanski, E.J. 1994. *A Step-by-Step Approach to Using the SAS System for Univariate and Multivariate Statistics*. Cary, NC: SAS Institute.

Hayward, M.L.A. and Hambrick, D.C. 1997. Explaining the premiums paid for large acquisitions: Evidence of CEO hubris. *Administrative Science Quarterly*, 42: 103–27.

Hitt, M.A., Harrison, J.S., and Ireland, R.D. 2001. *Mergers and Acquisitions: A Guide to Creating Value for Stakeholders*. New York: Oxford University Press.

Jemison, D.B. and Sitkin, S.B. 1986. Corporate acquisitions: A process perspective. *Academy of Management Review*, 11: 145–63.

KPMG. 1999. Unlocking shareholder value: the keys to success. *Mergers and Acquisitions: A Global Research Report*. November.

Lubatkin, M. 1983. Mergers and the performance of the acquiring firm. *Academy of Management Review*, 8: 218–25.

Lubatkin, M. 1987. Merger strategies and stockholder value. *Strategic Management Journal*, 8: 39–53.

Marks, M.L. and Mirvis, P.H. 1998. *Joining Forces: Making One Plus One Equal Three In Mergers, Acquisitions, and Alliances*. San Francisco: Jossey-Bass.

Mergerstat. 2000. Two tales can be told about the M&A market in 2000. *PR Newswire*, December 28.

Nahavandi, A. and Malekzadeh, A. 1988. Acculturation in mergers and acquisitions. *Academy of Management Review*, 13: 79–90.

Olie, R. 1994. Shades of culture and institutions in international mergers. *Organizational Studies*, 15: 381–405.

Pablo, A.L. 1994. Determinants of acquisition integration level: A decision-making perspective. *Academy of Management Journal*, 37: 803–36.

PricewaterhouseCoopers. 2000. PricewaterhouseCoopers forecast: While M&A outlook remains strong for 2001, acquirers look for more than size as they struggle with new economy growth model. *Business Wire*, December 18.

Ravenscraft, D.J. and Scherer, F.M. 1987. *Mergers, Sell-Offs, and Economic Efficiency.* Washington, DC: Brookings Institution.

Sauley, K.S. and Bedian, A.G. 1989. .05: A case of the tail wagging the distribution. *Journal of Management,* **15**(2): 335–44.

Schweiger, D.M., Csiszar, E.N., and Napier, N.K. 1993. Implementing international acquisitions. *Human Resource Planning,* **16**: 53–70.

Seth, A. 1990. Value creation in acquisitions: A re-examination of performance issues. *Strategic Management Journal,* **11**: 99–115.

Shrivastava, P. 1986. Postmerger integration. *Journal of Business Strategy,* 7: 65–76.

Singh, H. and Zollo, M. 1998. The impact of knowledge codification, experience trajectories and integration strategies on the performance of corporate acquisitions. *Academy of Management Best Paper Proceedings.*

Sirower, M.L. 1997. *The Synergy Trap: How Companies Lose the Acquisition Game.* New York: Free Press.

M&A Knowledge Transfer and Learning

Mergers and Acquisitions in Technology-Intensive Industries: The Emergent Process of Knowledge Transfer

Danna Greenberg, P.J. Guinan

Abstract

In technology-intensive industries, most acquisitions are undertaken with the expectation that the acquisition will lead to expanded technological capabilities and organizational innovation. The challenge behind this value-creation proposition is that the development of these innovative capabilities is dependent upon the sharing and leveraging of knowledge between the merging firms. Using a case study methodology to research three acquisitions among technology-intensive organizations, we focus on why knowledge transfer occurs following an acquisition and how the integration process impacts knowledge transfer. The findings from this study provide insight into the role individual organizational members play in supporting knowledge transfer and how the integration process influences the activity of these individuals.

Introduction

The end of the 1990s represented the fifth wave of mergers and acquisition activity in the United States, with over 62 percent of the M&As (measured in dollar volume) since 1980 occurring in 1999 and 2000 (Bahde 2001). In this last wave, technology-based industries such as computer hardware and software, electronics, biotechnology, and pharmaceuticals were frequently placed among the top 10 most active M&A industries according to the SDC's annual M&A almanac (Ranft and Lord 2000). M&As are an attractive growth strategy for technology-intensive organizations because they enable organizations to quickly enter new markets and/or quickly obtain a larger share of the market that an organization currently serves (Hitt et al. 1991). In these industries, the speed of competition has rendered organic growth to be excessively time-consuming.

Hence, acquisitions often represent a more viable strategy for gaining an advantage over one's competitors (Bresman, Birkinshaw, and Nobel 1999). The acquirer is able to save time and money by limiting its own R&D budget and relying on M&As to fulfill the same purposes of fueling innovation, growth, and knowledge expansion.

While in theory, acquisitions may appear to provide an organization with a viable strategy for stimulating new product development and innovation, the reality is that most acquisitions fail to achieve their anticipated returns. From a financial perspective, researchers have found that acquisitions frequently fail to achieve their financial goals, or to lead to increased shareholder wealth (Sirower 1997, Ashkenas and Francis 2000, Bahde 2001). From an organizational perspective, acquisitions can lead to high levels of stress (Cartwright and Cooper 1992) and increased turnover (Cartwright and Cooper 1990, Hambrick and Cannella 1993), which will hinder employee productivity following an acquisition.

For technology-intensive companies, achieving a successful acquisition is further complicated by the goals of the acquisition. To trigger innovative activities and expanded R&D following an acquisition, knowledge transfer must occur between the acquirer and the target following the acquisition. Unfortunately, most aspects of the acquisition process are more likely to hinder, not facilitate, knowledge transfer. For example, increased turnover among key managers following an acquisition results in the loss of their knowledge and expertise which, in turn, limits knowledge transfer (Cannella and Hambrick 1993). Following an acquisition, culture clash and feelings of demoralization often lead to employee resistance which further inhibits knowledge transfer and the realization of synergistic benefits (Larsson and Finkelstein 1999). The challenge for managers is to determine how to best manage the integration process so that organizational members are encouraged to participate in knowledge transfer activities which will, in turn, fuel the value-creation potential of the acquisition.

This study explores the issue by examining how the integration process influences future knowledge transfer activities between the target and the acquiring organizations. In particular, we were interested in why knowledge transfer occurs following an acquisition and how the acquisition process influences knowledge transfer. To address this question, we used a case study methodology to explore issues related to the acquisition process, knowledge transfer, and value creation in three technology-intensive acquisitions. An important component of this research design was that the selected case organizations were one to six years, post-acquisition announcement. Due to the complexities of the M&A change process, coupled with the amount of time required for any organization to learn to successfully collaborate with another, knowledge transfer is not likely to occur in the first few months following an acquisition (Bresman, Birkinshaw, and Nobel 1999). The findings from this study provide insight into the dynamics of the change processes that underlie an acquisition, as well as how these processes shape knowledge transfer between the merging partners.

Literature Review

Following the "process perspective" of M&A research, this study focuses on the process by which an acquisition unfolds and how the acquisition process impacts knowledge transfer between the merging organizations. The process perspective frames acquisitions as a series of decision-making steps each of which has an impact on the final outcome of the full acquisition process. Researchers have long understood that value creation following an acquisition must be studied by examining the actions that lead up to the acquisition decision along with the integration and management activities that follow the decision (Jemison and Sitkin 1986). While there may be a well-identified strategic and organizational fit underlying an acquisition, specific individuals in the organization manage the activities which ultimately do or do not result in value creation (Haspeslagh and Jemison 1991). This would suggest that individual manager actions, both during and after the integration process, are likely to influence knowledge transfer and value creation following an acquisition.

A definition of knowledge transfer

In the general management literature, concepts of knowledge transfer, knowledge creation, and knowledge combination have received increased attention from both academics and practitioners over the past few years. This increased focus comes from the assumption, which is partially supported by data, that success in today's marketplace is increasingly dependent on an organization's ability to become a master of knowledge management (Scott 1998, Hansen, Nohria, and Tierney 1999, Huseman and Goodman 1999). Mastery of knowledge management assists an organization in its pursuit of innovative and entrepreneurial growth strategies that are critical to the organization's survival (Nonaka and Takeuchi 1995).

One component of an organization's knowledge management strategy is knowledge transfer. Knowledge transfer refers to an organization's ability to assimilate, adapt, and improve on another organization's existing technological processes and products. This definition assumes that modification and further innovation of the existing technology is a component of the knowledge transfer process (Zander 1991). Pursuant to Bresman, Birkinshaw, and Nobel's (1999) findings, we suggest that knowledge transfer refers to knowledge that is shared from either or both directions following an acquisition. Knowledge transfer may move from the target to the acquirer, from the acquirer to the target, and ultimately back and forth. Reciprocal knowledge transfer, in which knowledge is transferred back and forth between the target and the acquirer, ,has the greatest influence on value creation since it is through this transfer process that new knowledge emerges (Bresman, Birkinshaw, and Nobel 1999).

Knowledge transfer and acquisitions

A fundamental reason for all acquisitions is the anticipation that the acquisition will result in value creation of some kind. From a knowledge transfer perspective, value creation results from the integrated organization's ability to share and leverage information, resources, and expertise in order to identify and implement new products and processes that will increase the competitive advantage of the organization. In the literature, this process has also been referred to as capability transfer where value creation is fundamentally dependent on the integrated organization's ability to create, transfer, assemble, integrate, and exploit knowledge assets (Haspeslagh and Jemison 1991, Inkpen 2000).

Because of this implicit connection between knowledge transfer and value creation, there has been an increase in research on knowledge transfer in M&As (i.e. Coff 1993, Lubatkin and Lane 1996, Singh and Zollo 1998, Birkinshaw 1999, Bresman, Birkinshaw, and Nobel 1999, Chaudhuri and Tabrizi 1999, Ranft and Lord 2000, Vermeulen and Barkema 2001). The focus of most of this research has been on disentangling the connection between knowledge transfer and value creation. Furthermore, the empirical research that has been conducted on this topic has primarily employed quantitative methods that rely on questionnaire data and the use of large data sets. Because of these conceptual and empirical limitations, most of the research on knowledge transfer and acquisitions has not captured the social and interpersonal strategies involved in the knowledge transfer process (Empson 2001a). As a result, existing research has not been able to provide much insight into why knowledge transfer does or does not occur in the context of an acquisition and the factors that influence this process (Bresman, Birkinshaw, and Nobel 1999).

Only recently have a few researchers begun to examine the factors that influence knowledge transfer in acquisitions. For example, Schoenberg (2001), in a study of knowledge transfer by European acquirers, found that an organization's ability to successfully transfer knowledge consistently fell short of expectations. Barriers such as limited absorptive capacity, poor relationships between the acquirer and the target, as well as causal ambiguity regarding the nature of the knowledge to be transferred, accounted for some of the difficulties. Bresman, Birkinshaw, and Nobel (1999) in their study of knowledge transfer in international acquisitions, found that there are two distinct patterns of knowledge transfer following an acquisition. Relevant to this study, these researchers found that tacit knowledge transfer (i.e. the transfer of technical know-how, technical expertise) is best facilitated by intensive communication during and after the integration process. A well-managed integration process that relies on visible leadership, communication, and the use of integrating mechanisms such as joint development teams, job rotations, and joint meetings will lead to higher levels of knowledge transfer (Bresman, Birkinshaw, and Nobel 1999).

The Bresman, Birkinshaw, and Nobel study (1999) underscores tacit knowledge transfer following an acquisition is primarily dependent upon individual organizational members, and the social relationships in which these individuals and their knowledge are embedded. These findings draw attention to the role that the creation of a new social community of practice has in facilitating knowledge transfer following an acquisition. The term, community of practice, refers to an informal group in which participants share understanding about what they are doing, and what that means for their organization and larger community (Lave and Wegner 1991). Communities of practice are not formally delineated organizational groups. Rather, they exist purely in the minds of the members and the relationships they have with each other (Liedtka 1999). Furthermore, communities of practice emerge over time among individuals who need to connect as they face similar challenges and try to achieve similar goals (Lesser and Prusak 1999).

While communities of practice have been identified as fundamental to the development and transfer of knowledge (i.e. Brown and Duguid 1991, Lave and Wegner 1991), the informal nature of a community of practice emphasizes the challenge that such a community poses for a newly integrated organization. To facilitate knowledge transfer following an acquisition, managers must facilitate the formation of a community of practice. However, because communities of practice cannot be formally created and managed, integration managers cannot simply dictate the formation of such a community through the redesign of new work groups. Instead, managers must find informal ways to encourage such a community to evolve on its own.

Two factors that may be particularly important in facilitating the emergence of a community of practice following an acquisition include the creation of a trusting climate and the development of a shared identity among organizational members from both the acquirer and the target. Often individual organizational members will only participate in knowledge exchange when they share a sense of identity or belonging with their colleagues (Kogut and Zander 1996). Trust is another prerequisite to the development of a community of practice, and to the flow of knowledge among organizational members (Davenport and Prusak 1998). Without trust, organizational members may be concerned about whether or not their knowledge-sharing activities will be recognized and rewarded by the organization (Davenport and Prusak 1998, Nahapiet and Ghoshal 1998). Unfortunately, the acquisition process, which is often disruptive and highly stressful, does not create a context for the establishment of trust and shared identity among the integrated organizations. The challenge is how to best manage the integration process so that it supports the development of trust and a shared identity that will facilitate the emergence of an integrated community of practice. Without the formation of this community of practice, knowledge transfer is not likely to occur following the acquisition.

Conceptual framework: Communities of practice facilitating knowledge transfer

Bower (2001) emphasizes that different types of acquisitions have fundamentally different value creation propositions that merit being studied and managed differently. In technology-intensive industries, the issue of knowledge transfer is particularly important to acquisitions as an organization's ability to compete is often dependent upon its abilities to develop innovative technologies which requires knowledge transfer, learning, and innovation. Increases in R&D capabilities, which frequently provide the rationale for acquisitions in technology-based companies, are inherently dependent on knowledge transfer (Hitt et al. 1991). Thus, for acquisitions in technology-intensive industries it is imperative that we develop a better understanding of why knowledge transfer does or does not occur following an acquisition.

Because there is limited research on the factors that influence knowledge transfer following an acquisition (Bresman, Birkinshaw, and Nobel 1999), we applied an inductive approach to carry out our research. Our primary focus was on understanding why knowledge transfer did or did not occur following an acquisition, and on the influence that the integration process had on these knowledge transfer activities. Although this was an inductive study, we did rely on a general conceptual framework to guide the design of our research.

Following from the communities of practice literature, this study is based on the premise that the formation of a community of practice is likely to facilitate knowledge transfer following an acquisition. Previous researchers have emphasized that knowledge transfer is fundamentally an interpersonal process (Leonard-Barton 1995,

Empson 2001a) and, as such, we were interested in the link that individuals might play in the relationship between communities of practice and knowledge transfer following an acquisition.

Methodology

To fully explore the complexity of the relationship between acquisitions and knowledge transfer, we used a multi-site, multi-researcher, case-based methodology (Yin 1984, Eisenhardt 1989). The strategy underlying case study research is to focus on understanding the unique dynamics present within single case settings of the phenomenon under investigation. Theory is generated through an inductive process of analyzing within-case data, and then searching for patterns across cases. Larsson (1993) has suggested that case methodology is particularly useful in the study of M&A, as it enables the researcher to explore the processes through which synergies are identified and actualized. In spite of Larsson's advocacy, a case methodology has only been used in a limited number of M&A research studies (i.e. Larsson 1989, Larsson and Finkelstein 1999, Empson 2001b).

Research sites

We used three selection criteria to identify the cases that form the basis for this study. First, to compare the similarities and differences across different types of technology-intensive industries, we stratified our cases across multiple industries. In the end, we selected research sites from three different technology-intensive industries: computer storage, computer hardware, and biotechnology. Our second selection criterion related to time lapse from the acquisition announcement. Because previous researchers have suggested that knowledge transfer is not likely to occur in the first few months following the acquisition close date (Bresman, Birkinshaw, and Nobel 1999), we wanted to study organizations that were at least one-year post-acquisition close. In the end, our research sites ranged from one year to six years post closing date. Finally, we selected research sites based upon preliminary discussions with the acquirer that part of the strategic rationale for the acquisition was an expectation that it would lead to the development of innovative products and processes. We stratified our sample using the first criterion (industry mix) and selected only those cases that met the second (time lapse) and third criteria (strategic intent). This approach is consistent with case study methodology, as it allows us to better explore the patterns that exist across the cases with the goal of improving the validity and generalizability of the findings from this study.

Research design

The three in-depth case studies that are presented here were developed using interview data along with archival data from public and privately held documents. Depending on where each case fell in the data collection cycle, between 10 and 40 organizational members were interviewed. For the first case (Case A in Tables 8.1 and 8.2), we interviewed more participants in order to obtain clarity on the specific factors that were

Table 8.1 Descriptive information regarding case studies

	Industry	Value-creation proposition	Revenue in year before acquisition
Case A:	Computer storage	Gain access to technological capabilities that would lead to product line expansion	Acquirer: $7 billion Target: $1.5 billion
Case B:	Hardware–software	Gain capabilities in the software and services end of the business. Increase competitive position in changing technological market	Acquirer: $72 billion Target: $1 billion
Case C:	Biotechnology	Gain access to scientific expertise in an emerging segment of the market	Acquirer: $353 million Target: $79 million

Table 8.2 Data description

	Case A: Computer storage	Case B: Software	Case C: Biotechnology
Target interviews	19	7	10
Acquirer interviews	20	3	4
Total interviews	39	10	14
Data collection timetable	1.5 years post closure	6 years post closure[1]	1 year post closure

[1] While this case was six years post closure, for the first four years following the acquisition the two firms were completely independent organizations. It was only in the past two years that the two organizations have been integrated and opportunities for collaboration and innovation have appeared.

influencing knowledge transfer following the acquisition. After the first case study was written and data analyzed, the researchers revised the interview protocol to focus more specifically on those aspects of the acquisition process that had emerged as being most relevant to knowledge transfer. Descriptive information for each of the three cases is presented in Tables 8.1 and 8.2.

All of the interviews followed a semi-structured format and lasted 60–90 minutes. The interviews focused on three general themes: the participants' perceptions of the acquirer and target companies at the time of the acquisition; the integration process; and collaborative behavior and knowledge transfer activities that had (or had not) occurred between the target and the acquirer following the acquisition. For each of the research sites, organizational members from different levels and departments from both the acquirer and the target company were interviewed in order to develop the internal validity of each case.

Data analysis

Data analysis began, using a within-case sampling frame (Miles and Huberman 1994). The interviews were transcribed and data were coded using the qualitative software package Atlas TI. Coding themes were developed based upon the specific research questions we began with, in addition to new themes emerging from the data. Once coding was completed, in-depth case studies were written for each of the three cases that highlighted the perceptions of the organizational members, integration process, and knowledge transfer opportunities that arose as a result of the acquisition. Data analysis continued with a between-case approach, in which the researchers looked for similarities and differences across the cases in order to develop a more robust theoretical frame.

During this period of data analysis, the researchers used a complement of insider and outsider perspective to help maximize data validation (Evered and Louis 1981). Part of the original research design was for the researchers to alternate in taking the lead role in data investigation for each of the research sites. This alternation process was particularly useful during data analysis, as one investigator had an insider perspective on the case while the other investigator had an outsider perspective. Once a theoretical frame was established for each of the cases, the researchers then discussed these interpretations with organizational members from the different research sites. These discussions helped the researchers further refine their theoretical frames and their interpretations of the data. This approach has been identified as a useful technique for developing clarity and validity in research that involves a cultural or interpretivist perspective (Louis 1981).

Results

In all of the cases we studied, the value-creation proposition that justified each of the acquisitions included the expectation that the acquisition would lead to innovative activities and increased R&D capabilities. The dealmakers who oversaw each acquisition explicitly stated that they had hoped the acquisition would enable the acquirer to expand its current product and/or service offerings, and to integrate complementary expertise from the merging organizations to develop new, innovative products and services. So, in order for these acquisitions to lead to new service and product offerings, knowledge transfer needed to occur between the merging partners.

In exploring the factors that influenced knowledge transfer following an acquisition, we found a few interesting patterns in our research. Most importantly, we found that knowledge transfer was primarily dependent on the actions of individual organizational members who chose to engage in knowledge transfer activities. While senior managers did not directly control the extent to which individual organizational members engaged in knowledge transfer activities, they could influence these individuals through their management of the integration process. When the integration process was managed such that it facilitated the emergence of communities of practice between the target and the acquirer, we found more instances of individual organizational members engaging in knowledge transfer activities. The community of practice facilitated more individuals to engage in knowledge transfer activity and it created a positive organizational climate in which other organizational members were more supportive of those individuals who were engaging in knowledge transfer activity.

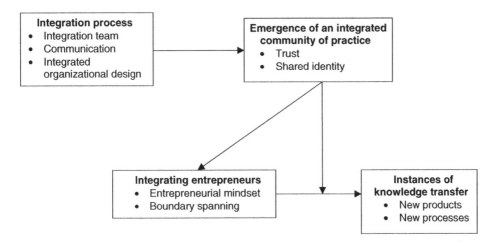

Figure 8.1 Conceptual framework

In Figure 8.1 we present a graphical overview of how the integration process influences individual behavior and knowledge transfer activities following an acquisition. Below, we describe in more detail the behavior and mindset of those organizational members who engaged in knowledge transfer activities. We then discuss how the integration process influenced the emergence of a community of practice which enabled these organizational members to build knowledge transfer opportunities.

Integrating entrepreneurs: Individuals creating knowledge transfer opportunities

Across all of our cases, the one consistent reason participants gave for why knowledge transfer activities occurred following an acquisition, was that knowledge transfer was primarily dependent on the actions of individual organizational members. Knowledge transfer opportunities arose because individual organizational members saw opportunities and chose to pursue these opportunities. The question that remained was: What distinguished those individuals who engaged in knowledge transfer activities from those who didn't and how did the integration process influence these individuals?

In trying to determine why some individuals were more likely to engage in knowledge transfer activities than others, we found that individuals who engaged in knowledge transfer activities were similar in two very important ways. First, these individuals had similar cognitive mindsets that enabled them to embrace new opportunities. We refer to this as an entrepreneurial mindset. Secondly, these individuals engaged in similar boundary-spanning behavior that built bridges between the necessary parties, which fueled knowledge transfer.

Because entrepreneurial mindset was one of the similarities among individuals who engaged in knowledge transfer activities, we refer to these individuals as integrating entrepreneurs. This term is adapted from Empson's work (2001b), where she used the term "integration entrepreneurs" to refer to those organizational members who advanced the integration process by engaging colleagues from the merging partners. It is important to note that in contrast to Empson's work, we use this term to refer to those organizational members who support value creation following the integration process by advancing knowledge transfer opportunities. In the following section, we discuss in greater detail the two characteristics these integrating entrepreneurs shared: an entrepreneurial mindset and engaging in boundary-spanning action.

Entrepreneurial mindset. Organizational members who engaged in knowledge transfer activities first and foremost had an entrepreneurial mindset. Entrepreneurial mindset describes individuals who are able to act quickly under pressure, think creatively about new products and services, behave flexibly when competitors strike, and take appropriate risks for appropriate rewards (Timmons 1999). Rather than focusing on the stress and uncertainty that might result from the acquisition (for both the target and the acquirer), these organizational members approached the acquisition as an opportunity for themselves and their team. The following quotes illustrate how participants from each of the cases either exhibited or described this mindset:

> *Case A*: "(Integrating entrepreneurs) are people who are aggressive, who are not set in their ways, who are open to change and new ideas, as long as those new ideas make sense from the – make sense to them from a corporate perspective – i.e. the profitability of the company, or success of the company, or success of their particular group. People who aren't stubborn" (Director, Engineering)

> *Case B*: "… and so the value creation is also what their product can do by being able to be used in other joint efforts on a go-forward basis. I think also that there are a lot of R&D folks whose expertise can blend into our group and projects that alone we could not have had the resources to fund" (Engineer)

> *Case C*: "They're (the individuals who engaged in knowledge transfer activity) just smart people looking for innovation … It wasn't that much of an extension of their normal working model" (Vice President, R&D)

Part of being opportunistic also meant that integrating entrepreneurs tended to be very objective, whether it was in evaluating organizational members, the technology, or the product opportunities of the merging partner. Integrating entrepreneurs were not territorial. They did not care if an idea or a team member came from their organization, or from that of the merging partner – they were simply focused on putting together the best team that would most effectively capitalize on new opportunities. These integrating entrepreneurs also tried to cultivate this mindset among their colleagues. The following quotes illustrate this component of entrepreneurial mindset:

> *Case A*: "He was very focused on specific talent: picking up a talent of a particular individual that they might not have had or one area that they might not have, he didn't care if it was our talent, their talent or an outside talent" (Senior Engineer)

Case B: "Most of them [sales teams] are very, very protective and territorial about it and what I saw in one sales leader for example, he could visualize the future and say, you know, it really is going to be good for everyone if we can work together and work closely together and the sooner we can the better" (Vice President, Sales)

Case C: "I learned the more you treat it like a merger the better you are. People who are more able to even-handedly pick talent from either side or even-handedly evaluate a system and kind of let the best process win, they did better [at creating knowledge transfer opportunities]" (Director, R&D)

The third component of this entrepreneurial mindset was integrating how entrepreneurs approached their acquisition partner, with a more complex perspective. Often organizational members in one of the acquisition partners would look at the financial performance, market position, or technological reputation of the other partner and assume these signs indicated the partner employed inferior organizational members who could not bring any value to the merging organizations. Organizational members who had an entrepreneurial mindset had a much more complex perspective of their merging partners. These organizational members recognized that poor organizational performance did not translate to poor individual performance. In fact, these organizational members often believed that poor organizational performance translated to good individual performance in spite of poor management. Organizational members with this complex thinking were able to approach their acquisition partner with a more open mindset enabling them to uncover untapped opportunities and hidden talent in the acquisition partner.

Case A: "I am one of those people who pursued relationships because I just, you know, I know that with that many people working at the acquirer, they can't all be idiots. There have got to be people who want to make something good happen and people who are worth knowing. All sorts of reasons to look for the opportunities to engage instead of hiding because I think people did to an extent" (Director, Marketing)

Case C: "You know, when you do these things, people come to rely on rocks. But what we found was that if you looked under lots of rocks we found great things that people hadn't even thought of – product opportunities!" (Director, Manufacturing)

In summary, organizational members with an entrepreneurial mindset saw the acquisition as an opportunity for developing and promoting new technologies and processes, expanding R&D, and pursuing new business opportunities. Having an entrepreneurial mindset meant that integrating entrepreneurs focused on identifying new opportunities as a result of the acquisition. They were open to all new ideas regardless of their origination, and they could evaluate their acquisition partner with a complex perspective that separated individual and organizational performance.

Boundary-spanning actions.   With this entrepreneurial mindset in hand, integrating entrepreneurs engaged in specific actions that facilitated knowledge transfer. While there were some differences in how these individuals approached knowledge transfer, the one common activity of the integration entrepreneurs was boundary spanning. Following the acquisition, integrating entrepreneurs pursued relationships with the merging partner that supported knowledge transfer and new value creation.

Previous research has suggested the central role that boundary-spanning managers play in the knowledge transfer process (Tushman and Scanlan 1981). Relative to the M&A literature, it has been suggested that the integration manager and other formal leaders need to act as boundary spanners to help the integration process (Bahde 2001). However, our findings indicate that boundary spanning is an important role, not just for formal leaders of the integration process, but also for individual organizational members. The bridges integrating entrepreneurs create connect individual organizational members who have complementary or supplementary knowledge so that they can build social relationships that support the knowledge transfer process.

It is particularly important to note the informal nature of these boundary-spanning activities. In all of our cases, the integrating entrepreneurs engaged in these activities, not because they were formally supported through meetings or training programs, but because individuals believed these relationships would support product and process innovations. The following quotes illustrate the informal nature of these boundary-spanning activities:

Case A: "In the media services group, they actually called up and said, 'Hey, we understand that you have some really neat servers. And right now we're buying servers from somebody else. And wouldn't it be better if we kind of kept it under our dome? Within the family? Great.' So we did it. They initiated the call. Also the whole engineering interaction – it really came about because my boss knew the General Manager and Director of that group of the division and was interacting with him. And said, 'Hey you're off trying to do this stuff and you're having some trouble. We do this for a living. Maybe we should get the groups together.' And so she hosted a meeting where myself and some of my counterparts went down – and we sat and chatted" (Engineer)

Case B: "… so it was really more two engineering teams in two different cities that said, 'Our challenge here is to bring these attributes to our database and the industry's leaders, in doing that, sit out on the West Coast, and we both work for the same company.' So it was actually at an engineering level that that connection was made" (Engineer)

Case C: "They [integrating entrepreneurs] are a little bit sensitive to the operational issues. If you really get how a business runs, you understand that A talks to B, B talks to … you know, if you understand all those linkages you are more apt to know how to short-circuit a new person into the existing processes. You are able to think systematically about what needs to happen to make these guys [the target employees] part of the team" (Vice President, R&D)

Integrating entrepreneurs supported the knowledge transfer process by building networks and relationships that enabled organizational members from the merging firms to come together, share knowledge, and develop new opportunities. A knowledge-based view of the firm stresses the importance of all employees who possess critical individual or team expertise and skills (Ranft and Lord 2000). Integrating entrepreneurs were essential for leveraging this expertise in the newly integrated organization. Fueled with their entrepreneurial mindset, integrating entrepreneurs built networks between the target and the acquirer so that organizational members could share knowledge and resources and begin generating new value opportunities.

In summary, these results recognize knowledge transfer occurred as a result of actions that individual integrating entrepreneurs chose to take. These integrating

Table 8.3 Case comparison

	Case A: Computer storage	Case B: Software	Case C: Biotechnology
Integration process	Barrier to emergence of a community of practice	Initially a barrier to emergence of a community of practice but changing	Facilitator to emergence of a community of practice
Integrating entrepreneurs	Few references to integrating entrepreneurs	Initially few references to integrating entrepreneurs	Large number of references to integrating entrepreneurs
Knowledge transfer activities	Low levels of knowledge transfer activity	Initially low levels of knowledge transfer activity though increasing	Immediate, high levels of knowledge transfer activity

entrepreneurs with their entrepreneurial mindsets, and their ability to create connections between the merging organizations, yielded knowledge transfer opportunities. It is important to note that our findings suggest that individual organizational members acting on their own initiative had the greatest influence on knowledge transfer following an acquisition. The question that remains is: How did the actions that were taken by senior managers during the acquisition process influence the integrating entrepreneurs?

Integration process: Creating a community that supports integrating entrepreneurs

While we did find examples of integrating entrepreneurs in all three cases, there was variance across the three cases in terms of both the quantity of integrating entrepreneurs who existed, as well as their ability to successfully engage other organizational members to support the knowledge transfer opportunities that they identified. As Table 8.3 outlines, the cases were categorized as low, medium, and high levels of knowledge transfer depending on the extent to which participants could identify integrating entrepreneurs and depending on the amount of knowledge transfer activities that were identified. Because of these differences, we then focused our data analysis efforts on identifying why there were substantially more instances of integrating entrepreneurs engaging in knowledge transfer activities in Case C: Biotechnology than in Case A: Computer storage or even Case B: Hardware–Software.

Based upon further analysis of participants' descriptions of the acquisition integration process and those factors that participants identified as influencing knowledge transfer, we found that differences across the three integration processes either facilitated or hindered integrating entrepreneurs and their ability to leverage knowledge transfer opportunities. When the integration process was managed in such a way that it enabled the emergence of a community of practice among the two organizations, integrating entrepreneurs were more successful at leveraging knowledge transfer opportunities (such as was found in Case C: Biotechnology). When the integration process was managed such that it hindered an integrated community of practice from forming, there were fewer instances of integrating entrepreneurs and the organization was less open to the activities of these individuals (as was found in Case A: Computer storage and to a lesser extent Case B: Hardware–Software). In the following section, we discuss how the integration process, and specifically the integration team, did or did not facilitate the emergence of an integrated community of practice in the cases we studied.

Integration team composition.   Often, the most visible and immediate symbol of the new social order following an acquisition is the integration team. One of the first decisions that must be made following an acquisition is: Who will lead the integration team, who will comprise the team, and how will the process unfold? Some organizations decide that the team and the decisions regarding integration should be made by the acquirer's organizational members while other organizations decide that these teams should be more jointly represented by both the target and the acquirer.

While the importance of the integration team has been discussed extensively in the acquisition literature (i.e. Bower 2001, Marks and Mirvis 1986), most researchers focus on the impact this team has on the success of the integration process. The need to appoint strong organizational leaders who are well respected and who can make important decisions has been highlighted as critical to managing a successful integration process. In this study, we also suggest the integration team is important because the structuring of the team can facilitate the emergence of an integrated community of practice. The following quotes illustrate how in the three cases the design of the integration team sent very different messages regarding the formation of communities of practice:

> **Case A**: "The team was created and when we started it we were just the acquirer's people. Then you were suppose to bring in – connect to your counterparts in the target – but they weren't on the team. They were the designated people beyond" (Director, Human Resources)

> **Case B**: "The approach that was taken was to ensure that the two organizations would be kept at arm's length to avoid any conflict in those corporate styles. The risk that was being managed was that by integrating the target into the acquirer quickly it would have caused people to leave the target organization. So the approach in terms of integration was to ensure that the acquirer brought the financial support to the target but allowed the target to continue in a way that wouldn't compromise the target's culture" (Associate Director, Engineering)

> **Case C**: "We immediately put a transition team in place and we took people from each of the functional areas within the target and put them on the transition team. And their counterparts within our organization were on the transition team. We met every week in person for about three months and we alternated between our site in Massachusetts (the acquirer) and the target's site in Connecticut" (Vice President, R&D)

As these quotes illustrate, the cases varied in the extent to which the two integration teams were equally represented by members from both the acquirer and the target. When the integration team was dominated by the acquirer or was managed such that the intent was to limit contact between the target and the acquirer, a clear message was sent to organizational members that management was not trying to develop an integrated community between the acquirer and the target (Cases A and B). In contrast, in Case C, a joint integration team with representation from both the acquirer and the target suggested that the merging partners would be seen as equals in the new organization. This message facilitated the emergence of a community of practice.

Integration team communication.   The integration team could also facilitate or hinder the emergence of a community of practice through the communication messages that they deliver both internally and externally to the organizations. As the following quotes illustrate, the communication messages delivered in each of the cases varied in the extent to which they did or did not support the development of a community of practice.

> *Case A*: "They [the integration team and senior managers] need to be very aware that anything that they say in the press in a public forum has a huge impact on morale, both positive and negative. It would have been very easy for them to say things positive about the target. It would have gone a long way for morale and kind of the trust, if you will, of the group" (Senior Developer)

> *Case B*: "A number of strong leaders at the target did not exemplify any interest in being integrated with the rest of the acquirer. That was demonstrated in their actions" (Sales Director)

> *Case C*: "What went well was we were able to get people to understand the strategic objectives of why we were putting the companies together and to get people excited about the potential of the companies coming together in a way that would make us more successful than we had been in the past" (Chief Scientist)

When the message was communicated that the integrating partners were not being viewed as equals or that an integrated organization would not be advantageous, these messages hindered other organizational members from forming an integrated community of practice.

Organizational members did not see value in creating a new, shared identity that would be the basis for the community of practice (Cases A and B). However, when a message was delivered that facilitated the formation of a new, shared identity between the target and the acquirer, it set the stage for the emergence of an integrated community of practice.

The integration team and the new organizational design.   Finally, the integration team also influences the emergence of a community of practice through the new organizational design that they create. As the integration team creates a new organizational structure, they decide who will take on what roles, who will report to whom, and how the differentiated groups will be integrated. The integration team also decides whether leadership positions in the acquirer should be taken on by formal leaders in the target, whether groups will be integrated from the two companies, and whether leaders from the two organizations may be transferred to create more linkages in the newly integrated organization. These design decisions are important, not only because they define the strength of the new organizational structure, but also because organizational structures guide organizational members' interpretations (Ranson, Hinings, and Greenwood 1980). As the following quotes illustrate, the different designs of the integrated organizations also sent different messages regarding the emergence of an integrated community of practice.

> *Case A*: "The greater the influence of people that have a relationship there, the greater the ability to make things happen. So it would have really helped if some of our senior guys had been given positions there (with the acquirer)" (Engineering Manager)

> *Case B*: "It's well known that the acquirer had kind of an arm's length relationship with us for the first few years of post acquisition. But I think we learned later that we probably missed out on opportunities to leverage one another. We overstepped the length of that distance" (Engineer)

> *Case C*: "We've tried – the rep level is very balanced. At the regional manager level, we have one of the target's regional managers and four of the acquirer's managers. Another of the target's managers had come over to run the marketing team ... so we've got a real mix of talents and we've leveraged those in a way that I think is synergistic" (Marketing Manager)

To summarize, the integration team, the communication they provided, and the structures they designed served as either a barrier or facilitator to the emergence of a community of practice. This community of practice then influenced integrated entrepreneurs and their ability to engage in knowledge transfer activities. In Case A: Computer storage, the appointment of the integration team and their approach to working with the target hindered the emergence of an integrated community of practice. Organizational members from the target and the acquirer were not treated as equals, which prevented trust and a shared identity from developing and prevented organizational members from creating an integrated community of practice. In Case B: Hardware–Software a slightly different message was sent. In this case, the design of the integration team sent the message to organizational members that the merging organizations would remain as separate and distinct entities. This separate structure prevented a shared identity from forming among organizational members, which hindered the emergence of an integrated community of practice. In Case C: Biotechnology the design of the integration team sent a very different message regarding the development of a community of practice. In this organization, the team composition, the communication the team delivered, and the new organizational design facilitated the formation of trust and a shared identity among organizational members. This in turn supported the emergence of an integrated community of practice among the acquisition partners.

As prior research has stated, without the development of a community of practice that is categorized by a trusting climate and a shared identity, it is difficult for an acquisition to result in knowledge transfer opportunities (Kogut and Zander 1996). The findings from our study support this premise. However, we also found that the community of practice does not directly influence knowledge transfer opportunities. Instead, the community of practice creates a climate for integrating entrepreneurs to appear and enables them to engage in knowledge transfer activities.

Discussion

The results from the three cases we profiled indicate that knowledge transfer following an acquisition primarily resulted from individual organizational members engaging in individual action. Through their entrepreneurial mindset and their boundary-spanning actions, integrating entrepreneurs created knowledge transfer opportunities following the acquisition. While senior managers' actions did not directly influence these integrating entrepreneurs, they did indirectly influence them through their management of the integration process. When the integration process was managed such that it supported the development of an integrated community of practice between the target and the acquirer, more integrating entrepreneurs appeared and they were more successful at influencing other organizational members to engage in knowledge transfer activities.

There are some limitations to this research. Most importantly, our case studies rely primarily on the use of qualitative data and not on the combination of qualitative and quantitative data that has been advocated by some researchers (i.e. Larsson 1993). In addition, given the retrospective nature of our study we had to rely on participants' memories of the integration process that may have occurred between one to five years previously. Hence, we believe future research on the relationship between the acquisition process and knowledge transfer would benefit from taking a longitudinal perspective. While we acknowledge these limitations, we believe the findings from this study do provide insight into why some acquisitions are more likely than others to yield knowledge transfer opportunities.

The importance of individuals in acquisition value creation

Discussions of value creation following an acquisition usually follow from a strategic perspective of mergers and acquisitions. This perspective emphasizes the structured, planned nature of the integration process, and emphasizes that when an acquisition is founded on a solid value proposition and that acquisition is well managed, the acquisition has a strong chance of resulting in value creation. Unfortunately, most acquisitions are not as successful as they might be. As such, researchers continue to look for ways to explain what actually does occur more accurately. The findings from our study suggest that value creation following an acquisition cannot be planned and managed; rather it is an emergent process. Value creation results from entrepreneurial integrators taking action to engage in the knowledge transfer process. These individuals engage in specific boundary-spanning activities that create new opportunities for the firm. The organization has very little to do with managing, organizing, or even directing the action of these individual organizational members.

Not only is the value-creation process more emergent than planned, the individuals who play the most significant role in influencing this process are not the ones who are most frequently studied. Academics and practitioners have frequently highlighted the important role that formal leaders and senior management play in managing and guiding the integration process to ensure that value is created. More recently, researchers have also focused on the leadership role of the integration managers who are formally charged with overseeing the integration process (Ashkenas and Francis 2000, Bahde 2001). Although these formal leaders do play an important role in managing the integration process and its influence on value creation, we also found that individual organizational members who are more informal leaders play an equally important role in this process. These individuals who are guided by their entrepreneurial mindset span boundaries, which facilitates communication, builds relationships, and generates knowledge transfer activities. Because of their intimate knowledge of which employees possess critical expertise and skills, these informal leaders are an important link for creating a new social order that facilitates knowledge transfer. Future research would benefit from understanding more about who these integrating entrepreneurs are, how they influence the knowledge transfer process, and ultimately how organizational leaders can create organizational structures and processes that facilitate this type of behavior.

Facilitating a community of practice: The link to knowledge transfer

While researchers have highlighted the influence of the integration process on knowledge transfer and value creation following an acquisition (Hitt et al. 1991, Haspeslagh and Jemison 1991), we have not developed strong theoretical frames for why or how this occurs. A recent exception is work by Ranft and Lord (2002) where they develop a series of propositions regarding the influence that speed, communication, autonomy, and retention of acquisition integration have on knowledge transfer. Similar to the work by Ranft and Lord (2002), the findings from this study provide new insight into the relationship between the integration process and knowledge transfer following an acquisition.

Specifically, we suggest that the formation of an integrated community of practice is the critical link between the integration process and knowledge transfer. While the integration process cannot dictate the formation of an integrated community of practice, a well-managed integration process can set the stage for such a formation. When the integration process is managed in such a way that it creates a climate of trust, and facilitates the formation of a shared social identity among organizational members, the integration process supports organizational members' creation of a community of practice between the acquirer and the target. This community of practice encourages the emergence of integrating entrepreneurs, and also creates a climate that supports the activities of these individuals. Future research would benefit from exploring further the link between the integration process and the formation of a community of practice. A number of important questions remain unanswered. How is the community of practice sustained over time? How quickly can a community of practice begin to form and to what extent will it influence people's desire from both the acquirer and the target to remain and support the new organization following the acquisition? Finally, if as we have suggested, these processes simply emerge over time due to critical individuals, how can the organization act in more formal ways beyond the integration team's role to facilitate the emergence of communities of practice and support knowledge transfer? Answers to these types of questions will not only further our conceptual understanding of the phenomenon, they will also influence acquisition management practice which is in need of pragmatic direction.

While there continues to be a great deal of research on mergers and acquisitions, our research emphasizes there are still important aspects of these change processes that are not well understood. In particular, we believe there should be a continued emphasis on the knowledge transfer process and not just whether it leads to value creation but how it occurs following a merger and how it leads to value creation. In addition, we believe there is a need to focus more on the emergent nature of value creation following an acquisition and how individuals and communities of practice factor into this process.

Note

This chapter was supported through a grant from Babson College, Center for Technology and Enterprise. In addition, the authors would like to acknowledge the assistance we received from Zachary Dorr, Denise Murray, Farshad Rafii, Mandi Rutledge, and Rene Treiser; and from our colleagues in the Boston Writing Forum: Erica Foldy, Tammy MacLean, Sharon Rogolsky, Jenny Rudolph, and Steve Taylor.

References

Ashkenas, R.N. and Francis, S.C. 2000. Integration managers: Special leaders for special times. *Harvard Business Review*, 6(78): 108–17.

Bahde, K.P. 2001. *Synergy is Created, not Imagined: Towards Theoretical Progress in the Integration of Mergers and Acquisitions*. Unpublished 2nd qualifying exam at Benedictine University.

Birkinshaw, J. 1999. Acquiring intellect: Managing the integration of knowledge-intensive acquisitions. *Business Horizons*, 42(3): 33–42.

Bower, J.L. 2001. Not all M&A are alike – And that matters. *Harvard Business Review*, 93–101.

Bresman, H., Birkinshaw, J., and Nobel, R. 1999. Knowledge transfer in international acquisitions. *Journal of International Business Studies*, 30(3): 439–62.

Brown, J.S. and Duguid, P. 1991. Organizational learning and communities-of-practice. *Organization Science*, 2(1): 40–57.

Cannella, A.A. Jr. and Hambrick, D.C. 1993. Effects of executive departures on the performance of acquired firms. *Strategic Management Journal*, 14: 137–52.

Cartwright, S. and Cooper, C.L. 1990. The impact of mergers and acquisitions on people at work: Existing research and issues. *British Journal of Management*, 1: 65–76.

Cartwright, S. and Cooper, C.L. 1992. *Mergers and Acquisitions: The Human Factor*. Oxford, UK: Butterworth Heineman.

Chaudhuri, S. and Tabrizi, B. 1999. Capturing the real value in high-tech acquisitions. *Harvard Business Review*, 77(5): 123–30.

Coff, R. 1993. *Corporate Acquisitions of Human-Asset-Intensive Firms: Let the Buyer Beware*. Unpublished doctoral dissertation, University of California, Los Angeles.

Davenport, T.H. and Prusak, L. 1998. *Working Knowledge: How Organizations Manage What They Know*. Boston, MA: Harvard Business School Press.

Eisenhardt, K.M. 1989. Building theories from case study research. *Academy of Management Review*, 14(4): 532–50.

Empson, L. 2001a. Mergers between professional services firms: Exploring an undirected process of integration. In C. Cooper and A. Gregory (eds.), *Advances in Mergers and Acquisitions*. New York: JAI Press, pp. 205–38.

Empson, L. 2001b. Fear of exploitation and fear of contamination: Impediments to knowledge transfer in mergers between professional services firms. *Human Relations*, **54**(7): 839–62.

Evered, R. and Louis, M.R. 1981. Alternative perspectives in the organizational sciences: "Inquiry from the inside" and "inquiry from the outside." *Academy of Management Review*, **8**: 385–95.

Hambrick, D.C. and Cannella, A.A. Jr. 1993. Relative standing: A framework for understanding departures of acquired executives. *Academy of Management Journal*, **36**: 733–62.

Haspeslagh, P.C. and Jemison, D.B. 1991. *Managing Acquisitions: Creating Value Through Corporate Renewal*. New York: Free Press.

Hansen, M., Nohria, N., and Tierney, T. 1999. What's your strategy for managing knowledge? *Harvard Business Review*, 106–16.

Hitt, M.A., Hoskisson, R.E., Ireland, R.D., and Harrison, J.S. 1991. Are acquisitions a poison pill for innovation? *Academy of Management Executive*, **5**(4): 22–34.

Huseman, R.C. and Goodman, J. 1999. *Leading with knowledge: The Nature of Competition in the 21st Century*. Thousand Oaks, CA: Sage.

Inkpen, A.C. 2000. Learning through joint ventures: A framework of knowledge acquisition. *Journal of Management Studies*, **37**(7): 1019–30.

Jemison, D.B. and Sitkin, S.B. 1986. Corporate acquisitions: A process perspective. *Academy of Management Review*, **11**(1): 145–63.

Kogut, B. and Zander, U. 1996. What firms do. Coordination, identity, and learning. *Organization Science*, **7**(5): 502–18.

Larsson, R.1989. *Organizational Integration of Mergers and Acquisitions: A Case Survey of Realization of Synergy Potentials*. Lund, Sweden: Lund University Press.

Larsson, R. 1993. Case survey methodology: Quantitative analysis of patterns across case studies. *Academy of Management Journal*, **36**(6): 1515–46.

Larsson, R. and Finkelstein, S. 1999. Integrating strategic, organizational, and human resource perspectives on mergers and acquisitions: A case survey of synergy realization. *Organization Science*, **10**(1): 1–16.

Lave, J. and Wegner, S. 1991. *Situated Learning*. Cambridge, UK: Cambridge University Press.

Leonard-Barton, D. 1995. *Well Springs of Knowledge: Building and Sustaining the Sources of Innovation*. Cambridge, MA: Harvard Business School Press.

Lesser, E. and Prusak, L. 1999. Communities of practice, social capital, and organizational knowledge. *Information Systems Review*, **1**(1): 3–10.

Liedtka, J. 1999. Linking competitive advantage with communities of practice. *Journal of Management Inquiry*, **8**(1): 5–16.

Louis, M.R. 1981. A cultural perspective on organizations: The need for and consequences of viewing organizations as culture-bearing milieux. *Human Resources Management*, **2**: 246–58.

Lubatkin, M.H. and Lane, P.J. 1996. Psst … The merger mavens have it wrong! *Academy of Management Executive*, **2**(4): 295–302.

Marks, M.L. and Mirvis, P.H. 1986. *Joining Forces: Making One Plus One Equal Three in Mergers, Acquisitions, and Alliances*. San Francisco: Jossey-Bass.

Miles, M. and Huberman, A.M. 1994. *Qualitative Data Analysis: An Expanded Sourcebook*. Thousand Oaks, CA: Sage.

Nahapiet, J. and Ghoshal, S. 1998. Social capital, intellectual capital, and the organizational advantage. *Academy of Management Review*, **23**(2): 242–66.

Nonaka, I. and Takeuchi, H. 1995. *The Knowledge Creating Company*. New York: Oxford University Press.

Ranft, A.L. and Lord, M.D. 2000. Acquiring new knowledge: The role of retaining human capital in acquisitions of high-tech firms. *Journal of High Technology Management Research*, 11(2): 295–319.

Ranft, A.L. and Lord, M.D. 2002. Acquiring new technologies and capabilities: A grounded model of acquisition implementation. *Organization Science*, 13(4): 420–42.

Ranson, S., Hinings, B., and Greenwood, R. 1980. Structuring of organizational structures. *Administrative Science Quarterly*, 25: 1–17.

Schoenberg, R. 2001. Knowledge transfer and resource sharing as value creation mechanisms in inbound continental European acquisitions. *Journal of Euromarketing*, 10(1): 99–114.

Scott, M. 1998. *The Intellect Industry: Profiting and Learning from Professional Services Firms*. New York: Wiley.

Singh, H. and Zollo, M. 1998. The impact of knowledge codification, experience trajectories, and integration strategies on the performance of corporate acquisitions. *Academy of Management Best Paper Proceedings*.

Sirower, M. 1997. *The Synergy Trap: How Companies Lose the Acquisition Game*. New York: Free Press.

Timmons, J.A. 1999. *New Venture Creation: Entrepreneurship for the 21st Century*. Boston, MA: Irwin McGraw-Hill.

Tushman, M.L. and Scanlan, T.J. 1981. Boundary-spanning individuals: Their role in information transfer and their antecedents. *Academy of Management Journal*, 24(2): 289–305.

Vermeulen, F. and Barkema, H. 2001. Learning through acquisitions. *Academy of Management Journal*, 44(3): 457–76.

Yin, R. 1984. *Case Study Research*. Beverly Hills, CA: Sage.

Zander, U. 1991. *Exploring a Technological Edge – Voluntary and Involuntary Dissemination of Technology*. Stockholm, Sweden: Stockholm School of Business.

CHAPTER NINE

Does It Pay to Capture Intangible Assets Through Mergers and Acquisitions?

Asli Musaoglu Arikan

Abstract

The resource-based view suggests that firm-specific intangible assets are more likely to be sources of sustainable competitive advantage. Mergers and acquisitions (M&A) allow access to the targets' asset bases. The purpose of this chapter is to determine the long-run performance effects of acquiring intangible versus tangible assets through M&A. Findings show that, on average, buyers of highly intangible targets experience an economic loss of 12 percent, whereas buyers of highly tangible targets break even over the five years following the announcements. The methodology used to measure long-run abnormal returns eliminates various biases associated with calculating cumulative abnormal returns over long horizons.

The resource-based view suggests that firm-specific intangible assets are more likely to be sources of sustainable competitive advantage (Barney 1991a, Wernerfelt 1984). How do firms come to possess intangible resources? Intangible (Itami, 1987, uses the term "invisible") assets are accumulated through either a direct route in which a firm takes explicit actions such as choosing a technology for research and development; or an indirect route (operations), in which assets are accumulated as byproducts of daily operations (Itami 1987). For example, Honda's experience in motorcycle production in the United States eased its entry into the automobile market (Pascale 1984).

Accumulation and maintenance of intangible assets through operations is a longer process, yet the results are arguably more reliable (e.g. word-of-mouth customer appreciation is much more effective than a television advertisement in convincing potential customers). Internal processes, such as R&D and employee training, develop intangible assets such as know-how, patents, innovativeness, employee commitment, and satisfaction. One of the direct methods of acquiring/developing intangible assets is through mergers and acquisitions. Acquiring firms come to possess the tangible and intangible assets of the target firms, but should the concentration of intangible assets matter at all regarding long-run post-event economic performance?

The existing literature on M&A and performance provides one consistent finding: On average, shareholders of target firms earn significant economic gains whereas shareholders of acquiring firms break-even (Jensen and Ruback 1983, Jarrell, Brickley, and Netter 1988). In fact, Jensen and Ruback (1983) interpret this general finding as evidence that the market for corporate control, "the arena in which alternative management teams compete for the rights to manage corporate resources" (1983: 6), is efficient.[1] It is important to take into account that the bulk of this literature looked at the daily stock returns in the couple of days around the M&A announcement. The fundamental reason why this approach was taken, is that the market is assumed to incorporate the expected net present value of the gains (losses) due to the M&A activity, which renders longer post-merger analysis irrelevant. If we relax the assumption of markets being perfectly efficient to semi-strong efficient,[2] and assume that agents in the markets for corporate control have private information, then there is the possibility of immediate reaction to a corporate announcement to deviate from the efficient outcome. It is widely accepted that managers have private information about their firm-specific resources, capabilities, and growth options. It is logical to assume that the M&A activity is a highly complex investment, which affects the acquirer in many aspects. It is also probable that the effects of M&A activity will unfold over a longer period after the event, thus warranting the interest in long-run performance following the M&A activity.

The purpose of this chapter is to determine the long-run performance effects of acquiring intangible assets versus tangible assets through M&A activity. The first section presents the theoretical background including the characteristics and the economic valuation of intangible assets. This is followed by theoretical background on M&A activity as a mechanism for firm growth. The second section discusses data, methodology, and the model. The third section presents the results and the final section discusses managerial and theoretical implications of the results.

Theoretical Background and Hypotheses

Assets fall into three categories (Lindenberg and Ross 1981): (1) those that are sold in the market and make up what is traditionally known as the capital stock; (2) special factors of production which lower costs relative to those of competitive or marginally competitive firms – such resources are valued at their cost-reducing abilities (e.g. a river whose water acts as a natural coolant); and (3) special factors of production that the firm possesses, which act as barriers of entry to the competitors and generate abnormal returns. Intangible assets are more likely to be in the third category, and such assets would have different economic value for different owner firms, thus creating resource heterogeneity and non-redeployability. Itami defines intangible assets as information-based resources such as technology, customer trust, brand image, corporate culture, and management skills (Itami 1987: 12). According to Itami (1987), the main difference between the tangible and intangible assets is that tangible assets, such as plant, equipment, raw materials, employees, financial capital have to be present for the business operations to take place whereas intangible assets, such as know-how, innovativeness, patents, brand equity, employee motivation and commitment, and customer service are necessary for competitive success.

Intangible sources of firm value are of a differential character, in that the advantage of those firms who own them may lead to competitive disadvantage of those who do not (Veblen 1908). Conversely, tangible resources would not lead to competitive advantage over firms that lack such resources. The main reason is that the price charged by the owners of those tangible resources in factor markets would be equal to the income that would be generated by the buyers of those resources in product markets. Also, if the assets of the target have high redeployability (high ratio of tangibles), then acquiring such targets would be, on average, equivalent to internally developing the same resources because the costs associated with both methods would be approximately the same.

There have been systematic efforts to distinguish the types of assets (tangible or intangible) and their effects on the firm's competitiveness (e.g. Hall 1992, 1993). Prahalad and Bettis (1986) emphasize a "dominant logic" as an intangible asset that could be shared between firms through diversification to create economic value. Firms that develop their core competency, defined as "the collective learning in the organization, especially how to coordinate diverse production skills and integrate multiple streams of technologies", are more likely to have a strategic advantage over their competitors (Prahalad and Hamel 1990: 82). According to the resource-based logic, resources that are rare, valuable, and inimitable are the real sources of competitive advantage (Barney 1991a, 1991b). Of these firm-specific resources, intangible assets are more likely to be the source of sustainable competitive advantage because it is difficult and more time-consuming to accumulate. Villalonga (1999) tests this assertion by using the predicted value from a hedonic regression of Tobin's q as a measure of resource intangibility and finds supporting results.

Intangible assets provide simultaneous uses and they are both inputs and outputs of business activities. Moreover, these intangible assets are likely to be causally ambiguous (Dierickx and Cool 1989) making them less likely to be imitated by competitors (Barney 1991a). Therefore, firms that seek to internalize intangible assets through acquiring highly intangible targets are, on the one hand, more likely to create future growth opportunities. On the other hand, they are more likely to suffer from potential pricing, integration, and maintenance problems of the targets due to causal ambiguity, complexity, and tacitness of the very same intangible assets.

Knowledge, a highly important firm-specific intangible asset, has been developed as a reason for the firm's existence (Conner and Prahalad 1996, Liebeskind 1996, Spender 1996) as well as the likely source of competitive advantage. Liebeskind conceptualized firms as structures to keep knowledge proprietary (1996).[3] Conner and Prahalad (1996) argued that absent opportunism firm organization would provide a better mechanism to allow an owner to provide his/her knowledge as an input in the team production setting, with higher value than in a market setting. As we know, information and knowledge are, although factors of production, unlikely to have a market clearing price because their economic value is context- and owner-specific. On the other hand, precisely this ambiguity may allow firms to create competitive advantage by accumulating productive intangible assets. Given this, how would a strategic factor market for knowledge and more generally for intangible assets work?

It could be that the firm is an internal market for knowledge that decreases the inefficiencies of the market for knowledge. Once an individual offers his/her knowledge to the team production, the internal processes would translate it into a firm-specific knowledge base (Kogut and Zander 1992). Highly specific knowledge would be harder to transmit because fewer parties other than the innovator can benefit from the application of that knowledge (Henderson and Cockburn 1996, McEvily and

Chakravarthy 2002). If the firm is an accumulation of idiosyncratic knowledge that is valuable, how can other firms access the focal firm's specific knowledge base to enhance their current knowledge stock? One of the direct methods is to pursue M&A activity and try to internalize knowledge-intensive targets. Such target firms are necessarily the ones with highly intangible asset stocks.

M&A activity alters the composition of firm assets through large-scale investments. Since governance is costly, the general rule is to reserve complicated forms of financing for complicated investments (Williamson 1991). "Expressed in terms of asset specificity, fungible assets can be leased, semi-specific assets can be debt financed, and equity is the financial form of last resort – to be used for assets of a very non-redeployable kind" (Williamson 1991: 84).[4] Non-redeployability also suggests that the value of the assets in its first-best use is significantly higher than the value of the same assets in its second-best use. Therefore, we would expect non-deployable assets that are financed by equity to be intangible assets. It is also the case that firms with highly intangible assets have unrealized growth potential for the future. One would ask why would the shareholders of the highly intangible target firms sell their claims if the firm has truly valuable growth opportunities? Conversely, why would the acquirer be willing to finance the target's existing growth opportunities when there is collateral value associated with the target's asset base that could compensate the buyer as an insurance policy would?

Lang, Stulz, and Walkling (1989) state that well-managed bidders (high Tobin's q) benefit positively from tender offers, especially if the targets were poorly managed (low Tobin's q). Also, well-managed targets benefit less than the poorly managed targets from a tender offer. There are two possible explanations for this finding (Lang, Stulz, and Walkling 1989). First, already well-managed targets cannot be improved further through takeovers. Second, the bidder succeeds in acquiring a high q target because the bidder overpaid for a target that is, in fact, not as valuable. Both explanations need the assumption that the motivation for the takeover is to improve the quality of the management of the target firm. However, there is another possible reason why firms would want to buy targets with high intangibles to internalize those firms' growth potential. Bidder firms aim to grow through buying highly intangible targets ($q' > 1$) to fund otherwise not funded, positive net present value (NPV) projects.[5] Acquirers who buy targets with less deployable (highly intangible) assets foresee some positive NPV projects that only the merged company could undertake.

Intangible assets of a firm, such as R&D projects, patent stocks, and human capital are more likely to be undervalued by the market when another company buys them. Such assets would generally have high firm specificity and therefore lower second-best use which, in turn, leads to the undervaluation. Overall, because intangible assets are more likely to be non-redeployable, the market would discount post-merger market value of equity of the acquirer. Moreover, buying a firm with high intangibles is a more noisy way to obtain a particular subset of intangible assets: buyers also get additional baggage. An alternative and more precise way would be to develop intangible assets internally through firm-specific processes such as employee training and R&D. In this case, because the direct method of internal development would be more precise the abnormal returns are expected to be higher when compared to the abnormal returns to the acquirers of highly intangible targets. One would puzzle over highly synergistic acquisitions even though the target's assets are highly intangible. The only assumption required to follow through with this logic is the following: the potential for synergies is equally likely to exist for both the acquirers of highly intangible targets as well as highly tangible targets therefore the level of intangible assets and thus the non-deployability tips the scale. However, the theory is agnostic about the average direction of this deviation.

Hypothesis 1a: Firms that obtain intangible resources by engaging in M&A activity, on average, will generate negative long-run performance.

Hypothesis 1b: Firms that obtain intangible resources by engaging in M&A activity, on average, will generate positive long-run performance.

One can extend these discussions and findings in the context of M&A and expect that if a firm is buying a highly intangible target, the market reaction is more likely to be less efficient, thus the long-run abnormal returns will be statistically different than zero. On the other hand, if a firm is buying a highly tangible target, the market reaction is more likely to be more efficient, thus the long-run abnormal returns will not be statistically different than zero.

Hypothesis 2:   Firms that obtain tangible resources by engaging in M&A activity, on average, will break even.

Methodology

Event studies are commonly used to gauge the performance implications of major corporate events or decisions, such as earning announcements, acquisitions, stock splits, or seasoned equity offerings. The main concern in these event studies is to determine whether there are abnormal returns associated with the firm-specific events. There is considerable variation among these studies regarding the calculation of abnormal returns and the statistical tests carried out to detect the presence of abnormal returns. In this study, modified Tobin's q measure is used as a proxy for the concentration of valuable intangible assets in the target firms. The analysis is concerned with measuring the abnormal economic performance of the buyers in the long run. The most important step in measuring abnormal performance is to define a theoretically sound benchmark to proxy the expected (average) performance. In this section the discussion and construction of the related variables will be provided. The methodology for calculating long-run buy-and-hold abnormal returns is briefly presented. Also, a brief discussion of the traditional method of calculating long-run abnormal returns and the shortcomings of this method will be discussed.[6] Finally, the data and the test for the hypotheses will be explained.

Valuation of intangible assets

In this chapter, we use Tobin's q (Tobin 1969, Lang, Stulz, and Walkling 1989) as an indicator of the target's intangible assets (Daniel, Hirshleifer, and Subrahmanyam

2001). True q ratio of ith firm is defined as the market value of all financial claims on the firm, MV_i, relative to the firm's total assets calculated as the sum of the ith firm's replacement values of tangible assets T_i and intangible assets I.

$$q_i \equiv \frac{MV_i}{T_i + I} \qquad (9.1)$$

In competitive markets with linear homogeneous production technology that employs optimal level of capital stock, the ith firm's true equilibrium q ratio will be equal to 1 (Megna and Klock, 1993). The MV_i of the target firm is measured as the sum of all outstanding claims on the firm including book value of debt D_i and preferred stock P_i, and market value of common equity C_i. Assuming market efficiency, the firm's future growth potential based on its current asset base is incorporated in its current stock price. Book value of total assets is denoted as A_i.

$$M_i \equiv D_i + P_i + C_i \qquad (9.2)$$

$$D_i \equiv (\text{Current liabilities} - \text{Current assets}) + \text{Book value of inventories} \\ + \text{Long-term debt}$$

Since we do not have the theorized homogeneity in real life due to differences in tax provisions, depreciation schedules, heterogeneous production functions due to firm-specific resources and capabilities, etc. the true equilibrium value of ith firm's q defined by equation (9.1) is unobservable. Therefore one observes:

$$q'_i \equiv \frac{MV_i}{T_i} \qquad (9.3)$$

The replacement cost of tangible assets of the ith firm is approximated by A_i, book value of total assets, because the replacement value of intangible assets is not reflected in the A_i. Chung and Pruitt (1994) developed this approximation. It is not as theoretically correct as the Lindenberg and Ross' (1981) algorithm because the replacement value of assets is not as accurate, but both are highly correlated (Lee and Tompkins 1999, Bharadwaj, Bharadwaj, and Konsynski 1999). Also, the advantage of this approximation is that bidder firms and the investors are most likely to use this simpler formula that requires publicly available financial and accounting data. It is reasonable to assume that the observed q' values will approximate the portion of market value of the firm explained by the firm's tangible assets. If q' is greater than 1 then there are firm-specific valuable intangible assets contributing above and beyond the firm's tangible assets. A q' that is less than 1 would suggest that the firm's tangible resources and capabilities are underutilized or that there are value-destroying intangible resources (e.g. bad management). Such intangible resources, in theory, would have negative replacement value.[7]

Traditional event methodology

The traditional approach in corporate event studies is to calculate cumulative abnormal returns (CAR). A security's performance can only be considered "abnormal" relative to a particular benchmark (Brown and Warner 1980). Therefore, a model generating normal returns (ex ante expected returns) has to be specified. Almost exclusively, all event studies of this kind apply the capital asset pricing model (CAPM) or market model to estimate the normal returns. The method focuses on average market model residuals of the sample securities for a number of periods around the event date. The null hypothesis is such that if there are no significant effects associated with the corporate event, CARs will be a random walk, such that the average residual in the event time are independent and identically distributed, with a mean of zero.

Generally these studies identify $\tau = \pm 5$ or some other shorter window of analysis around the event date of $t = 0$. The main argument behind this identification is that the stock prices reflect the discounted economic value of all future expectations. As discussed earlier, M&A activity is an event that is much more complex than any other corporate event such as an earnings announcement. Also the nature of the event is conducive to exacerbate any potential investor biases such as overconfidence. Therefore, studies as early as 1974 have started looking at longer post-event periods to gauge long-run performance effects of M&A activity (e.g. Mandelker 1974, Dodd and Ruback 1977, Langetieg 1978, Asquith 1983, Bradley, Desai, and Kim 1983, Malatesta 1983, Loderer and Martin 1992, Agrawal, Jaffe, and Mandelker 1992, Gregory 1997, Loughran and Vijh 1997, Rau and Vermaelen 1998).[8] All of these studies used CAR and overall document negative CAR for mergers and positive CAR for tender offers. Also, most of these studies document a less than 3 percent CAR in magnitude for combined M&A activity with varying signs.

Barber and Lyon (1997) documented four types of biases when using the CAR method to determine long-run abnormal returns: (1) measurement bias in the calculation of long-run abnormal returns that causes negatively biased t statistics; (2) new listings and survivor biases occur because sampled firms are tracked for a long post-event period, but firms that constitute the index (e.g. S&P500, equally weighted or value-weighted market indexes) typically include firms that begin trading subsequent to the event month or firms that are delisted subsequently; (3) rebalancing bias arises because the compound returns of a reference portfolio (proxied by a market portfolio, e.g. equally weighted market index) are generally calculated assuming periodic (e.g. monthly) rebalancing to maintain equal weights; and (4) skewness bias arises because the distribution of long-run abnormal stock returns is positively skewed, which also contributes to the misspecified test statistics.

Two other sources of bias that affect the test statistics in long-run performance studies are due to the cross-sectional dependence between firms and the validity of the asset pricing model used to estimate abnormal returns. Since, in this chapter, the expected returns are not estimated by a model such as CAPM, the validity of the model is an irrelevant issue. However, cross-dependence might be a source of bias in the setup of this chapter, although all other sources of bias are eliminated. The main problem is that cross-sectional dependence inflates test statistics because the number of sample firms overstates the number of independent observations. It is especially problematic if there is calendar date clustering (e.g. a high number of announcements per a specific event date) or industry clustering (there are more than 75 industries with no significant clustering of M&A activity in the sample). As long as there is no additional industry clustering or unusual pre-event return performance, the approach used in this chapter will not have the biases due to cross-sectional dependence. Moreover, reference portfolios are formed in each sample year, which also accounts for any cross-sectional dependence due to the event year. An alternative method for calculating long-run buy-and-hold abnormal returns (BHAR) that eliminates these biases using reference portfolios formed by similar firms in terms of their size, as well as their book-to-market ratios, to proxy expected returns to a firm that engages in M&A will be discussed further in detail.

Calculating long-run buy-and-hold abnormal returns

The first issue is to decide on an unbiased measure of long-run abnormal returns that reflects the investor behavior accurately. CARs and BHARs answer two different questions (Barber and Lyon 1997). For example, a test of null hypothesis that the 12-month CAR is zero is equivalent to a test of the null hypothesis that the mean monthly abnormal return of sample firms during the one-year post-event period is equal to zero. On the other hand, the null hypothesis that the one-year BHAR is equal to zero would test whether the mean annual abnormal return is equal to zero. Of course, for detecting/testing long-run abnormal returns the second null hypothesis is relevant. $BHAR_{it}$ are calculated as the difference between the return on buy-and-hold investment in the sample firm and the return on a buy-and-hold investment in an asset portfolio with an appropriate expected return. As shown below the calculation of $BHAR_{it}$, unlike CAR, takes into account the monthly compounding (Barber and Lyon 1997, Lyon, Barber, and Tsai 1999).

$$BHAR_{it} = \prod_{t=1}^{r}[1 + R_{it}] - \prod_{t=1}^{r}[1 + E(R_{it})] \qquad (9.4)$$

This method eliminates the measurement bias due to the realistic compounding. Also, it is imperative to state that this difference in compounding makes CAR a biased estimator of $BHAR_{it}$. Barber and Lyon (1997) compared one-year CAR and one-year BHAR for a random sample of 10,000 observations. Both CAR and BHAR are calculated using equally weighted market index. The authors compared annual CAR and BHAR per portfolio for 100 portfolios, each of which has 100 stocks. Given that, on average, the returns on individual securities are more volatile than the return on the market index, CAR is understated when BHAR is above zero, and overstated when BHAR is below zero (Barber and Lyon 1997). The other biases discussed above stem from the way the reference portfolios are constructed.

The reference portfolios are constructed to eliminate new listings and rebalancing biases (Lyon, Barber, and Tsai 1999). Fifteen reference portfolios are formed based on acquirer firm size and book-to-market ratios in the sixth event month of each sample year (1988, 1989, 1990, 1991). The portfolio membership of each firm in the sample is updated every six months for 10 times in the 60-month post-event period to account for the confounding effects of other corporate events. The returns of the 15 size/book-to-market portfolios are tracked for the period of $\tau = 60$ months.

Long-run returns on each reference portfolio are calculated by first compounding the returns on securities constituting the portfolio and then summing across securities:

$$R_{pst}^{bh} = \sum_{i=1}^{n_s} \frac{\prod_{t=s}^{s+\tau}(1 + R_{it}) - 1}{n_s} \tag{9.5}$$

where n_s is the number of sampled securities traded in month s, the beginning period for the return calculation. The return on this portfolio represents a passive equally weighted investment in all securities constituting the reference portfolio in that period s. With this method there are no new listings and rebalancing biases because there are no out-of-sample new firms added subsequent to period s. $BHAR_{it}$ is calculated using equation (9.4) and the $E(R_{it})$ is proxied by equation (9.5), which were in essence formed by matched control firm technique. Lyon, Barber, and Tsai (1999) show that the use of reference portfolios based on the control firm approach yields well-specified test statistics in both random and size samples.[9]

Sample

For the analysis, recapitalizations, self-tender offers, and repurchasing of common shares are excluded from the sample. A total of 413 M&As that were identified from the Thompson Financial Securities Data, during 1988–91, have stock returns for the preceding 60 months after the announcement date and have target information to calculate q'. This might potentially limit us to draw inferences conditional on the survival of the acquirers. However, because the abnormal returns are not calculated by using a regression model, tests of equality as well as tests to detect abnormal returns would not be affected. Moreover, the benchmark performance for each firm in the sample is also formed within the sample, eliminating any survivorship bias in the calculation of abnormal returns. Financial and accounting data are obtained from COMPUSTAT and the stock returns data is extracted from CRSP tapes using the WRDS database.

Missing returns of the acquirers are replaced with mean return to the monthly reference portfolio return that the company belongs to based on its last reported return. It is in a sense reinvesting the returns from the delisted stock, for that month, on the reference portfolio that the stock belongs to. After excluding the acquirers of target firms for which q' could not be calculated due to non-reported balance sheet items, there were 109 acquirers in $y = 1988$. After calculating $BHAR_{it}$ using equation (9.4), the acquirers were divided into two groups based on the type (high or low q') of targets they bought. Of the 109 acquirers, there are $n_{g1} = 75$ acquirers that bought target firms with $q' \leq 1$ (group $j = 1$), and $n_{g2} = 34$ acquirers that bought target firms with $q' > 1$ (group $j = 2$). For each group j, average monthly $BHAR_{jt}$ are calculated for 60 post-event months as:

$$BHAR_{jt} = \frac{\sum_{i=1}^{n_{jt}} BHAR_{ij}}{n_{gj}} \quad \text{for } t = 1 \ldots 60 \text{ and } j = 1, 2 \tag{9.6}$$

The calculation of $BHAR_{it}$ for the other sample years in the sample period is carried out in the same manner. The resulting pooled dataset has 24,780 firm $\times$ month observations. The frequency statistics per sample year are as follows:

$y = 1988$	$n_s = 109$,	$n_{g1} = 75$,	$n_{g2} = 34$
$y = 1989$	$n_s = 110$,	$n_{g1} = 64$,	$n_{g2} = 46$
$y = 1990$	$n_s = 95$,	$n_{g1} = 47$,	$n_{g2} = 48$
$y = 1991$	$n_s = 99$,	$n_{g1} = 70$,	$n_{g2} = 29$
$y = $ pooled	$n_s = 413$,	$n_{g1} = 256$,	$n_{g2} = 157$

Variables

In Tables 9.1–9.4 various descriptive statistics are presented for the variables used in the analysis as well as some representative variables such as advertisement stock/sales (advstsls); R&D stock/sales (rdstsls); plant, property, and equipment/sales (ppesales); and plant, property, and equipment/assets (ppeasset). The descriptions of the variables are provided in Table 9.1.

Descriptive statistics for the variables are presented in Table 9.2. In this chapter q' is used to approximate the concentration of intangible assets in target firms. However, there are other related variables that have been widely used in the literature to approximate for intangible assets, such as mainly approximating the returns to R&D and advertisement and selling expenditures in terms of net sales. Of course, one has to use the COMPUSTAT data to get the book values reported for the relevant variables. It is logical to assume that the true market values of these intangible assets are more likely to deviate from their book values when compared to other accounts that keep record of more tangible assets such as plant, property, and equipment. Therefore, using book values of R&D and advertisement and selling expenditures would be a less accurate way to determine the value attributable to intangible assets. It would also be appropriate to classify the target firms into highly tangible versus low tangible targets by using the ratio of ppeasset, however, the proportion of missing data would be higher. The additional advantage of using q' is that one would get at the market valuation of intangible assets rather than the book values. However, one has to acknowledge the possibility of high market value, thus high q' due to risk premium. Therefore, it is reasonable to incorporate other proxies for intangible assets and systematic risk factors. If we look at the correlation matrix in Table 9.3, we observe that the advertisement stock/sales is positively correlated $(0.130, p = 0.008)$ with the group membership, q'_{rank}.

We can conclude that it is more likely to have a highly intangible target when that target has a higher ratio of advertisement expenditure accounting for the net sales. It is reasonable to assume that much of advertisement expenditure directly affects brand equity. Moreover, plant, property, and equipment/assets variable is equally and negatively correlated with advertisement stock/sales $(-0.242, p = 0.002)$ and R&D stock/sales $(-0.241, p = 0.002)$, which would be in line with the argument that firms with high advertisement and R&D expenditures over sales, such as consulting firms or high-technology firms, would be less likely to have highly tangible assets such as plant, property, and equipment. One would question the relevance of

Table 9.1   Variables

Variable name	Variable description
Advertisement stock/sales (advstsls)	Target's average advertisement stock ($) over the past five-year period before the announcement (depreciation rate is assumed to be 15%) is scaled by the target's average net sales ($) over the past five-year period before the announcement date
R&D stock/sales (rdstsls)	Target's average R&D stock ($) over the past five-year period before the announcement (depreciation rate is assumed to be 15%) is scaled by the target's average net sales ($) over the past five-year period before the announcement date
Plant, property, equipment/ sales (ppesales)	Target's book value of plant, property, and equipment ($) is scaled by the net sales ($) for the last fiscal-year end before the announcement date
Plant, property, equipment/ assets (ppeasset)	Target's book value of plant, property, and equipment ($) is scaled by the book value of total assets ($) for the last fiscal-year end before the announcement date
Common equity (market value) (C_{it} ($ million))	Acquirer's monthly market value of equity ($) is calculated by multiplying the common shares outstanding (# million) and the stock price per share, for the 60-month period after the announcement date
Common equity (book value) (bookvl ($ million))	Acquirer's quarterly book value of common equity ($) for the 15-quarter (60 months) period after the announcement date. It is assumed that the book value of common equity stays constant during a given quarter
Book-to-market ratio of common equity (btm)	Acquirer's book value of common equity ($) is scaled by the market value of common equity ($) for the 60-month period after the announcement date
Common equity (market value) (Lnmkt)	Natural logarithm of C_{it} ($ million) used for scaling
Tobin's q (q')	Modified Tobin's q is calculated based on Chung–Pruitt approximation
Dichotomy of high vs. low q (q'_{rank})	If $q' < 1$ then $q'_{rank} = 1$, indicating target firms with low intangibles, whereas if $q' > 1$ then $q'_{rank} = 2$, indicating target firms with high intangibles

R&D expenditure as a measure of intangible assets. A better measure would be to construct patent stocks for that subsample, which would allow a more fine-grained classification and understanding of the performance effects of acquiring intangible assets through M&A activity in, especially, high-technology environments.

In Table 9.4 there are some interesting results. In the theoretical setup, we argued that the type of asset-base of the target would have a differential effect on the abnormal returns to the acquirers in the long run. It is important to stress the need to look at the long-run performance to gauge for performance differences between acquirers of highly intangible versus highly tangible targets, because even if we have similar

Table 9.2 Descriptive statistics

	Variable	N	Mean	Std. Dev	Minimum	Maximum
Target Firm	q'	413	1.22	1.41	−0.49	13.07
	q'_{rank}	413	1.38	0.49	1.00	2.00
	advstsls	413	0.01	0.03	−0.02	0.17
	rdstsls	410	0.07	0.45	−0.01	8.43
	ppesales	162	0.67	0.92	0.01	5.16
	ppeasset	162	0.41	0.24	0.01	1.32
Acquirer Firm	C_{it}	24,720	51,844	277,164	0.00	11,333,063
	btm	24,699	1.46	13.43	0.00	385.62
	bookvl	24,780	1,503	3,359	0.00	42,832
	lnmkt	24,699	7.23	2.85	−1.98	16.24
	refrbh	24,780	0.42	0.66	−0.67	5.82
	$BHAR_{it}$	24,780	−0.05	0.96	−6.24	24.62
	$BHAR^q_{it}$	24,780	0.00	0.89	−6.66	24.34

Acquirer firm's variables are calculated monthly for the entire 60-month period after the announcement date. Target firms' variables are calculated using COMPUSTAT and CRSP databases using the last fiscal year-end data before the announcement date.
$BHAR^q_{it}$: For a more conservative test, buy-and-hold abnormal returns are calculated by using reference portfolios that are formed by a three-tier ranking in the order of target's q'_{rank}/size/book-to-market.

Table 9.3 Correlation matrix for target variables

		q'	q'_{rank}	advstsls	rdstsls	ppesales	ppeasset
q'		1.000					
	p-value						
	N	413					
q'_{rank}		0.570****	1.000				
	p-value	< 0.0001					
	N	413	413				
advstsls		0.040	0.130**	1.000			
	p-value	0.423	0.008				
	N	413	413	413			
rdstsls		0.018	0.014	−0.032	1.000		
	p-value	0.713	0.771	0.522			
	N	410	410	410	410		
ppesales		−0.015	−0.017	−0.171*	0.101	1.000	
	p-value	0.845	0.833	0.030	0.202		
	N	162	162	162	162	162	
ppeasset		−0.023	0.044	−0.242**	−0.241**	0.613****	1.000
	p-value	0.770	0.581	0.002	0.002	< 0.0001	
	N	162	162	162	162	162	162

The target firm's variables are assumed to be constant during the 60-month period after the announcement.
**** Significant at the $p = 0.0001$ level. *** Significant at the $p = 0.001$ level. ** Significant at the $p = 0.01$ level. * Significant at the $p = 0.05$ level.

Table 9.4 Correlation matrix

	Target firm's variables						Acquirer firm's variables					
	q'	advstsls	rdstsls	ppesales	ppeasset	C_{it}	btm	bookvl	lnmkt	R^{bh}_{psT}	$BHAR_{it}$	$BHAR^{q}_{it}$
C_{it}	0.038****	0.088****	0.012	−0.024	−0.086****	1						
p-value	< 0.0001	< 0.0001	0.062	0.019	< 0.0001							
N	24,720	24,720	24,540	9,720	9,720	24,720						
btm	−0.016	0.058****	0.009	−0.020	0.000	−0.020	1					
p-value	0.012	< 0.0001	0.178	0.046	0.963	0.002						
N	24,699	24,699	24,519	9,719	9,719	24,699	24,699					
bookvl	0.033****	0.175****	−0.023***	0.012	0.030**	0.153****	0.209****	1				
p-value	< 0.0001	< 0.0001	0.0002	0.249	0.003	< 0.0001	< 0.0001					
N	24,780	24,780	24,600	9,720	9,720	24,720	24,699	24,780				
lnmkt	0.082****	0.091****	−0.044****	−0.034**	−0.086****	0.400****	−0.112****	0.376****	1			
p-value	< 0.0001	< 0.0001	< 0.0001	0.001	< 0.0001	< 0.0001	< 0.0001	< 0.0001				
N	24,699	24,699	24,519	9,719	9,719	24,699	24,699	24,699	24,699			
R^{bh}_{psT}	0.013*	0.010	−0.013*	−0.029**	−0.037***	0.158****	−0.040****	0.058****	0.245****	1		
p-value	0.045	0.118	0.045	0.004	0.000	< 0.0001	< 0.0001	< 0.0001	< 0.0001			
N	24,780	24,780	24,600	9,720	9,720	24,720	24,699	24,780	24,699	24,780		
$BHAR_{it}$	−0.065****	0.050****	−0.019*	−0.030*	0.031*	0.037****	−0.005	0.010	0.034****	0.261****	1	
p-value	< 0.0001	< 0.0001	0.004	0.003	0.002	< 0.0001	0.448	0.120	< 0.0001	< 0.0001		
N	24,780	24,780	24,600	9,720	9,720	24,720	24,699	24,780	24,699	24,780	24,780	
$BHAR^{q}_{it}$	−0.042****	0.067****	−0.024***	−0.020*	0.058****	0.027****	−0.005	−0.001	0.043****	0	0.819****	1
p-value	< 0.0001	< 0.0001	0.000	0.043	< 0.0001	< 0.0001	0.452	0.934	< 0.0001	1	< 0.0001	
N	24,780	24,780	24,600	9,720	9,720	24,720	24,699	24,780	24,699	24,780	24,780	24,780

The target firm's variables are assumed to be constant during the 60-month period after the announcement. **** Significant at the $p = 0.0001$ level. *** Significant at the $p = 0.001$ level. ** Significant at the $p = 0.01$ level. * Significant at the $p = 0.05$ level. + Significant at the $p = 0.1$ level.

synergies between the two types, the processes which firms need to go through to realize those synergies would be different across these two types of M&A. The bottom line is that in the case of highly tangible targets there is very little that is unknown. However, in the case for highly intangible targets, such as high-technology firms, it is a matter of acquirer's firm-specific capability even to pinpoint the source of economic value because it would not be in the accounting reports. The most important result in Table 9.4 is the relationship between q' of the target and the $BHAR_{it}$ of the acquirer. There is a negative and significant relationship between the level of intangibles of the target before the acquisition and the buy-and-hold long-run abnormal returns, $BHAR_{it}$, to the acquirer of that target (-0.065, $p < 0.0001$). Other variables of the target firms that are used commonly to proxy intangible assets are also significantly correlated with the $BHAR_{it}$. These findings support the need to understand the performance implications of acquiring intangible assets through M&A.

As a more conservative setup, the reference portfolios are formed after acquirers are separated into two groups based on whether the targets were high or low on intangible assets. In each group the method described in the previous section for reference portfolio construction is performed. The buy-and-hold abnormal returns calculated in this fashion are denoted as $BHAR_{it}^q$. If the target's intangible assets have any effect on the buyer's post-even long-run performance by a priori accounting for, this fact should decrease the correlation between $BHAR_{it}$ and q'. Results show that the correlation between $BHAR_{it}^q$ and q' is -0.042 ($p < 0.0001$).

Results

The methodology provides the abnormal returns to an acquiring firm above and beyond the expected returns that would be generated by firms with the same size/book-to-market ranking that employ the same strategy of M&A. Figures 9.1–9.5 show striking differences between the monthly average abnormal returns for each group of acquirers (buyers of highly intangible and tangible targets) in years 1988–91. In each figure, there is a downward trend in the average buy-and-hold abnormal returns to the acquirers of highly intangible targets in the 60-month period after the merger announcement. However in Figure 9.4 there seems to be an outlier month that corresponds to 1996.[10] In Table 9.5, the following null hypothesis, regarding the equality of medians across two time series in each year, is tested for $y = 1988, \ldots,$ 1991, pooled:

$$H_0 : BHAR_{1y} = BHAR_{2y}$$

$$H_a : BHAR_{1y} \neq BHAR_{2y}$$

where $BHAR_{1y}$ is the median of the 60-month time series of average buy-and-hold abnormal returns to the firms that acquired highly tangible targets ($q' \leq 1$) in the year y. Similarly, $BHAR_{2y}$ is the median of the 60-month time series of average buy-and-hold abnormal returns to the firms that acquired highly intangible targets

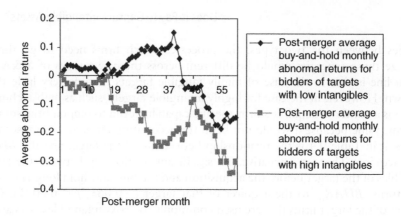

Figure 9.1 Average monthly abnormal returns to the acquirers with announcement year of 1988

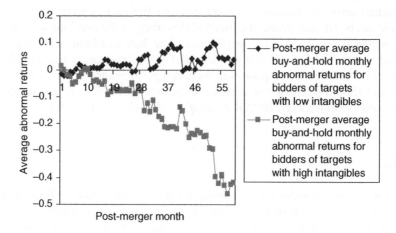

Figure 9.2 Average monthly abnormal returns to the acquirers with announcement year of 1989

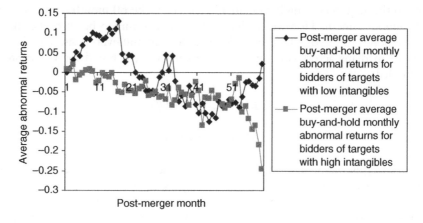

Figure 9.3 Average monthly abnormal returns to the acquirers with announcement year of 1990

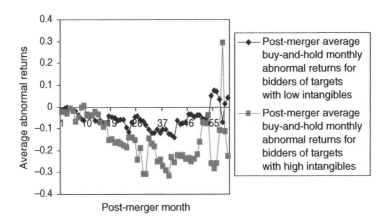

Figure 9.4 Average monthly abnormal returns to the acquirers with announcement year of 1991

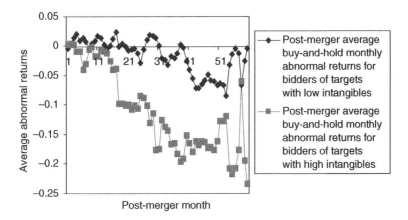

Figure 9.5 Average monthly abnormal returns to the pooled acquirers with announcement years in 1988–1991

Table 9.5 Test of median equality for the 60-month average buy-and-hold abnormal returns

	1988	1989	1990	1991	1988–1991
N					
	60	60	60	60	60
$BHAR_{jy}$ (j = 1, low intangibles)	0.018	0.021	−0.015	−0.046	−0.005
$BHAR_{jy}$ (j = 2, high intangibles)	−0.081	−0.121	−0.049	−0.135	−0.122
Wilcoxon / Mann-Whitney	7.109****	9.067****	3.126**	3.315***	7.041****
Med. Chi-square	43.200****	83.333****	6.533*	4.800*	34.133****
Adj. Med. Chi-square	40.833****	80.033****	5.633*	4.033*	32.033****
Kruskal-Wallis	50.579****	82.259****	9.786**	11.003***	49.613****
van der Waerden	48.222****	72.583****	11.402***	11.106***	47.643****

**** Significant at the $p = 0.0001$ level. *** Significant at the $p = 0.001$ level. ** Significant at the $p = 0.01$ level. * Significant at the $p = 0.05$ level.

Table 9.6 Descriptive statistics for the average monthly buy-and-hold abnormal returns ($BHAR_{j,t}$)

	$BHAR_{1,1988}$	$BHAR_{1,1989}$	$BHAR_{1,1990}$	$BHAR_{1,1991}$	$BHAR_{1,pooled}$	$BHAR_{2,1988}$	$BHAR_{2,1989}$	$BHAR_{2,1990}$	$BHAR_{2,1991}$	$BHAR_{2,pooled}$
Mean (H_0: Mean = 0)	0.040****	0.016***	0.032**	−0.060****	**0.001**	−0.097****	−0.066****	−0.031****	−0.118****	**−0.071******
Median	0.024	0.013	0.041	−0.060	0.002	−0.091	−0.060	−0.034	−0.140	−0.085
Maximum	0.102	0.067	0.130	−0.001	0.023	−0.001	0.014	0.019	0.006	0.004
Minimum	−0.016	−0.022	−0.074	−0.121	−0.032	−0.250	−0.183	−0.083	−0.307	−0.176
Std. Dev.	0.033	0.022	0.056	0.033	0.014	0.078	0.052	0.027	0.089	0.059
Skewness	0.515	0.515	−0.130	−0.239	−0.578	−0.665	−0.600	0.080	−0.397	−0.229
Kurtosis	1.850	2.889	1.919	2.477	2.613	2.229	2.699	1.908	2.197	1.693
Jarque–Bera (H_0: Normal Dist.)	3.577	1.611	1.854	0.753	2.226	3.546	2.295	1.827	1.914	2.880
Probability	0.167	0.447	0.396	0.686	0.329	0.170	0.317	0.401	0.384	0.237
N	36	36	36	36	36	36	36	36	36	36

**** Significant at the $p = 0.0001$ level. *** Significant at the $p = 0.001$ level. ** Significant at the $p = 0.01$ level.

For the $BHAR_{1,pooled}$ series the following null hypothesis regarding the series mean is tested, and we fail to reject. H_0: Mean = 0 (t statistic = 0.31 and p value = 0.76).
For the $BHAR_{2,pooled}$ series the following null hypothesis regarding the series mean is tested, and rejected. H_0: Mean = 0 (t statistic = −7.25 and p value = 0.0001).

($q' > 1$) in the year y. Buy-and-hold long-run abnormal returns, generally, have positively skewed distributions that would violate the normality assumptions, thus negatively biasing the t-statistics (Barber and Lyon 1997). Therefore, test of equality is carried out for the median value rather than the mean value for the series. Overall, nonparametric tests are more powerful for detecting abnormal performance (Barber and Lyon 1996) when compared to the parametric test. The key test statistic reported is one of Wilcoxon signed-ranks nonparametric test,[11] although other equality tests[12] are also reported in Table 9.5. Based on the t-statistics and the associated probabilities, we can reject the null hypothesis at the $\alpha = 0.05$ significance level, for each sample year as well as the pooled series, that the abnormal returns, on average, would be the same for both strategies of buying highly tangible and intangible targets. This result supports the theoretical argument that the concentration of intangible assets in the target firm has a direct relationship to the long-run abnormal returns to the acquirers.

As discussed above, normality of the distribution of long-run buy-and-hold abnormal returns degenerates as we further increase the number of months. Therefore, the sample is restricted to a 36-month period to test for abnormal returns. In Table 9.6, results of the test for normality[13] lead one to fail to reject the null hypothesis of normality. Thus, it is appropriate to carry out the equality of mean tests. In the right-hand side of Table 9.6 results regarding hypotheses 1a and 1b are presented. The null hypothesis is that acquirers of highly intangible targets, on average, would earn zero abnormal returns against the alternative hypotheses that are stated in hypotheses 1a and 1b. Test statistics for this test are calculated for a 60-month series of $BHAR_{2y}$, where $y = \{1988, 1989, 1990, 1991, \text{pooled}\}$. As presented in Table 9.6, the null hypothesis is rejected with at least $\alpha = 0.05$ significance level for each sample year as well as the pooled series. Overall, we can reject the null hypothesis that the mean abnormal return is zero for the acquirers of targets with $q' > 1$. Moreover, hypothesis 1a is supported: Acquirers of highly intangible targets, on average, earn negative abnormal returns (for this sample the range is between -0.031 and -0.118).

This leads to hypothesis 2, which in essence tests whether the average monthly returns for acquirers of low intangibles, $q' \leq 1$, is equal to zero against the alternative hypothesis that the average monthly return for acquirers of low intangibles, q', is not equal to zero. In Table 9.6, the left-hand side panel reports the test statistics that were calculated for a 60-month series of $BHAR_{1y}$, where $y = \{1988, 1989, 1990, 1991, \text{pooled}\}$. As presented, the null hypothesis is rejected for each sample year. It appears that the buy-and-hold abnormal returns to the acquirers of highly tangible targets are dependent upon the event year. Like the stock market, trading assets in markets for M&A have a time-specific component that has to be taken into account when making comparisons across time periods.

In this chapter, due to the method used in the construction of the reference portfolios, in a particular year, y, the time-fixed effects on the abnormal returns calculated in that sample year would be purged out. However, there are macroeconomic business cycles, spanning over multiple years that were not accounted for. Whatever is left that presents itself as statistically significant differences across sample years would be generated by the random effects of the sample year, y. An alternative method would be to construct portfolios by taking into account the business cycles and first grouping acquirers based on the period in which they announced the M&A activity. If we look at the pooled sample and test to see what is happening on average (across sample years) we see that the mean of $BHAR_{1,pooled}$ is equal to 0.001 (t-statistic = 0.31), which fails to reject the null hypothesis. Therefore, hypothesis 2 is supported: Acquirers of low intangible targets, on average, break even (zero abnormal returns). As a robustness check when the same test is carried out with the complete dataset, lumping both sets of acquirers together, the mean of the time series of monthly long-run buy-and-hold abnormal returns is not statistically significant, which confirms the stylized fact that acquirers break even at best.

Discussion

Intangible assets are more likely to be valuable, rare, and hard to imitate, which makes such firm-specific assets potential sources of sustainable competitive advantage. How do firms come to have intangible assets? One method of accumulating intangible assets is through M&A activity. Given the stylized fact that acquirers, on average, break even at best, what would be the performance implications of such corporate activity that acquires highly intangible assets? Both management and financial economics literature are agnostic about the predicted performance outcome of engaging in M&A activity to accumulate intangible assets. Theoretically, intangible assets are more likely to create the potential for growth opportunities. Thus, firms that acquire highly intangible targets try to buy a bundle of growth potentials. However, because, on average, intangible assets are more likely to be non-redeployable without losing significant value of their first-best use, acquirers' post-M&A economic values are more likely to be discounted.

The results show a significant difference between the two types of acquirers. Firms that buy highly intangible targets lose, on average, 12 percent of their economic value over the 60 months following the M&A activity. On the other hand, firms that buy highly tangible targets, on average break even in the long run. Overall, the market for intangible assets seems to be less efficient than the market for tangible assets, in the sense that long-run performance of acquirers will be a result of either a correction of initial expectations of investors or unexpected revelations of unrealized but expected synergies. In future studies, incorporating the financial economics literature helps us tie up some of the loose ends. Daniel and Titman (2001) provide a behavioral explanation and show that investors overreact to intangible information. The findings of this study might be interpreted in this framework as follows: Buyers of highly intangible targets are overvalued at the time of the announcement because investors are overconfident in their ability to evaluate the expected synergies of the M&A activity when the target firm is highly intangible. There is surely more research to be done to understand the dynamics of this corporate activity.

This study empirically shows that engaging in M&As that result in acquiring intangible assets destroys economic value. This is a surprising result in the sense that intangible assets are more likely to provide valuable and new future growth opportunities. Given the findings of this study, one can ask whether or not firms would be better off using M&A activity to utilize their current intangible assets (by buying highly tangible targets), and realize already known growth opportunities, rather than trying to buy intangible assets. Does this mean firms that choose to internally develop intangible assets for future growth opportunities are, on average, more likely to generate positive abnormal returns? If so, highly intangible firms would "cash in" when they become targets because the true market value of the intangible assets cannot be determined through secondary markets such as the stock markets. When such targets are acquired, because the process requires a period of information disclosure and negotiations the market value of the target is appreciated, thus leading to the only too well-known premiums to the targets' shareholders. Clearly, we need to look at the types of intangible assets in this context and their differential effects on acquirer performance. Also, why would the firms still continue to buy highly intangible targets? It might be that those firms would have lost even more economic value if they had tried to develop the same highly intangible asset base of the target internally.

For this sample of buyers, engaging in M&A to buy highly intangible targets, on average, resulted in negative and significant long-run returns. Given this general base, some firms are better at creating value by buying highly intangible targets, because there is a wide variation among this negative mean of long-run performance. Conversely, some firms are worse at doing the same transaction. This heterogeneity in post-event long-run performance of the buyers allows us to conceptualize and further research a firm-specific governance capability that would be a source of competitive advantage. The next step is to identify the components of such a capability and research the possible differences among governance capabilities such as forming alliances and spot market transacting. What is the role of various types of intangible assets in the post-merger long-run abnormal returns and corporate strategy? Can a firm be good at executing multiple governance forms simultaneously or is specializing better?

Notes

I would like to thank Ilgaz Arikan, Brad Barber, Jay Barney, David Hirshleifer, Anita McGahan, Ralph Walkling, Karen Wruck, and the participants at the OSU Strategy Seminar 2001, and M&A Summit 2002 for their helpful comments. The usual caveats apply.

1. For a comprehensive review of this literature refer to Jensen and Ruback 1983, and Jarrell, Brickley, and Netter 1988.
2. Semi-strong efficient markets incorporate all the publicly available information to the stock price, whereas strong efficiency in markets assumes that all the public and private information of agents is incorporated in the stock prices.
3. This assumes, in essence, that there is a fully efficient market for knowledge, and that without the firm the knowledge would have been diffused which is in essence similar to Porter's idea of entry barriers.
4. Emphasis is not present in the original.
5. If high q' measures the growth opportunities stemming from intangible assets, above and beyond the tangible assets, why would the target firm be willing to sell the firm?

For target firms with high intangibles, as the degree of non-redeployability increases, it will be inefficient for debt holders to finance new investments because the increasing risk of default, coupled with high uncertainty regarding the flow of project cash flows, would lead expected value of the debt holders' claims to decline. In such cases target firms would have to forego some of the positive NPV projects because of financing. Where projects face market breakdowns it is efficient to finance it through equity. Therefore, equity financing is an endogenous response to governance needs of suppliers of finance (in this context the bidder firms) who invest in non-redeployable projects. These suppliers are the residual claimants who are awarded "control" over the board of directors.

6. Barber and Lyon (1997) provide evidence that the common techniques used to calculate short-run abnormal returns, when applied over a longer horizon, are conceptually flawed and/or lead to biased test statistics.

7. If we can fully explain the market value of a firm based on its tangible resources then the firm's q' is equal to 1. Megna and Klock state (1993) that the equilibrium value of q' for any firm will change from year to year as there are changes in the mix of the old capital, new capital, and intangible capital, as well as changes in the macroeconomic and regulatory environment. Another source of change in q' are M&As, which are most likely to alter the mix of a firm's asset base.

8. Related studies (Mandelker 1974, Dodd and Ruback 1977, Langetieg 1978, Asquith 1983, Bradley, Desai, and Kim 1983, Malatesta 1983, Agrawal, Jaffe, and Mandelker 1992, Loderer and Martin 1992, Gregory 1997, Loughran and Vijh 1997, Rau and Vermaelen 1998) are reviewed in detail by Robert F. Bruner (2001).

9. Also, if size/book-to-market portfolios are formed by increased number of groupings (thus with lower number of firms in each group) the precision of the reference portfolios increases. In fact this technique can approach to the rule of matching a control firm with 70–130 percent of its size and/or book-to-market ratio. There are 15 size/book-to-market portfolios in this study. The range of number of firms in each portfolio is between 5–7 and the firms in each portfolio are within 70–130 percent range of their size and book-to-market ratios.

10. When the t-statistics are recalculated for 1991 to test the equality between Med_{1t} and Med_{2t} with a restricted sample of 50 months the null hypothesis is still rejected at the $\alpha = 0.01$ significance level. Similar results are obtained when the rest of the t-tests are run based on 50-month samples.

11. Suppose we compute the absolute value of the difference between each observation and the mean and then rank these observations from high to low. The Wilcoxon test is based on the idea that the sum of the ranks for the samples above and below the median should be similar. The P value for the normal approximation to the Wilcoxon T-statistic is reported after being corrected for both continuity and ties.

12. "Kruskal–Wallis one-way ANOVA by ranks" is a generalization of the Mann–Whitney test to more than two subgroups. The test is based on a one-way analysis of variance using only ranks of the data. The Kruskal–Wallis test statistic is calculated by the chi-square approximation (with tie correction). "Chi-square" test for the median is a rank-based ANOVA test based on the comparison of the number of observations above and below the overall median in each subgroup. This test is also known as the median test. Under the null hypothesis, the median chi-square statistic is asymptotically distributed as [(Number of groups) − 1] degrees of freedom.

13. Jarque–Bera is a test statistic for testing whether the series is normally distributed. The test statistic measures the difference of the skewness and kurtosis of the series with those from the normal distribution.

References

Agrawal, A., Jaffe, J.F., and Mandelker, G.N. 1992. The post-merger performance of acquiring firms: A re-examination of an anomaly. *Journal of Finance*, **67**(4): 1605–21.

Asquith, P. 1983. Merger bids uncertainty and stockholder returns. *Journal of Financial Economics*, **11**: 51–83.

Barber, B.M. and Lyon, J.D. 1996. Detecting abnormal operating performance: The empirical power and specification of test-statistics. *Journal of Financial Economics*, **41**(3): 359–99.

Barber, B.M. and Lyon, J.D. 1997. Detecting long-run abnormal stock returns: The empirical power and specification of test statistics. *Journal of Financial Economics*, **43**(3): 341–72.

Barney, J.B. 1991a. Firm resources and sustained competitive advantage. *Journal of Management*, **17**: 99–120.

Barney, J.B. 1991b. The resource-based view of strategy: Origins, implications, and prospects. *Journal of Management*, Special Theory Forum, **17**: 197–211.

Bharadwaj, A.S., Bharadwaj, S.G., and Konsynski, B.R. 1999. Information technology effects on firms' performance as measured by Tobin's *q*. *Management Science*, **45**(6): 1008–24.

Bradley, M., Desai, A., and Kim, E.H. 1983. The rationale behind interfirm tender offers: Information or synergy? *Journal of Financial Economics*, **11**: 183–206.

Brown, S.J. and Warner, J.B. 1980. Measuring security price performance. *Journal of Financial Economics*, **8**: 205–58.

Bruner, R.F. 2001. *Does M&A pay? A Survey of Evidence for the Decision-Maker*. Darden Business School Working Paper.

Chung, K.H. and Pruitt, S.W. 1994. A simple approximation of Tobin's *q*. *Financial Management*, **23**(autumn): 70–4.

Conner, K.R. and Prahalad, C.K. 1996. A resource-based theory of the firm: Knowledge versus opportunism. *Organization Science*, **7**(5): 477–501.

Daniel, K., Hirshleifer, D., and Subrahmanyam, A. 2001. Overconfidence arbitrage and equilibrium asset pricing. *Journal of Finance*, **56**(3): 921–65.

Daniel, K. and Titman, S. 2001. *Market Reaction to Tangible and Intangible Information*. Kellogg Scholl Working Paper.

Dierickx, I. and Cool, K. 1989. Asset stock accumulation and sustainability of competitive advantage. *Management Science*, **35**: 1504–11.

Dodd, P. and Ruback, R. 1977. Tender offers and stockholder returns: An empirical analysis. *Journal of Financial Economics*, **5**: 351–74.

Gregory, A. 1997. An examination of the long run performance of UK acquiring firms. *Journal of Business Finance and Accounting*, **24**: 971–1002.

Hall, R. 1992. The strategic analysis of intangible resources. *Strategic Management Journal*, **13**(2): 35–144.

Hall, R. 1993. A framework linking intangible resources and capabilities to sustainable competitive advantage. *Strategic Management Journal*, **14**(8): 607–18.

Henderson, R. and Cockburn, I. 1996. Measuring competence? Exploring firm effects in pharmaceutical research. *Strategic Management Journal*, **15**: 63–84.

Itami, H. 1987. *Mobilizing Invisible Assets*. Cambridge, MA: Harvard University Press.

Jarrell, G., Brickley, J.A., and Netter, J.M. 1988. The market for corporate control: The empirical evidence since 1980. *Journal of Economic Perspectives*, **2**(1): 49–68.

Jensen, M.C. and Ruback, R. 1983. The market for corporate control: the scientific evidence. *Journal of Financial Economics*, **11**: 5–50.

Kogut, B. and Zander, U. 1992. Knowledge of the firm, combinative capabilities, and the replication of technology. *Organization Science*, **3**(3): 383–98.

Lang, R., Stulz, R., and Walkling, R.A. 1989. Managerial performance: Tobin's q and the gains from successful tender offers. *Journal of Financial Economics*, **24**: 137–54.

Langetieg, T.C. 1978. An application of a three-factor performance index to measure stockholder gains from merger. *Journal of Financial Economics*, **6**(4): 365–83.

Lee, D.E. and Tompkins, J.G. 1999. A modified version of the Lewellen and Badrinath measure of Tobin's q. *Financial Management*, **28**(1): 20–31.

Liebeskind, J.P. 1996. Knowledge strategy and the theory of the firm. *Strategic Management Journal*, **17** (Winter Special Issue): 93–107.

Lindenberg, E.B. and Ross, S.A. 1981. Tobin's q ratio and industrial organization. *Journal of Business*, **54**(1): 1–32.

Loderer, C. and Martin, K. 1992. Post-acquisition performance of acquiring firms. *Financial Management*, **21**: 69–79.

Loughran, T. and Vijh, A.1997. Do long-term shareholders benefit from corporate acquisitions? *Journal of Finance*, **52**: 1765–90.

Lyon, J.D., Barber, B.M., and Tsai, C. 1999. Improved methods for tests of long-run abnormal stock returns. *Journal of Finance*, **54**(1): 165–200.

Malatesta, P. 1983. The wealth effect of merger activity and the objective functions of merging firms. *Journal of Financial Economics*, **11**: 155–81.

Mandelker, G. 1974. Risk and return: The case of merging firms. *Journal of Financial Economics*, **1**: 303–35.

McEvily, S.K. and Chakravarthy, B. 2002. The persistence of knowledge-based advantage: An empirical test for product performance and technological knowledge. *Strategic Management Journal*, **23**: 285–305.

Megna, P. and Klock, M. 1993. The impact of intangible capital on Tobin's q in the semiconductor industry. *The American Economic Review Papers and Proceedings of the Hundredth and Fifth Annual Meeting of the American Economic Association*, **83**(2): 265–9.

Pascale, R.T. 1984. Perspectives on strategy: the real story behind Honda's success. *California Management Review*, **26**: 47–72.

Prahalad, C.K. and Bettis, R.A. 1986. The dominant logic: A new linkage between diversity and performance. *Strategic Management Journal*, **7**: 485–501.

Prahalad, C.K. and Hamel, G. 1990. The core competence of the corporation. *Harvard Business Review*, **68**: 79–91.

Rau, R.P. and Vermaelen, T. 1998. Glamour, value and the post-acquisition performance of acquiring firms. *Journal of Financial Economics*, **49**: 223–53.

Spender, J.C. 1996. Making knowledge the basis of a dynamic theory of the firm. *Strategic Management Journal*, **17** (Winter Special Issue): 109–22.

Tobin, J. 1969. A general equilibrium approach to monetary theory. *Journal of Money Credit and Banking*, **1**: 15–29.

Veblen, T. 1908. On the nature of capital: investment intangible assets and the pecuniary magnate. *Quarterly Journal of Economics*, **23**(1): 104–36.

Villalonga, B. 1999. *Intangible Resources and the Sustainability of Competitive Advantage*. UCLA Working Paper.

Wernerfelt, B. 1984. A resource-based view of the firm. *Strategic Management Journal*, **5**: 171–80.

Williamson, O.E. 1991. Comparative economic organization: The analysis of discrete structural alternatives. *Administrative Science Quarterly*, **36**(2): 269–96.

Culture and Leadership in M&As

CHAPTER TEN

Leadership and the M&A Process

Sim B. Sitkin, Amy L. Pablo

Abstract

Merger and acquisition research has identified the importance of leadership as a critical determinant of M&A activities and outcomes. However, surprisingly little systematic attention has been paid to conceptualizing or studying the effect of leadership on M&A success – either in the academic or in the practitioner literature. In this chapter, we apply a recently proposed leadership framework to suggest how M&A leaders can effectively focus their actions on the problems and facilitating factors arising in the M&A process.

Introduction

Although scholars and practitioners recognize that acquisitions frequently fail to live up to their potential (Larsson and Finkelstein 1999, Sirower 1997), the impact of leadership on acquisition processes and outcomes has not been well developed, or even widely recognized. A review of scholarly and practitioner-focused writing on M&A suggests that others have only occasionally noted the critical import-ance of leadership in M&A success and failure. And, even in those cases where leadership's impact has been acknowledged, past work on M&A has neither examined nor proposed any details concerning what constitutes M&A leadership, or how it might make a difference. In this chapter, we apply a recently proposed leadership framework to advance past research on M&A by suggesting how leadership can effectively focus attention on the problems and facilitating factors arising in the M&A process.

Although the M&A process has been generally underexplored as a factor affecting the outcomes of mergers and acquisitions, research does provide guidance concerning a variety of impediments that might arise in the formulation and implementation of a corporate renewal strategy founded on the use of M&A. While these impediments do not occur to the same extent in all cases, we suggest that M&A process issues and effects can be better understood when we incorporate leadership into our analysis.

Table 10.1   Two samples of M&A key issues

Bower (2001)	Business Week (1995)
1. Acquirer paid too much	1. Inadequate due diligence
2. Friendly deals done using stock perform well	2. Lack of strategic rationale
3. CEO's fall in love with deals and then don't walk away	3. Unrealistic expectations of synergies
	4. Paid too much
4. Integration is hard, but a few do it well consistently	5. Conflicting corporate cultures
	6. Failed to move quickly enough to integrate

Attention to Leadership in the M&A Literature

A review of the academic and practitioner literatures on M&A reveals that discussions of the primary determinants of M&A processes and outcomes rarely even mention leadership. Instead, when they do refer to leadership, they tend to focus exclusively on a highly rationalized notion of strategy development. As shown in Table 10.1, where the literature has identified key M&A factors, the treatment of leadership-related issues has remained narrow ("pay too much") or vague and indirect ("fall in love", "integration is hard"). Although they are not exhaustive, the two lists are representative and illustrate how M&A commentaries sometimes mention leadership, but largely neglect it. Furthermore, in these (and similar) writings, there is little or no direct mention of leadership. Where authors do talk about leadership, they tend to focus very specifically and prescriptively on actions that managers should take, without describing how and what needs those actions meet.

The process perspective on M&A is concerned with how various impediments and facilitators in decision making and behavior evolve over time, and why the evolution occurs as it does. In the capabilities-based view of M&As as a tool for corporate renewal, managers are presumed to be willing to exert leadership to develop a new vision for the combined firms. "The issue of *leadership* and the development of organizational purpose is at the heart of many authors' arguments about the primary responsibilities of senior executives and general managers" (Haspeslagh and Jemison 1991: 356, emphasis added). In their treatise on managing M&As to create value through corporate renewal, Haspeslagh and Jemison (1991: 156) *do* recognize the important effect of leadership on M&A success, noting the criticality of institutional leadership as "the only broad force available to counteract the effects of uncertainty, insecurity, and value destruction, which affect all managers and employees". They conclude their advocacy of the importance of leadership in M&A by contending that "acquisitions are a revealing litmus test that highlight the quality of leadership" (Haspeslagh and Jemison 1991). Despite their strong advocacy, they do not explore any specific ways that leadership might make the difference they recognize as so significant. Unfortunately Haspeslagh and Jemison's relative neglect of the details of leadership's role is reflective of the M&A literature in general, including other authors utilizing the process perspective (e.g. Pablo, Sitkin, and Jemison 1996, Larsson and Finkelstein 1999, Birkenshaw, Bresman, and Hakanson 2000). Overall, the M&A literature contains barely glancing attention to specific ways in which the appropriate application of leadership capabilities can be used to effectively design and implement acquisitions.

Broad pronouncements concerning the criticality of leadership are not, however, universally accepted. There remain some authors who explicitly denigrate the role of leadership as a causal factor in explaining M&A performance. An example is Ashkenas and Francis (2000: 9) who assert that "the business leader's very position of authority often limits his or her ability to facilitate integration". However, as argued in Sitkin and Pablo (2003), while leadership may be less crucial in specific circumstances, when we look beyond attributing explanations for a *single* M&A event or outcome and instead look at how the M&A process is guided, the M&A leadership role clearly draws upon particular sets of value- and knowledge-based capabilities that can help the organization to be more effective. Thus, the process perspective represents an especially apt lens through which to examine the specific leadership attributes that might make managers more effective in this role.

Organizational combinations such as mergers or acquisitions represent a major trans-formational event for organizations and the people in them. Kotter has argued that such significant organizational change requires leadership that facilitates coherence and adaptability (Kotter 1996), both of which have been identified as essential for M&A success (Jemison and Sitkin 1986a). In one of the most well-known and influential early works on the topic of M&A implementation, Kitching (1967) supports these factors as crucial to M&A success stressing the importance of change management to ensure adequate focus in gaining control in the post-acquisition situation.

Current mutual adjustment theories of acquisition performance (Pablo 1994, Isaacs 1999) take into account not only those factors that indicate the *potential* for value creation, but also the processes through which value is *actually* created as synergistic benefits come to be realized. As Hitt, Harrison, and Ireland (2001) note with respect to achieving synergy in post-acquisition integration, managerial actions over and above control are an essential foundation of the value-creation process.

In the acquisitions literature, integration is traditionally largely defined by the degree of intrusion of the acquiring company into the acquired organization (e.g. Sales and Mirvis 1984, Finkelstein 1986, Walsh 1987, Larsson 1989). While the acquiring organization may also experience change as a result of the acquisition, the traditional focus of integration practice and research reflects a primary concern with the extent to which the acquiring organization makes changes in the acquired organization. In this sense, integration has been conceptualized as a varying degree of boundary disruption initiated by the acquiring organization to create mechanisms within the acquired company that facilitate the achievement of parent company goals. This perspective on acquisition integration is one of administrative control, which focuses on integration as the use of formal authority mechanisms to coordinate the goal-directed activities of organizational subunits (March and Simon 1958).

More recent conceptualizations of integration (e.g. Pablo 1994) do not view integra-tion as change solely initiated by an acquiring organization to gain administrative control, but rather as a more complex and interactive mutual adjustment process between the two organizations. From this perspective, integration includes significant change on the part of the acquiring organization, as well as the acquired organization (Haspeslagh and Jemison 1991). This mutual adjustment conceptualization of integration takes into account the relative difficulties of managing given varying degrees of boundary disruption. Engaged mutuality may be managerially more difficult to implement than either a hands-off or an all-encompassing approach, because it implies the need for judgment (e.g. selectivity and restraint in terms of where the acquiree's boundaries will be disrupted and where they will be preserved), and involvement on the part of the acquirer (Bastien and Van de Ven 1986, Haspeslagh and Jemison 1991) – both of which are consistent with a leadership-focused conception of M&A. While leadership may have been necessary, even under unidirectional conceptions of the integration process, it is fundamental to the newer and more ambiguous and emergent conception of M&A.

Why the lack of attention to leadership in M&A literature?

Perhaps the simplest explanation for the lack of attention to leadership in M&A literature is that a literature cannot be expected to incorporate everything. In the *academic* literature, M&A research has drawn from the disciplines of economics and sociology (rather than psychology) for its theoretical and empirical focus. These disciplines tend to mention leadership issues only in passing, rather than making them a core focus, as would be more consistent with the discipline of psychology. Even organizational scientists who have focused on M&A have tended to study cultural fit or the compatibility of other organizational attributes, referring to leadership issues only incidentally. Thus, because of its disciplinary roots, research on M&A has tended to stress the analysis of a number of important issues other than leadership, including firm *valuation* and *financial* performance, *strategic* fit, *organizational* fit, and the management of the M&A *process*. Even in writing utilizing the process perspective (the most recent of the M&A research streams and the one with the strongest ties to psychology), how M&A processes and mechanisms might be enabled through the appropriate use of leadership capabilities has been overlooked.

The process perspective on M&A

Most M&A research has focused on the economics of corporate restructuring. However, a substantial and relatively newer body of research has focused on strategic and organizational aspects of M&A activity that are more directly relevant to M&A leadership. Of particular relevance is the M&A "process perspective" (Jemison and Sitkin 1986a), which combines strategic and organizational views to examine how characteristics of the process itself affect M&A activities and outcomes (see Figure 10.1). The process perspective identifies cognitive and agency problems that affect M&A decision making, and highlights how organizational hubris and fear can affect interactions between two firms in both the pre- and post-combination periods. For example, Jemison and Sitkin (1986a, 1986b) identified cognitive limitations in their development of the process perspective, which they used to explain how activity segmentation

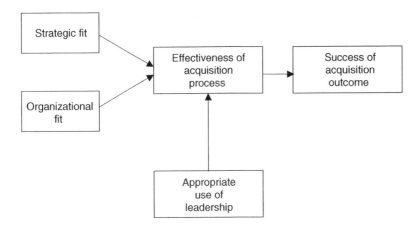

Figure 10.1   Application of leadership to the M&A process

enters into the early phases of M&A processes due to the diverse specializations required to complete a transaction, the time available to decision makers, and the secrecy that must surround the event resulting in potential exclusion of important information.

Other process-related issues influencing pre-acquisition decision making are agency problems of involved decision makers that can result in an escalating momentum to complete the deal when not all information has been adequately taken into account. Finally, when ambiguity is being used strategically by both parties to the negotiations, a potentially high level of uncertainty may remain once the deal is closed. This ambiguity can result in post-acquisition lack of agreement about expectations for success between the involved firms, ultimately resulting in poor performance of the acquisition (Shanley and Correa 1992). Given these conditions, it is not surprising that an acquirer might impose its own administrative systems without due consideration of whether they are really the most appropriate, with this arrogance/defensiveness likely creating the conditions to breed acquiree resistance.

Issues of how risk affects the acquisition process throughout have also been explored to examine how candidate choices are made, how negotiations proceed, and how integration is executed, with risk perception and propensity theorized to have a cascading effect from start to finish (Pablo, Sitkin, and Jemison 1996). The process perspective also highlights why, in order for capabilities to be transferred between organizations in the post-acquisition organization (and value created), the "right" atmosphere must exist. This includes bilateral organizational and cultural understanding, mutual willingness to cooperate, transfer and absorptive capabilities between the firms, adequate slack, and comprehension of M&A synergy dynamics (Haspeslagh and Jemison 1991).

The process perspective on acquisitions has been influential in current research on M&A, but even in this stream of work – where the relevance of leadership is so readily apparent – little attention has been paid to theorizing about or studying leadership.

Figure 10.2   Six-dimension integrative model of leadership
Source: From Sitkin, Long, and Lind (2001)

A Leadership Framework Applied to the M&A Process

Drawing upon Sitkin, Long, and Lind's (2001) integrative model of leadership, Sitkin and Pablo (2003) discussed how the six essential dimensions of effective leadership apply to the M&A context (see Figure 10.2). Personal leadership refers to the idea that it matters that a leader conveys to other organizational members who he/she is, including a sense of personal vision, values, emotions, and beliefs. Relational leadership emphasizes the important role of the leader in forging strong ties with individuals in the organization. Contextual leadership involves creating the situational conditions that enable organizational members to focus and be effective. Inspirational leadership involves building the desire for greatness or excellence by raising expectations and the acceptance of challenges, with enthusiasm and confidence. Supportive leadership involves making others aware of pressing organizational problems and making them secure enough in their own capacity to take appropriate corrective action. Finally, firms are institutional ships and require symbolic leadership at the helm, with the leader acting as steward of the institution, honoring and protecting deeply held community values. In this stewardship role, it is important for leaders to be the chief integrator and balancer, insuring that the multiple elements of leadership described here are drawn together and effectively balanced for a particular situation.

In this chapter, we explore the specific applicability of each of these dimensions to create a better understanding of how leadership affects the M&A process, as

Table 10.2   Key M&A process issues and related leadership dimensions

Key M&A process issues	Relevant leadership dimensions
Instilling a new sense of purpose	*Personal leadership* • personify the new merged entity • let people know who the leader is as a person • convey vision and values
Interface management	*Relational leadership* • context supportive of strategic capability transfer • organizational atmosphere respectful of inter-firm differences • drive to join forces and commit to the new entity
Building credibility	*Contextual leadership* • creates processes that facilitate cooperation and coordination • community builder • creates shared identity through new processes, procedures, and structures that reflect new integration rather than old silos
Choice	*Inspirational leadership* • accepts (even relishes) challenges of M&A • focuses on opportunities as well as threats to success • drives stretch targets and high expectations • builds momentum for aspirational speed, and high strategic and operational goals
Interactions and integration	*Supportive leadership* • builds security • inculcates a sense of collective capability • does not whitewash tough news or decisions, but is honest while being appreciative and supportive
Decision making	*Stewardship leadership* • accepts responsibility for the whole not just favorite parts • assumes role as personification of the new combination and efforts to join forces • expects and moves others to see themselves as responsible for making the new organization work

conceptualized in the M&A process perspective literature. Our analysis is intended to serve two functions. First, by incorporating an explicit model of leadership to revisit M&A process concepts, we hope that key problems in the pre- and post-acquisition stages can be better understood and more effectively studied. Second, we hope to contribute to the understanding of leadership more generally by applying a general model to a phenomenon of significant organizational importance.

Key issues in the M&A process

In the sections that follow, we will examine how the various elements that occur in the process of making and managing mergers and acquisitions can be improved on through the application of appropriate leadership elements. These are summarized in Table 10.2.

Instilling a new sense of purpose.   Process problems in the post-acquisition integration period set in when managers are rigidly fixed in their expectations of what will happen, irrespective of the realities of the situation. Personal leadership can be a strong force in helping the organization adjust to the actualities of post-acquisition requirements. In this context, it matters who the leader is, what their vision is, and how they convey to organizational members who they are, their values, their emotions, and their personal beliefs. The role of the "institutional leader" as communicator of "vision and purpose", including the need to "recognize and address … and articulate new purpose for the combined firms serves to focus and motivate members of the newly formed organization to *want* to be associated with it." Haspeslagh and Jemison (1991: 198) similarly highlight the importance of a leader to manage the integration process: "To manage the integration process, a single manager has to be clearly in the lead."

The neglected importance of this leadership dimension (in practice as well as theory) can be seen in Haspeslagh and Jemison's (1991) description of J&J's acquisition of Depuy ($3.7 billion), where it was a "surprise" that the leader was a "lightning rod for many people's emotions." The importance of this dimension to M&A lies in how personal leadership fosters the loyalty and motivation necessary to create positive emotions and overcome indifferent or negative responses so typical of M&A situations, and thus builds commitment to the organization. Tetenbaum highlights the importance of the leader in her 1999 article, outlining seven key practices for achieving integration and synergies, suggesting that persons merit being followed because of their qualities of "high energy and resilience under stress, their knowledge and experience in translating intent into action, their credibility, and decisiveness". Similarly, Guth (2002) reflects the importance of personal leadership where linking to leaders' values pulls emotions and expectations from dim prospects to strong belief in the possibilities of positive outcomes.

Interface management for value creation.   Preparing the post-acquisition organization for integration requires a transitional stage during which organizational members are readied for strategic capability transfer. Relational leadership is central to this process in creating an organizational atmosphere where there is mutual understanding and a willingness to participate in organization building. Relational leadership concerns building the organization through interpersonal relationships – by fostering interpersonal cooperation and connection, building a shared sense of understanding, and establishing emotional connection and accessibility. Ashkenas and Francis (2000: 112–13) capture this dimension in their description of the Texas Instruments/Unitrode merger as involving building "social connections" through language and culture. Haspeslagh and Jemison's (1991) notion of "interpersonal leadership" as involving helping members to "develop, understand, and embrace the acquisition's purpose" and "to see their role in it" also reflects this idea. Tetenbaum (1999) also acknowledges the need for strong interpersonal and conflict management skills and, in fact, cites managing the information flow as a critical factor in the overall success of an M&A. The tasks associated with these leadership activities are relational in nature, and include communication with employees and attendance of executive staff at events relating to the integration team and customers.

Building credibility in the post-acquisition organization.   What Sitkin, Long, and Lind (2001) refer to as contextual leadership focuses on the role of the leader in creating a milieu that enables organizational members to form a sense of community that allows them to function more effectively as individuals and a collectivity. By focusing, simplifying, and creating a sense of coherence leaders can enable a collective sense of community to emerge, fostering a positive organizational identity that members wish to be a part of (see the description of the Electrolux acquisition of Zanussi in Haspeslagh and Jemison 1991). Leaders have to be credible in building a context about which they can communicate why they have made certain decisions if they are to generate the necessary acceptance and commitment to action among those who are charged with implementation.

Within the M&A literature, this notion has been captured in descriptions of leaders as the chief community builder and architect of the organization's structure, process, and culture (leader as "master designer" (Pablo 1995)). Also under this rubric, we would include such typical M&A issues as redesigned rules, goals, measures, HR policies/procedures, symbols, and ceremonies (Galpin and Herndon 2000), as well as designing the "structure within which the team could function effectively," providing a "road map to help people see the work ahead," and creating common tools, measures, project management discipline to build a sense of coherence. In Tetenbaum's (1999) recipe, this involves building organizational capability and having the right people in the right place at the right time to achieve strategic goals. It means establishing success indicators consistent with business strategy in such a way as to create strategic alignment through the use of appropriate systems and procedures to build strategic leverage and thus produce desired performance. In Galpin and Herndon's (2000) terms, this leadership activity would involve systems for regular integration updates and a planned basis for accountability and recognition in creating and adhering to a new culture.

Choice.   The choices managers make in entering into M&A relationships reflect their competitive stance and how they have chosen to allocate their corporate resources (Haspeslagh and Jemison 1991). Inspirational M&A leadership is an important influence at this point because it determines the direction of the newly combined entity. Through inspirational leadership, a desire for greatness, for excellence by raising expectations, and the acceptance of challenges with enthusiasm and confidence can be engendered at a critical time in the organization's history. Jemison and Sitkin (1986b) describe how Loral Corp CEO, Bernard Schwartz, led his organization to learn to excel by reaching to be worthy of individual stretch acquisition targets as part of a systematic acquisitive strategy. Schwartz identified as an acquisition target the "crown jewel" of a related industry segment and was disciplined enough to inspire and sustain the pursuit of this goal across two intended preparatory acquisitions to position the firm to purchase his ultimate (and original) target.

According to Guth (2002) leadership can be inspirational when it effectively utilizes *logos* (making people aware of how achieving the goals of the organization link to their own goals), *pathos* (linking goals to positive emotions), and *ethos* (linking to the values represented by the leader) to create the new organization's collective mind reflecting knowledge, values, and emotions. Guth suggests that through these "rhetorics" of inspiration, motivation can be used to overcome indifferent or negative responses to the M&A and build commitment to the organization.

Interactions and integration dynamics.   Early in the execution of M&A, the process of building a strong foundation by putting operations on an even keel, taking stock and establishing control, and strengthening the acquired organization (Haspeslagh and Jemison 1991) is enabled through supportive leadership. Providing supportive leadership throughout the M&A process involves making others feel secure enough to take risks by fostering a sense of acceptance, security, personal efficacy, confidence, and willingness to rely on collective understanding. GE Capital created an integrating manager role to fulfill this function in its acquisitions of Gelco in the 1980s and the UK's Burton Group in 1991 by building "connective tissue" that helped each side "understand" the other – by bridging, explaining, and translating (Ashkenas, DeMonaco, and Francis 1998).

In any major change situation, people go through a number of stages, including denial, acknowledgment, and finally acceptance (Kubler-Ross 1997). As part of these stages, individuals' ability to deal with risk and risk-taking will cycle from fear and risk aversion to confidence and opportunity seeking. This is especially applicable to M&A (Pablo, Sitkin, and Jemison 1996). As Haspeslagh and Jemison (1991: 248) advise M&A leaders: "Encourage learning … immediate results may not be as important as a contribution to the company's overall capabilities and options." Tetenbaum (1999) and Marks and Mirvis (1985) similarly stress the importance of handling "post-merger drift" by recognizing that people have experienced a major psychological shock and that, in order to move from total absorption with self to being engaged in the combined entity, significant support is required.

Decision making.   A variety of cognitive and motivational impediments frequently occur during M&A decision making as a result of the nature of the process itself. First, it is complex and requires the input of a number of specialists at different points in time. As all of these individuals may not be members of either of the parties to the transaction, their particular concerns and levels of attention to central issues will be uneven, and the final product may resemble a Frankenstein-like creation rather than the creative improvement envisioned by the deal's designers. Fragmented perspectives resulting from the variety of players, ambiguous expectations reflecting the differences in interpretations of meanings and information, and multiple motives illustrating the diversity of goals held within the organizations are a predictable hazard of the M&A game (Jemison and Sitkin 1986a, 1986b) and, without strong stewardship leadership, may be the rocks on which the combination founders.

Firms are institutional ships and can benefit from symbolic leadership at the helm, with the leader acting as steward of the institution, articulating and communicating to all members of the decision-making team the tacit values and mental models they use to make acquisition plans and decisions (Pablo 1995). According to Galpin and Herndon (2000), part of the leader's role is to foster in others a sense of personal responsibility to the whole and a level of actionable understanding of what is intended so that each member can act in a way that advances movement toward the organization's goals in the acquisition strategy.

Institutional leadership is especially critical in the M&A context because there is such a tendency for value to be destroyed when guidance is lacking (Haspeslagh and Jemison 1991). Mezias, Grinyer, and Guth (2001) note that the leader must personally symbolize the collective identity of the member and the institution. Without such a stewardship role, the firm behaves like a rudderless ship, having lost a sense of identity, a sense of core values, and a sense of individual responsibility for the whole. Haspeslagh and Jemison (1991: 133) highlight the importance of this dimension by describing its absence among financial services executives: "We were cast adrift ... There was no support for us within the firm and nobody understood what we are ... No instruction except to make money." The multifaceted nature of organizational life makes it important for leaders to play the role of chief integrator and balancer, insuring that the multiple elements of leadership described here are drawn together and weighted most effectively for the particular situation.

Discussion

The message for acquisition researchers is clear. Work needs to be done to examine the leadership dimensions present in various acquisition situations, and performance associated with those same acquisitions. Specifically, in order to better understand variations in acquisition performance, an important first step is understanding whether the full set of leadership dimensions proposed here is present, the application of those leadership dimensions, and the effects of those leadership applications.

This research could be carried out in a number of ways. Comparative case study research could be used to evaluate leadership differences between high performing M&A and poorly performing M&A. Based on the findings from that work, measurement of the leadership dimensions should be more understandable, and a survey methodology could be used to examine larger samples of M&A and establish some leadership effect findings that are generalizable. Finally, research in this area would need to be expanded longitudinally to examine the relationships among leadership dimensions and needs at different points in the M&A process, for example in making integration design decisions, carrying out integration implementation activities, and institutionalizing the combined organizational form so as to be able to draw clearer linkages among these variables process issues and performance. If this research were effectively carried out, it would be the first to actually perform empirical research using the process perspective on M&A.

Conclusion

In a worldwide survey of 190 executives conducted by Watson Wyatt for the years 1998–99, 73 percent of respondents cited leadership as the key reason for M&A success (Galpin and Herndon 2000). Yet M&A research has ignored leadership issues. In this chapter, we provide the beginnings of a theory-guided framework for understanding how leadership can influence the M&A process. Our exploration of how specific theoretically based leadership dimensions can mitigate M&A process problems contributes to the further development of the acquisition literature, particularly as we have built upon and extended the reach of the process perspective on acquisitions.

Notes

An earlier version of the paper was presented at the M&A Summit, Calgary, Canada, June, 2002 and at the Academy of Management meeting in Denver, Colorado, August 2002.

References

Ashkenas, R.N., DeMonaco, L.J., and Francis, S.C. 1998. Making the deal real: How GE Capital integrates acquisitions. *Harvard Business Review*, **76**(1): 165–77.

Ashkenas, R.N. and Francis, S.C. 2000. Integration managers: Special leaders for special times. *Harvard Business Review*, **78**(6): 108–17.

Bastien, D.T. and Van de Ven, A.H. 1986. *Managerial and Organizational Dynamics of Mergers and Acquisitions.* Discussion Paper #36, Strategic Management Research Center, University of Minnesota.

Birkenshaw, J., Bresman, H., and Hakanson, L. 2000. Managing the post-acquisition integration process: How the human integration and task integration processes interact to foster value creation. *Journal of Management Studies*, **37**(3): 395–425.

Bower, J. 2001. Not all M&As are alike – and that matters. *Harvard Business Review*, **79**(3): 92–101.

Business Week. 1995. The case against mergers. 30 October: 122–38.

Finkelstein, S. 1986. *The Acquisition Integration Process.* Working Paper, Columbia University.

Galpin, T. and Herndon, M. 2000. *The Complete Guide to Mergers and Acquisitions: Process Tools to Support M&A Integration at Every Level.* San Francisco: Jossey-Bass.

Guth, W. 2002. *A Cognitive Anatomy of Strategic Leadership for Superior Firm Performance.* Presentation at University of Calgary, October, 2001.

Haspeslagh, P. and Jemison, D.B. 1991. *Managing Acquisitions.* New York: Free Press.

Hitt, M.A., Harrison, J.S., and Ireland, R.D. 2001. *Mergers and Acquisitions: A Guide to Creating Value for Shareholders.* New York: Oxford University Press.

Isaacs, W. 1999. *Dialogue and the Art of Thinking Together.* New York: Currency/Doubleday.

Jemison, D.B. and Sitkin, S.B. 1986a. Acquisitions: The process can be a problem. *Harvard Business Review*, March–April: 107–16.

Jemison, D.B. and Sitkin, S.B. 1986b. Corporate acquisitions: A process perspective. *Academy of Management Review*, **11**(1): 145–63.

Kitching, J. 1967. Why do mergers miscarry? *Harvard Business Review*, **45**: 84–107.

Kotter, J. 1996. *Leading Change.* Boston, MA: Harvard Business School Press.

Kubler-Ross, E. 1997. *Death and Dying.* New York: Simon & Schuster.

Larsson, R. 1989. Organizational integration of mergers and acquisitions. *Lund Studies in Economics and Management 7*, Lund University Press.

Larsson, R. and Finkelstein, S. 1999. Integrating strategic, organizational, and human resource perspectives on mergers and acquisitions: A case survey of synergy realization. *Organization Science*, **10**(1): 2–26.

March, J.G. and Simon, H.A. 1958. *Organizations.* New York: Wiley.

Marks, M.L. and Mirvis, P.H. 1985. Merger syndrome: Stress and uncertainty. *Mergers and Acquisitions*, **20**(2): 50–5.

Mezias, J., Grinyer, P., and Guth, W. 2001. Changing collective cognition: A process model for strategic change. *Long Range Planning*, **34**(1): 71–95.

Pablo, A.L. 1994. Determinants of acquisition integration level: A decision-making perspective. *Academy of Management Journal*, **37**(4): 803–36.

Pablo, A.L. 1995. The case of post-acquisition integration design decisions. *International Journal of Value-Based Management*, **8**: 149–61.

Pablo, A.L., Sitkin, S.B., and Jemison, D.B. 1996. Acquisition decision-making processes: The central role of risk. *Journal of Management*, **22**(5): 723–46.

Sales, A.L. and Mirvis, P.H. 1984. When cultures collide: Issues in acquisition. In J.R. Kimberly and R.E. Quinn (eds.), *Managing Organizational Transitions*. Homewood, IL: Irwin.

Shanley, M.T. and Correa, M.E. 1992. Agreement between top management teams and expectations for post-acquisition performance. *Strategic Management Journal*, **13**(4): 245–67.

Sirower, M.L. 1997. *The Synergy Trap*. New York: Free Press.

Sitkin, S.B., Long, C.P., and Lind, E.A. 2001. *The Pyramid Model of Leadership*. Working paper, Fuqua School of Business, Duke University.

Sitkin, S.B. and Pablo, A.L. 2003. The neglected importance of leadership in mergers and acquisitions. In G.K. Stahl and M. Mendenhall (eds.), *Mergers and Acquisitions: Managing Culture and Human Resources*. Stanford, CA: Stanford University Press.

Tetenbaum, T.J. 1999. Beating the odds of merger and acquisition failure: Seven key practices that improve the chance for expected integration and synergies. *Organizational Dynamics*, Autumn: 22–36.

Walsh, J.P. 1987. *Performance from Diversification by Acquisitions: Effects of Acquisition Integration*. Working Paper, Amos Tuck School of Business Administration, Dartmouth College.

The Role of CEO Charismatic Leadership in the Effective Implementation of Mergers and Acquisitions

David A. Waldman

Abstract

This chapter attempts to form a theoretical model showing how CEO charismatic leadership processes may be central to the effective implementation of a merger or acquisition. Key mediating variables are introduced including organizational integration, cultural integration, and employee resistance to change. In addition, the potentially moderating effects of pre-merger differentiation are described. The model specifies a number of propositions linking CEO charismatic leadership, the mediating variables, and the effectiveness of an M&A. In addition, research possibilities are considered regarding the appropriate testing of the model.

Introduction

The performance of mergers and acquisitions (M&As) has not kept up with their growth in the world of business. A high percentage of M&As either fail or do not realize expectations. In an attempt to understand this disparity, Morosini (1998) noted that in the area of post-M&A performance, most research has focused on strategic and financial issues. However, as discussed by Larsson and Finkelstein (1999), it is becoming increasingly clear that research models that focus on such issues cannot adequately address the human elements that can make or break the successful implementation of an M&A. These elements include such factors as organizational and cultural integration, retention of top talent, new approaches to work, reducing resistance to change, and the minimization of stress.

Leadership is a logical driver of the human elements associated with an M&A implementation, and thus, its ultimate success. Unfortunately, leadership issues have taken a back seat in scholarly efforts. To be sure, leadership is often heralded as a key ingredient, and anecdotal evidence abounds (e.g. Morosini 1998). However, research has not systematically examined leadership variables in the M&A implementation process. The overall goal of this chapter is to identify a theoretical model of chief executive officer (CEO) leadership and empirical issues that need to be considered.

Two boundary conditions are relevant to the theoretical model presented in this chapter. First, the focus is on the strategic M&As that are formed on the pre-merger expectation of developing synergies between merging firms (Healy, Palepu, and Ruback 1997). In contrast, financial M&As are not the focus of this chapter. Financial M&As are based on pure transaction or the buying of a stream of revenues for the purpose of better asset management; few if any synergies are expected. Second, by focusing on CEOs, M&As for which the CEO is the top decision-maker accountable for successful implementation are addressed. In contrast, some acquisitions may be relatively small in relation to the overall size of the acquiring firm, in which case a lower level business unit manager may be the one accountable.

The potential importance of CEO leadership is not a new consideration in the management literature. Indeed, it has been recognized as an essential ingredient for the continual revitalization of organizations (Tichy and Devanna 1986, Peters 1987). Further, there is growing evidence that CEO leadership qualities can predict firm performance (Agle and Sonnenfeld 1994, Waldman et al. 2001, Waldman and Javidan 2002). But can CEO leadership have a significant effect on the successful implementation of an M&A? A consideration of the nature of leadership at the strategic level will help provide answers to this question.

Leadership at the strategic level: The upper echelons perspective

Over the past 20 years, the field of strategic management has become increasingly concerned with top-level managers and their effects on strategy formulation and firm performance. Upper echelons theory was first put forth in the work of Hambrick and Mason (1984), and since then it has been widely cited and expanded somewhat under the rubric of strategic leadership (Finkelstein and Hambrick 1996, Cannella and Monroe 1997). The essence of this theory is that strategic choices and change, such as M&As, are determinants of firm performance. Further, strategic decisions clearly represent what Mischel (1977) referred to as a "weak situation" in that the choices of decision makers (e.g. the decision to engage in an M&A) can vary widely. This allows them to insert aspects of themselves (e.g. leadership qualities) into such choices and their implementation (Finkelstein and Hambrick 1996, House and Aditya 1997).

In its earlier development, Hambrick and Mason (1984) focused on background and demographic characteristics of CEOs. These included such variables as age, functional track, formal education, and socioeconomic background. At the outset, Hambrick and Mason (1984: 196) recognized the limitations of demographic and background variables in that they "may contain more noise than purer psychological measures." That is, psychological measures were seen as potentially more direct in terms of revealing the types of CEO values, beliefs, and behavioral inclinations relevant to strategy formation and performance, i.e. to fill in the "black box" created by an exclusive focus on demographic and background variables (Finkelstein and Hambrick 1996: 46).

In line with this notion of psychological measures, emerging charismatic leadership theory may provide new possibilities for the upper echelons perspective in general, and the leadership of a merger or acquisition in particular. The definition of charismatic leadership used here is based largely on the work of House and colleagues (e.g. House and Shamir 1993) and Conger (e.g. Conger and Kanungo 1998). Specifically, charisma can be defined as a *relationship* between an individual (leader) and one or more followers based on leader behaviors and attributes combined with favorable attributions on the part of followers. Key behaviors on the part of the leader include: (1) providing a sense of mission or purpose based on opportunities and constraints in the larger environment; (2) articulating an inspirational vision that challenges the status quo and is based on powerful imagery and values; (3) showing determination when accomplishing goals or change; (4) communicating high performance expectations; and (5) hands-on involvement and leading by example. As will be described further below, all of these behaviors may be relevant to the effective implementation of an M&A. Examples of key attributes include self-confidence, optimism, ability to articulate in an eloquent manner, and high energy levels. Favorable attributional effects on the part of followers include the generation of confidence in the leader, making followers feel good in his/her presence, the alleviation of stress or uncertainty, and strong admiration or respect.

The application of charismatic leadership to M&As may indeed be timely. Yukl (1999) criticized recent theorists of organization-based, charismatic leadership for focusing too heavily on dyadic processes rather than leader influence over group and organizational processes. He listed examples of the latter as including the extent of coordination of inter-related group activities, mutual trust and cooperation among members across groups, and member agreement regarding objectives and priorities. Each of these examples would seem to be relevant to the effective implementation of an M&A. In addition, Beyer (1999) suggested that more charismatic theory and research should be devoted to achieving organizational level change and outcomes, an assertion agreed upon by House (1999). In summary, it seems clear that a focus on M&A implementation processes could help move the field of charismatic leadership forward in a beneficial direction.

CEO Charismatic Leadership in an M&A Implementation

At the outset, it is important to note that effective, charismatic leadership is not a given in an M&A, and indeed, the context may often preclude it. Specifically, Marks and Mirvis (1998) noted that in an acquisition (or when there is a lead party in a merger), the acquirer may take on an air of superiority. This could cause the acquirer to look at the acquiree and its policies and systems in a condescending manner. The upshot would be a lack of charismatic leadership perceptions and attributions on the part of the acquiree.

With that said, it is essential to delineate the specific behaviors and attributes that are relevant to the potential role of CEO charisma in the implementation of a merger or acquisition. Recent books by Morosini (1998) and Marks and Mirvis (1998) demonstrate similar ideas about CEO leadership, both stressing elements of the charismatic leadership paradigm. For example, Marks and Mirvis (1998) discuss the importance of positive vision coupled with an articulation of the principles, values, and priorities behind a merger or acquisition. Vision is also prominent in the discussion of M&A leadership recently presented by Gadiesh et al. (2002). The role of vision in strategic leadership is not especially new, and it has already been articulated in the literature (e.g. Robbins and Duncan 1988, Westley and Mintzberg 1989). However, what is not as clear is the distinction between vision *process* and *content* (Larwood et al. 1995).

This distinction may be quite relevant to the charismatic leadership involved in an M&A implementation. Process elements of vision are in line with the charismatic behaviors mentioned above. Specifically, they include enthusiastic or eloquent articulation geared toward energizing followers. Content elements are perhaps not so obvious, although it is clear that the content of charismatic vision emanates from values and beliefs of the leader (Conger and Kanungo 1998). As noted by Gadiesh et al. (2002), the content of an M&A vision must clearly specify its purpose and what the M&A plans to achieve. Pablo and Javidan (2002) refer to this as strategic intent. Pablo and Javidan (2002) define strategic intent in terms of how merger partners augment or complement each other's strategy, thereby contributing to the goals of the combined firm. Strategic intent can be characterized according to a variety of themes such as growing economies of scale, building adjacent businesses, broadening the scope of products or technologies, and perhaps even redefining a business or industry (Gadiesh et al. 2002).

The common denominator of all these themes is value creation. Without a clear theme or content specifying value creation, an M&A vision is not likely to energize and build confidence among followers, i.e., not be charismatic in nature. Pablo and Javidan (2002) provide an example of a large Canadian firm that purchased another large Canadian firm solely as a defensive move to preempt American competitors from purchasing the latter. The strategic intent of the purchasing CEO's vision was not a motivating force in the merger's implementation, and Pablo and Javidan attribute much of the subsequent failure of the M&A to this problem.

Other behaviors and attributes are also relevant to CEO charismatic leadership during an M&A implementation. Marks and Mirvis (1998), as well as Morosini (1998), stress the importance of leading by example, presenting fact-based and well-reasoned arguments to employees at various hierarchical levels, and building trust and confidence. Indeed, it may be important for the emergent CEO of an M&A process to not just engage in the glamorous activities associated with negotiating a deal, but also maintain involvement by performing the many externally and internally oriented activities required to steward such a major organizational change (Marks and Mirvis 1998). External activities are geared toward such constituents as stockholders and industry analysts. More forgotten are those activities involving internal constituents, i.e., lower level managers and employees. Gadiesh et al. (2002) stress the need for continuous, enthusiastic "crusading" to get the vision across. They also suggest that such hands-on leadership cannot be delegated to multiple people, i.e. the CEO must stay engaged in the process by maintaining face-to-face

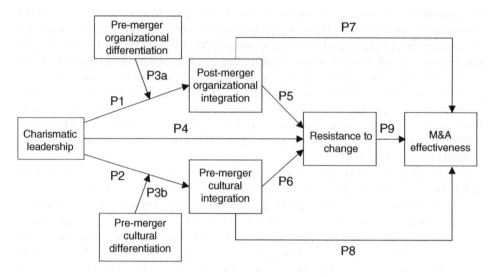

Figure 11.1   A model of CEO charismatic leadership and M&A implementation effectiveness

contact. Gadiesh et al. provide the example of how Rolf Borjesson, CEO of Rexam, a UK packaging company, has provided such involvement for acquisitions in both Europe and the United States.

It is interesting to note that these latter activities and constituents are relevant to the work of Cannella and Monroe (1997). They proposed that CEO charisma and inspirational leadership are important, not so much because of their effect on choice of strategies, e.g. the decision to engage in an M&A process, but rather because of their effect on the implementation of the strategic decisions and changes that top managers make. They argued that when such leadership is lacking, employees will not have the motivation or clear direction to pursue change.

As noted above, leadership theorists have espoused a number of charismatic leadership models with largely similar content (e.g. Bass 1985, Conger and Kanungo 1998, House and Shamir 1993). However, it is possible that some relevant behavior components may be missing with regard to CEO charisma specifically in the implementation of an M&A. For example, I will argue below that information sharing may be a key charismatic behavior instilling confidence and trust, while reducing resistance to change on the part of lower level managers and employees.

Let us now focus attention on the mediating mechanisms and variables that can help us understand the effects of CEO charismatic leadership on the ultimate success of an M&A process. A model of CEO charismatic leadership and M&A implementation effectiveness is shown in Figure 11.1. The model highlights the potential importance of two types of integration: (1) organizational; and (2) cultural. It also highlights pre-merger differentiation as a potentially moderating influence, as well as the necessity of overcoming employee resistance to change. These issues are addressed in the discussion below, which goes on to form a number of propositions (as shown in Figure 11.1), and then proceeds to delineate research possibilities.

Organizational and Cultural Integration

In an M&A, differences in organizational elements are likely to be evident early on. One of the partnering firms may be highly centralized in its operations; the other, highly decentralized. One firm may be highly bureaucratized, while the other is more organic. Further, one firm may stress reward conformity (e.g. salary-based pay), while the other stresses pay variability based on performance. It follows that organizational integration is likely to be an important aspect of an M&A process (Pablo 1994). Organizational integration can be defined as the unification of relevant organizational elements (i.e. structures, operating procedures, reward systems, and so forth) between merging firms through the use of conciliatory processes. Conciliatory processes are those that are not enigmatic or arbitrary, but instead are transparent and entail criteria for change that are explicit and clear. It should be noted that this definition differs somewhat from that of Larsson and Finkelstein (1999), who did not emphasize actual unification or conciliatory processes, and instead focused simply on the degree of interaction or coordinative efforts in an M&A, e.g. the extent of usage of transition teams. However, as noted by Marks and Mirvis (1998), transition teams may put forth much effort but end up drifting aimlessly or succumbing to politics and self-serving power agendas, rather than seeking and building synergies. It is proposed that a conceptualization that deals more precisely with actual unification through conciliatory processes is more likely to be predictive of implementation effectiveness.

Morosini (1998) warned firms not to rely on external entities, e.g. management consultants, to oversee organizational integration processes. Instead, it may be essential for senior management to provide a clear, motivational vision that energizes individuals (e.g. integration task force members) and focuses them on what is expected in terms of a desired end state, as well as conciliatory processes. Further, through "execution orientation" it is necessary for senior management, including the CEO, to maintain constant direct involvement in organizational integration (Morosini 1998: 149). In other words, in line with the thinking of Cannella and Monroe (1997), the CEO may need to spend proportionately more time in a hands-on mode (e.g. "road shows") stimulating ideas regarding integration, as opposed to simply engaging in strategic thinking (Gadiesh et al. 2002). In short, the following proposition is suggested:

Proposition 1 (P1):   CEO charismatic leadership will foster organizational integration in an M&A.

In addition to organizational differences, cultural differences may also be present. Cultural integration can be complex because it may involve not only the cultures of two organizations, but in the case of an international M&A, it also involves the blending of national cultures. Because of these cultural differences, merging firms may have substantial differences in terms of norms, values, and beliefs. Integration would thus involve the unification of these cultural elements through conciliatory processes.

Cultural differences could spawn alternative perspectives and culture clashes, especially on the part of the acquiree, which may see itself as the loser in the combination. How exactly might cultural differences manifest themselves? Pablo and Javidan (2002) provide the example of differences in partners' risk propensities, which occurs when they have opposing tendencies to take or avoid risks. Less conservative firms in terms of risk propensity tend to have the accompanying values of individual freedom and initiative, while more conservative firms tend to value compliance and stability. Indeed, Pablo and Javidan attribute problems in the Daimler–Chrysler merger largely to risk-propensity differences. They further note that underlying societal cultural differences can also come into play in the case of cross-national mergers. For example, firms from societies high on uncertainty avoidance are likely to prefer making choices based on certain outcomes, rather than taking risks to maximize gains. Further, they are likely to engage in detailed planning in anticipation of unknown events. In contrast, firms from societies low on uncertainty avoidance will have more of a tendency to accept risk and assume an action-orientation, rather than engaging in intensive or detailed planning.

The bad news is that there is an inverse relationship between perceived cultural differences (i.e. lack of integration) and shareholder gains (Chatterjee et al. 1992). The good news is that although organizational culture change typically takes a number of years to be realized, the time period may be substantially shortened in the event of an M&A. The "unfreezing associated with a combination gives executives a head start in culture change" (Marks and Mirvis 1998: 195). Such change may be necessary to achieve integration.

Leadership may be essential to ensure the ultimate integration of cultures. Morosini (1998) suggested that leadership efforts directed toward cultural integration should not wait until implementation, but rather should be considered in the planning phase. He cited a quote from Colin Marshall of British Airways stressing that it is important early on to find a partner who shares basic organizational values including approaches to selection, training, communicating, and leading. As the M&A progresses, a number of authors have recommended that senior management should respect pre-merger cultures, including that of the acquiree. For example, Morosini (1998: 158) described the 1987 merger of the European firms of ASEA and Brown Boveri. He noted how the CEO, Percy Barnevik, spent much time "radically shaking the merging companies' old values and structures ... almost single-handedly replacing them with totally new corporate values and organizational designs." As an example, Barnevik was intent on making the newly formed entity, ABB, more globally oriented. However, Morosini also commented upon the seeming paradox of how Barnevik was simultaneously intent on maintaining many of the merging companies' historic characteristics (e.g. extensive local market knowledge and business approaches/values known to work).

Marks and Mirvis (1998) also stressed the importance of treading lightly on a pre-merger culture, even if the ultimate intention is to absorb a firm and assimilate its culture. As stated by Dr. von Pierer, the CEO of Siemens, "... it's important that the buying company doesn't try to overrun and completely change the corporate culture in the acquired company" (Javidan 2002). Such consideration is likely to generate reciprocal respect for the acquirer's culture, as well as for senior management. From a leadership perspective, the generation of respect and trust is an essential element in the formation of a charismatic relationship (Bass 1985).

Sales and Mirvis (1984) classified three possible levels of acculturation in an acquisition. First, cultural *pluralism* allows partners to coexist, thus maintaining their separate cultures. Second, cultural *integration* occurs when the partner firms become unified through conciliatory processes. Third, cultural *assimilation* occurs when one firm's culture absorbs the other. Considered below are the ramifications of inappropriately forcing one culture onto another, as could potentially occur in the case of cultural assimilation. For now, we simply will consider what constitutes effective cultural integration and the role of charismatic leadership.

The Sales and Mirvis (1984) conceptualization of cultural integration may be the most desired route if the ultimate goal is to achieve breakthrough combinations and synergies. As noted earlier, such M&As are the focus of the current model. On the other hand, cultural pluralism may make the most sense when the combining firms display vastly different cultures and more modest or gradual integration is desired, or what Marks and Mirvis (1998: 201) would refer to as "one plus one equals two". Such is the case when the pre-merger driver is purely financial in nature.

As shown in Figure 11.1, a key ingredient of successful integration may be the nature of the leadership driving it. As noted above, a charismatic CEO will generate trust and respect by avoiding hasty or forceful assimilation. He/she will pursue acculturation in accordance with espoused values and the articulation of an appealing, future-based vision of the merged company. That vision will be repeated in a number of different forums and media by an energetic, charismatic CEO throughout the implementation period, thus showing his/her determination in making the integration successful. Further, the CEO will model or reward the desired end state by building a cohesive top management team aligned toward achieving the desired level of integration (Waldman and Yammarino 1999). Such alignment helps to demonstrate credibility and conciliation, and it shows that all of the senior management staff are on board to achieve integration. In sum, it is expected that:

Proposition 2 (P2):   CEO charismatic leadership will foster cultural integration in an M&A.

Pre-merger differentiation

Yukl (1999) was critical of charismatic leadership theories in organizations and their emphasis on universal applicability. He suggested that "more attention is needed to identify facilitating and limiting conditions for charismatic leadership" (Yukl 1999: 301). This theme has also been echoed by Beyer (1999) and Shamir and Howell (1999). However, with the exception of Waldman and Yammarino's (1999) conceptualization of the moderating effects of perceived environmental uncertainty, very little emphasis can be seen in the literature with regard to contextual determinants of the effectiveness of charismatic leadership.

Beyer (1999) proposed that more attention should be paid to contextual issues in a longitudinal manner. Mergers and acquisitions represent phenomena for which the longitudinal context is likely to be relevant to the effectiveness of CEO charismatic leadership. Specifically, I propose that the pre-merger context in terms of organizational and cultural differentiation is likely to serve as a moderating influence.

This notion follows from the differentiation and integration model put forth by Lawrence and Lorsch (1969). The essence of that model is that the higher the degree of differentiation, the more difficult it is to achieve integration within an organization. Lawrence and Lorsch (1969: 13) proposed that it was management's responsibility to achieve integration through "supplemental integrating devices" such as cross-unit teams or even whole units of individuals whose basic purpose is to achieve integration among other units.

There are three obvious differences between the model proposed here and that of Lawrence and Lorsch (1969). First, in the current model, the focus of differentiation is between firms, rather than within one firm. Second, the concept of differentiation is extended beyond organizational structure or procedures to include culture. Third, CEO charismatic leadership can be seen in the current model as an integrating mechanism. It is interesting to note that earlier models of leadership may have precluded its specific consideration by Lawrence and Lorsch (1969) as such a mechanism. Hunt (1999) suggests such possibilities in his historical consideration of charismatic leadership theory in relation to earlier paradigms that did not focus as much on change processes.

Organizational mechanisms (e.g. autonomous transition teams) or even external entities (e.g. management consultants) may suffice in an effort to achieve organizational integration when pre-merger differentiation is low. Under such circumstances, the merging firms are largely mirror images of each other in terms of structures, procedures, and human resource systems. At most, transactional forms of leadership could help in terms of monitoring and rewarding effective transition behavior and actions (Bass 1985, Bass and Avolio 1990).

However, when pre-merger differentiation is high, charismatic leadership may be necessary to establish a clear vision of the new organization and how structures, procedures, and systems will need to change to be in line with that vision. Moreover, the leader will need to be an enthusiastic champion to make sure that effective integration comes to fruition (Morosini 1998, Gadiesh et al. 2002). In the Pablo and Javidan (2002) example described above, the acquiring company had performance evaluation and compensation systems designed to encourage entrepreneurial activity and variable-based pay. In contrast, the acquiree's systems did not encourage entrepreneurship, and an emphasis on base salary was standard among employees. Without charismatic leadership to establish a clear vision, there was a lack of effective organizational integration.

In a similar manner, achieving effective cultural integration will not be an especially challenging issue when pre-merger differentiation is low since the cultures will be able to meld together without a great deal of leadership stimulus. Conversely, when pre-merger differentiation is high, charismatic leadership may be essential to set the future tone in terms of values and beliefs, to articulate the extent to which cultural pluralism may be allowed and for what length of time, and so forth. Again, using the Pablo and Javidan (2002) example, the acquiring company had a high-risk propensity, while the acquiree did not. Since the post-merger CEO provided little in the way of an inspirational vision, effective cultural integration was also not achieved. Along these lines, Morosini (1998) stressed the importance of elements of charismatic leadership in his consideration of cross-national mergers. This should not be surprising given the high likelihood of pre-merger cultural differentiation in such mergers. In sum, the above arguments suggest that:

Proposition 3a (P3a):   CEO charismatic leadership will be highly predictive of organizational integration in an M&A when there is a high degree of pre-merger organizational differentiation; conversely, CEO charismatic leadership will be minimally predictive of organizational integration when there is a lack of pre-merger organizational differentiation.

Proposition 3b (P3b):   CEO charismatic leadership will be highly predictive of cultural integration in an M&A when there is a high degree of pre-merger cultural differentiation; conversely, CEO charismatic leadership will be minimally predictive of cultural integration when there is a lack of pre-merger cultural differentiation.

Understanding and overcoming resistance to change

As shown in Figure 11.1, resistance to change may be a key mediating variable in understanding the effective implementation of an M&A. But why is resistance such a likely occurrence? Marks and Mirvis (1998) focus their attention on the stress accompanying an M&A. They note that stress in an M&A is due to such factors as a highly uncertain future, job insecurity, a loss of personal control, and simply the notion that change in and of itself is stressful, whether or not that change will ultimately evolve into something for the better. Larsson and Finkelstein (1999) suggest that the greatest stress and resistance should logically be seen on the part of the acquiree. It may suffer from the "merger syndrome" in which its employees "mourn a corporate death" and are more likely to not see change as a positive event (Marks and Mirvis 1986: 41). Unfortunately, the manifestations of resistance can include absenteeism, disobedience, voluntary turnover (including some of the firm's better employees), and even sabotage.

Much of the resistance to change may be due to faulty leadership practices emanating from the top (i.e. the CEO leadership may seem invisible, and when in sight the CEO as well as lower level leaders may "seem harried and circumspect" (Marks and Mirvis 1998: 93)). As an alternative, I propose that CEO charismatic leadership may be shown in an effort to reduce resistance to change. Such leadership affects success indirectly by first helping to alleviate the stress and uncertainty associated with the major change associated with an M&A process. Waldman et al. (2001) and Waldman and Yammarino (1999) illustrated the potential importance of uncertainty as a factor in the relationship between CEO charisma and firm performance. In the realm of an M&A, a state of shock is liable to permeate a firm involved in such a process, especially a firm that is acquired. As noted above, stress and uncertainty can build because of feelings of loss of control, insecurity, and being overwhelmed by change, thus fostering resistance to change.

The CEO can help alleviate the uncertainty and resistance by engaging in a number of charismatically oriented behaviors. First, the CEO can display empathy and understanding of people's fears, as well as by being positive and even displaying a sense of humor at times. Bass (1985) considered the importance of such individualized consideration in his theory of transformational leadership. Some might argue that because of its high management level, the CEO position cannot be responsible for reaching out to individuals who are many layers removed. However, cases such as Mary Kay Ash and Sam Walton illustrate CEOs who reached out in a personal manner to many of their individual employees through such practices as speeches and management by walking around (Hughes, Ginnett, and Curphy 1996). While not all employees may be reached, various authors have stressed the symbolic effects of such leadership behavior because of how favorable stories and sagas are likely to be passed on through social contagion processes (Gardner and Avolio 1998, Waldman and Yammarino 1999).

Second, the CEO can make an intellectual case for why people should let go of the past organization and ways of thinking about and doing things. Further, providing a vision of a new and better organization helps divert individuals' attention from what they are giving up, and it generates confidence that management has a real picture of where the new firm is heading.

Third, Yukl (1999) criticized charismatic leadership theory for not including information sharing as an important behavioral component. He noted that followers are likely to find the sharing of sensitive information an empowering influence. Indeed, it may be an important action on the part of a charismatic CEO attempting to reduce resistance to change in an M&A implementation. Conversely, Morosini (1998) pointed toward the necessity of keeping information secret during the pre-combination phase of an M&A. Secrecy could be maintained by avoiding the use of external management consultants or outside experts. Morosini argued that any leakage of information could lead to various entities such as the press reporting innuendo and half-truths. The end result is likely to be misunderstandings on the part of such important constituents as shareholders of the merging firms. As well, the share price of the targeted firm is likely to increase.

However, the situation changes during actual combination, and especially, during the implementation of an M&A. Keeping information secret from employees only serves to heighten the aforementioned cloud of uncertainty. People begin to wonder what exactly management is trying to hide, and imaginations are likely to suggest the worst in terms of reorganizations, job loss, and so forth. Unfortunately, the upshot is likely to be strong negative reactions including resistance to change (Marks and Mirvis 1983).

Accordingly, it is proposed that especially during the implementation, information secrecy or what might be termed the "mushroom theory of management" should be kept to a minimum. Simply stated, the mushroom theory suggests that the best practice is to keep employees in the dark, feed them a lot of manure (figuratively), and hope that they'll grow and be productive within the M&A. Unfortunately, such a strategy will only serve to undermine the trust and confidence that are so important in the establishment of a charismatic leadership relationship. An approach more in line with charismatic leadership would be for the CEO to be specific and candid, thereby clearing up unknowns and rumors. As proposed by Marks and Mirvis (1998), the CEO should share both good and bad news, thereby avoiding the patronization of individual employees. Moreover, the CEO should be visible and available to discuss concerns. In sum, these arguments would suggest:

Proposition 4 (P4):   CEO charismatic leadership will alleviate employee resistance to change in an M&A.

Organizational integration may also affect employee resistance. It should be noted that Larsson and Finkelstein (1999) found no significant relationship between integration and resistance. However, as discussed above, their measure of integration did not emphasize the actual unification or conciliatory processes, and instead focused simply on the degree of interaction or coodinative efforts. Indeed, merging firms may drift aimlessly and succumb to politics and self-serving agendas on the part of individuals, rather than seeking to build organizational synergies, economies of scale, and so forth.

If the integration proceeds in a manner perceived to be transparent, fair, and justified, resistance is likely to be minimal. Conversely, a failure to effectively integrate may exacerbate resistance and associated problems. For example, transition managers and task forces may submit to political gamesmanship, deals, and forced or autocratic change. Although some individuals may make personal gains in the process, the vast majority of employees are likely to view such dealings in a cynical manner, thus only serving to fuel their resistance to change. In short:

Proposition 5 (P5):   Organizational integration will alleviate employee resistance to change in an M&A.

As mentioned earlier, cultural assimilation occurs when one firm essentially attempts to absorb the culture of another. There is a natural tendency for the dominant firm (i.e. the acquirer) to attempt to engage in assimilation and see itself as the "winner", while the acquiree is seen as the "loser". Unfortunately, such thinking may lead to put-downs emanating from both sides, especially the acquirer. For example, in an acquisition described by Marks and Mirvis (1998: 191), "the 'seasoned hands' at the parent company felt obliged to teach the 'greenhorns' in the entrepreneurial shop a thing or two about running a 'real' business." The inevitable result is likely to be resistance to change on the part of this acquiree which views its entrepreneurial, organic culture as being under threat.

In contrast, effective cultural integration will include conciliatory processes that emphasize mutual respect for each other's culture and an attempt to look for synergies. Pre-merger cultures are likely to be respected, and in some instances, cultural pluralism (i.e. co-existence of cultures) may even be allowed in the short-run to ease the integration process. In short, it is expected that:

Proposition 6 (P6):   Cultural integration will alleviate employee resistance to change in an M&A.

Predicting M&A effectiveness

Increasing evidence points toward organizational integration as being a key ingredient of the effective implementation of an M&A (Haspeslagh and Jemison 1991, Pablo 1994,

Larsson and Finkelstein 1999). Significant interaction and coordination are necessary if firms are to be able to attain true synergies as a result of their merger. Successful integration should foster enhanced economies of scale, the transfer of information and technologies between firms, the sharing of best practices (e.g. human resource practices), and so forth. On the other hand, poor organizational integration may be accompanied by such unproductive problems as high transition management costs (Marks and Mirvis 1998). In short, it is expected that:

> Proposition 7 (P7):   Organizational integration will lead to the effective implementation of an M&A.

Cultural integration is also directly relevant to understanding M&A implementation effectiveness. Research has shown that shareholder gains are dependent on the degree of cultural fit between the merging firm's top management (Chatterjee et al. 1992). In the joint alliance arena, Serapio and Cascio (1996) point toward culture clashes as a key element in the demise of the alliance between AT&T and Olivetti. Resistance to change has already been identified as an important mediating variable between cultural integration and M&A effectiveness. It is likely that culture clashes also spawn misunderstandings, lack of communication, and unproductive conflicts between the merging firms or partners. On the other hand, cultural integration based on conciliation is likely to involve a reconsideration of important values, beliefs, and norms on the part of both firms as they move ahead with the building of their new, combined entity. Ideally, the new partners will mutually identify cultural elements worth saving, versus those that should be discarded. In sum:

> Proposition 8 (P8):   Cultural integration will lead to the effective implementation of an M&A.

Finally, there is growing evidence that resistance to change itself should have a direct effect on M&A implementation (Chatterjee et al. 1992, Datta 1991, Larsson and Finkelstein 1999). Employee resistance is likely to be accompanied by unproductive reticence, overt hostility, and employee turnover. Unfortunately, all such outcomes are likely to inhibit the synergistic implementation of an M&A.

The potential connection between employee resistance to change and M&A outcomes is in line with recent work involving strategic human resource management (HRM). Much of that work stresses that HRM configurations in firms need to provide a fit with strategic directions in order to realize firm effectiveness. The pursuit and implementation of a merger or acquisition inherently involve strategic change, and as such, will necessitate human-capital-enhancing configurations to maximize employee development and problem-solving capabilities, while minimizing resistance to change (Youndt et al. 1996). As noted by Delery and Doty (1996), this type of HRM configuration is likely to include extensive benefits and services to those who may be outplaced (e.g. terminated) as a result of an M&A. Such practices will help alleviate employee resistance to change and further the pursuit of M&A synergistic outcomes. Alternatively, HRM configurations that do not stress employee development or practices to reduce employee resistance are less likely to yield favorable M&A outcomes. In sum, these arguments suggest that:

Proposition 9 (P9):   Employee resistance to change will have a negative effect on the successful implementation of an M&A.

Research possibilities

There are a number of research strategies that can be employed to test the model and propositions that have been put forward here. Three such strategies are outlined here: (1) case method; (2) case survey method; and (3) survey combined with interview methods. Numerous examples of the case method to study M&A implementation can be found in the literature (e.g. Ravenscraft and Scherer 1987). Relatedly, it is interesting to note how systematic, qualitative studies of top management teams and CEOs have grown in number over the past 15 years. For example, Eisenhardt (1989) performed a multiple case study of the microcomputer industry and showed how decision-making and leadership styles of CEOs could be readily identified. The advantage of case methodology lies in the depth or richness of data that can be collected on a particular firm or M&A (Yin 1989). It is also advantageous when research questions are more exploratory in nature. However, the present model and propositions are not so exploratory or inductively formed. More deductively based research has already been conducted in the areas of CEO charismatic leadership (e.g. Agle and Sonnenfeld 1994, Waldman et al. 2001), as well as aspects of organizational integration and employee resistance to change and their effects on M&A implementation (e.g. Larsson and Finkelstein 1999). Accordingly, it would appear that case study methodology might not be very appropriate as a means of examining the current model and propositions.

Larsson and Finkelstein (1999) touted the use of case survey methodology. This approach is potentially appropriate when numerous case studies already exist in the research area in question, as is the case with regard to M&A implementations. It involves identifying a sample of relevant case studies, developing a coding scheme to convert qualitative case information into quantifiable variables, having multiple raters code the data, and statistically analyzing the coded data (Larsson and Finkelstein 1999). The primary advantage of the case survey approach is that it pools together case information to allow for deductive hypothesis testing. As such, the case survey method helps form a bridge between qualitative and quantitative research (Jick 1979).

On the other hand, the case survey method relies on information available in existing case write-ups. As revealed in the work of Larsson and Finkelstein (1999), with regard to organizational integration, this approach only appeared to allow for quantitative estimates of the degree efforts put forth. However, the model presented above stresses actual unification and conciliatory processes, not simply the degree of interaction or coordinative efforts. This methodology may also preclude the assessment of other necessary variables. For example, CEO charismatic leadership measures are typically obtained directly from followers (e.g. Waldman et al. 2001), although it is possible to measure leader charisma based on written materials (e.g. House, Spangler, and Woycke 1991). A further problem is that since the case survey method relies on existing case information, there may be a bias toward M&As that have already been studied and published, thus potentially limiting the generalizability of results.

A third methodology that might potentially overcome some of these problems is the use of surveys combined with interview methods. It is recognized that survey approaches may yield relatively low response rates, especially when they involve mail-outs to high-level managers (e.g. Datta 1991, Waldman et al. 2001). There is also the potential problem of common method variance or single-source bias when a number of constructs are assessed in the same survey using data collected from the same respondents (Podsakoff and Organ 1986). With these problems duly noted, a possible procedure will be presented that could produce fruitful results.

First, it is proposed that survey measures should be used to assess CEO charismatic leadership, and indeed, such measures already exist in the literature (e.g. Conger and Kanungo 1998, Waldman et al. 2001). Even though these measures exist, it is clear that additional item construction may be necessary to adequately assess CEO charisma in an M&A (e.g. items to assess information sharing versus secrecy). As specified further below, other measures depicted in Figure 11.1 could be gleaned from coded interview data.

Second, there are the related issues of when, and from whom, to collect survey as well as interview-based measures. It is probably desirable to assess leadership, integration, and employee resistance measures in a retrospective manner, perhaps a year after making the M&A deal, thus allowing respondents time to reflect. These respondents should be relatively high-level managers, although it is probably not necessary to obtain information directly from CEOs, which would likely be difficult in any event (cf. Finkelstein and Hambrick 1996). The respondents should be solicited from both firms involved in a respective M&A process. This would allow for an assessment of agreement between the various respondents of the two initial organizations. For example, outcomes could be problematic if the acquiring firm rates the CEO (who also came from that firm) as charismatic, while respondents from the acquired firm do not.

Third, if the survey/interview approach is used, the actual procedures of organizational entry and data collection on the part of researchers would become critical. Researchers might enter a post-merger organization through a high-level contact manager. That manager might take responsibility for distributing surveys to a small sample of managers from each of the pre-merger firms (e.g. perhaps six surveys per pre-merger firm). The sole purpose of these survey data might be to collect information regarding CEO charisma. Measures of organizational and cultural integration, as well as employee resistance to change, could then be collected through interviews or surveys conducted with the contact manager and a few other individuals highly involved in the M&A process. Any interview data collected could subsequently be coded and quantified for analyses, along with the survey data. The advantage of these procedures is that high response rates are likely to be achieved, unlike the somewhat low response rates typical of mail-out surveys (e.g. Waldman et al. 2001). Moreover, because data are solicited from multiple sources using multiple methods, the common method/single-source bias problems mentioned above would be reduced (Podsakoff and Organ 1986). These problems would be further reduced through the use of archival information and objective databases to obtain pre-merger differentiation and outcome performance data, respectively.

Conclusions

The fact that so many M&As evolve with less than satisfactory performance suggests that opportunities exist for researchers to form a better understanding of M&A implementation effectiveness. Heretofore, M&As have been studied primarily through strategic management, economic, and financial lenses. While research of a more organizational nature has been growing, it now appears that some key variables, such as CEO leadership behavior, may be examined in an attempt to more fully develop research models.

At the same time, I agree with Larsson and Finkelstein (1999), who suggest that organizational, human resource, and strategic explanations for M&A success should be considered simultaneously. The omission of key strategic variables, such as the combination potential of merging firms, might lead to the underspecification of research models. At the very least, such variables will need to be included as control variables in research designs that attempt to move the field forward in a multidisciplinary manner.

Note

David Waldman is also an Affiliated Faculty member of the Department of Management at Arizona State University Main in Tempe, USA.

References

Agle, B.R. and Sonnenfeld, J.A. 1994. Charismatic chief executive officers: Are they more effective? An empirical test of charismatic leadership theory. In D.P. Moore (ed.), *Academy of Management Best Papers Proceedings*, pp. 2–6.

Bass, B.M. 1985. *Leadership and Performance Beyond Expectations*. New York: Free Press.

Bass, B.M. and Avolio, B.J. 1990. *The Multifactor Leadership Questionnaire*. Palo Alto, CA: Consulting Psychologists Press.

Beyer, J.M. 1999. Taming and promoting charisma to change organizations. *Leadership Quarterly*, **10**: 307–30.

Cannella, A.A. Jr. and Monroe, M.J. 1997. Contrasting perspectives on strategic leaders: Toward a more realistic view of top managers. *Journal of Management*, **23**: 213–37.

Chatterjee, S., Lubatkin, M., Schweiger, D., and Weber, Y. 1992. Cultural differences and shareholder value in related mergers: Linking equity and human capital. *Strategic Management Journal*, **13**: 319–34.

Conger, J.A. and Kanungo, R.N. 1998. *Charismatic Leadership in Organizations*. Thousand Oaks, CA: Sage.

Datta, D.K. 1991. Organizational fit and acquisition performance: Effects of post-acquisition integration. *Strategic Management Journal*, **12**: 281–97.

Delery, J.E. and Doty, D.H. 1996. Modes of theorizing in strategic human resource management: Tests of universalistic, contingency, and configurational performance predictions. *Academy of Management Journal*, **39**: 802–35.

Eisenhardt, K.M. 1989. Making fast strategic decisions in high-velocity environments. *Academy of Management Journal*, **32**: 543–76.

Finkelstein, S. and Hambrick, D.C. 1996. *Strategic Leadership: Top Executives and Their Effects*. Minneapolis/St. Paul: West Publishing.

Gadiesh, O., Buchanan, R., Daniell, M., and Ormiston, C. 2002. The leadership testing ground. *Journal of Business Strategy*, **23**(2): 12–17.

Gardner, W.L. and Avolio, B.J. 1998. The charismatic relationship: A dramaturgical perspective. *Academy of Management Review*, **23**: 32–58.

Hambrick, D.C. and Mason, P.A. 1984. Upper echelons: The organization as a reflection of its top managers. *Academy of Management Review*, **9**: 193–206.

Haspeslagh, P.C. and Jemison, D.B. 1991. *Managing Acquisitions: Creating Value Through Corporate Renewal*. New York: Free Press.

Healy, P.M., Palepu, K.G., and Ruback, R.S. 1997. Which takeovers are profitable? Strategic or financial. *Sloan Management Review*, **38**(4): 45–57.

House, R.J. 1999. Weber and the neo-charismatic leadership paradigm: A response to Beyer. *Leadership Quarterly*, **10**: 563–74.

House, R.J. and Aditya, R. 1997. The social scientific study of leadership: Quo vadis? *Journal of Management*, **23**: 409–74.

House, R.J. and Shamir, B. 1993. Toward an integration of transformational, charismatic, and visionary theories of leadership. In M. Chemmers and R. Ayman (eds.), *Leadership: Perspectives and Research Directions*. New York: Academic Press, pp. 81–107.

House, R.J., Spangler, W.D., and Woycke, J. 1991. Personality and charisma in the U.S. presidency: A psychological theory of leader effectiveness. *Administrative Science Quarterly*, **36**: 364–96.

Hughes, R.L., Ginnett, R.C., and Curphy, G.J. 1996. *Leadership: Enhancing the Lessons of Experience*. Boston, MA: Irwin/McGraw-Hill.

Hunt, J.G. 1999. Transformational/charismatic leadership's transformation of the field: A historical essay. *Leadership Quarterly*, **10**: 129–44.

Javidan, M. 2002. Siemens CEO Heinrich von Pierer on cross-border acquisitions. *Academy of Management Executive*, **16**(1): 13–15.

Jick, T.D. 1979. Mixing qualitative and quantitative methods: Triangulation in action. *Administrative Science Quarterly*, **24**: 602–11.

Larsson, R. and Finkelstein, S. 1999. Integrating strategic, organizational, and human resource perspectives on mergers and acquisitions: A case survey of synergy realization. *Organization Science*, **10**: 1–26.

Larwood, L., Falbe, C.M., Kriger, M.P., and Miesing, P. 1995. Structure and meaning of organizational vision. *Academy of Management Journal*, **38**: 740–69.

Lawrence, P.R. and Lorsch, J.W. 1969. *Developing Organizations: Diagnosis and Action*. Reading, MA: Addison-Wesley.

Marks, M.L. and Mirvis, P.H. 1983. *Situational and Personal Factors Influencing Employee Response to Corporate Merger*. Paper presented at the annual convention of the American Psychological Association, Anaheim, CA.

Marks, M.L. and Mirvis, P.H. 1986. The merger syndrome. *Psychology Today*, **20**(10): 36–42.

Marks, M.L. and Mirvis, P.H. 1998. *Joining Forces: Making One Plus One Equal Three in Mergers, Acquisitions, and Alliances*. San Francisco: Jossey-Bass.

Mischel, W. 1977. The interaction of person and situation. In D. Magnusson and N.S. Ender (eds.), *Personality at the Crossroads: Current Issues in Interactional Psychology*. Hillsdale, NJ: Erlbaum.

Morosini, P. 1998. *Managing Cultural Differences: Effective Strategy and Execution across Cultures in Global Corporate Alliances*. New York: Elsevier Science.

Pablo, A.L. 1994. Determinants of acquisition integration level: A decision-making perspective. *Academy of Management Journal*, **37**: 803–36.

Pablo, A.L. and Javidan, M. 2002. Thinking of a merger ... Do you know their risk propensity profile? *Organizational Dynamics*, **30**: 206–22.

Peters, T. 1987. *Thriving on Chaos*. New York: Alfred A. Knopf.

Podsakoff, P.M. and Organ, D.W. 1986. Self-reports in organizational research: Problems and prospects. *Journal of Management*, **12**: 531–44.

Ravenscraft, D.J. and Scherer, F.M. 1987. *Mergers, Sell-offs, and Economic Efficiency*. Washington, DC: Brookings Institution.

Robbins, S.R. and Duncan, R.B. 1988. The role of the CEO and top management in the creation and implementation of strategic vision. In D.C. Hambrick (ed.), *The Executive Effect: Concepts and Methods for Studying Top Managers*. Greenwich, CT: JAI Press, pp. 137–62.

Sales, A.S. and Mirvis, P.H. 1984. When cultures collide: Issues in acquisitions. In J.R. Kimberly and R.B. Quinn (eds.), *Managing Organizational Transitions*. Burr Ridge, IL: Irwin.

Serapio, M.G. Jr. and Cascio, W.F. 1996. End-games in international alliances. *Academy of Management Executive*, **10**(1): 62–73.

Shamir, B. and Howell, J.M. 1999. Organizational and contextual influences on the emergence and effectiveness of charismatic leadership. *Leadership Quarterly*, **10**: 257–83.

Tichy, N.M. and Devanna, M.A. 1986. *The Transformational Leader*. New York: Wiley.

Waldman, D.A. and Javidan, M. 2002. Charismatic leadership at the strategic level: Taking a new look at upper echelons theory. In B.J. Avolio and F.J. Yammarino (eds.), *Monographs in Leadership and Management* (2nd vol.). New York: Elsevier Science, pp. 173–99.

Waldman, D.A., Ramirez, G.G., House, R.J., and Puranam, P. 2001. Does leadership matter? CEO leadership attributes under conditions of perceived environmental uncertainty. *Academy of Management Journal*, **44**: 134–43.

Waldman, D.A. and Yammarino, F.J. 1999. CEO charismatic leadership: Levels-of-management and levels-of-analysis effects. *Academy of Management Review*, **24**: 266–85.

Westley, F. and Mintzberg, H. 1989. Visionary leadership and strategic management. *Strategic Management Journal*, **10**: 17–32.

Yin, R. 1989. *Case Study Research: Design and Methods*. Beverly Hills, CA: Sage.

Youndt, M.A., Snell, S.A., Dean, J.W. Jr. and Lepak, D.P. 1996. Human resource management, manufacturing strategy, and firm performance. *Academy of Management Journal*, **39**: 836–66.

Yukl, G. 1999. An evaluation of conceptual weaknesses in transformational and charismatic leadership theories. *Leadership Quarterly*, **10**: 285–305.

CHAPTER TWELVE

The Impact of Perceived Uncertainty on Culture Differences in the Post-Acquisition Process to Strategy Realization

Vera Hartog

Abstract

This study sets out to develop an understanding of why and how in the post-acquisition integration process, culture differences impact strategy realization. Based on clinical research, the effect of culture differences was explored in multiple integration settings within a single multinational corporation. This pointed to various degrees of perceived organizational and perceived personal uncertainty associated with different integration approaches impacting on commitment to organizational goals. A controlled laboratory experiment validated perceived uncertainty causing an individual change on the socially constructed variable culture, which affects employees' behavior, such that it negatively impacts the process to strategy realization. The theoretical and practical relevance of these findings is discussed, as are directions for further research.

Introduction

Mergers and acquisitions (M&A) as a strategy for growth, by their sheer size and number, carry strategic importance for companies, industries, and the economy as a whole. M&A are a select opportunity to enhance a firm's capabilities (Haspeslagh and Jemison 1991), and though a well-traveled, not proven road to value creation (Chatterjee 1992, Datta 1991). Success depends on companies' ability to achieve their specific synergy goals by integrating their specific organizations, sharing their specific resources, and reconfiguring their organization toward value-creation processes. The needed inter- and intra-company cooperation, turning potential into achievement, reinforces the need to regard strategy formulation and implementation as aspects of the same objective (Nahavandi and Malekzadeh 1988, Datta and Grant 1990, Larsson and Finkelstein 1999).

The study develops an understanding of why, and how, culture differences impact strategy realization in mergers and acquisitions (M&A). The following three premises set the framework of the research area: (1) M&A are a select opportunity to enhance a firm's capabilities (Haspeslagh and Jemison 1991); (2) the post-acquisition integration process is a crucial factor in M&A, whereby management of the post-acquisition integration process is generally considered important in achieving organizational objectives (Pablo 1994, Schweiger and Walsh 1990); (3) culture is found to be a plausible explanation for obstructions in the post-acquisition integration process (Nahavandi and Malekzadeh 1988, Very, Lubatkin, and Calori 1996).

Weick (1985) argues that culture and strategy are overlapping constructs. Culture in an organizational setting serves two critical functions. It solves both problems of external adaptation (defining objectives) and those of internal integration, namely how opportunities and threats in the environment are dealt with. Social scientists have defined culture in a myriad of ways. "Culture gives you a set of codes to deal with phenomena in a social environment" (Nelson 1994). Schein (1985) defines culture as a set of shared, taken for granted implicit assumptions, which determine how a group perceives, thinks about, and reacts to changing environments. Hofstede (1994) considers culture the collective programming of the mind, which distinguishes the members of one group or category of people from another.

Impact of Culture on the Post-Acquisition Integration Process

In value-creating M&A, post-acquisition integration is the vehicle to transfer competencies and to share knowledge and skills between organizations (Haspeslagh and Jemison 1991, Jemison and Sitkin 1986). Though cultural diversity offers the opportunity to use the competencies and knowledge contained in each organization to the benefit of the combined company, clashing cultures throughout the corporate structure are found to poison an integration process and subsequently prevent synergy from being achieved (Shrivastava 1986, Weber, Shenkar, and Raveh 1996).

Two phenomena have made culture harder to come to terms within present-day M&A. The first is the growing number of cross-border (Datta and Puia 1995), cross-business (e.g. retail and investment banking), and cross-industry (e.g. banking and insurance) M&A. Not only do employees have different norms, values, and attitudes, they filter the environment and acts of others through the lenses of their own experience. Cross-border M&A are even less likely to succeed than within country M&A (Hofstede 1991): accommodating both national and organizational cultures results in "double layered acculturation" (Barkema, Bell, and Pennings 1996).

The second phenomenon is the growing importance of human capital, the primary "raw material" of the service industry (Davis 1984, Devine and Hirsch 1998). In providing a service there is both a high "personal" factor (Irons 1994) and a high level of interaction. In such an environment, the acquired business' resentment over loss of autonomy and its subsequent resistance to change (Dess, Picken and Janney 1998), are detrimental to achieving organizational objectives. Assimilating the staff of merging or acquired companies is a matter of strategic importance in the realization of synergies (Walsh 1988).

Failure to integrate cultures makes for an organizational void soon filled with dilemmas and conflicts, thus making for a situation where culture clashes are unavoidable (Nahavandi and Malekzadeh 1988, Sales and Mirvis 1984). Furthermore, Bloor and Dawson (1994) caution that culture clashes between members of different subcultures will likely evolve from a dormant level to an overt one if business is no longer "as usual".

The post-acquisition integration process is not only a complex situation of change, concerning a wide range of behaviors and processes, but the long-term success of a merger or acquisition also depends to a large extent on management of the human dimension (Devine and Hirsh 1998). Sommer, Bae, and Luthans (1996) state that employees' willingness to invest in the organization depends on their feelings of security and investiture. A number of researchers consider uncertainty to impact on organizational commitment: unpredictability throughout an organization and feelings of loss make people feel insecure, incompetent, and powerless to contribute (Begley 1998, Devine and Hirsh 1998). Conversely, Porter et al. (1974) define commitment to organizational goals as comprising a strong desire to remain in the organization, a strong belief in, and acceptance of the organization's goals and values, and a willingness to exert considerable effort on behalf of the organization.

Nahavandi and Malekzadeh (1988) and Larsson (1989, 1990) found employee reactions to M&A to be predominantly negative, largely because of the acculturation that occurs within the integration process. This reaction to acculturation is termed "employee resistance". Though culture is defined as setting one group of people apart from another, employee resistance to change in an acculturation process is considered to be a universal aspect of behavior. Weick (1996) wrote a most intriguing article using wild fires as an allegory for organizational studies. The historic events in the article illustrate the dynamics of dramatic, instant, and unexpected changes. Weick describes a situation where all of a sudden the fire-officers' framework of operation changed drastically. In retrospect, the fire-officers failed to reframe in a timely manner from fire-fighting to running for their life. On two similar occasions, this difficulty in adapting to changing circumstance did cost 23 men and four women their life. The lack of adaptation to change with one's life at stake makes for a divergence from the view that resistance to change is a purely rational process, within the conscious control of individuals.

Empirical research investigating non-rational adaptive action is not found in the management sciences but it is a prominent domain of research in the field of behavioral and cognitive neuroscience. At the beginning of the last century, Cannon (1915) stated that above a critical level of stress, corrective efforts were affected to such an extent that adjusting to a changing environment was seriously impaired. Uncertain situations perceived as stressful, trigger a complex neuro-endocrine cascade leading to adrenal gland reactions, which exert a striking influence on cognitive behavior (Krugers et al. 1997). Under conditions of uncertainty, organisms do not passively respond to consequences of stress. The human body reacts by activating a complex repertoire of behavioral and physiologic responses (Douma 1999).

Integrating theory based on analytical research literature, though covering a wide area of scientific fields, does not result in the establishment of a process resting solely on extant knowledge. Prior research stops short of explaining why and how culture differences impact on strategy realization in M&A.

Realization of strategy

In M&A, the realization of strategy is based on the achievement of strategic task objectives through exploitation of the synergy potential. There are a fair number of definitions but basically synergy is the value created by businesses working together as part of an organization, compared to the value the businesses would have created operating independently (Goold and Campbell 1998).

The strategic motives for M&A are manifold, furthermore it is possible that it is not one single motive that leads to a merger or acquisition. Taking situation-specific synergy goals into account does pose hurdles for large comparative studies, but realistically strategy realization depends on companies' ability to achieve their specific synergy goals by integrating their specific organizations, sharing their specific resources, and reconfiguring their organization toward value-creation processes. In this study, realization of strategy is determined by post-acquisition integration bridging the gap between synergy potential and synergy achieved.

This study diverges from prior research in arguing that the absence of culture clashes in the post-acquisition integration process is not enough of a condition to lead to realization of strategy. It is taken into account that organizational objectives, in most M&A, do change post acquisition and hence, constitute a situation where business is not as usual. Viewing employees' commitment to organizational goals on a continuum, "0" would constitute business "as is", resistance to change would constitute "−1", and what is required for strategy realization, extra-role behavior, "+1".

Extra-role behavior is defined in the literature as the willingness to exert considerable efforts on behalf of the organization (Lau and Woodman 1985). Successful organizational adaptation requires employees' support and enthusiasm for the new strategy, rather than just overcoming resistance (Piderit 2000), or continuing business on the same footing as before the merger or acquisition. The skills and expertise embodied in the employees of the acquired company are critical to the sustained success of the consolidated organization (Ravenscraft 1990); organizations have to respond quickly to evolving circumstances (Bartlett and Ghoshal 1995). Notwithstanding the fact that in the post-acquisition integration process not all required employee input can be foreseen, contractually regulated or directly rewarded, organizations depend on internal sources of advantage in an environment where external markets become increasingly efficient (Peteraf 1993).

An exploratory field study

An exploratory field study was conducted, within an M&A context, to explore the relationship of post-acquisition integration, culture, and realization of strategic goals. This work was done in 14 business units of Wegener NV, a Dutch listed company in the newspaper and direct marketing industry. In structured interviews held at the

Table 12.1   Culture differences in the Wegener acquisition of VNU Newspapers

Wegener	VNU Newspapers
Cost oriented	Revenue oriented
Centralized	Responsibility low in the organization, cooperative
Manuals, comfortable with rules and regulations, rigid	Dealing with uncertainty as a challenge, do not like bureaucracy
Procedural, disciplined, up to length of articles	Entrepreneurial, at times thrived on chaos
Obey	Think – dare – do – persist
Hierarchic, top management is right, fall in line, top-down, one boss who knows what is best	More freedom, liberal, equality, consensus, coordinate, commitment, open relationships between hierarchic levels
Submissive employees, do not speak up at meetings, different formal and informal behavior	Free spirits, taking initiatives, "a man a man, a word a word"
Managers not seen on the work floor	Personal interest in well-being of employees
Sit on the fence, political, hidden agendas	Open culture, knowledge easily shared
Lack of communication	Open communication, open doors
Problem situations smoldering like a moor fire, subsurface and unexpectedly flaring up	Problem situations out in the open
Work hard – roll up your sleeves	Meetings, committees, consensus

corporate and three other hierarchical levels, culture differences between the acquisition partners were found to be considerable (Table 12.1).

This field study showed that, contrary to expectations, respondents did not find the culture differences problematic and/or affecting the various post-acquisition integration processes. Thus, regardless of the degree to which different cultures came into contact with each other in the different integration approaches, respondents did not object to adapting to the culture of the partner as long as the post-acquisition process was perceived to be fair, honoring employees' past commitment to organizational goals, and free from opportunistic behavior.

The distinguishing factor between the different integration approaches is the level of autonomy granted and interdependencies required. From exploring the different integration approaches it was learned that the different integration approaches make for different combinations of high and low perceived organizational and personal uncertainty (Table 12.2).

Preservation stands for low interdependence and high autonomy. The acquired company is only integrated to a modest degree and preserves its way of doing business. *Symbiotic* acquisitions reflect high interdependence and at the same time a high need for organizational autonomy. *Absorption* represents the most complete integration. The acquirer absorbs the acquired business directly and assimilates it into its culture. An absorption instantaneously creates redundant functions as two formerly separate entities become one (Haspeslagh and Jemison 1991). Whereas Haspeslagh

Table 12.2   Matrix of integration approaches and subsequent levels of uncertainty

Post-acquisition integration	Perceived organizational uncertainty	Perceived personal uncertainty
Preservation	Low	Low
Symbiosis	High	Low
Absorption	Low	High
Predicament	High	High

and Jemison's framework deals with three clear choices of integration approach, there can also be a situation where no clear choice has been made. This situation will be referred to as *predicament*. This integration approach is characterized by a high level of perceived organizational uncertainty combined with a high level of perceived personal uncertainty.

In the field study, perceived uncertainty, stemming from organizational change in the integration approaches, was a major issue. Respondents described it impacting the post-acquisition integration process to the extent that it affected commitment to organizational goals and subsequently strategy realization. They considered uncertainty as a processual phenomenon of post-acquisition integration, reflecting both perceived organizational and perceived personal uncertainty. Perceived organizational uncertainty comprises the future of the company, knowing and understanding of what the goals are, the availability of resources to accomplish the goals set, legitimate concern for the protection of value drivers, and the industrial and economic environment in which the organization operates. Perceived personal uncertainty includes among other things, job security, honoring psychological contracts, altered career expectations, job satisfaction, new colleagues, work practices and/or business systems, and opportunistic behavior of others.

Research framework

This study diverges from earlier research findings in that obstructions to cooperation are not assumed to stem entirely from formerly independent organizations coming into contact with one another. If culture differences between acquisition partners obstruct post-acquisition integration, then the degree of culture differences between the acquisition partners and the degree of contact between the acquisition partners are of a determining nature. In this study, empirical work was conducted to investigate specifically how organizational and personal uncertainty change individuals' responses to cultural dimensions relating to goal-directed behaviors. In the specific M&A framework for investigation discussed earlier and shown at Figure 12.1, it is hypothesized that dimensions of culture are affected by perceived uncertainty created by the integration approach implemented, ultimately impacting commitment to organizational goals and strategy realization. It is argued that above a certain level, perceived uncertainty causes a reaction outside the conscious control of individuals, affecting extra-role behavior, notwithstanding earlier collective programming of the mind. The specific framework for investigation allows for how and why the

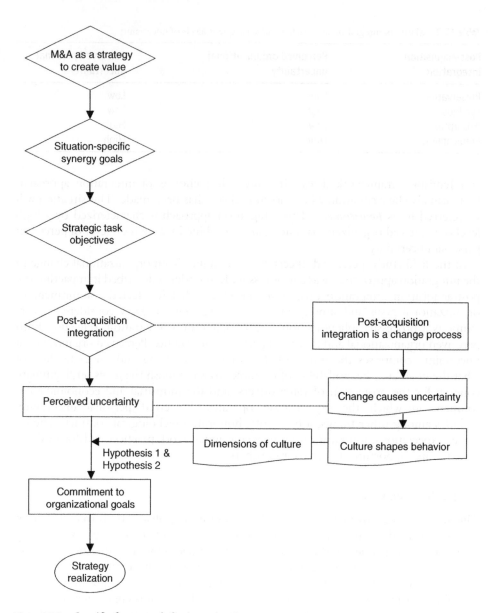

Figure 12.1   Specific framework for investigation

dimensions of culture moderate the behavioral outcomes of post-acquisition integration and, ultimately, strategy realization for the firm.

Strategy realization requires employees' commitment to organizational goals and
in M&A this requires extra-role behavior. Extra-role behavior (Lau and Woodman
1985) is expected to be present in varying degrees within a certain range. A within-
person change on the dimensions of culture would reflect how culture impacts
goal-directed behavior and ultimately strategy realization. Assuming the different

combinations of perceived organizational and personal uncertainty have a dissimilar impact on the dimensions of culture, we predict different levels of extra-role behavior exhibited by individuals. If culture shapes behavior, and if both behavior and employee performance are influenced by uncertainty, different perceptions of uncertainty should lead to changes in behavior measured along the dimensions of culture (Hofstede and Bond 1988).

In order to understand why and how culture contributes to strategy realization, the following hypothesized relationships are tested in a controlled laboratory experiment.

Hypotheses

The following hypotheses test the perspective that the dimensions of culture are a dynamic contextual dependent variable in the post-acquisition integration process.

Null hypothesis 1:   Dimensions of culture will not differ between the integration approaches.

Null hypothesis 2:   The median of the answers given on the same questions in the different integration approaches does not differ between the integration approaches.

The acceptance of the null hypotheses would signify that the study provides no evidence to suggest that there is a significant within-person difference on the dimensions of culture under conditions of change.

Methodology

The controlled laboratory experiment is an explorative, quantitative research method using vignettes, in this study, manipulating the post-acquisition integration approaches. The matrix in Table 12.2 allows for the controlled laboratory experiment to constitute what in mathematical statistics is defined as a true random experiment (Hogg and Craig 1970), capturing respondents' reactions to different perceptions of reality. It excludes any boundary conditions, other than perceived uncertainty, which are likely to be present in unaccounted for sources of variance specific to respondents' real-life situations. The psychometrics of the study described build on Hofstede's (1980) research and are here tailor-fitted to post-acquisition integration.

Designing the sample

Not adhering to a mathematical definition of "random", the sample is random to the extent that a process outside the control of the researcher selected the respondents. The sample was collected over a period of several months commencing at the end of 2001 and extending to April 2002. All respondents were drawn from the business community: students were not part of the sample. The organizations in the sample were accessed based on personal introduction of earlier professional contacts. Lacking

Table 12.3   Demographic characteristics of the sample

	Demographic characteristics of sample
Gender	female $n = 334$; male $n = 468$
Age	$<25\ n = 56$; 25–30 $n = 95$; 31–35 $n = 188$; 36–40 $n = 117$; 41–45 $n = 140$; 46–50 $n = 99$; 51–55 $n = 73$; $>55\ n = 34$
Nationality	Belgian $n = 194$; British $n = 61$; Bulgarian $n = 190$; Dutch $n = 208$; South African $n = 105$; of assorted nationalities $n = 44$
Tenure (years)	$<2\ n = 120$; 2–5 $n = 144$; 6–10 $n = 195$; $>10\ n = 343$
Function	manager of managers $n = 94$; manager of non-managers $n = 176$; individual contributors $n = 195$; operators/admin staff/other $n = 337$
Education	vocational $n = 84$; technical $n = 127$; high school $n = 176$; university $n = 411$; other $n = 4$
Field	economics $n = 82$; education $n = 29$; engineering $n = 258$; administration $n = 84$; sociology $n = 23$; marketing and sales $n = 34$; languages $n = 18$; IT $n = 14$; law $n = 22$; other $n = 238$
Congruence field and function	yes $n = 524$; no $n = 204$; not applicable $n = 74$
Job market	expecting to find a job within one month $n = 397$; within a year $n = 225$; finding a job with great difficulty $n = 180$

a pre-existing sampling frame, the sample is homogeneous in respect that respondents were undergoing or subject to a pending merger or acquisition. The sample is heterogeneous based on demographic characteristics. It is deliberately composed of dissimilar respondents for external validity not to pose a problem. Table 12.3 presents the demographic characteristics of the sample.

Unit of analysis

The unit of analysis is the integration approaches described by Haspeslagh and Jemison (1991) plus the added "predicament" (high level of perceived organizational uncertainty combined with a high level of perceived personal uncertainty). To account for random errors, the sequence of the vignettes representing the integration approaches has been altered (1/2/3/4, 2/4/1/3, 3/1/4/2, and 4/3/2/1).

Design of vignettes

In general, vignettes allow for a great amount of background information and detail to be built into hypothetical but recognizable situations. For the purpose of this study four vignettes were written (Table 12.4). These were evaluated by a diverse group of academics familiar with the use of questionnaires. This resulted in the vignettes being brought back to a bare minimum in text and being devoid of emotional string pulling.

Table 12.4   Integration approaches and vignettes

Integration approach	Vignette
Preservation	In this case you work for a company which has been acquired for its specific specialist knowledge. The acquiring company leaves the management in the hands of the present incumbents. Though ambitious in its goals for the next three years, it is a matter of fact that the means to attain the proposed goals have been made available.
Symbiosis	Consider working for an organization which has been bought by a supplier. By optimizing and aligning the operations of both companies it is expected to enhance profitability. It has been agreed that the acquirer will not directly be involved in the operations, though often there is a request to provide further information. Frequently external experts are hired to search for coordination benefits between both companies. Immediately following the acquisition you have been informed in a personal conversation that you are a valuable and difficult to replace employee.
Absorption	Imagine that you work for a company, which is one of the best in its sector. A while ago your company was acquired by a competitor. The new owner will invest in the company, the future of the company is not at stake. Though you have not received a lot of information, the company is full of talk about pending cost-cutting exercises. You and your colleagues fear that mass lay-offs cannot be prevented. The operations of your division will be managed from one of the regional offices of the acquirer. It is known throughout the industry that it is cheaper to concentrate all operations at one location.
Predicament	Imagine about a year ago your company was acquired by a foreign party. In contrast to the initial expectations of substantial synergies, massive losses have been incurred. Many of your colleagues have left the company, and just about everybody is updating their resume. Cooperation with the acquirer is fraught with miscommunication and friction. Of late, you no longer know what is expected of you. Before the dust settles there seems to be yet another round of reorganization. Due to circumstances, you spend a great deal of your time reassuring employees, rather than being able to perform your own job adequately.

To test whether the integration approaches displayed levels of perceived organizational and perceived personal uncertainty as designed, seven retired U.S. Air Force officers, five Belgian engineers, three Bulgarian, and two South African business people completed the manipulation test. The 17 respondents evaluated the four vignettes to which either a high or a low level of both perceived organizational and perceived personal uncertainty had to be assigned. The number of answers to be given amounted to a total of $(17 \times 4 \times 2)$ 136 answers. One form only mentioned perceived organizational uncertainty (so carried four errors), four forms had two errors and 12 were in line with the design, which is 91.18 percent.

The non-parametric Kendall's coefficient of concordance was used to test the measurement of agreement between raters. At 0.737 it established sufficient agreement between the evaluators.

Design of scales

All of the items on the questionnaire (shown in Table 12.5), other than the questions soliciting demographic data, were measured on a seven point Likert-type scale ranging from 1 (strongly agree) to 7 (strongly disagree). The same set of questions followed each vignette. The scale is considered as a single-item component measuring the dimensions of culture.

Validity. Reference content validity, the dimensions of culture are described in Table 12.5. Based on Geert Hofstede's (1991) book *Cultures and Organisations: Software of the Mind* the questions are tailor fitted to reflect the type of behavior required for value to be created (predictive validity). The actual order of the questions in the controlled laboratory experiment is different from that in Table 12.5.

Construct validity concerns the extent to which a measure behaves as expected based on theory (DeVellis 1991) and in a multi-item measure is internally consistent. Prior specification of general notions permits researchers to measure constructs more accurately (Eisenhardt 1989). The three practitioners, who helped design the vignettes, were given a list of 60 questions plus a description of the five key constructs in the scale. Based on how well the questions reflected what they were intended to measure as well as the ease with which the questions would be understood, taking into account the different nationalities and levels throughout the hierarchies, resulted in a questionnaire with 10 questions following each case. Testing the questionnaires, it took more than an hour to fill in the form.

Reliability. Based on 802 questionnaires, and recoding the questions numbered 7 and 8 (Table 12.5), the following Cronbach's alphas were found: preservation (0.72), symbiosis (0.78), absorption (0.79), and predicament (0.72). Subsequently, the degree to which the measures are free from error are acceptable (Nunnally 1978). The same scale showing a different Cronbach's alpha, notwithstanding that each vignette in the questionnaire was responded to by exactly the same sample, is remarkable.

The Kaiser–Meyer–Olkin measure of sampling adequacy was used to test the underlying structure in the scale. It was established at preservation (0.85), symbiosis (0.85), absorption (0.79), and predicament (0.80). It can be safely argued that all scales point to an underlying structure in the scale (Norusis 1988). It is emphasized that the scale did not cause differences in strength of the scale structure, as identical scales were tested.

Translation of the questionnaire

The questionnaire was distributed in three languages (English, Dutch, and Bulgarian). Per language version, two native speakers whose working language is English were involved in translating and re-translating the questionnaire.

Table 12.5 Dimensions of culture, content and questions

Dimensions of culture	Content and questions
Uncertainty avoidance (UAI)	The extent to which individuals are able to tolerate uncertain, ambiguous, or unknown situations. Low Hofstede (1991) scores suggest people are less cautious, more likely to take risks, and apt at making fundamental innovations. Employees' beliefs that change will yield negative outcomes impact the readiness and receptivity of organizations to adapt to new initiatives in organizational change.
	In the strategy implementation phase uncertainty avoidance is considered to affect the degree to which employees will risk being noticed.
	1. In this situation, I would choose not to rock the boat and think twice before offering creative solutions.
	2. I would not be surprised if absenteeism was high.
Masculinity/ Femininity (MAS)	"Masculine" cultures favor ambition, assertiveness, and the desire to achieve recognition by succeeding in one's career. "Feminine" cultures in contrast value modesty in people and are characterized by a concern for the quality of life.
	In a post-acquisition integration approach it is assumed that the more masculine the culture the less the employees would be inclined to let groups benefit from their expertise, skills, and qualities if they were not certain it benefited their own career.
	3. I would be surprised if cooperation between divisions would be smooth.
	4. In the above-described situation, I would not be inclined to share specific professional knowledge.
Individualism/ Collectivism (IDV)	In a business context, individualism is characterized by the loosely knit social framework and crystallized in employer–employee contracts and negotiations more accurately than by tactic group conformity. It defines the extent to which it is acceptable that personal values deviate from the accepted values within the group. Social behavior is strongly influenced by rules in an organization with a collective cultural orientation (Triandis 1995).
	In a post-acquisition integration process individualism is determined by the manner and degree to which employees relate to groups, put their own interests before the group, and willingness/ ability to depend on others.
	5. I would not consider voluntary overtime.
	6. I would find it risky to depend on colleagues to achieve goals.
Power/Distance (PDI)	Power/Distance (PDI) measures the extent to which inequality is expected and accepted in society and organizations.
	For the purpose of this study the following two questions relate to whether inequality based on hierarchical position affects the post-acquisition integration process (checking for large PDI acceptance). Questions 7 and 8 were re-coded, for analytical purposes, but intentionally posed the way they were.

Table 12.5 *Continued*

Dimensions of culture	Content and questions
	7. Working for the company described, I would find substantial differences in job security between management and work floor acceptable.
	8. Should I have a better approach, I would come forward without hesitation.
Long-term/Short-term Orientation (LTO)	Long term is an orientation toward the future. It stands for a high regard of virtues in particular perseverance, stable relationships with business partners, loyalty, and thrift. "Keep your nose to the grind stone and all will be well"-like. Short term stands for the fostering of virtues related to the past and present, in particular respect for traditions, preservation of "face", and fulfilling social obligations like reciprocation of favors.
	In an M&A situation a long-term view stands for loyalty toward the company and expecting psychological contracts to be adhered to.
	9. I would not assume that earlier made career promises would be adhered to.
	10. I would not feel loyal to a company as described in the vignette.

Distribution of the questionnaire

A master copy of the questionnaire was sent by email or registered mail to existing business contacts and to executives accessed based on personal introduction. The selection criteria for the points of contact was their organization going through a post-acquisition integration process or being subject to a pending merger or acquisition. The questionnaires were handed out and collected during courses, at meetings and briefings, as much as possible taking a hierarchical representation into account.

Results

Null hypothesis 1: Dimensions of culture will not differ between the integration approaches

The non-parametric Friedman test was used to test for the range of the questions per integration approach, to be equal. Null hypothesis 1 is rejected with a 99 percent confidence interval and a probability of $p = 0.000$ that the differences are caused by chance alone.

Null hypothesis 2: The median of answers given on the same questions in the different integration approaches does not differ between the integration approaches

With the non-parametric Friedman test, the median is compared per set of same questions across the integration approaches, resulting in 10 tests. Null hypothesis 2 is

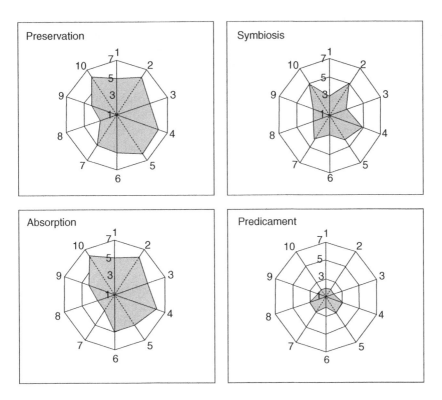

Figure 12.2   Radar graphs depicting the bandwidth of the culture dimensions along the integration approaches ($n = 802$)

rejected with a 99 percent confidence interval. The results establish that the data collected vary to such an extent that the sample is refuted to come from the same population. The null hypothesis for the question "Working for the company described, I would find substantial differences in job security between management and work floor acceptable" was refuted at a $p = 0.001$ error level. With a probability of $p < 0.000$ the null hypothesis was refuted on the other nine questions. The results suggest that perceived organizational and personal uncertainty do cause a within-person change on the culture dimensions as measured in the questionnaire.

In the radar graph, at Figure 12.2, the numbers around the circle represent the questions from 1 to 10 (re-ordered and re-coded) and the numbers on the radius represent the answers 1 (strongly agree) to 7 (strongly disagree). The area on the radar graph in the preservation post-acquisition integration approach shows most extra-role behavior, while certainly in the predicament case an extreme lack of extra-role behavior is illustrated. There is found to be a negative relation between perceived uncertainty and behavior conducive to the realization of strategy.

It is brought to the attention that the answers on the scale ranging from 1 (strongly agree) to 7 (strongly disagree) show the degree to which a certain type of behavior is present. It is present in answers ranging from 7 (strongly disagree) to 5 (somewhat disagree). A neutral situation is where respondents answered 4 (neither agree nor disagree). Respondents have to overcome, at best, a hesitation in the answers ranging from 3 (somewhat agree) to 1 (strongly agree). The re-coding of the questions allows for interpreting all of the dimensions in the same manner.

Starting from preservation with both low perceived organizational and personal uncertainty, the results show a more stable range on absorption than on symbiosis. The range illustrates a considerable decrease in extra-role behavior in the predicament integration approach, where perceived organizational and perceived personal uncertainty are both high. On questions 1, 2, 3, 4, 6, 8, 9, and 10 there is no narrowing of the range in comparing preservation to absorption. The latter post-acquisition integration approach with a low perceived organizational and a high perceived personal uncertainty. Offering creative solutions, absenteeism, cooperation between divisions, sharing of specific professional knowledge, depending on colleagues to achieve goals, stepping forward with a better approach, the assumption that earlier career promises are adhered to, and loyalty to the company are not affected by high perceived personal uncertainty.

Especially questions 1, 3, and 6 (offering creative solutions, cooperation between divisions, and depending on colleagues to achieve goals) are seriously affected by high perceived organizational uncertainty. Question 5 (considering voluntary overtime) is affected by high personal uncertainty and even to a larger extent by high perceived organizational uncertainty. Considering overtime is not resilient to the effects of perceived uncertainty, neither is question 7 (the acceptance of substantial differences in job security). However, the acceptance of power distance is more affected by high perceived personal uncertainty (absorption) than by high perceived organizational uncertainty (symbiosis).

Discussion and Implications

The primary theoretical contribution of this study is the establishment of why and how, in the post-acquisition integration process, culture differences impact the realization of strategy. In general, the dimensions of culture as described by Hofstede (1980, 1991) influence employees' participation in bridging the gap between synergy potential and synergy achieved. The dimensions of culture are found to be a moderating variable rather than an independent factor in the post-acquisition integration approach. A within-person change on the dimensions of culture, stemming from a change in the levels of autonomy granted and interdependence required, explains why culture impacts strategy realization. The effects of this within-person change on commitment to organizational goals resolve how culture impacts strategy realization. Culture is found to be a socially constructed variable, which in the post-acquisition integration process is impacted at an individual level, regardless of earlier programming of the mind. Uncertainty as it is perceived, stemming from organizational change in the post-acquisition integration processes, has an inverse relation to behavior conducive to realization of strategy.

The research results contribute to knowledge in the field of strategy, organizational behavior, and social psychology by validating that dependent on context the dimensions of culture become dynamic. Research findings also illustrate that in the post-acquisition integration process perceived uncertainty is a dual construct and a context-dependent process variable. Particular to the field of strategy is that the absence of resistance to change nor employees continuing to perform their daily routines is enough of a condition to bridge the gap between synergy potential and synergy achieved. Extra-role behavior is the critical factor in the post-acquisition integration process toward strategy realization. The scale applied in the controlled laboratory experiment, measuring the dimensions of culture, shows the discretionary nature of extra-role behavior.

Of practical relevance for business leaders is that it is not necessarily the degree of culture differences between acquisition partners, nor the degree cultures come into contact with each other, nor these culture differences originating cross-business, cross-industry or cross-border that explain the impact of culture on strategy realization. The effect of perceived uncertainty on the post-acquisition integration processes is such that the importance of management action cannot be overstated. The inverse relation between the level of perceived uncertainty and employees' extra-role behavior seriously impacts strategy realization. Any integration approach can show a pattern of high perceived organizational and high perceived personal uncertainty if no clear choices are made or if internal communication is lacking. In the post-acquisition integration approach, business is not as usual and the requirements for strategy realization have not yet crystallized to the extent that they can be incorporated in job descriptions, work procedures, structures, and processes. Extra-role behavior to a large extent being discretionary and in the span of control rather than under the control of business leaders is an important finding. The more employees' activities consist of actions that are non-fragmented, non-routine, and require interaction, the more strategy realization hinges on leadership creating an environment where value can be created. It is not so much that culture differences are incompatible, the effect of perceived uncertainty on extra-role behavior is such that employees throughout the hierarchy do not make the opening moves. The obstruction to cooperation is not so much employee resistance as that there is no platform for transfer of competencies, for sharing of knowledge and skills, or an environment for cooperation.

Limitations

The sample of the questionnaire is neither random nor has it been possible to test for non-reply. As stated earlier, in management research judgment samples are more common than probability samples (Thietart et al. 2001). The number of respondents is sufficiently large, and deliberately composed of dissimilar respondents for external validity not to pose a problem.

Eight questions following the vignettes are measuring personal behavioral intentions, while two are measuring the behavior of colleagues. Asking a direct question reference absenteeism was considered too intrusive to gather answers that were not influenced by considerations of "social correctness". The question on cooperation between divisions being smooth was purposely phrased as such cooperation is more of a group effort than that of a solitary individual.

In this study, the most widely used analytical tool to establish reliability, Cronbach's alpha, and the Kaiser–Meyer–Olkin measure to determine sampling adequacy have been used. The use of these mean-based tests on ordinals is considered an acceptable risk as they test the scale applied. They are not used to interpret the controlled laboratory experiment results. Taking into account that the answers following the different vignettes were drawn from a true replicated sample, comparing the results of the reliability tests across the vignettes warrant attention. The application of mean-based statistics to an ordinal scale might not be without penalty or alternatively it might be that environmental contexts affect reliability tests.

Further research

This study is only the first step toward a better understanding of how and why culture differences impact strategy realization. Research into whether one or some dimensions of culture are clean in their effect while others are more of a moderating nature and/or their interrelation is deemed important. Further analysis of the data is deemed worthwhile but at the moment impaired by the unconventional premise that the difference between a discrete and a continuous solution space is such that it might seriously affect the meaningfulness of analytical statistical results.

In this context, it will be a contribution to the management literature to explore whether, and how, historic events influence perceptions of uncertainty in a present situation. And, whether and how, tolerance for absorbing impact within certain boundaries explains differences in the performance of firms. It is expected that current and historic organizational *modus operandi* and external environmental factors will determine these factors in specific change situations. The impact of these on strategy realization in addition to perceived uncertainty stemming from changing levels of autonomy and required amount of interdependence should be taken into account.

It was a core premise of the chapter that strategies and their implementation are an integral part of strategy realization. Investigating the generalizability of the research findings to other organizational change efforts might not be without significance in explaining differences in firms' performance.

Notes

The author gratefully acknowledges the insightful contributions by Professor Philippe Haspeslagh, the enlightening discussions on analytical and mathematical statistics with Jan Vons, and access to the field of neuroscience provided by Theo van Kooten of the University of Groningen.

References

Barkema, H., Bell, J., and Pennings, J. 1996. Foreign entry, cultural barriers, and learning. *Strategic Management Journal*, **17**: 151–66.
Bartlett, C. and Ghoshal, S. 1995. Rebuilding behavioral context: Turn process reengineering into people rejuvenation. *Sloan Management Review*, **37**(1): 11.
Begley, T. 1998. Coping strategies as predictors of employee distress and turnover after an organizational consolidation: A longitudinal analysis. *Journal of Occupational and Organizational Psychology*, **71**(4): 305–29.
Bloor, G. and Dawson, P. 1994. Understanding professional culture in organizational context. *Organization Studies*, **15**(2): 275.
Cannon, W. 1915. *Bodily Changes in Pain, Hunger, Fear, and Rage*. New York: Appleton.
Chatterjee, S. 1992. Sources of value in takeovers: Synergy or restructuring – implications for target and bidder firms. *Strategic Management Journal*, **13**: 267–86.
Datta, D. 1991. Organizational fit and acquisition performance: Effects of post-acquisition integration. *Strategic Management Journal*, **12**: 281–97.
Datta, D. and Grant, J. 1990. Relationships between type of acquisition, the autonomy given to the acquired firm and acquisition success: An empirical analysis. *Journal of Management*, **16**(1): 29–44.
Datta, D. and Puia, G. 1995. Cross-border acquisitions: An examination of the influence of relatedness and cultural fit on shareholder value creation in U.S. acquiring firms. *Management International Review*, **4**: 337.
Davis S. 1984. *Managing Corporate Culture*. Cambridge, MA: Ballinger.
Dess, G., Picken J., and Janney, J. 1998. Subtracting value by adding business. *Business Horizons*, **41**(1): 9–18.
Devine, M. and Hirsch, W. 1998. *Mergers and Acquisitions: Getting the People Bit Right*. Horsham, UK: Roffey Park Management Institute.
DeVellis, R. 1991. *Scale Development: Theory and Applications*. Newbury Park: Sage.
Douma, B. 1999. *Stress, Learning and Hippocampal Plasticity*. Thesis, Rijksuniversiteit Groningen, The Netherlands.
Eisenhardt, K. 1989. Building theories from case study research. *Academy of Management Review*, **14**(4): 534–50.
Goold, M. and Campbell, A. 1998. Desperately seeking synergy. *Harvard Business Review*, September–October: 130–43.
Haspeslagh, P. and Jemison, D. 1991. *Managing Acquisitions: Creating Value through Corporate Renewal*. New York: Free Press.
Hofstede, G. 1980. *Culture's Consequences: International Difference in Work-Related Values*. Beverly Hills, CA: Sage.
Hofstede, G. 1991. *Cultures and Organizations: Software of the Mind*. Berkshire, UK: McGraw-Hill.
Hofstede, G. 1994. *Uncommon Sense About Organizations: Case Studies and Field Observation*. Thousand Oaks, CA: Sage.
Hofstede, G. and Bond, M. 1988. The Confucius connection: From cultural roots to economic growth. *Organizational Dynamics*, **16**(4): 4–21.
Hogg, R. and Craig, A. 1970. *Introduction to Mathematical Statistics*. New York: Macmillan.
Irons, K. 1994. *Managing Service Companies: Strategy for Success*. Harlow, UK: Addison-Wesley.
Jemison, D. and Sitkin, S. 1986. Corporate acquisitions: A process perspective. *Academy of Management Review*, **11**(1): 145–63.

Krugers, H., Douma, B., Andringa, G., Bohus, B., Korf, J., and Luiten, P. 1997. Exposure to chronic psychosocial stress and corticosterone in the rat: Effects on spatial discrimination learning and hippocampal protein Kinase Cy immunoreactivity. Department of Biological Psychiatry and Department of Animal Physiology, Graduate School for Behavioral and Cognitive Neurosciences: University of Groningen, The Netherlands. *Hippocampus*, 7: 427–36.

Larsson, R. 1989. *Organizational Integration of Mergers and Acquisitions: A Case Survey of Realization of Synergy Potential*. Lund: Lund University Press.

Larsson, R. 1990. *Coordination of Action in Mergers and Acquisitions*. Lund: Lund University Press.

Larsson, R. and Finkelstein, S. 1999. Integrating strategic, organizational, and human resource perspectives on mergers and acquisitions: A case survey of synergy realization. *Organization Science*, 10(1): 1–26.

Lau, C. and Woodman, R. 1995. Understanding organizational change: A schematic perspective. *Academy of Management Journal*, 38(2): 537.

Nahavandi, A. and Malekzadeh, A. 1988. Acculturation in mergers and acquisitions. *Academy of Management Review*, 13(1): 79–90.

Nelson, C. 1994. *Managing Globally: A Complete Guide to Competing Worldwide*. Burr Ridge, IL: Irwin.

Norusis, M. 1988. *SPSS/PC+ Advanced Statistics TM V2.0*. USA: SPSS Inc.

Nunnally, J. 1978. *Psychometric Theory* (2nd ed.). New York: McGraw-Hill.

Pablo, A. 1994. Determinants of acquisition integration level: A decision-making perspective. *Academy of Management Journal*, 37(4): 803–36.

Peteraf, M. 1993. The cornerstone of competitive advantage: A resource-based view. *Strategic Management Journal*, 14(3): 179–91.

Piderit, S. 2000. Rethinking resistance and recognizing ambivalence: A multidimensional view of attitudes towards an organizational change. *Academy of Management Review*, 25(4): 783–94.

Porter, L., Steers, R., Mowday, R., and Boulian, P. 1974. Unit performance, situational factors, and employee attitudes in spatially separated work units. *Organizational Behavior and Human Performance*, 15: 87–98.

Ravenscraft, D. 1990. The merger game: Playing against the odds. In D. Fair and C. de Boissieu (eds.), *Financial Institutions and Europe under New Competitive Conditions*. Dordrecht: Kluwer.

Sales, A. and Mirvis, P. 1984. When cultures collide: Issues in acquisition. In J. Kimberly and R. Quinn (eds.), *New Futures: The Challenge of Managing Corporate Transitions*. Homewood, IL: Irwin.

Schein, E. 1985. *Organizational Culture and Leadership: A Dynamic View*. San Francisco: Jossey-Bass.

Schweiger, D. and Walsh, J. 1990. Mergers and acquisitions: an interdisciplinary view. In K. Rowland and G. Ferris (eds.), *Research in Personnel and Human Resource Management*. Greenwich, CT: JAI Press.

Shrivastava, P. 1986. Postmerger integration. *Journal of Business Strategy*, 7(1): 65–76.

Sommer, S., Bae, S., and Luthans, F. 1996. The structure-climate relationship in Korean organizations. *Asia-Pacific Journal of Management*, 12: 23–36.

Thietart, R.A. et al. 2001. *Doing Management Research: A Comprehensive Guide*. London: Sage.

Triandis, H. 1995. *Individualism and Collectivism*. Boulder, CO: Westview Press.

Very, P., Lubatkin, M., and Calori, R. 1996. A cross-national assessment of acculturative stress in recent European mergers. *International Studies of Management and Organisation*, 26(1): 59.

Walsh, J. 1988. Top management turnover mergers and acquisitions. *Strategic Management Journal*, **9**(2): 173–83.

Weber, Y., Shenkar, O., and Raveh, A. 1996. National and corporate culture fit in mergers/acquisitions: An exploratory study. *Management Science*, **42**(8): 1215–27.

Weick, K. 1985. Cosmos vs. chaos: Sense and nonsense in electronic contexts. *Organizational Dynamics*, **14**(2): 51–64.

Weick, K. 1996. Drop your tools: an allegory for organizational studies. *Administrative Science Quarterly*, **41**(2): 301.

Research in M&As

CHAPTER THIRTEEN

When We Study M&A, What Are We Learning?

Joseph L. Bower

Abstract

In this chapter, the author reviews the scholarly work of researchers studying the complex phenomena of mergers and acquisitions through the twentieth century (and beyond), and examines what they have learned from their many years of inquiry. While acknowledging the valuable groundwork that has been laid, he contends that until we draw on multiple bodies of theory and include a mix of methods in our research, we will not be learning that much new. He exhorts us to deal with differences among types of M&A, explore meaning "on-the-ground" of engaging in these transactions, and pay close attention to identification and measurement of the huge variety of variables important to M&A outcomes. Otherwise, findings are of questionable value, and it really is not clear what we have learned.

Introduction

In the United States, the scholarly study of mergers begins with the economists' concern with the consequences of concentration in manufacturing. Reasoning that monopolistic industry structure led to a series of exploitative practices such as predatory pricing, Congress passed the Sherman Anti-Trust Act in 1898 and empowered the Department of Justice to enforce it. Noting that concentration was often the result of a series of mergers, economists recommended and Congress passed in the form of the Clayton Act legislation that made illegal mergers or acquisitions that would significantly lessen competition. The Federal Trade Commission was empowered to review mergers. In the context of these public policy concerns, economists have continued to examine M&A activity and its consequences for competition.[1] The idea that the structure of industry influenced directly the conduct of firms and hence their performance, continued to shape thinking about competition well into the 1960s. It was only the scholars of management whose case research demonstrated that the strategies of individual firms might differ substantially from each other and that might make a difference to industry performance.[2]

Skipping over nearly six decades of work that elaborated the structure–conduct–performance paradigm, economists in the 1980s began to concern themselves with the external competitiveness of industry. They noticed that lower prices and improving quality were sometimes associated with industry structure that looked tightly oligopolistic. This healthy result was counter-intuitive. It was also apparent that world trade was linking markets in ways that challenged conventional industrial organization definitions of markets which were almost always national. It was hard to ignore that in the U.S. car market, Toyota and Nissan had made a mockery of the "market power" of the "Big Three" auto producers. In Japan in particular, economists considered how much competition was enough to generate robust rivalry and what conditions were likely to produce hyper-competition and destructive price wars.[3]

In the United States, M&A captured the attention of two major groups of scholars who joined industrial organization economists in examining consolidations. The first group was financial economists who discovered that M&A activity lent itself quite well to "event studies." *Given the assumption that security markets were perfectly efficient in their pricing of company shares, then the wisdom of managers in merging or acquiring could be measured by examining how the market reacted to the news of an M&A event.* The assumption is emphasized because it is preposterous from a strategic perspective. An extensive literature developed that is considered below.

The second group of scholars studied the competitive strategies of particular firms. Business histories and case studies described the building of firms through acquisitions. A group of scholars following Wrigley[4] studied different patterns of diversification noting that the divisions of some firms were closely related at even an operating level, while others were highly unrelated except for the fact of a single legal and financial parent. Much of the study of diversification involved growth by acquisition.[5] This work called attention to the different management challenges that would be posed by these different diversification strategies.

In the mid-1970s, management scholars began to consider whether such diversity and a strategy of acquisition was a good thing for the companies involved. Kenneth Andrews opined that making a success of unrelated diversification was implausible.[6] A decade later, Michael Porter published an empirical study of that question in the *Harvard Business Review* in which he noted that over the 1950–86 period, of 33 large prestigious U.S. companies, most had divested many more acquisitions than they had kept. His implicit conclusion was that this was evidence that the majority of decisions were unsound. There followed a whole series of papers by financial economists examining post-merger performance.[7]

The problem, of course, is that selling a company a decade after buying it is not evidence that the purchase was a mistake. It all depends on why one bought it. Often companies buy firms to accelerate entry into a geographic market, or development of a technological competence, or expansion of production capacity. The fact that at a later date, one no longer needs that unit does not mean the original move was wrong. This is critical to understanding why the studies conducted with the lens of industrial organization economists or corporate finance or capital markets will not necessarily tell those of us interested in strategic management anything very interesting about M&A.

The same kind of question can be raised with the event studies, the approach to mergers taken by most financial economists. Indeed, my own view is that a recent paper by Shleifer and Vishny (in press[8]) will substantially alter our interpretation of most of these studies. Whereas event studies assume the perfect efficiency of *markets*, Shleifer and Vishny presume the perfect rationality of *managers*. Markets they take to be irrational are subject to significant short-term swings of emotion. The price of a particular company can be higher or lower than a manager knows to be justified by its circumstances. These irrational premiums or discounts go to zero in the long term. Under these circumstances, when a manager knows that his unjustified premium is higher than the unjustified premium of a target, it makes sense to buy using stock. In turn, a manager will demand cash when his company's premium is lower than the value he knows to be correct.

This model is consistent with most of the empirical studies of M&A by financial economists. But the interpretation is entirely different, much closer to a managerial perspective. The deals are largely successful in the sense that rational managers are making sensible decisions, even when the premiums they pay are quite high. AOL's purchase of Time-Warner may have been a classic example. But the perspective is still not strategic.

The problem with these two lines of argument is that it leaves us without a clear conclusion. When we study M&A, we are not learning that much new. We don't know that many deals failed because they were unwound, and we don't know that they failed because a high premium was paid. The problem with the Shleifer and Vishny study is that while it predicts well which mergers are undertaken, it fails to deal with the well-documented problems of implementation. There is the special case where the financing of the purchase premium causes such problems that bankruptcy follows.[9] Most would take that as clear evidence of failure. Although not documented, there is a clear pattern of bankruptcy following peaks of highly leveraged mergers. And *Moody's* indicates that M&A was the largest source of event risk in the 1980s.[10] But bankruptcy aside, to get M&A studied properly we will have to ask managements what they had in mind when they made the decision to buy or mate with another company and whether things worked out.

Some of you will recognize this argument as related to my recent article in the *Harvard Business Review*.[11] There I use the resources, processes, values model to show that the task of implementing an M&A transaction varies widely in difficulty depending on the strategy driving the merger. A within-country geographic roll-up poses far fewer problems than using M&A as a substitute for R&D.[12] Philippe Haspeslagh and David Jemison also made distinctions among mergers, but sorted along differences in the task of implementation rather than strategy per se.[13]

My argument today goes further. A reading of the research on M&A published in the last three years reveals as a pattern the two fundamental problems identified in the previous discussion. The meaningfulness of research on M&A that adopts a performance hypothesis is limited by non-strategic measures of performance. At the same time, studies that examine from a strategic perspective the problem of implementing a merger or acquisition seem almost always to use qualitative non-economic measures of performance.

Many papers are written as if their authors think that they are making such a contribution. But they treat all mergers as if they are the same, or they treat mergers made in the conditions in the 1960s as if they were similar to mergers made in the 1980s or 1990s. They often ignore the huge personal gains available to U.S. executives of selling organizations that have large stock option packages. They are often written in apparent ignorance of the substantial case literature of mergers and restructuring. Those writing about the human aspects of mergers seem to not recognize the importance of the deal financial context: Was it hostile and is there a great deal of new debt?

It may be very difficult, but to be truly helpful, research should deal with both managements' strategic *and* economic objectives in undertaking a deal. And the research should be informed by some understanding of what it means to acquire a firm and integrate its activities into one's own. Otherwise, it really isn't clear what we have learned. Put more formally, where so many variables are important to the various outcomes of interest, they must be identified correctly and measured or controlled for findings to be more than interesting speculation.

Against that standard, I want to use the remainder of this chapter to discuss a sample of papers that I reviewed in preparing this work. I culled 75 papers in refereed journals dealing with M&A from the past three years of the ABI/Inform database. From this list, I chose for reading 16 (see Appendix A) that had a managerial focus as evidenced by abstract. If your work is not included, you should not be offended since my approach to sampling was arbitrary despite my intent to be reasonable.

Research on M&A

The work on M&A can be categorized into three broad categories. The first is one version or another of empirical attempts to determine whether mergers work for the buyers and sellers. The second is a study that uses M&A events to examine another phenomenon of primary interest such as organizational learning or foreign direct investment. The third are studies of merger implementation where success is measured by a strategic goal such as acquisition of R&D capability or a social goal such as acculturation. As this categorization suggests, some studies are purely descriptive, while others implicitly or explicitly have prescriptive implications.

The work I examined ranged from a case study of the Pharmacia acquisition of Upjohn by Terry Belcher and Lance Nail in the *International Review of Financial Analysis* to a survey of worldwide merger booms by Frederic Pryor in the *Journal of Economic Issues*. To make my point, I have chosen four papers that I really liked. Had they been informed by a better understanding of the phenomenon, they would have been much better papers.

Takeovers, objectives and shareholder wealth

The first paper I chose was Mark Walker's "Corporate takeovers, strategic objectives, and acquiring firm shareholder wealth."[14] It appealed to me because he thought that not all M&A were the same and used categories somewhat similar to mine to examine mergers between 1980 and 1996 (whereas my study was 1997–99). The differences in the data were instructive. Vertical integration had more or less disappeared by the late 1990s. He lacked a category to pick up mergers motivated by industry over-capacity, but far fewer mergers sought "increased market share," his category. If we add my product line extension and industry convergence categories, it is more or less the same as his two diversification categories in some respects, but the late 1990s saw almost no unrelated diversification.

Now we are ready. What does Walker do after getting the data organized? He performs a five-day event study to determine the change in shareholder wealth for the buyer. His results conform to those of most event studies – acquirers lose wealth – and the differences by category are not dramatic. But more important than the uninteresting finding is the uninteresting question. Why would one expect that the market's reaction over 16 years ranging from economic depression, a sky-high dollar, and the rust bowl to a technology-led new economy be the same with respect to firm strategies – assuming the market's assessments were efficient? Given who does the assessing – security analysts – why would one assume that they could assess the various strategies equivalently well, or that the strategies would be viewed in the same way across huge changes in the macro-economy. In short, just because the data are numbers, what is there to suggest that they are comparable?

With this audience in mind, I chose the next three papers from sources closer to home.

Foreign direct investment

Jaideep Anand and Andrew Delios have written about "Absolute and relative resources as determinants of international acquisitions."[15] In a truly ingenious study, they compare inward investment to the United States by Japanese, German, and UK firms where the move involved either technology or marketing capability to see whether the method is by acquisition or "greenfield." They learn that where the capabilities involved are not fungible, the mode of entry is determined by the absolute level of capabilities in the United States. But where the capabilities are fungible, the mode chosen depends on the relative level of capability.

The paper is a contribution to our understanding of foreign direct investment. But we cannot learn from the paper the strategic intent of the investors. Nor can we say anything about the wisdom of the investments because performance data were not gathered. By way of contrast, a couple of years earlier, Walter Kuemmerle was studying the way German, Japanese, and U.S. high technology firms invested in R&D capability.[16] Because his data were firm specific, including interviews, he was able to document strategic intent. This led to the concept of technology extending and technology exploiting investments. The nature of the inward investment reflected the investor's desire to use its technology in a new market or to acquire new technology for the home (or global) market. The success of the investments reflected the extent to which the firms had organized to achieve the different objectives.

So what do we learn? In the first case we are able to predict whether foreign direct investment will take the form of greenfield investments or acquisitions. In the second, we can advise a firm on how to organize and manage a multinational network of research capabilities. We learn different things because we have different data. Kuemmerle visited the firms and gathered data. So we can learn about strategic management. Anand and Delios used government publications so we can learn about industry behavior.

Acquisitions as a learning catalyst

Next, Freek Vermeulen and Harry Barkema have done an interesting study of a very original question.[17] They have asked whether organic growth through "greenfield" extensions has a drawback in a kind of path-dependent ecological entropy that can be offset by a dollop of acquisitions. Think acquisitions as "ruile" in the soup.

They extend this intriguing idea to consider the kinds of acquisitions (new domain or not) and the number of acquisitions in relationship to preceding "greenfields." Their data were a longitudinal database (1966–94) on the subsidiaries of large Dutch firms ($n = 1,349$ after Akso, Philips, Shell, and Unilever were dropped). Their hypotheses are significantly corroborated, forcing all of us to think about acquisitions in a new way: not only are they difficult to pull off, but also if you do pull them off, your chances of future growth and prosperity go up.

The authors are properly cautious about their findings. My wish is that they had complemented their empirical work with a small set of cases so that they could have told us a little more about the learning associated with acquisitions. To begin, one wonders whether the same finding would hold up in a large country where "greenfield" growth takes one across significant market and industrial boundaries. Growth within Holland does not pose strong cultural challenges. More generally, while the authors cite literature such as Nelson and Winter to argue why their hypotheses make sense, it would be interesting to know precisely which aspects of the firm are stretched in a healthy way by acquisition – resources, processes, or values (RPV).

Using the RPV model deductively, I would reason that resources are less likely to run down or rigidify than processes or values. One can recognize superior goods or capability when they are regularly traded. Anecdotal evidence would suggest that without serious benchmarking, it is much easier to exaggerate the relative effectiveness of one's own processes and to leave one's values unquestioned. But it would be much better if these speculations were tested by careful surveys and case studies. In other words, we have learned from Vermeulen and Barkema that we may want to think more positively about the effects of acquisitions, but it would be helpful to know why. Then they wouldn't have to be so cautious about their findings.

Post acquisition

A different slant on post-acquisition activity is provided by Julian Birkinshaw, Henrik Bresman and Lars Hakanson in "Managing the post-acquisition integration process: How the human integration and task integration processes interact to foster value creation."[18] The authors separate post-acquisition process into two categories (exclusive but not necessarily exhaustive): those involved in achieving operational synergies, and those involved in creating a positive attitude toward the integration. The one they call task integration, the other human integration.

Happily for me today, they begin their paper by acknowledging and reviewing relevant literature from financial economics, strategic management, organizational behavior, and process perspective. Richly informed by this theory, they gained access to three significant companies that had made at least two recent acquisitions and studied implementation over four years. The measures of performance included both economic measures such as change in R&D output, realization of technology transfers, and post-acquisition market position as well as qualitative and sociometric indications of organizational integration and interpersonal respect.

Their findings represent patterns that emerge strongly from the data. The power of the findings comes from the richness of the data, for there are only nine companies studied. But there are multiple interviews and many questionnaires. What do we learn? Acquisition success is a function of both human and task integration and these follow trajectories over time. Poor human integration will often block task integration, leading to the normative implication that managers cannot drive task integration faster than their success with human integration.

The finding is not completely new, but neither is it conventional wisdom. The authors cite Greenwood and Haspeslagh and Jemison. They also acknowledge that their finding may be limited to the situations where the strategic intent involves symbiosis. My guess is that the student who examines their propositions across strategic intent will discover that their finding holds. In any event, we certainly learn something we can use.

Conclusion

In developing this talk, I do not think I have been very subtle. If one wants to learn something meaningful from the study of as complex a matter as the mating of two companies, then it is important to draw on the several relevant bodies of theory and to gather the data necessary to control or inform oneself on the variables that are important. This will almost always involve complementary empirical and case analysis. So that we not imagine this to be an impossible challenge I would remind you that for the last several years the prize-winning doctoral theses at our section of the Academy exemplify this kind of study.

More than a decade ago, Haspeslagh and Jemison did a very good job of laying out the difficulties associated with making M&A work.[19] It is not clear to me that most people writing in the field have fully accepted what they said. Since then there have been numerous good case studies of mergers so that we can understand much more clearly what might be involved in making them work.

What we have learned is that the acquisition of one ongoing company by another is a complex economic, social, and political activity. Except when the underlying purpose is acquiring assets to shut them down, or to break up the target into saleable components worth more than the purchase price, the social and political forces are important. I believe this is why the Birkinshaw et al. paper discussed above is so interesting.

Human integration and task integration do interact and one can't move faster on task than the people will permit without destroying social fabric.

I hope this conference can contribute to the establishment of a norm: that people writing about M&A as a subject as opposed to a convenient block of data helpful for studying something else, read the clinical literature of the field before proceeding. If we are able to do that, we will have accomplished a great deal.

Notes

1. See for example: The National Bureau of Economic Research. 1955. *Business Concentration and Price Policy*. Princeton; Stigler, G. 1968. Monopoly and oligopoly by merger, in *The Organization of Industry*, Chicago: The University of Chicago Press, pp. 95–107; and Scherer, F.M. 1980. *Industrial Market Structure and Economic Performance*, 2nd edition. Boston, MA: Houghton Mifflin.
2. Kenneth Andrews developed the first industry case series, Note on the Swiss Watch Industry and accompanying cases in 1959. This model shaped the next decade of work in the field of business policy. Michael Porter successfully formalized the ideas deduced from a decade's work by Harvard Business School case writers and faculty in *Competitive Strategy*, 1978. Prentice Hall.
3. See for example Shinohara, M. 1982. *Industrial Growth, Trade, and Dynamic Patterns in the Japanese Economy*. Toyko: University of Tokyo Press, pp. 45–52.
4. Wrigley, L. 1967. *Divisional Autonomy and Diversification* [doctoral thesis]. Boston, MA: Harvard Business School; Rumelt, R. 1974. *Strategy, Structure, and Economic Performance*. Division of Research. Boston, MA: Harvard Business School; and Christensen H.K. and Montgomery C.A. 1981. Corporate economic performance: Diversification strategy versus market structure. *Strategic Management Journal*, 2: 327–43.
5. Salter, M.S. and Weinhold, W.A. 1979. *Diversification Through Acquisition*. New York: Free Press. US anti-trust law until the 1980s was interpreted by the courts in a way that blocked horizontal acquisitions. As a consequence, most M&A activity was of the sort studied by Salter and Weinhold.
6. Andrews, K.R. 1971. *The Concept of Corporate Strategy*. Homewood, IL: Dow Jones Irwin, p. 86.
7. For example: Asquith, P. 1983. Merger bids, uncertainty, and stockholder returns. *Journal of Financial Economics*, 11: 51–83; Banerje, A. and Owens, J.E. 1992. Wealth reduction in white knight bids. *Financial Management*, 21: 48–57; Healy, P., Palepu, K., and Ruback, R. 1983. Do mergers improve corporate performance? *Journal of Financial Economics*, 31: 135–75; Jensen, M.C. and Ruback, R. 1983. The market for corporate control: The scientific evidence, *Journal of Financial Economics*, 11: 5–50; and Servaes, H. 1991. Tobin's q and the gains from takeovers. *Journal of Finance*, 46: 409–19.
8. Shleifer, A. and Vishny, R.W. 2001. Unpublished monograph.
9. Marc Sirower (1997) has carefully analyzed the costs of awkward financing in *The Synergy Trap*. New York: Free Press.
10. Hilderman, M. 2000. Event risk's four horsemen of the apocalypse. *Moody's Investors Service Global Credit Research*, November.
11. Bower, J.L. 2001. Not all M&A are alike – and it matters. *Harvard Business Review*, March.
12. Indeed, recent field research underway in some leading hi-tech acquirers suggests that some of the examples of the latter category of transaction that I use in my article have worked out badly.

13. Haspeslagh, P.C. and Jemison, D.B. 1991. *Managing Acquisitions: Creating Value Through Corporate Renewal.* New York: Free Press.
14. Walker, M.M. 2000. Corporate takeovers, strategic objectives, and acquiring-firm shareholder wealth. *Financial Management,* Spring: 53–66.
15. Anand, J. and Delios, A. 2002. Absolute and relative resources as determinants of international acquisitions. *Strategic Management Journal:* 119–34.
16. Kuemmerle, W. 1999. Foreign direct investment in industrial research in the pharmaceutical and electronics industries – Results from a survey of multinational firms. *Research Policy,* 28(2–3): 179–93.
17. Vermeulen, F. and Barkema, H. 2001. Learning through acquisitions. *Academy of Management Journal,* 44(3): 457–76.
18. Birkinshaw, J., Bresman, H., and Hakanson, L. 2000. Managing the post-acquisition integration process: How the human integration and task integration processes interact to foster value creation. *Journal of Management Studies,* 37(3): 395–425.
19. Haspeslagh and Jemison, op cit.

Appendix A – M&A Papers Reviewed for this Report

Anand, J. and Delios, A. 2002. Absolute and relative resources as determinants of international acquisitions. *Strategic Management Journal,* 23: 119–34.
Ang, J. and Kohers, N. 2001. The take-over market for privately held companies: The US experience. *Cambridge Journal of Economics,* 25: 723–48.
Belcher, T. and Nail, L. 2000. Integration problems and turnaround strategies in a cross-border merger: A clinical examination of the Pharmacia–Upjohn merger. *International Review of Financial Analysis,* 9(2): 219–32.
Birkinshaw, J., Bresman, H., and Hakanson, L. 2000. Managing the post-acquisition integration process: How the human integration and task integration processes interact to foster value creation. *Journal of Management Studies,* 37(3): 395–425.
Blonigen, B.A. and Taylor, C.T. 2000. R&D intensity and acquisitions in high-technology industries: Evidence from the US electronic and electrical equipment industries. *Journal of Industrial Economics,* 68: 47–70.
Chatterjee, R.A. 2000. The financial performance of companies acquiring very large takeover targets. *Applied Financial Economics,* 10: 185–91.
Ernst, H. and Vitt, J. 2000. The influence of corporate acquisitions on the behaviour of key inventors. *R&D Management,* 30(2): 105–19.
Hayward, M.L.A. 2002. When do firms learn from their acquisition experience? Evidence from 1990–1995. *Strategic Management Journal,* 23: 21–39.
Kane, E.J. 2000. Incentives for banking megamergers: What motives might regulators infer from event-study evidence. *Journal of Money, Credit, and Banking,* 32(3): 671–705.
Kohers, N. and Kohers, T. 2001. Takeovers of technology firms: Expectations vs. reality. *Financial Management,* 30(3): 35–54.
Krishnan, H.A. and Park, D. 2002. The impact of work force reduction on subsequent performance in major mergers and acquisitions – An exploratory study. *Journal of Business Research,* 55(4): 285–92.
Larsson, R. and Lubatkin, M. 2001. Achieving acculturation in mergers and acquisitions: An international case survey. *Human Relations,* 54(12): 1573–607.
Pryor, F.L. 2001. Dimensions of the worldwide merger boom. *Journal of Economic Issues,* 35(4): 825–40.

Scott, C.L. and Switzer, J.A. 2001. Are cash acquisitions associated with better post combination operating performance than stock acquisitions? *Journal of Banking and Finance*, **25**(6): 1113–38.

Shleifer, A. and Vishny, R.W. *Stock-Market Driven Acquisitions*. Harvard University and the University of Chicago, Revised June 2001.

Vermeulen, F. and Barkema, H. 2001. Learning through acquisitions. *Academy of Management Journal*, **44**(3): 457–76.

Walker, M.M. 2000. Corporate takeovers, strategic objectives, and acquiring-firm shareholder wealth. *Financial Management*, **29**(1): 53–66.

CHAPTER FOURTEEN

Where We've Been and Where We're Going

Mansour Javidan, Amy L. Pablo, Harbir Singh,
Michael Hitt, David Jemison

Abstract
On the final day of M&A Summit 2002, a panel of speakers discussed the issues related
to research on M&As. Harbir Singh provided a brief summary of the existing literature
and some future directions. Dave Jemison summarized the core issues and major findings that had been discussed during the conference. Michael Hitt presented a series of
questions that need research attention to move the field forward. After the panel presentations and discussions, the audience was broken up into groups. Each group was asked
to identify their "burning research questions" and propose methodologies that would
help find the answers to those questions. This chapter is based on the discussions by the
panel and the groups. It first provides a brief overview of the literature on mergers and
acquisitions as it has evolved to date and identifies some of the strengths and weaknesses
of the various perspectives and the work done in those paradigms. It then highlights the
key issues, questions, and research possibilities discussed during the session. The chapter
is designed to inform and energize further research on this very important topic.

Where We've Been...

That mergers and acquisitions (M&As) are a major and ongoing element of our corporate landscape goes without saying. In just the last decade of the twentieth century,
approximately $12 trillion worth of these transactions took place around the world
(Picot 2002)! In the current century, M&As continue at a tremendous rate both in
terms of activity and value. For example, as noted by Javidan and Vallally (2002),
nearly 37,000 mergers and acquisitions occurred globally in 2000 at a value of
approximately $3.5 trillion. Half of the publicly held companies received takeover
bids in the 1980s. However, as both scholars and practitioners recognize, M&As
frequently fail to live up to their potential (Sirower 1997, Larsson and Finkelstein 1999,

Ashkenas and Francis 2000), and there has been a raft of work trying to explain these outcomes that ultimately has not given us many answers. To quote Professor Joseph Bower, "When we study M&A, we're not learning that much new" (2002).

History

During the past century, there have been five major waves of merger activity (Rudolph 2000, Gaughan 2002). These cycles are associated with technological, economic, or regulatory shocks in industries as described below. The first wave of merger activity (1897–1904) in the early twentieth century has been described as "mergers for monopoly" in which consolidation of firms in basic industries (e.g. transportation, oil, and steel) took place. A second wave ("mergers for oligopoly" – 1916–29) occurred when firms were aligned through vertical integration into holding companies that owned other companies which would be engaged in production of a product (e.g. General Motors). The context of this cycle was the post-World War I economic boom when plentiful investment capital and lenient securities laws were in place. By the end of this period, government concerns about abuses of the market and the power wielded by large firms had resulted in the creation of a stricter antitrust environment with the passage of the Sherman and Clayton acts addressing unfair business practices and creation of cartels. The stock-market crash of 1929 put an end to these early merger waves.

The booming economy of the 1960s saw the emergence of conglomerates (Scherer 1986) as unrelated businesses merged to diversify and achieve competitive advantage through leveraging of assets and capabilities into other fields. Despite a strict antitrust political environment, a historically high level of merger activity occurred during this period. In fact, because of tough anti-trust laws, firms with the necessary financial resources seeking to expand were left with virtually no other alternative than to form conglomerates.

With the negative performance results evidenced by conglomerates starting in the late 1960s, merger activity (although declining in the high-interest rate environment of the 1970s) took on a new character – that of the hostile takeover. Companies began using increasingly aggressive behavior in their pursuit of potential takeover targets, and those targets began erecting stronger and stronger defenses. The 1980s saw the ballooning of the market for corporate control in which mergers and acquisitions were used as a tool to take over management of firms deemed to be performing less than optimally. In this period of "merger mania", the hostile takeover (often financed through leveraged buyouts) became common. This "fourth wave" (Fray, Down, and Gaylin 1985) of acquisition activity that began in the late 1970s and continued in the 1980s was best known for the "hostile" takeovers, corporate raiders, and mega-deals financed by easy credit (Smith 1991) that occurred during the period.

In the 1990s, the fifth merger wave of the twentieth century (which has continued into the twenty-first century) came into existence and, because of the huge size of the deals, it is known as the period of the "megamerger". The 1990s, however, have brought to the forefront different trends in merger and acquisition activity. The pattern, which is emerging from the shadows of the more sensational consolidations, is one of organizational combinations driven by corporate strategy. These combinations are typically friendly, negotiated transactions between corporations with common business interests, and are seen as vehicles for growth and change as opposed to acquisitions as isolated events.

The literature

The academic literature that has been spawned as scholars seek to develop insights into these major economic events largely falls into several major schools of thought: the capital markets school, the strategic management school, the organizational behavior/theory school, and the process school (Haspeslagh and Jemison 1991).

The capital markets school is most concerned with the question of the market for corporate control and whether and for whom value is created from M&A. It also examines agency issues, the role of investors, and public vs. private firms. The strategic management school examines types of acquisitions, how to select them, and their performance for particular firms. In the organizational behavior/theory school, researchers are concerned with how acquisitions affect organizations and the individuals in them. They examine the issues of knowledge management and acquisition capability. The acquisition process researchers want to know how the acquisition process itself affects acquisition outcomes.

In the *capital markets school*, economists claim that shareholders of the acquiring firm tend to lose from mergers, with earnings of firms in mergers declining after combination (Goldberg 1983, Ravenscraft and Scherer 1987). Financial economist researchers use event-study methodology to assess whether wealth has been created from an acquisition transaction based on changes in the firms' market prices after the deal has been announced. Jensen and Ruback (1983) and Weston and Chung (1983) present excellent reviews of this work; in general, these studies have found that gains from acquisition accrue to shareholders of acquired but not acquiring organizations. Recent exemplar studies in this area finding that on average, abnormal returns to acquirers are negative but not significant include Jarrell and Poulsen (1989), Kaplan (2000), Mitchell and Stafford (2000), and Andrade, Mitchell, and Stafford (2001). Recent work has shown that unlike their U.S. counterparts, Canadian bidding firms produce positive returns (Eckbo and Thorburn 2001). This work comes from the perspective of the market for corporate control in which bidding processes are used to determine who will win control of the firm's resources (Singh 2002).

Shleifer and Vishny (1988 and 2001) coming from a managerialist/agency perspective, have focused on how managerial preferences take precedence over shareholder interests resulting in non-value maximizing behavior that needs to be controlled, and hostile takeovers, despite the inherent readjustment hardships they imply, may be just what the doctor ordered to redistribute wealth appropriately.

In the *strategic management school*, research using either accounting-based or stock-market-based measures has produced a variety of studies relating acquisition performance to acquisition motives and strategies (e.g. Lubatkin 1983, Kusewitt 1985, Singh and Montgomery 1987, Shelton 1988). To a large extent this work focuses on diversification strategy and how related and unrelated acquisitions perform relative to each other. Seth (1990) in her paper examining value creation in acquisitions, presents an excellent review of studies in this area from 1980 forward. While the results of these studies have been inconclusive, Seth concludes by raising the question of how acquisition implementation issues may impact on realizing the potential for synergy creation.

Later researchers using realized-profit measures have found mixed results as well. In *The Synergy Trap*, Sirower (1997) reveals that only if the NPV of the realized synergies from a merger more than pay for the premium paid will a merger be financially successful. Healy, Palepu, and Ruback (1997) found in some strategic circumstances (friendly, stock-based purchase of a related business) returns were positive while hostile, non-strategic deals did no better than break even. In another study, Morosini, Shane, and Singh (1998) used growth rate in sales to assess M&A performance but it is unclear whether increase in sales was necessarily reflective of successful integration. Acquisition experience has also been an area of interest in the strategy field (Singh and Zollo 1998, Hayward 2002). Similar to the studies on diversification strategies, the evidence on the effect of acquisition experience and learning is mixed (Hayward 2002, Hitt, Harrison, and Ireland 2001). There may be a nonlinear relationship between prior experience and acquisition performance in the sense that high levels of experience may breed rigidity. Furthermore, experience recorded as codified knowledge is more helpful than that in the form of tacit knowledge (Singh and Zollo 1998). Acquisition activity has been found to have a negative relationship with other elements of strategic direction such as firm innovation and R&D inputs and outputs (Hitt, Hoskisson, and Ireland 1990).

Interestingly, as noted by Bower (2002 and chapter 13 in this book), who also provides an excellent overview of recent M&A research, it is critical to look at the whole picture of what's going on in the acquisition to understand the outcomes. Studies looking only at economic results miss understanding the strategic and managerial motives behind the acquisition, the financial implications of the financing, and the integration issues implied by all of these.

The *organizational behavior/theory school* of acquisition research comes from basically two major directions: how people respond to acquisition situations and how acquisitions impact on the organization and the people in it. The primary focus in the first instance comes from a psychological perspective in that an acquisition is a traumatic transformational event for people in organizations creating a sense of loss, lack of trust, stress, uncertainty, and the associated resulting behavioral problems (e.g. Buono and Bowditch 1989, Marks and Mirvis 1985 and 2001, Harris and Sutton 1986, Buono, Bowditch, and Lewis 1985, Schweiger and Walsh 1990).

The acquisition's impact on the organization and the people in it can occur in a number of ways including organizational structures and working relationships (Shanley and Correa 1992), disruption of culture (Sales and Mirvis 1984, Nahavandi and Malekzadeh 1988), career disruption (Jick 1979, Walsh 1988), and loss of status in the organization (Hambrick and Cannella 1993). Napier (1989) provides a good review of HR issues in mergers and acquisitions. For example, it has been shown that turnover of top management of the acquired firm is usually higher than expected (Walsh 1989) and is generally disruptive to performance (Hambrick and Cannella 1993).

Evolution of the process school

To a large extent earlier research streams generally ignored issues of post-acquisition management, relegating questions of implementation to "black box" status, concentrating instead on whether mergers *on average* function in desirable ways (Bradley, Desai, and Kim 1983, Jensen and Ruback 1983). Thus, these literatures focused on acquisition potential and the realization or failure to realize that potential, but did not suggest a managerial mechanism for mediating the gap between potential and performance. Organizational research and the more organizationally oriented strategy research suggest that the key mediating mechanism is integration (Shrivastava 1986, Finkelstein 1988, Jemison 1988a and 1988b, Larsson 1989).

In acquisitions, integration serves to coordinate and control the activities of the combining organizations so as to realize the potential of the interdependencies which motivated the acquisition (Shrivastava 1986). However, the necessary organizational conditions must be created for this potential to be realized (Jemison 1988a and 1988b, Haspeslagh and Jemison 1991). Thus, integration also involves issues of conflicting interests between the acquiring and the acquired firms (Shrivastava 1986).

Shanley (1987) describes the conflict that frequently results in M&A situations from a political perspective, as follows. In a traditional organization, when subunit and organizational goals come into conflict, the organization is able to maintain control because subunit members have internalized organizational as well as subunit goals. Also, control is enhanced because the organization, being familiar with the business and activities of the subunit, can easily assess whether organizational goals are being pursued. In acquisition situations, however, subunit members have not necessarily internalized parent goals, and parent firms may have insufficient understanding of subunit activities to gauge whether parent goals are being pursued. Thus the agency problems of the marketplace, apparently solved by the acquisition, may recur within the organization after the acquisition. In such a situation, the parent will take actions including the exercise of power to ensure that its goals in the acquisition are being pursued.

Larsson's (1989) discussion of synergies points out the delicate balance that must be achieved in integration. The concept of synergy, ubiquitous in the acquisition literature, relates to the effect of the whole being greater than the sum of its parts (Fuller 1975, Hitt, Harrison, and Ireland 2001) as a result of interdependencies between the parts (Porter 1985). In acquisitions, these interdependencies can result both in potential benefits, which motivated the acquisition, and potential dysfunctions embodied in coordination costs and conflict (Finkelstein 1988, McCann and Galbraith 1981). Thus, synergies in acquisitions can take on both a positive and a negative nature. Higher levels of integration are theoretically associated with greater realization of the potential of interdependencies. However, higher levels of integration may also result in greater realization of negative synergies due to the negative impact of organizational differences and incompatibility (Walsh 1989).

In sum, then, while integration is the mediating mechanism between acquisition potential and acquisition performance (Larsson 1989, Pablo 1994), the degree or level of integration is an important concept because it reflects the tradeoff between the beneficial and dysfunctional consequences, or the positive and negative "synergies", of integration.

The literature that is relevant to post-acquisition management and integration can be divided into two major groups: that which focuses on the task of achieving business performance objectives, and that which focuses on issues of interorganizational conflict and adjustment between the acquiring and acquired organizations.

Achieving business performance objectives

Works in this area come primarily from the strategic management and business policy literatures. These works are largely prescriptive and concentrate on two themes. The first is the operational implementation of the strategic fit identified in the formulation of the acquisition strategy. The second is the maintenance of strategically critical capabilities and resources within the acquired organization.

Implementation of strategic fit.   One of the most well-known and influential works on the topic of implementing strategic and operating fit is that of Kitching (1967). In this study, Kitching sought to study acquisition performance and to understand the underlying causes for variations in acquisition performance. Based on his findings, Kitching suggested the importance of installing "managers of change" to handle the critical areas needing change to accomplish the tasks of the acquisition. He stressed the need to quickly establish effective management relationships between the acquiring and acquired companies, including the appointment of an executive to "ride herd", the communication of clear reporting procedures, and the installation of a system of controls.

Searby (1969) continued in Kitching's tradition by suggesting the need for quick and decisive action in taking control of the acquired organization. He suggested the importance of maintaining momentum immediately after the acquisition by consolidating financial functions, systems, and procedures. The consolidation of personnel and physical plant, along with integration of operations and technologies were recommended for the realization of full, long-term profit potential in the acquisition. Searby focused on the need to identify likely areas of interdependency between the two organizations and then to move quickly to manage them and realize their potential. A similar focus was taken by Leighton and Tod (1969) in their arguments for acquisition group managers.

Howell's (1970) research suggested a conceptual scheme by which acquisitive managers could plan the acquisition process in its entirety, from strategy formulation through integration. Based on his work, Howell developed a framework for classifying different types of acquisitions along functional lines and tailoring integration activities accordingly. He identified acquisitions as having primarily a financial, marketing, or manufacturing focus and suggested that each had implications for organizational positioning relative to the parent, integration opportunities (areas of interdependency), and planning and control systems.

Ansoff et al. (1971) similarly found that planning enhanced organizations' ability to implement post-acquisition change activities and realize the potential implied by their acquisition objectives. Most recently, Bower (2001) suggested that M&A strategies are indeed quite different depending on the motivations underlying them, and that different managerial behaviors will be required to carry out successful implementation of these very different types of acquisitions.

Preservation of critical capabilities.   Works focusing on the second major theme, preserving capabilities and resources in the acquired organization critical to the objectives of the acquisition, include that of Yunker (1983). He argues for as much autonomy for the acquired organization as possible, with intervention only occurring in the instance of important problems. Otherwise, the acquisition may "lose the qualities that made it interesting to the acquirer in the first place" (Yunker 1983: 3). Shrallow (1985) similarly argued that for an acquisition to succeed, it was necessary to identify and preserve the "critical values" of the acquiree, defined as "those elements, tangible or intangible, which are the foundation of the successful management, operation, financial performance and growth... of a given company" (Shrallow 1985: 32). The nature of those critical values, then, has implications for the extent and nature of acquiring firm intervention.

In 1987, Haspeslagh and Farquhar developed a contingency model that incorporated both strategic fit and organizational capabilities needs addressing the more complex dimensions of strategic buyers who anticipate benefits based on a long-term relationship with the acquired organization. The management of this relationship is therefore critical to the success of the acquisition.

While studies of the business performance of acquisitions have been inconclusive (e.g. Jensen and Ruback 1983, Lubatkin 1983 and 1987, Singh and Montgomery 1987), much of the evidence suggests that the intended strategic benefits of acquisition are often not realized (e.g. Meeks 1977) raising questions about the management of the post-acquisition relationship (e.g. Scherer 1986). In addition to failures to achieve desired strategic outcomes, the negative impacts of acquisitions on the employees and managers of acquired firms have also received a great deal of attention (e.g. Levinson 1970, Hayes 1979, Jick 1979, Magnet 1984, Marks and Mirvis 1986, Schweiger and DeNisi 1987, Buono and Bowditch 1989, Sinetar 1981). Given the importance of acquisitions and the questions that have been raised about them, it is not surprising that in recent years, researchers have begun to focus on the management of post-acquisition relationships between acquiring and acquired organizations as a potentially fruitful area of research.

One of the most important issues in this relationship is the question of how the acquiring and acquired organizations are to be integrated in the post-acquisition period. Following an acquisition, some degree of interorganizational integration is necessary (Jemison 1988a, Jemison and Sitkin 1986a, Haspeslagh and Jemison 1991) but the issue of *what* level the organization chooses and ultimately, implements, is critical to both organizational and strategic outcomes (Pritchett 1987, McCann and Gilkey 1988, Buono and Bowditch 1989, Walsh 1989, Haspeslagh and Jemison 1991).

The process school.   Research from the process perspective recognizes not only the importance of strategic and organizational fit in determining acquisition outcomes, but it also recognizes the effect of the acquisition process itself as a potentially important determinant (Jemison and Sitkin 1986b). Elements of how decision-making and integration processes evolve are added to the mix. The research presented in Haspeslagh and Jemison's prize-winning 1991 book is situated in this paradigm. Pablo's (1994) work on integration decision making is rooted in this tradition because it allows for a better understanding of relationships between design decisions, implementation activities and processes, and acquisition outcomes.

A number of additional researchers have taken up this perspective because it adds to the richness of understanding how mergers and acquisitions really work, and provides a framework whereby more integrative models of M&A performance can be built. For example, Larsson and Finkelstein (1999) were able to empirically examine the impact of integration processes in combination with strategic fit and HR elements on acquisition performance. This integrative model was found to be highly explanatory of synergy realization, earning praise from Kathleen Eisenhardt:

> This paper is exciting because it synthesizes several theoretical perspectives into an integrative model and addresses a very significant topic – mergers and acquisitions – with a sharp eye towards clear managerial relevance and with innovative methods. I expect it to become a defining paper in M&A research (Larsson and Finkelstein, 1999: 1).

More recently, Birkinshaw, Bresman, and Hakanson (2000) examined how human and task integration processes can be managed to most effectively foster value creation. This paper was singled out by Bower (2002) as being reflective of the kind of M&A research from which "we certainly learn something we can use".

Because acquisition research has been characterized by a high degree of fragmentation, there is not one tightly connected theoretical perspective on how to look at this important subject. Rather, prior research from a number of perspectives has culminated in four largely unrelated theoretical models that represent the current state of theory in this area. These models reflect the particular interests of many diverse groups of scholars, and we hope that this brief overview provides some understanding of the many different questions that people are asking, the variety of methodologies being used, and the accumulation of findings that combine to create yet other sets of questions.

Where We're Going…

As we pointed out in the Introduction chapter, there is an interesting paradox: Corporations and executives are obviously in love with M&As. They have been buying up other companies at dizzying speed. At the same time, the academic and consulting worlds are quite pessimistic about M&As. There may be many reasons for such a disconnect, but in our minds, a key reason is the lack of research. Many scholars are working on various aspects of M&A but our collective understanding of this phenomenon is still rather limited. There are still many unanswered questions and confusing findings. An important objective of the M&A Summit 2002 was to help energize and focus research attention on the key issues. To this end, Michael Hitt and Harbir Singh each made a presentation and the participants worked in groups to identify research issues and directions. Below is a consolidated summary of their work. We'll use Michael Hitt's process framework to present their ideas. The typical M&A process is shown in Figure 14.1.

To understand the M&A process, one needs to start with the strategic thinking underlying it. A merger or an acquisition is usually a step in implementing a particular strategy. From a rational perspective, firms typically examine their opportunities, identify their broad strategies, and examine the range of options that would help implement their strategies. M&As are one such option. So the process starts with the firm's strategy and its attempts to identify potential target companies. Of course, it is also possible to be approached by potential target companies with the invitation

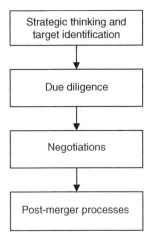

Figure 14.1   M&A process framework
Source: Hitt (2002)

to bid. In such cases, the firm can take a strategic approach or an opportunistic approach. Under the latter approach, the firm is interested in the financial gains it may receive as a result of the transaction even though there may be no strategic drivers for it. Our discussion here is mostly related to the strategic M&As and not the ones that are pursued for short-term gain.

The next step in the process is due diligence, where the acquiring firm attempts to ensure it is making the right decisions and that it has a thorough understanding of the target firm, its potential upside and downside, and its proper valuation. Negotiating the deal follows when the due diligence process does not raise fatal concerns and once the firms are ready to engage in serious negotiations. Assuming that the negotiations are successful and a price is agreed on, depending on the type of deal, both firms need approval by their boards of directors and their shareholders. The acquiring firm needs to get the required regulatory approvals, and start the process of post-acquisition integration. This is the process designed to help achieve the expected benefits of the merger. Related to this process is the notion of knowledge and organizational learning that is usually expected to take place as part of the integration process.

Below, we will identify the important research questions involved at every stage of the M&A process and will make some observations about effective and useful research methodologies. The following information is based on the presentations by Michael Hitt, Harbir Singh, and Dave Jemison, as well as the work by the teams of participants at the M&A Summit.

Strategic thinking underlying M&As

An important and under-explored issue is the role that M&As play in implementing strategies. It is conventional wisdom that firms view M&As as a way of implementing their strategies. But how do they do that? At what point do they start focusing on

M&A as a possible course of action? What role do industry shocks such as technological change or regulatory change play in the firm's decision making? How do firms compare M&As with other strategic options like alliances? What criteria do they use in making such comparisons? How do they go about identifying and screening potential M&A targets? Synergies and strategic fit are usually mentioned as the main drivers, but how do firms define synergy and fit and how do they measure it in identifying and evaluating target companies? Which executives play what role at this stage? Is it mostly a finance group project or is it run by business units and line people? What role do consultants and investment bankers play? What other motives are driving decision making at this stage? What other expectations do decision makers have in exploring merger possibilities?

This stage in the M&A process is more of a black box to researchers. There is much prescriptive work but little empirical and descriptive research. It is simply unclear to what extent the decisions made in this phase contribute to success or failure of M&As. Is it possible that mergers fail because they were triggered by the wrong strategies, or were they the wrong means for implementing a solid strategy?

Due diligence

This is the stage where the acquiring company has a short list of potential targets and needs to make an assessment of each target's assets and resources, both tangible and intangible, their potential value, and a reasonable premium and price to propose. An effective due diligence process should lead to a solid understanding of the strengths and weaknesses of the target firm and a reasonable premium to be paid. Many unanswered questions exist in regard to this phase: What criteria do firms use in evaluating the target firm? Who does the actual evaluation? What information is collected? How does the acquiring firm balance the need for more information with the need to prevent leakage? How are intangible assets evaluated? What is the impact of the size of the target firm on the evaluation process? Are there differences between private and public sector acquisitions? Are there differences between for profit and nonprofit sectors? What risk management framework is used by decision makers? What is the impact of regulatory and political constraints? How many executives and managers get involved from the two firms? How long does this phase take? What role do consultants and investment bankers play? What are the typical mistakes made and why? What other issues, such as organizational politics, play a role? How does signal processing work at this stage? The conventional wisdom in the finance literature is that the premium paid for an acquisition is as big as or bigger than the expected benefits from the merger. How do executives calculate the expected benefits and the premium? What impact does previous experience have? How do they use their previous merger experience in making these calculations? How do they learn from other companies' experience? What percentage of the target companies being studied are rejected at this stage? What type of information leads to withdrawal on the part of the acquiring firm? What is the threshold for pursuing the target firm? There is some evidence that acquiring firms keep pursuing a target firm even in the face of negative information uncovered during this stage. What dynamics drive the reluctance to stop the pursuit? What are the attributes of an effective due diligence process?

The due diligence process represents a high potential area for researchers. It is a critical phase in the M&A decision-making process and has been rather under explored. Its complex and multidimensional characteristics make it an important topic of study but one that is hard to access for researchers.

Negotiating the deal

The information collected and the decisions made by the acquiring firm during the previous stage constitute the input to this phase. This is when the negotiators from the two sides need to agree on the premium, the price, and the conditions of the sale. While there is substantial research on typical negotiation processes, there is rather limited information on M&A negotiations. Research is needed to better understand the motives of the individual players at this stage: The two CEOs, the boards of directors, the executive teams, the institutional investors, the consultants, and the investment bankers. How long does the negotiation take? How do the two sides prepare for the negotiations? What role does previous experience have? Does the size of the acquisition have an impact on the size of the premium agreed to? Does the type of payment (i.e. cash vs. stock) and types of conditions have an impact on the price? What is the difference between friendly takeovers and hostile takeovers? Under what conditions should the acquiring firm attempt each option? It may very well be that the seeds of failure in acquisitions are planted at this stage through over-payment or unworkable conditions. For example, a particular type of acquisition which used to be very popular but is now banned in the United States is the notion of the pooling arrangement. This form of merger has potentially substantial tax benefits and can make very large acquisitions possible for the acquiring firm, but it imposes various constraints on management decision making after the merger. As a result, it can cause major post-merger problems or lead to outright failure.

Post-merger processes

This is probably the most talked about phase in M&As but like other stages, lacks sufficient rigorous empirical research. Many questions need to be answered: How does the acquiring firm go about realizing the expected synergies? Does it make a difference whether integration teams and integration managers are appointed? What are the different levels and categories of integration? Is it easier to integrate some parts of the firms than others? Why? What are the leadership challenges in managing the integration process? What are the attributes of effective leaders managing post-merger integration? What drives the integration decision making? How do firms decide what to integrate and what not to integrate? What is an effective integration process? Does the integration process differ depending on the type of industry and whether the two firms are in the same industry or from different industries? What causes integration processes to fail? What is the role of speed of integration? How fast or slow? What determines the appropriate speed? What factors inside and outside the firm impact the outcome of the integration process? In what ways? What determines the relationship between the management teams of the acquired and acquiring company? What should that relationship be? How big is the issue of retention of employees and executives of the acquired firm? How much freedom should be provided to managers of the acquired firm? What determines that? Are there differences in the process depending on whether the acquisition was hostile or friendly? What is the impact of the acquisition on the two firms' customers and employees? Does the relative size of the two firms have an impact? What is it? What is the role of previous experience? How do firms monitor their integration process? What is the process of knowledge internalization and diffusion throughout the post-merger firm? How is trust built in the new firm? What is cultural distance and how can it be measured? What is the impact of cultural difference between the two firms? Is cultural distance always dysfunctional? Can it be an advantage? What types of acculturation processes exist and under what conditions are they effective? How long does a process of integration take? What forces help determine the length of time? Related to the issue of integration is the special case of cross-border mergers. Why do firms engage in cross-border mergers? What are the consequences of differences in national cultures and contexts? Are there special issues in terms of firm differences in cross-border mergers? In-depth understanding of the questions listed here will provide valuable insights into this complex process and should help pave the way for better implementation of mergers and acquisitions.

Merger outcomes

Perhaps the most controversial issue in mergers is that of merger outcomes: Do they fail or succeed? Do they add shareholder value for the acquiring and target firm shareholders? While these are logical and simple questions, their answers are anything but simple or forthcoming. The starting point is the definition of success. How is it defined and measured? Is it possible to study the outcome of a single acquisition which is then incorporated and integrated within the acquiring firm? Is it possible to isolate the long-term effects of a merger? Are we better off studying the effect of strategies implemented through mergers vs. other options such as internal development? Is it possible and desirable to measure success of M&A through objective and subjective metrics? Or through output, process, and input measures?

The issue of defining and measuring merger outcome is a major impediment currently holding research back. For the field to move forward, there is a need to break this logjam. Innovative ideas are needed to spearhead the research. Once a more effective metric and methodology are developed, researchers can start focusing on what determines success in mergers. Do companies track their own success in M&As? How? What is the role of industry? Past experience? Various elements of the M&A process discussed above? Does size matter? Why and how? What is the track record of M&As compared to other strategic options? While much work has been done on the outcome of mergers, there is no consensus on outcome metrics and no single piece of work addresses the issue of measuring success in a fully satisfactory way. As a result, different researchers have reached different and at times contradictory conclusions.

Research design and methodology

Despite its importance, M&A research seems to be somewhat limited. During the period 2001–2002, fewer than 10 articles on the topic appeared in the top three management journals: the *Academy of Management Journal*, the *Academy of Management Review*, and the *Strategic Management Journal*. The most important issue in regard to research in the area is that the subject of M&A is by nature a multilevel, multi-stage, and multidisciplinary construct. Researchers, on the other hand, tend to use single-level, single-stage, and single-disciplinary approaches because that is what they are typically trained in and because it is easier to do. As a result, most of the work in the area tends to be narrowly focused and fails to capture the dynamic and complex nature of the constructs. The M&A Summit speakers and participant teams made the following suggestions in regard to how we can conduct more effective research on M&As.

To begin with, it is important to develop and demonstrate a strong understanding of the phenomena and constructs in question. This can be achieved by a close working relationship between practitioners and researchers or consultants. Scholars need to better understand the realities of M&As and the people involved in them. They need a more in-depth picture of what actually happens and why. At the same time, the field of mergers and acquisitions suffers from a lack of well-developed theoretical frameworks. It will benefit from stronger conceptual work that clarifies the theoretical dynamics involved and will also profit from a better grounding of the M&A concepts in the more established general theories in other disciplines. As a new field of inquiry, M&A research is in need of work that leads to paradigm development.

There is also a strong need for multidisciplinary research. To be effective, M&A research requires cross-disciplinary constructs, models, and methodologies. Perhaps the most efficient way of achieving this is through cross-disciplinary teams of researchers. While managing large multidisciplinary teams entails a variety of challenges, as evidenced by the GLOBE project, it can generate valuable outputs. The GLOBE (Global Leadership and Organizational Behavior Effectiveness) research program is a team of over 150 researchers spanning 62 countries who have been working together for the past nine years to study leadership across cultures (House et al. 1999, House et al. 2002).

The current literature on M&A seems to be dominated by event-study methodologies. The conflicting findings and the theoretical shortcomings in this approach point to the need for new and innovative thinking and methodologies. Qualitative and longitudinal studies will help in paradigm development, but the critical work is in the area of operationalizing and measuring the dynamic constructs involved in M&As. M&A scholars need to put more collective energy and effort into this area to be able to make significant progress.

To close, in this chapter, we have provided the reader with many tantalizing questions and some thoughts on what needs to be done to find the answers to those questions. Our hope is that we have been able to prompt further development of this important field of inquiry.

References

Andrade, G., Mitchell, M., and Stafford, E. 2001. New evidence and perspectives on mergers. *Journal of Economic Perspectives*, **15**(2): 103–20.

Ansoff, H.I., Brandenburg, R.G., Portner, F.E., and Radosevich, R. 1971. *Acquisition Behavior of U.S. Manufacturing Firms, 1946–1965*. Nashville, TN: Vanderbilt University Press.

Ashkenas, R. and Francis, S.C. 2000. Integration managers: Special leaders for special times. *Harvard Business Review*, November/December: 108–17.

Birkenshaw, J., Bresman, H., and Hakanson, L. 2000. Managing the post-acquisition integration process: How the human integration and task integration processes interact to foster value creation. *Journal of Management Studies*, 37(3): 395–425.

Bower, J.L. 2001. Not all M&A's are alike – and that matters. *Harvard Business Review*, 79(3): 92–101.

Bower, J.L. 2002. *When We Study M&A, What Are We Learning?* Keynote address, M&A Summit 2002, Calgary, Canada.

Bradley, M., Desai, A., and Kim, E.H. 1983. The rationale behind interfirm tender offers: Information or synergy. *Journal of Financial Economics*, 11: 182–206.

Buono, A.F. and Bowditch, J.L. 1989. *The Human Side of Mergers and Acquisitions: Managing Collisions Between People, Cultures, and Organizations.* San Francisco: Jossey-Bass.

Buono, A.F., Bowditch, J.L., and Lewis, J.W. 1985. When cultures collide: The anatomy of a merger. *Human Relations*, 38: 477–500.

Eckbo, B. and Thorburn, K.S. 2001. Gains to bidder firms revisited: Domestic and foreign acquisitions in Canada. *Journal of Financial and Quantitative Analysis*, 35(1): 1–25.

Finkelstein, S. 1988. *Managerial Orientations and Organizational Outcomes: The Moderating Roles of Managerial Discretion and Power.* Unpublished Doctoral Dissertation, Columbia University.

Fray, L.L., Down, J.W., and Gaylin, D. 1985. Acquisitions and divestitures. In W.D. Guth (ed.), *Handbook of Business Strategy.* Boston, MA: Warren, Forham, and Lamont.

Fuller, R.B. 1975. *Synergetics.* New York: Macmillan.

Gaughan, P.A. 2002. *Mergers, Acquisitions, and Corporate Restructurings.* New York: Wiley, pp. 23–56.

Goldberg, W.H. 1983. *Mergers: Motives, Modes, Methods.* Aldershot, England: Gower.

Hambrick, D.C. and Cannella, A.A. 1993. Relative standing: A framework for understanding departures of acquired executives. *Academy of Management Journal*, 36(4): 733–62.

Harris, S.C. and Sutton, R.I. 1986. Functions of parting ceremonies in dying organizations. *Academy of Management Journal*, 29: 5–30.

Haspeslagh, P.C. and Farquhar, A.B. 1987. *The Acquisition Integration Process: A Contingent Framework.* Presented at the Seventh Annual International Conference of the Strategic Management Society.

Haspeslagh, P. and Jemison, D.B. 1991. *Managing Acquisitions.* New York: Free Press.

Hayes, R.H. 1979. The human side of acquisitions. *Management Review*, 68(11): 41–6.

Hayward, M.L.A. 2002. When do firms learn from their acquisition experience? Evidence from 1990–1995. *Strategic Management Journal*, 23(1): 21–39.

Healy, P.M., Palepu, K.G., and Ruback, R.S. 1997. Which takeovers are profitable? Strategic or financial. *Sloan Management Review*, 38(4): 45–57.

Hitt, M.A., Harrison, J.W., and Ireland, R.D. 2001. *Mergers and Acquisitions: Guide to Creating Value for Stakeholders.* Oxford: Oxford University Press.

Hitt, M.A., Hoskisson, R.E., and Ireland, R.D. 1990. Mergers and acquisitions and managerial commitment to innovation in M-form firms. *Strategic Management Journal*, 11(Special Issue): 29–47.

House, R.J., Hanges, P.J., Ruiz-Quintanilla, S.A., Dorfman, P.W., Javidan, M., Dickson, M.W., and Gupta, V. 1999. Cultural influences on leadership and organizations: Project GLOBE. In W.H. Mobley, M.J.Gessner, and V. Arnold (eds.), *Advances in Global Leadership.* Stamford, CN: JAI Press, pp. 171–233.

House, R.J., Javidan, M., Hanges, P., and Dorfman, P. 2002. Understanding cultures and implicit leadership theories across the globe: An introduction to Project GLOBE. *Journal of World Business*, 37(1): 3–10.

Howell, R.A. 1970. Plan to integrate your acquisitions. *Harvard Business Review*, **49**: 66–76.

Jarrell, G. and Poulsen, A. 1989. The returns to acquiring firms in tender offers: Evidence from three decades. *Financial Management*, **18**(3): 12–19.

Javidan, M. and Vallally, L. 2002. *Failure in Mergers and Acquisitions: Measurement and Dynamics*. Paper presented at the 22nd Annual International Conference of the Strategic Management Society, Paris, France.

Jemison, D.B. 1988a. Value creation and acquisition integration: The role of strategic capability transfer. In G. Liebcap (ed.), *Corporate Restructuring through Mergers, Acquisitions, and Leveraged Buyouts*. Greenwich, CT: JAI Press.

Jemison, D.B. 1988b. *Process constraints on strategic capability transfer during acquisition integration*. Working Paper No. 88/89-5-1, Graduate School of Business, University of Texas at Austin.

Jemison, D.B. and Sitkin, S.B. 1986a. Acquisitions: The process can be a problem. *Harvard Business Review*, March–April: 107–16.

Jemison, D.B. and Sitkin, S.B. 1986b. Corporate acquisitions: A process perspective. *Academy of Management Review*, **11**: 145–63.

Jensen, M.C. and Ruback, R.S. 1983. The market for corporate control: The scientific evidence. *Journal of Financial Economics*, **11**: 5–50.

Jick, T.D. 1979. *Process and Impacts of a Merger: Individual and Organizational Perspectives*. Unpublished doctoral dissertation, Cornell University.

Kaplan, S.N. 2000. Mergers and productivity. *National Bureau of Economic Research Conference*. University of Chicago.

Kitching, J. 1967. Why do mergers miscarry? *Harvard Business Review*, **45**: 84–107.

Kusewitt, J.B. 1985. An exploratory study of strategic acquisition factors relating to performance. *Strategic Management Journal*, **6**: 151–69.

Larsson, R. 1989. Organizational integration of mergers and acquisitions. *Lund Studies in Economics and Management 7*, Lund University Press.

Larsson, R. and Finkelstein, S. 1999. Integrating strategic, organizational, and human resource perspectives on mergers and acquisitions: A case survey of synergy realization. *Organization Science*, **10**: 1–26.

Leighton, C.M. and Tod, G.R. 1969. After the acquisition: Continuing challenge. *Harvard Business Review*, **47**: 90–102.

Levinson, H. 1970. A psychologist diagnoses merger failures. *Harvard Business Review*, March–April: 138–47.

Lubatkin, M. 1983. Mergers and the performance of the acquiring firm. *Academy of Management Review*, **8**: 218–25.

Lubatkin, M. 1987. Merger strategies and stockholder value. *Strategic Management Journal*, **8**: 39–53.

Magnet, M. 1984. Help! My company has just been taken over. *Fortune*, July 9: 44–51.

Marks, M.L. and Mirvis, P.H. 1985. Merger syndrome: Stress and uncertainty. *Mergers and Acquisitions*, **20**(2): 50–5.

Marks, M.L. and Mirvis, P.H. 1986. The merger syndrome. *Psychology Today*, **10**: 36–42.

Marks, M.L. and Mirvis, P.H. 2001. Making mergers and acquisitions work: Strategic and psychological preparation. *Academy of Management Executive*, **15**(2): 89–92.

McCann, J.E. and Galbraith, J.R. 1981. Interdepartmental relations. In P.C. Nystrom and W.H. Starbuck (eds.), *Handbook of Organizational Design*. New York: Oxford University Press.

McCann, J.E. and Gilkey, R. 1988. *Joining Forces: Creating and Managing Successful Mergers and Acquisitions*. Englewood Cliffs, NJ: Prentice Hall.

Morosini, P., Shane, S., and Singh, H. 1998. National cultural distance and cross-border acquisition performance. *Journal of International Business Studies*, **29**(1): 137–58.

Meeks, G. 1977. *Disappointing Marriage: A Study of the Gains from Merger*. Cambridge, UK: Cambridge University Press.

Mitchell, M.L. and Stafford, E. 2000. Managerial decisions and long-term stock price performance. *Journal of Business*, **73**(3): 287–329.

Nahavandi, A. and Malekzadeh, A. 1988. Acculturation in mergers and acquisitions. *Academy of Management Review*, **13**: 79–90.

Napier, N.K. 1989. Mergers and acquisitions, human resource issues and outcomes: A review and suggested typology. *Journal of Management Studies*, **26**: 271–89.

Pablo, A.L. 1994. Determinants of acquisition integration level: A decision-making perspective. *Academy of Management Journal*, **37**: 803–36.

Picot, G. 2002. *Handbook of International Mergers and Acquisitions*. New York: Palgrave.

Porter, M.E. 1985. *Competitive Advantage: Creating and Sustaining Superior Performance*. New York: Free Press.

Pritchett, P. 1987. *Making Mergers Work*. Homewood, IL: Dow Jones-Irwin.

Ravenscraft, D.J. and Scherer, F.M. 1987. *Mergers, Sell-Offs, and Economic Efficiency*. Washington, DC: Brookings Institution.

Rudolph, R.G. 2000. A short history of mergers and acquisitions. *CPCU Journal*, Spring: 14–18.

Sales, A.L. and Mirvis, P.H. 1984. When cultures collide: Issues in acquisition. In J.R. Kimberly and R.E. Quinn (eds.), *Managing Organizational Transitions*. Homewood, IL: Irwin.

Scherer, F.M. 1986. Mergers, sell-offs, and managerial behavior. In L.G. Thomas (ed.), *The Economics of Strategic Planning*. Lexington, MA: Lexington Books.

Schweiger, D.M. and DeNisi, A. 1987. *The Effects of Communication with Employees Following a Merger: A Longitudinal Field Experiment*. Paper presented at the National Meeting of the Academy of Management, New Orleans, LA.

Schweiger, D.M. and Walsh, J.P. 1990. Mergers and acquisitions: An interdisciplinary view. In K.M. Rowland and G.R. Ferris (eds.), *Research in Personnel and Human Resource Management*, Vol. 8. Greenwich, CT: JAI Press.

Searby, F.W. 1969. Control post-merger change. *Harvard Business Review*, **5**: 139–45.

Seth, A. 1990. Value creation in acquisitions: A re-examination of performance issues. *Strategic Management Journal*, **11**: 99–115.

Shanley, M.T. 1987. *Acquisition management approaches: An exploratory study*. Unpublished doctoral dissertation, University of Pennsylvania.

Shanley, M.T. and Correa, M.E. 1992. Agreement between top management teams and expectations for post-acquisition performance. *Strategic Management Journal*, **13**(4): 245–67.

Shelton, L.M. 1988. Strategic business fits and corporate acquisition: Empirical evidence. *Strategic Management Journal*, **9**: 279–87.

Shliefer, A. and Vishny, R.W. 1988. Value maximization and the acquisition process. *Journal of Economic Perspectives*, **2**(1): 7–20.

Shliefer, A. and Vishny, R.W. 2001. *Stock Market Driven Acquisitions*. Unpublished monograph.

Shrallow, D. 1985. Managing the integration of acquired operations. *Journal of Business Strategy*, **6**(1): 30–6.

Shrivastava, P. 1986. Postmerger integration. *Journal of Business Strategy*, **7**: 65–76.

Sinetar, M. 1981. Mergers, morale, and productivity. *Personnel Journal*, **60**: 863–7.

Singh, H. 2002. *Progress and Opportunity on Research in Acquisitions*. Keynote address, M&A Summit 2002, Calgary, Canada.

Singh, H. and Montgomery, C.A. 1987. Corporate acquisition strategies and economic performance. *Strategic Management Journal*, **8**(4): 377–86.

Singh, H. and Zollo, M. 1998. The impact of knowledge codification, experience trajectories, and integration strategies on the performance of corporate acquisitions. *Wharton Financial Institutions Center Working Paper*, pp. 1–43.

Sirower, M.L. 1997. *The Synergy Trap: How Companies Lose the Acquisition Game*. New York: Free Press.

Smith, R. 1991. Wall Street dismantles much of its M&A machinery. *The Wall Street Journal*, C1, January 2.

Walsh, J.P. 1988. Top management turnover following mergers and acquisitions. *Strategic Management Journal*, **9**: 173–83.

Walsh, J.P. 1989. Doing a deal: Merger and acquisition negotiations and their impact upon target company top management turnover. *Strategic Management Journal*, **10**: 307–22.

Weston, J.F., and Chung, K.S. 1983. Do mergers make money? A research summary. *Mergers and Acquisitions*, **18**(3): 40–8.

Yunker, J.A. 1983. *Integrating Acquisitions*. New York: Praeger.

Index

Printed and bound by CPI Group (UK) Ltd, Croydon, CR0 4YY

23/04/2025

14660966-0002